Praise for *The Prologue*

"Alexander Mirtchev's sweeping exploration of the changing energy landscape looks far into the future and outlines issues that will occupy scholars and policymakers for decades to come."

—**The Hon. Henry Kissinger**, Chairman, Kissinger Associates; Former Secretary of State and National Security Advisor

"Dr. Alexander Mirtchev's new book, *The Prologue: The Alternative Energy Megatrend in the Age of Great Power Competition*, provides a timely and truly inspired perspective on 21st century global security challenges. It has long been clear that security challenges of the 21st century are much broader and more holistic than they were in the last century when major power competition was largely defined by military power. Dr. Mirtchev's book helps the reader unpack the complex relationship between economics, the alternative energy megatrend, security, and defense and the implications for the unfolding major power competition. Faced with this daunting complexity, Dr. Mirtchev urges policymakers to undertake the essential task of any successful strategist: to prioritize objectives to align ends with means and be smart. Fundamentally, *The Prologue* offers a valuable new framework for international strategic analysis and course of action."

—**General James L. Jones**, USMC (Ret.), Executive Chairman Emeritus, Atlantic Council; 32nd Commandant, USMC; Former National Security Advisor to the U.S. President; Former Supreme Allied Commander Europe

"With the advancements in alternative energy technology at the beginning of the 21st century, energy security thinking and planning will never be the same. Alexander Mirtchev's profoundly original book *The Prologue* reveals the new dilemmas that will challenge policy makers in all major economies and provides for dealing with the new realities in a smart way."

—**The Hon. Judge William H. Webster**, Chairman, Homeland Security Advisory Council; Former Director, CIA; Former Director, FBI

"Dr. Alexander Mirtchev has written an extraordinary book that is far ahead of any other contemporary analysis in connecting the cross currents of global security, international economic competition, and—above all—alternative energy. His *Prologue* belongs in the hands of any serious policymaker and will undoubtedly be studied at the nation's top universities and war colleges. A masterpiece of original thought!"

—**Adm. James G. Stavridis** USN (Ret.), Operating Executive, The Carlyle Group; Chair of the Board of Counselors, McLarty Associates; Former Supreme Allied Commander Europe; Former Dean, Fletcher School of Law and Diplomacy at Tufts University

"Alexander Mirtchev's book is a fascinating read."

—**Lt. General Guy Swan**, CEM, CPP, Ret., Executive Director,
Institute of Land Warfare

"I found your book most stimulating. I look forward to seeing the reception."

—**The Rt Hon. Lord Robertson**, Port Ellen, KT, GCMG, FRSE, PC;
Former Secretary General, NATO

"Alexander Mirtchev has provided a thorough examination of a possible significant future, in which the implications of alternative energy source developments come to dominate national, economic, and environmental security and world geopolitics. The thesis in the book is one that needs to be understood by global policy makers, not least in China."

—**Prof. Sir David Omand**, Former UK Security and Intelligence Coordinator;
Author, *Securing the State*

"Alexander Mirtchev's book, *The Prologue*, introduces a not just original but smart methodology that provides for a breakthrough study. By defining alternative energy development as a trend and analyzing its drivers, the book allows a balanced perspective on issues that have remained beyond the radar screen of economic policy and planning, as well as a new understanding of the upcoming challenges, making it an essential read for both policy makers and business leaders."

—**Sir Richard Evans**, Former CEO, BAE Systems

"The ongoing revolution in the energy industry is a comparable discontinuity to what occurred when Internet was developed for communications. Not just energy's business model will change but both geopolitics and the competitiveness of many markets will be redefined. Alexander Mirtchev's work is a very accurate and absolutely a 'must-read' analysis of this transformation, which will impact everyone's life."

—**Prof. Giuseppe Recchi**, Chairman, Telecom Italia, Former President, ENI

The
PROLOGUE

THE ALTERNATIVE ENERGY MEGATREND IN THE AGE OF GREAT POWER COMPETITION

ALEXANDER V. MIRTCHEV

PRESS

A POST HILL PRESS BOOK

The Prologue:
The Alternative Energy Megatrend in the Age of Great Power Competition
© 2021 by Alexander V. Mirtchev
All Rights Reserved

ISBN: 978-1-64293-553-0
ISBN (eBook): 978-1-64293-554-7

Cover art by Cody Corcoran
Interior design and composition by Greg Johnson, Textbook Perfect

Post Hill Press
New York • Nashville
posthillpress.com

Published in the United States of America
1 2 3 4 5 6 7 8 9 10

CONTENTS

FOREWORD   xvii

SUMMARY   xx

ACKNOWLEDGMENTS   xxii

INTRODUCTION   xxiii

AUTHOR'S NOTE   xvii

PART 1. About the Prologue: Introducing the Modern Alternative Energy as a Socio-Political, Techno-Economic, and Ideological Megatrend in a Universally Securitized World   **1**

  I. Setting the stage—how is the 21st century world becoming universally securitized?   2

    1. Exploring and mastering the new security contexts.

    2. How is securitization possible and enacted in a universally securitized world?

    3. The alternative energy megatrend's multiple security connotations.

  II. The grand entrance—modern alternative energy assuming the mantle of a socio-political, techno-economic, and ideological megatrend.   9

    1. The promise of alternative energy technologies: turning dreams and visions into reality?

      (1) Hydropower: the ancient renewable competitor to fossil fuels.

      (2) Wind, solar, biofuels, geothermal: established technologies that must pass the test of modern times.

      (3) Tidal, wave, hydrogen, nuclear fusion, Earth's magnetic field, and solar-from-orbit: experimental precursors of upcoming linear advancements.

    2. The trend's emerging identity as a factor in the Grand Energy Game: the mutually reinforcing and converging drivers behind the trend.

      (1) The insatiable demand for energy: coalescence of demand-supply calculations into a future energy vision.

      (2) The expansion of dominant environmental concerns: the imperatives for a "new habitat" here and now.

(3) The economic growth dictum: alternative energy as a stabilizer against economic risks.

(4) The global technological revolution: a precondition and challenge.

(5) The quest for new military capabilities: reshaping strategic and tactical approaches and practices in line with the emerging security context.

(6) The new empowerment for the new times: state, community, and individual aspirations.

(7) The ethical imperative: the moral impetus driving the trend as a "morally superior" form of energy.

(8) The policies and regulations: integrating the drivers into a trend and transforming them into a phenomenon vastly surpassing its own drivers.

(9) The ever-continuing social construction of the megatrend: impact, invention, and reinvention.

III. A very brief history of alternative energy's future—contemporary constructions charting alternative energy's progress.   32

1. The historicity: how the modern construction of alternative energy, its past and future have been shaped.

2. The "Golden Age" redux: envisaging alternative energy's "glorious past" from antiquity to the Age of Enlightenment.

3. The re-conceptualization: the juxtaposition with fossil fuels enabling the envisioning of practical alternative energy applications from the Industrial Revolution to the latter half of the 20th century.

4. The transformation: the post-Cold War paradigm shift in the context of globalization and the global technological revolution.

5. Achieving the impossible: The impact of the Fourth Industrial Revolution and Artificial Intelligence on the alternative energy megatrend.

6. The delayed arrival of the future: assuring the marvelous prospects of alternative energy.

IN CONCLUSION: How have alternative energy developments in the 21st century evolved into a socio-political, techno-economic, and ideological megatrend in a universally securitized world?   45

PART 2. Geopolitics: Charting a Complex Megatrend in a Globally Securitized World Under the Gathering Storm of Old and New Great Power Rivalries   47

I. The Equilibrium—plotting one more variable, the megatrend, on the geopolitical system in flux.   48

1. The megatrend: shedding a new light on the equilibrium.

2. Core-Periphery dynamics: the megatrend as a counterweight between multiplying power centers.

3. East-West rivalries: how the megatrend is reshaping past Western hegemony along new lines of contention and cooperation.

4. The North-South divide: the megatrend's projected iterations altering divisions and alignments.

5. Top-down build-up and bottom-up pressures: changes in state–society relations.

II. The resources—rethinking the political topography of energy.   63

1. Solar: generating power potential for the South and beyond.

2. Wind: game-changing potential?

3. Biofuels: national interest-driven competitive advantages.

4. Hydropower: proven performance with limited scope for future expansion.

5. Geothermal and tidal sources: holding promise for many but still at the experimental stage.

6. Space-based sources of energy: the new frontier.

7. Rare earth elements: another area of potential conflict.

III. The old and some new actors—the cast of the Great Energy Play.   71

1. The dynamic and interconnected networks: fluid balances of multidimensional alliances and divisions.

   (1) The changing power endowments of 21st century actors.

   (2) Upending the balances.

   (3) Modifying the actor's geopolitical stances.

2. State actors: emerging postures and the pursuit of untested options.

   (1) Power projection tactics.

   (2) The alternative energy megatrend increasing the pressures on policymaking.

3. Non-state actors: deriving new powers and moving toward the spotlight.

   (1) Non-state actors: a diverse world of assorted initiatives and inspired approaches.

   (2) Shifting relationship paradigms.

IN CONCLUSION: The megatrend reveals 21st century security complexities that are rapidly reshaping geopolitical divisions and stances in the age of new Great Power Competition.   83

PART 3. The Alternative Energy Megatrend's Trajectory Across the Transforming Energy, Defense, Environmental, and Economic Security Domains   86

I. The modern age of energy security—factoring in the alternative energy megatrend.   86

1. The broadening scope of energy security: new approaches to securing energy and new threats to stability.

(1) Adding new dimensions to energy security.

(2) The technological revolution's impact on energy security: adding momentum to new approaches.

2. The viability of alternative energy technologies: the challenges to be addressed to ensure the alternative energy megatrend's future energy security relevance.

(1) Intermittency impediments: in search of timely delivery.

(2) Transmission shortfalls: improving the current grid.

(3) Storage capacity restrictions: needing more power...greater density.

(4) Imperfect infrastructure: adapting new applications and demands of energy efficiency.

3. The megatrend as an attitude modifier: offering a new slant on socio-political perceptions, attitudes, and energy relations.

(1) Energy imperialism: reshaping the ties that bind consumers to producers.

(2) Resource nationalism: the megatrend's effect on fossil fuel suppliers' perceived leverage.

(3) Anti-American and anti-Western attitudes: highlighted overtones of the megatrend.

4. Energy securitization: a new means of projecting power?

(1) Alternative energy-derived geopolitical empowerment: new dimensions of "soft power"?

(2) The deterrence factor: accruing the geopolitical tools and capacity to signal and dissuade.

(3) Adding geopolitical leverage: one more "bargaining chip" on the table, or something more?

5. Nuclear power: charting a possible roadmap for the future of the alternative energy megatrend.

(1) Nuclear power: a possible template for alternative energy developments.

(2) Anti-nuclear sentiments and non-proliferation efforts: alternative energy offered as a substitute for nuclear power.

(3) The question of the post-proliferation world: a potential weaponization of renewables through the looking glass of nuclear power's dual use.

II. 21st century national defense transformation—the influence of the alternative energy megatrend.   **116**

1. The expanding defense mandate: the perspective of the alternative energy megatrend.

2. Alternative energy: an element of the growing spectrum of technologies spurring defense transformation.

(1) The impact of technological advances on defense transformation.

(2) Alternative energy: a potential game-changer in Great Power Competition.

3. The transformation of defense strategies: the megatrend highlights new capabilities, missions, and areas of strategic engagement and cooperation.

4. The defense benefits promised by alternative energy: not just adapting to the new strategic environment, but rather new forms of power projection and cooperation.

(1) Optimizing the military's energy supply, use, and logistics: near-term tactical benefits and long-term defense energy security.

(2) Powering the warfighter: force multiplier in front-line operations and the progenitor of new warfighting capabilities.

(3) The anticipated unintended side effects: improving society's technological base through defense sector-induced technological advancements.

5. Practical uptake of renewables by defense establishments worldwide: U.S. maintaining a leading role.

(1) Defense-generated demand: fueling the overall alternative energy market.

(2) The U.S. Department of Defense: directives, policies, and initiatives.

(3) U.S. Navy, Air Force, and Army: the military's renewable energy programs in practice.

(4) NATO approaches: new challenges driven by the evolving global security environment.

(5) China: leading with a long-term vision.

(6) Uneven developments in the rest of the world: sufficient momentum yet to be gained.

6. The uneasy question of renewables' viability: do they meet defense requirements?

(1) Core impediments: operational, security, and infrastructure.

(2) Institutional inertia: the disconnect between operations and strategy and institutional impediments.

(3) The technological integration impediments.

(4) The cost of alternative energy defense integration: foreseeable short-term burdens and potential long-term advantages.

III. Environmental security revisited—the alternative energy megatrend redefining the securitization of the global habitat.   152

1. The modern redefinition of environmental security: the emergence of actionable environmental policies promised by alternative energy.

(1) Environmental security: broadening the concept of securitizing the global habitat and concomitant political considerations.

(2) Alternative energy redefining the policy toolkit: providing practical means for mitigating environmental threats.

(3) The effect of societal values on environmental security: the megatrend's impact on the discourse.

2. Environmental policies: an emerging cross-border renewable energy regulatory framework.

(1) Conventional alternative energy-related environmental policies: quotas, subsidies, fixed pricing, and emission restrictions.

(2) The build-up toward an expansive environmental regulatory framework: the alternative energy megatrend propelled by the coalescing global governance architecture.

3. "Greening" geopolitics: the megatrend as a focal point for strengthening environmental security-related cooperation and competition.

(1) Cooperation and alliances for peace: factoring the alternative energy megatrend into global eco-realignments.

(2) Discord and conflicts: divergent interests and new points of contention.

(3) The environmental viability of alternative energy applications: the overlooked issue of "green geopolitics."

4. The megatrend's role in mitigating environmental security challenges.

(1) Emerging environmental security priorities in a universally securitized world: transforming policy goals into practical securitization mechanisms.

(2) The coalescing shape of future environmental security threats.

IV. Global economic security—the alternative energy megatrend highlighting a growing reliance on geo-economic statecraft in the competition escalation.   185

1. The evolution of economic security: the alternative energy megatrend's foothold in economic security considerations.

(1) The securitization of the global economy understood through the prism of alternative energy developments.

(2) A stabilizing factor: reinforcing economic resilience.

(3) A disruptive factor: economic losses, uncertainties, tensions, and conflicts.

2. Leviathan as a market-maker: economic imperatives and policy tools propelling the alternative energy megatrend.

(1) In pursuit of economic growth: costs, productivity, and new jobs.

(2) Technological advancements: pursuing alternative energy-related transformations.

(3) Policy toolkit: fiscal, regulatory, and financing incentives.

3. The alternative energy market: emerging at the juncture of the private and public sectors.

(1) The emerging alternative energy market: worldwide investment patterns.

(2) Market-making strategies: from incentivizing public-private cooperation to integrating alternative energy into a global marketplace.

(3) Economic viability: will the market lose out for facilitating the megatrend's future economic security contribution?

4. Geo-economics in a universally securitized world: the promise and the warnings of the alternative energy megatrend.

(1) From geopolitics to geo-economics and back: the megatrend highlighting the drifting emphasis on sources of power projection.

(2) The rising importance of geo-economics: what does the alternative energy megatrend's evolution reveal about upcoming economic security considerations?

IN CONCLUSION: How does the alternative energy megatrend affect the future of the energy, defense, environmental, and economic security domains?   227

PART 4. The Metamorphoses: The Alternative Energy Megatrend's Inevitable Demise and Future Security Trajectory   **233**

I. Charting the megatrend's future course.   234

1. The demise?

2. The ascent?

3. The dynamics.

II. The progression of the alternative energy megatrend—making headway in a multi-centric world in the new age of Great Power Competition.   245

1. The Americas: broadening energy security considerations and new avenues of power projection.

(1) The United States: energy security, environmental, and economic imperatives.

(2) Canada: maximizing potential.

(3) Latin America and the Caribbean: Brazil aiming to maintain its frontrunner status.

2. Europe: a millennial strategy.

(1) The European Union: the durability of the consensus on energy security challenges.

(2) Russia and other non-EU countries: moving beyond testing the waters from the shore.

3. China: pursuing regional hegemony via a broader strategy of national development and security with renewables-related geopolitical leadership.

4. Asia-Pacific: pursuing alternative energy developments to match the regional hegemon.

(1) India: energy, economic, and environmental security considerations amid the pursuit of regional and global positioning.

(2) Japan: searching for a sustainable energy model in the aftermath of Fukushima.

(3) Australia: addressing energy security considerations with respect to reliance on natural resources for economic and national security.

5. The Greater Middle East and Africa: experimentation restricted by the dominance of fossil fuels in the Middle East and the "Grand Energy Game" replayed in Africa.

(1) The Greater Middle East: ambitious projects constrained by inconsistent commitment.

(2) Israel: rapid technological advancements driven by security considerations.

(3) Africa: testing alternative energy pilot projects in the background of new power plays for resources.

(4) South Africa: finding its place at the BRICS table.

III. Rebalancing U.S. policies for the new age of Great Power Competition—prioritization imperatives in the universally securitized world.   271

1. Factoring the new and upcoming security complexities of the alternative energy megatrend's progression: the securitization policies.

2. Proactively shaping the emerging security context of the Great Power Competition: the tentative emergence of new principles underpinning the global security architecture.

3. Policy prioritization: avoiding the pitfalls in formulating desirable securitization goals in the age of Great Power Competition.

IN CONCLUSION: What are the plausible scenarios for the megatrend's linear and nonlinear developments in the new iteration of Great Power Competition?   288

AUTHOR'S NOTE   **291**

**The Epilogue to THE PROLOGUE: Is the Alternative Energy Megatrend
a Search for a 21st Century Arcanum?**   **292**

    1. Some contemporary parallels: recurring patterns in the unending pursuit
of advancement and empowerment.

    2. The "differentia specifica" of the modern meanings: a securitized habitat
and mastery over nature within reach for everyone and everywhere.

ENDNOTES   **299**

INDEX   **370**

ABOUT THE AUTHOR   **387**

FOREWORD

As the post-Cold War geopolitical and geo-economic frameworks buckle, Dr. Alexander Mirtchev's new book, *The Prologue: The Alternative Energy Megatrend in the Age of Great Power Competition*, provides a timely and inspired perspective on 21st century global security challenges. Through the prism of the alternative energy megatrend, *The Prologue* analyzes the nexus of geopolitics, national security, and energy in the context of the new Great Power Rivalry and related Grand Energy Game.

The intersection of energy, geopolitics, and security is, of course, an age-old story. During my time as the Supreme Allied Commander Europe (SACEUR) from 2003–2007, I found myself wrestling with the implications of energy and geopolitics, as well as the proper role of a traditional defense alliance like NATO in addressing energy security. President Putin's natural gas cutoffs on East Europe as a geopolitical tool had real implications for the security and resilience of our allies, but NATO itself had a limited mandate and limited tools to help allies in need. The threats posed by non-traditional actors concerned us as well, including the risk of a major terrorist attack on energy facilities.

During my time as national security advisor to President Obama in 2009–2010, framing energy security appropriately was one of my key priorities. During the transition between administrations, as we deliberated upon the ideal National Security Council (NSC) structure that would best serve the President, I sought to ensure that energy security had its proper place as a strategic issue in national security debates. It has been a life-long observation that the United States has never had a comprehensive energy strategy that takes into account the wider range of economic, security, and geopolitical factors that Dr. Mirtchev explores in *The Prologue*.

In the decade since my time in government concluded, the alternative energy megatrend has continued to develop, and the geopolitical and technological landscape has continued to evolve. In The Prologue, Mirtchev analyzes power dynamics of the current and upcoming geopolitical complexities, as well as the impacts on economic and environmental security. One of the book's biggest draws is its exploration of where the alternative energy megatrend fits into the 21st century transformation of defense capabilities, doctrines, and policies in the context of today's Great Power Rivalry. Nuclear energy also plays a role in the analysis—not as a green solution to environmental challenges—but as a potential road map for the future evolution of the megatrend.

To be clear, this is not another alternative energy study. Instead, Mirtchev posits that by diving into the complexities of the alternative energy megatrend one might glimpse the future, a future where universal securitization could "replace traditional defense with terms like the economy, health, the environment, or international law, making security an all-inclusive matter."[1] But, by his own admission, simply embracing universal securitization is not enough; it will overwhelm policymakers, leaving the system unworkable.

We may have already approached this threshold. The modern national security advisor and NSC structure struggles to integrate non-traditional security challenges and is overwhelmed by crisis management, leaving national security principals little bandwidth for the kind of strategic thinking or holistic assessments that a major power competition environment requires. One of the key conclusions in Dr. Mirtchev's work is that dynamic prioritization is essential to any workable security framework.

In examining these complexities, The Prologue addresses some key questions: Why and how have contemporary alternative energy developments evolved into a global socio-political, techno-economic, and ideological megatrend? How is the transforming world of the early 21st century becoming universally securitized? What does the alternative energy megatrend reveal about modern and upcoming approaches toward energy security in the evolving Grand Energy Game? How does the alternative energy megatrend redefine environmental security and contribute to the greening of geopolitics? What is the future security trajectory of the alternative energy megatrend in the context of the Fourth Industrial Revolution and, in particular, the irreversible rise of Artificial Intelligence? Why does dynamic prioritization become imperative in a universally securitized world? What could be the shape and focus of the approaches, strategies, and policies necessary to benefit from the transforming 21st century security landscape?

THE PROLOGUE

Fundamentally, *The Prologue: The Alternative Energy Megatrend in the Age of Great Power Competition* offers a valuable new framework for international strategic analysis and a course of action. It challenges our preconceived notions about the alternative energy megatrend and what the megatrend tells us about 21st century security dynamics, as well as provides for innovative solutions for the unfolding new Great Power Competition.

General James L. Jones, USMC (Ret.)
Executive Chairman Emeritus, Atlantic Council; 32nd Commandant, USMC; Former National Security Advisor to the U.S. President; Former Supreme Allied Commander Europe

SUMMARY

This Woodrow Wilson Center Project identifies and charts the unfolding security trajectory of an early 21st century unpredictable global phenomenon: the ascent of alternative energy as a socio-political, techno-economic, and ideological megatrend in the context of the ongoing global technological revolution, the world in disequilibrium and the new Great Power Competition.

This competition designates a significant shift toward rivalry between major powers that have the capabilities to be a critical threat to each other. These great powers have amassed sufficient military, political, economic, and ideological capacities to be able to exert influence and compete on a global scale and/or in strategic areas, challenging the relative preeminence and potentially displacing the U.S. global leadership.

Through the prism of the alternative energy megatrend's trajectory in a world of profound transformation, the study analyzes the upcoming global security challenges that are geopolitical, geo-economic, defense- and nuclear-related, and environmental in nature. On this basis, the study outlines the 21st century global security transformations and the approaches, strategies, and policies relevant to these developments.

The study addresses the following questions:

- How is the transforming world of the early 21st century becoming universally securitized?
- Why and how have contemporary alternative energy developments evolved into a global socio-political, techno-economic, and ideological megatrend?
- What are the geopolitical, geo-economic, defense-related, and environmental security implications of the alternative energy megatrend in the new Grand Energy Game?

- What are the attributes and drivers of this socio-political, techno-economic, and ideological megatrend?
- What questions does the alternative energy megatrend raise about the modern understanding of geopolitical dynamics?
- What does the alternative energy megatrend reveal about modern and upcoming approaches toward energy security in the evolving Grand Energy Game?
- Where does the alternative energy megatrend fit into the 21st century transformation of defense capabilities, doctrines, and policies of the Great Power Rivalry?
- How does the alternative energy megatrend redefine environmental security and contribute to the "greening" of geopolitics?
- What does the alternative energy megatrend reveal about the transformation of global economic security calculations and the rise of geo-economics?
- How will nuclear energy evolve in the upcoming post-proliferation world, and could it be a frame of reference for the megatrend?
- What is the future security trajectory of the alternative energy megatrend in the context of the Fourth Industrial Revolution and, in particular, the irreversible rise of Artificial Intelligence?
- What does the megatrend reveal about the future global security context, and why does its prioritization become imperative in a universally securitized world?
- And finally, what could be the shape and focus of the approaches, strategies, and policies necessary to benefit from the transforming 21st century security landscape?

This study endeavors to answer these questions by proposing the conceptual framework of the modern universally securitized world. Via this universal securitization concept, the study posits prerequisites for dynamic security prioritization strategies and policies.

The study makes the case for an intelligent and vigorous pursuit of innovation and an expeditious entry into the realm of the unknown as a significant dimension of the new Great Power Competition. Such a pursuit could contribute to energy rebalancing, military capabilities, environmental safety, economic growth, and global stability. Most importantly, it could ultimately further human knowledge, prosperity, liberty, and dignity.

ACKNOWLEDGMENTS

I would like to express my gratitude to several friends and colleagues for their advice, critique, and support: the Hon. Henry Kissinger, Gen. James L. Jones (Ret.), Stephen Hadley, the Hon. William H. Webster, Adm. James G. Stavridis USN (Ret.), Lord Truscott of St. James's, Prof. Shirley M. Tilghman, the Hon. William Sessions, Rachel E. Kyte CMG, Lt. Gen. Guy Swan, CEM, CPP (Ret.), the Rt Hon. Lord Robertson of Port Ellen KT GCMG PC FRSA FRSE, Prof. Sir David Omand, Sir Richard Evans, Lionel Barber, Prof. Giuseppe Recchi, Kal Dimitrov, and Kristal Alley.

Also, I would like to acknowledge the support of several institutions and their leaders: Jane Harman, Director, President, and CEO of the Wilson Center; Dr. Karin von Hippel, Director-General of the Royal United Services Institute (RUSI); Prof. Michael Clarke, former Director-General of the Royal United Services Institute; and Prof. Mark J. Rozell, Founding Dean of the Schar School of Policy and Government at George Mason University.

INTRODUCTION

"Human felicity is produced not so much by great pieces
of good fortune that seldom happen, as by little advantages
that occur every day."

Benjamin Franklin[2]

This is not just another alternative energy study. Rather, this study
identifies the ascent of modern and upcoming alternative energy development as a techno-economic, socio-political, and ideological 21st century
megatrend. It charts the security-related trajectory of this relatively new
global phenomenon: a discernible flow of interacting socio-political, technological, economic and ideological developments that influence and are
influenced by the future of the Grand Energy Game and beyond.

Centrally, through the prism of the alternative energy megatrend's trajectory, this Woodrow Wilson Center Project analyzes the upcoming global
security transformations and challenges that are geopolitical, geo-economic,
defense-related, environmental, and ideological in nature. On this basis, the
study outlines the new millennium approaches, strategies, and policies relevant to these developments and the evolving Great Power Competition.

First, this study relies on the time-tested hermeneutic tradition of examining new phenomena via the viewpoint of a transforming character—in
this case, the alternative energy megatrend. Like the character of Apuleius's
Golden Ass who enables the audience to visualize the Roman world through
his perspective,[3] the analysis of the alternative energy megatrend similarly
furnishes the opportunity to assess contemporary and evolving security
complexities. Through the lens of this analysis, new knowledge and tools
of understanding emerge that not only highlight what is new and different
but allow the new reality that is presented to be better assimilated within

the societal understanding and common sense that govern ideas and notions. Thus, this book examines current and upcoming global security transformations and challenges through the prism of the alternative energy megatrend and suggests approaches to address them.

Second, this study applies an integrated, multidisciplinary approach,[4] to accommodate the multidimensional nature, evolution, impact, and continuous new findings and iterations in alternative energy. From there it assesses the diverse scope and implications of global security transformations by utilizing theories from various disciplines such as economics, sociology, political economy, energy studies, defense studies, political geography, foreign policy, and international legal studies, as well as the philosophies of science and technology. To provide a comprehensive presentation of the alternative energy megatrend's many facets, this book also builds on a wide range of historic facts, studies, and statistics. Such an approach engenders a balanced and thorough picture of the developments, meanings, and impacts of modern alternative energy developments germane to the shifting power balances of the global security landscape.

Third, this study introduces the conceptual framework of the modern universally securitized world and the relevant dynamic prioritization. A dynamic field of mutually interacting threats have amplified and/or transformed the security considerations of today's globalized, interdependent, and ever-multiplying actors. The study respectfully utilizes certain elements of securitization theory and goes beyond those tenets to introduce the concepts of universal securitization and security prioritization in the new age of Great Power Competition.[5]

The subject of the study—the alternative energy megatrend—is multifaceted and is unfolding and transforming as techno-economic, socio-political, and ideological in nature. It has vastly outpaced its own underlying technological developments and applications.

This trend has already assumed the mantle of a global game-changer with far-reaching promises and pitfalls that go far beyond actual technological capabilities. It has already begun to shape the way production choices are made and energy is distributed. It now plays a transformative role regarding societal values, political-economic priorities, and commercial practices. Perhaps most importantly, it has become an integral part of the collective human imagination and aspirations worldwide.

It is evolving in the age of a new Great Power Competition,[6] which marks a significant shift toward rivalry between major powers that have the capabilities to be a critical threat to each other. These great powers[7] have amassed sufficient military, political, economic, and ideological capacities, allowing them to exert influence and compete on a global scale and/or in strategic areas.

These powers have established, or will attempt to establish and consolidate, regions of dominance. From the perspective of the challengers, the final game is modifying and eventually changing the balance of power via disrupting and, in the longer run, displacing U.S. global leadership. Obviously, this would put a strain on the very concept of America's relative preeminence.

Despite these developments and a torrent of studies on new energy sources, the security context surrounding developments in alternative energy remains mostly uncharted territory. Notably absent from these studies is a thoughtful analysis of the trend's geopolitical, geo-economic, defense, and environmental security implications.

This book endeavors to answer the following key questions raised by these developments, while also revealing ongoing and upcoming global security transformations. These questions determine the structure of the book, which hopefully provide for a multi-dimensional discussion of the global security transformations and the alternative energy megatrend's security repercussions in a universally securitized world.

- How is the transforming world of the early 21st century becoming universally securitized?
- Why and how have contemporary alternative energy developments evolved into a global socio-political, techno-economic, and ideological megatrend?
- What are the geopolitical, geo-economic, defense-related, environmental security, and ideological implications of the alternative energy megatrend?
- What are the attributes and drivers of this socio-political, techno-economic, and ideological megatrend?
- What questions does the alternative energy megatrend raise about the modern understanding of geopolitical dynamics?
- What does the alternative energy megatrend reveal about modern and upcoming approaches toward energy security in the evolving Grand Energy Game?
- Where does the alternative energy megatrend fit into the 21st century transformation of defense capabilities, doctrines, and policies of the Great Power Competition?

- How does the alternative energy megatrend redefine environmental security and contribute to the "greening" of geopolitics?
- What does the alternative energy megatrend reveal about the transformation of global economic security calculations and the rise of geo-economics?
- How will nuclear energy evolve in the upcoming post-proliferation world, and could it be a frame of reference for the megatrend?
- What is the future security trajectory of the alternative energy megatrend in the context of the Fourth Industrial Revolution and, in particular, the irreversible rise of Artificial Intelligence?
- What does the megatrend reveal about the future global security context, and why does its dynamic securitization and respective prioritization become imperative in a universally securitized world, in particular during the age of Great Power Competition?
- And finally, what could be the shape and focus of the approaches, strategies, and policies: from technological empowerment, via power projection to cooperation with allies and partners, that will be necessary to benefit from the transforming 21st century security landscape?

In answering such questions, the study makes the case for an intelligent and vigorous pursuit of innovation and an expeditious entry into the realm of the unknown as a significant dimension of the new Great Power Competition.

Thus, this book aims to be forward looking and nuanced and, therefore, provide a theoretically deeper and more realistic and pragmatic understanding of current and future imperatives that underpin the notion and practices of national security. Such pursuit could contribute to energy rebalancing, military capabilities, environmental safety, economic growth, and global stability. Most importantly, it could ultimately further human knowledge, prosperity, liberty, and dignity.

AUTHOR'S NOTE

When first considering undertaking this study a few years ago, I was at the Washington, D.C., National Gallery of Art on a Sunday afternoon, looking at Roy Lichtenstein's "Cow Triptych (Cow Going Abstract)."

This triptych shows three consecutive paintings of a cow, each gradually zooming closer and simultaneously transforming and becoming abstracted through decomposition, restructuring and reimagining. In other words, the first image had nothing to do with the third. Or did it?

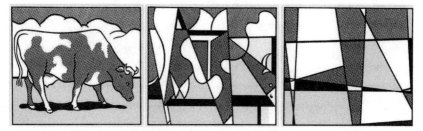

© "Cow Triptych (Cow Going Abstract)," Roy Lichtenstein, 1974

It occurred to me that the current and envisioned developments of the alternative energy megatrend and its security implications evolve in an analogous manner, with the second iteration being a recognizable outgrowth of the first, rather pastoral image, and the progression from the first to second iteration being more or less predictable. The result of the third iteration is unexpected, as the context is not only transformed beyond recognition, but represents a distinct new reality. Using this analogy, the alternative energy megatrend is currently more or less leaving the first canvas and entering the second, into the new, and hopefully not brave, 21st century world.

That is to say that the current developments are just a glorious prologue for the things to come. And the things to come are obscured not just by clouds but most probably (and expectedly) far beyond our current visions and imaginations.

Thus, the big question is how by focusing closely on these and other upcoming developments we reveal new approaches, strategies, policies, and practices that can ultimately further human knowledge, prosperity, dignity, and freedom.

PART 1

About The Prologue: Introducing the Modern Alternative Energy as a Socio-Political, Techno-Economic, and Ideological Megatrend in a Universally Securitized World

"How, from a fire that never sinks, or sets, would you escape?"

Heraclitus[1]

Why and how have modern alternative energy technologies, resources, applications, and their surrounding notions coalesced into a 21st century socio-political, techno-economic, and ideological megatrend?

The following chapters examine the gradual redefinition of society's historical understanding of energy and posit that the transformation of alternative energy into a modern megatrend is founded on an introspective rationalization of renewable energy. The analysis looks at the re-conceptualization of alternative energy throughout the turbulent 20th and 21st centuries. It ascribes the alternative energy megatrend's formation to modern transformation processes, such as globalization and the global technological revolution, against the backdrop of the post-Cold War paradigm shift.

In this book, modern alternative energy developments are defined as a trend composed of a group of evolving and converging socio-political and techno-economic drivers set in a socio-cultural context. The book posits that these drivers propel the trend and determine its future evolution.

More than any other phenomena, the alternative energy megatrend could be analyzed as a socially constructed phenomenon.[2] It is a consequence

1

of the convergence of knowledge and actions by diverse participants of global society, which in isolation could not create such a phenomenon, but in the aggregate provide it with ongoing momentum and presence.

Arguably, the trajectory of the alternative energy megatrend foreshadows the future global security landscape. The book explains the new and upcoming security context by positing the notion of universal securitization which corresponds to the broadening range of multiplying and mutually interacting threats and actors in a profoundly transforming world.

In the following chapters these elements are intentionally presented as static, which facilitates their understanding. In reality they are dynamic, chaotic and fluid in an anarchic environment.

I. Setting the stage—how is the 21st century world becoming universally securitized?

The analysis of the security trajectory of the alternative energy megatrend in the following chapters will draw the likely shapes of the future global security landscape. The following chapters explain this context by positing the notion of universal securitization.

As mentioned, the notion of universal securitization tries to grasp the 21st century's increasingly interconnected and mutually influenced globalized world in transition. This interconnectedness includes ever multiplying actors with ever multiplying agendas, competition, confrontations, and alliances in a new security context. At the same time, this interconnectedness implies that securitizing a single issue is impossible without creating spill-over into other issues, sectors and processes.

1. Exploring and mastering the new security contexts.

The new security context follows a transition from the previously dominant Westphalian system of relations between states to a post-Westphalian order governed by new ideas, notions, ambitions, and priorities that allows for virtually any theme to be labeled as a security issue. Domains of security are no longer restricted by "a spatial demarcation between those places in which the attainment of universal principles might be possible and those in which they are not."[3]

The notion of a world that became de facto universally securitized is reinforced by the evolution of the notion of security, which is growing to incorporate an expanding field of threats and actors. This has led to the

2

broadening of the concept of security, which is typically expressed through the demarcations of narrow and broad security.

The concept of narrow, or core, security considerations—which in classical international relations theory involves the defense of a state and its resources[4]—focuses predominantly on actions undertaken by one actor in relation to another. These actions form dynamic interactions with the ultimate outcome of military confrontation. Core security focuses on the high politics of inter-state relationships that rely on maintaining equilibrium by striking a balance between the major powers. The equilibrium is also maintained by emphasizing actors' perceived strategic interests and the means, particularly military ones, to achieve them.[5] Narrow security threats thus predominantly include hostile actions taken by a specific state toward another nation-state.[6] These threats continue to be identified with the need to ensure "the integrity of the nation's territory, of its political institutions and of its culture."[7]

After the end of the Cold War, the more traditional, narrow definition of security expanded to include issues beyond threats to the survival of the state, resulting in the concept of broader security.[8] Security considerations now increasingly incorporate not just the need for survival of nations and society as territorially distinguished groups, but also the preservation of certain expectations of welfare—social, economic, cultural, and physical—for individuals and communities. Broader security thus comprises fields such as the environment,[9] the economy,[10] demographic pressure and immigration, transnational crime, water security, human rights, justice, and anti-organized crime collaboration.[11] These and other security threats fall within the paradigm of human security, which integrates what was traditionally considered to represent sub-national threats to state legitimacy and civilian populations.

Energy touches on most, if not all, of the broader security fields. As Henry Kissinger noted "[a]t its core the energy system is again on an unsustainable path, threatening the political, economic, and social stability necessary for continued world progress. Energy security endures as a central and concerning feature of the current landscape."[12]

With this in mind, this study approaches the analysis of the modern and emergent security environment through the prism of the alternative energy megatrend by utilizing key elements of securitization theory, in particular the securitization actors, the referent objects to be securitized, and the audiences that acquiesce to the securitization action.

An increasing number of actors are claiming a legitimate place in security interactions. This dynamic field of securitization actors influences cross-border agendas and establishes power structures that augment pressures toward regionalization.[13] They have the power and legitimacy to convince pertinent audiences that addressing existential threats is a vital priority. Through their actions, these actors impose a shared understanding of what constitutes a threat and an appropriate response.

Securitization theory holds that securitization is a process of socio-political discourse. As an issue moves from the realm of politics toward the security sphere, it becomes associated with an implied need for resources and attention beyond what it would normally enjoy in daily politics. In other words, the securitizing actor is "talking security."[14]

During the Cold War, the bipolar hegemony of the two major powers—the United States and the Soviet Union—limited the range of actors capable of undertaking independent securitization measures. However, in the 21st century, there is a growing plethora of actors capable of undertaking securitization actions. This increasing number of securitization actors results in a gradual convergence of national security agendas and emerging regional security agendas.[15] It also widens the scope of security considerations that form these agendas. States distinguish between internal and external threats, and respond alone or form regional alliances that modify existing security perceptions and measures.[16] In this security operating environment, the repercussions of human activities are no longer limited by geographical distance or boundaries; changes in one field or sector inevitably affect other fields, even those that may appear unrelated.[17]

The new powers emerging onto the global scene include a range of non-state actors, such as international organizations, political and social movements, and interest groups. These are further altering the way actors interact, and how inter-state conflict and security are perceived and managed. Non-state actors influence the security debate by designating security resources as existentially threatened. Threats and responses therefore are determined by the perspectives of the relevant actors, resulting in an evolution of existing security notions and approaches that are at the heart of universal securitization.

Despite the growing influence of non-state actors, states will likely remain the dominant actors in the security field. However, they will be so with a modified and, arguably, diminished ability to exert their power through securitization.[18] With the balance of power between states as a mechanism of peace and security becoming less relevant, the result is that "there are too many powers to permit any of them to draw clear and fixed lines between allies and adversaries."[19]

Securitization in this context is also made more complex by the exponential growth of objects to be securitized. This phenomenon places new demands on actors and poses new difficult security choices in applying limited resources. Determining which objects to securitize first is therefore less clear, as harm to one object, e.g., infrastructure, international trade, the environment, or energy supplies, can affect others, e.g., economic wellbeing, health, or military power.

This poses a dilemma for securitization. It requires an evaluation of whether or not a threat exists objectively or subjectively, what the anticipated impact of the threat is, whether or not an ability to securitize the threat exists, and whether securitizing such a threat would have positive or negative repercussions for a wider set of referent objects.[20] As a result, core national security considerations have been joined on the security agenda by a number of broader security issues that tend to be described sometimes as "low politics,"[21] such as the environment, poverty, financial markets, and economic development. As security threats to referent objects "transcend national borders [and] are already beginning to break down the sacred boundaries of national sovereignty,"[22] security policies generate ripples that cross into different fields and induce unanticipated outcomes.

Further, there is an increasing number of securitization audiences, which includes individuals, business and political elites, military leaders, opinion-makers, communities, national populations, and broader civil society. These audiences are presented with actors' positions on a given threat and a respective action to securitize this threat. In this context, a useful simplification of the securitization audience is to consider it as a global community of individuals, groups, and entities, whose interests, values, and goals intersect. Successful securitization requires that, by accepting the proposed designation of security threats, the audience also accepts the implications of the proposed action.

With the conditional removal of the geography-based authority and restrictions that determined past interests, security is evolving beyond the spatial orientation of discursive practices.[23] In order for a securitization act to be considered legitimate, it must be framed in terms that are not only understandable but also approved by the growing, often global, target audience.[24] The corollary is that the legitimacy of securitization actions will reflect the expanded notions of insecurity held by the target audience, resulting in the multiplicity of objects to be securitized.

5

The security context is increasingly "universalized" by a notable blurring of the distinction between securitization actors and audiences. Audiences are becoming less passive, pointing to the growing importance of societal pressure for policymaking. Audiences present their own position on threats, referent objects, and securitization actions, and can project their own values onto securitization processes. The threats audiences wish to be protected against are dynamically interconnected, with the added complexity that some actors' securitization actions represent security threats for others, such as the interrogation of suspected terrorists, which is perceived by some audiences as a threat against the object of human rights protection. Constituencies approving securitization actions thus do not merely accept them but can sometimes influence the shape and implementation of the securitization process, as well as impact the security of other constituencies.[25]

Modern securitization audiences are also evolving. Some represent specific ideas that transcend national identities and borders, driven by diverse agendas to actively exert pressure on state actors on issues ranging from climate change to immigration. The new audiences also include political groups, parties, and organizations that are themselves agents of the main securitization actor, the state. Universal securitization may thus be viewed not just as a relationship between institutions, but also as an emancipation of the securitization audiences—the ability to achieve security that is linked to people and not confined to states.[26]

The dynamic between the securitization actors, objects, and audiences shapes and is in turn affected by an increasingly universalized security context. Simply put, a confluence of conditions dictates the extent to which a given object is perceived to be existentially threatened and enables securitization actors to assess the threat and determine whether audiences accept, or even demand, that the object be securitized.[27] The security context is shaped by both established and new notions of what threatens security. The complex 21st century security environment is thus characterized by conflicting practical securitization approaches as "strategy chasms [that grow] at a worrying pace...because these material and ideological differences reinforce one another."[28]

The evolving global security environment necessitates universal securitization. Threats and their mitigation in the new environment are more context-driven and dependent on myriad circumstances, including socio-political pressures, requirements imposed on actors and a pre-history of existing practices. Universal securitization represents an evolution of practical means and approaches that is beyond a socio-political process designating issues as security referent objects and determining the existence of risk. Instead, it creates the foundation for a transition to a new set of methods and practices that not only move security issues outside traditional frameworks of governance and political processes of debate but changes the rules of the game.[29] In a universally securitized world, it would be fully viable to replace traditional defense with terms like the economy, health, the environment, or international law, making security an all-inclusive matter.[30]

2. How is securitization possible and enacted in a universally securitized world?

Mitigating the continuously broadening scope of threats requires a deeper understanding and integration of all elements of the securitization process. The universally securitized world thus exacerbates the Hobbesian security dilemma, which holds that the choice of an actor to act preemptively and inimically against other actors is the most rational one. The multiplicity of actors, threats, and referent objects makes it more difficult to anticipate securitization outcomes.[31]

In this universally securitized world, it may behoove a state to act against another under a widening spectrum of circumstances. Securitization actors still act on behalf of themselves and their audiences to achieve specific outcomes. However, they increasingly use tools that modify rules and institutions to alter anticipated outcomes and prevent perceived threats. This is how cross-border securitization policies emerge.[32]

When suggesting universal securitization, broadening the concept of security too far risks making the term meaningless, potentially obstructing the ability of securitization actors to formulate actual policy and distinguish vital risks from non-threatening occurrences.[33] In order to address the inability to securitize everything, securitization theory attempts to posit that desecuritization could often lead to more beneficial outcomes. However, this approach provides relatively limited application.[34]

The process of making rational choices in a universally securitized world is affected by merging goals that multiple actors pursue.[35] This merging creates a pattern that constitutes the global security architecture. The analysis of the alternative energy megatrend thus highlights the security context of a universally securitized world, where fewer choices with measurable outcomes are available for actors to make in pursuit of rational security goals. In other words, the universally securitized world makes it more problematic to achieve order in society.[36] The alternative energy megatrend will be used as a prism through which the issue of how securitization is enacted in a universally securitized world could be fully addressed.

3. The alternative energy megatrend's multiple security connotations.

Currently, the presence of renewables in the energy mix is limited; therefore, the direct security repercussions of alternative energy technologies and resources are narrow. The contention of this book, however, is that having emerged as a 21st century socio-political, techno-economic, and ideological megatrend, alternative energy creates security resonances that have their own security trajectory. Furthermore, assessing the evolution of alternative energy developments provides a useful frame of reference for assessing the growing complexities of 21st century security considerations.

Alternative energy developments have intrinsic direct security implications. Alternative energy itself is not simply a referent object that can be securitized, but also a potential source of threats that requires securitization. Making alternative energy the subject of security analysis entails mitigating the immediate security concerns arising from the introduction of alternative energy technologies, securing the resulting energy system from harm and interference, and preventing adverse effects on the ability to produce and distribute renewable energy. Although not currently part of national security agendas, the following chapters demonstrate that the megatrend has a security imprint that is immediately felt in sectors such as geopolitics, energy, defense, the environment, and the global economy.

When actors securitize the megatrend, they exercise power with inevitable consequences for the security of other actors in multiple realms, including environmental, economic, and technological. A number of these security repercussions prompt policy reaction, as they can be destabilizers. The securitization of the megatrend's drivers, attributes, and their socio-political and socio-economic effects provides a fuller picture of the security impact of the megatrend and allows for the creation of securitization imperatives. In a sense, the megatrend itself is securitized almost by default, as it progresses within the security context of the universally securitized world.

The following analysis is premised on the understanding that the alternative energy megatrend's security impact creates its own socio-political framework that is more than the sum of the security threats emanating from it. Modern scientific and technological advances are replacing established policy imperatives, determined as much by the practical benefits technologies provide as by the knowledge they engender. The trajectory of the megatrend illustrates the increasingly complex terrain that policy-makers must navigate to cope with expanding security threats, proving the utility of the framework of universal securitization as a strategic tool with tangible applications.

The alternative energy megatrend can be considered a symptom of a revolution in global strategic relations. The analysis of the megatrend demonstrates how security complexities will be significantly affected by the world system, which is in a state of disequilibrium. With the conclusion of the last hegemonic cycle after the end of the Cold War, the transition to a new cycle is in full swing. But hegemons have been unable to estab-lish a clear-cut dominance. The previous hegemons are facing competition from new powers, the inertia of institutional rigidity, the erosion of their own economic and production base, and the rising cost of global rule enforcement.

Competitive geopolitical struggles traditionally mark the transition from one paradigm to another; they bring about and are sometimes pre-saged by the emergence of global trends. Historically, such transitions from one hegemonic cycle to another have been accompanied by war. While it will inevitably play a role in reshaping the future world order, this does not imply that the current transition will also engender violence. In a post-Westphalian decentralized world order, global approaches to secu-ritization will require a gradual transition of focus onto selected security fields and sectors, such as geopolitics, energy, defense, the environment, and the economy.

II. The grand entrance—modern alternative energy assuming the mantle of a socio-political, techno-economic, and ideological megatrend.

Why and how have modern alternative energy technologies and their mutually reinforcing drivers coalesced into a 21st century socio-political, techno-economic, and ideological megatrend?

A megatrend can be defined as a confluence of processes and events that interact and generate a "general shift in thinking or approach affect-ing countries, industries, and organizations."[37] Trends are an integration of changes in societal relations and structure brought on by the aggregate actions of social groups, communities, and political agents. They are the result of actors converging to pressure those in positions of influence to action. Trends involve several drivers—events, actions, objects, relations, and developments—that, by way of their interaction, result in a new phenomenon.

Alternative energy developments have coalesced into a trend exhibiting specific attributes that characterize them as a 21st century megatrend: a global scope that transcends geographical borders; demonstrated impacts on the actions of state and non-state actors, as well as on wider society; and a progression that alludes to longevity and has acquired an aura of permanence. Following a brief overview of existing technologies with their proven achievements and limitations, this chapter focuses on the converging and mutually reinforcing drivers that propel and constitute the megatrend and charts the development of alternative energy from ancient times through the Middle Ages, European Enlightenment, and Industrial Age.

The transformation of renewables into a trend has been influenced by society's changing understanding of energy sources since their emergence as an "alternative" to fossil fuels following World War II and during the Cold War. The processes that shaped societal perceptions and engendered the trend include globalization, fragmentation tendencies, the emergence of a multi-centric world system, and the momentum of the global technological revolution.

The themes explored here chart the lines for analyzing the alternative energy megatrend through the evolving notion of security. In later chapters, this will serve as a benchmark for determining how to approach security in the rapidly changing 21st century global security context.

1. The promise of alternative energy technologies: turning dreams and visions into reality?

The renewable energy technologies at the heart of the megatrend—hydropower, wind, solar, and biomass—are already impacting energy balances; and a range of experimental technologies—tidal, wave, hydrogen, Earth's magnetic field, and solar-from-orbit—capture the imagination as the shape of things to come. The ongoing technological revolution bolsters expectations of turning alternative energy from a dream of clean, limitless, and affordable energy into a technologically feasible, commercially viable, and environmentally friendly solution. A brief overview of the available technologies provides a glimpse into the reality behind this dream, shedding light on their proven achievements and on the issues inhibiting their wider practical uptake, as well as on their most obvious security implications.

(1) Hydropower: the ancient renewable competitor to fossil fuels.

Large-scale hydropower is a proven energy source with over 16% share of global electric power generation and 71% of all renewable electricity.[38] Hydropower has changed the energy fortunes of some countries. In Norway, an impoverished nation a century ago, hydropower plants were built on a vast scale. Today they furnish virtually all of the country's electricity and are largely responsible for—along with its sizeable oil production—Norway's energy independence. Hydroelectric resources offer obvious advantages to the countries that benefit from them.

The extent to which large-scale hydropower can help address environmental threats and mitigate climate change is controversial. Many large-scale dam projects have been criticized for altering wildlife habitats, obstructing fish migration, and affecting water quality and flow patterns. Some hydropower plants have turned out to be outright failures and environmental disasters. The Three Gorges Dam, for example, built on the Yangtze River in China drew widespread concerns around environmental and social impacts, including social tensions due to the relocation of masses of people.[39]

Large-scale hydropower's social and environmental challenges, and its potential to generate geopolitical conflict, prevent the technology from being a one-stop solution to global energy shortages. Its expansion capacity is also limited by natural restrictions, such as the availability of water resources. Additionally, developing hydroelectric resources can be prohibitively expensive.[40] Despite these drawbacks, countries like Canada, China, India, Brazil, and other emerging and developing countries are still undertaking ambitious large-scale hydropower projects, many of them funded by the World Bank and other international institutions.

Another type of hydropower project, called "run of the river," does not require large impoundment dams, and is therefore used to minimize environmental impacts. Although "run of the river" is less harmful to the environment, the system is less efficient as it relies on river flows that fluctuate. Small-capacity hydropower[41] is another option for some countries. Even though smaller plants tend to be less economically competitive than larger plants, interest in developing small hydropower remains high in China, the United States, and several countries in Southern and Eastern Europe. Developing small-capacity hydropower can involve building new structures or attaching power plants to existing dams, as is being done in the United States.

From a traditional security standpoint, the development of hydroelectric infrastructure across large rivers that cross several countries has created geopolitical tensions.[42] This is clearly evident in the strained ties between downstream Uzbekistan and the upstream countries of Tajikistan and Kyrgyzstan. Another salient example is the Three Gorges Dam in China, which threatens water access in many neighboring countries, including India, Bangladesh, Myanmar, Laos, Thailand, Cambodia, and Vietnam. Resolving such disputes is increasingly difficult as upstream countries seek to rectify their energy deficits by constructing hydropower stations and plants that downstream countries fear could deprive them of water.

(2) Wind, solar, biofuels, geothermal: established technologies that must pass the test of modern times.

In addition to hydropower, there are several renewable energy sources that are considered "established," which are currently at the heart of the megatrend. Leading the list are wind, solar power, biofuels, and geothermal.

Wind energy harnesses the power of the wind to propel the blades of wind turbines,[43] a well-known procedure that possibly originated in Persia and was brought to Europe by 12th century Crusaders.[44] Wind energy capacity is continuously growing and, in certain countries, growth is rapid.[45] Countries with high wind energy production are therefore able to reduce their dependency on fossil fuels. In 2016, wind energy covered an estimated 10.4% of EU demand and equal or higher shares in at least 11 EU member states, as well as in Uruguay and Costa Rica.[46]

Nevertheless, there are several well-documented challenges associated with wind power. These include lack of transmission infrastructure, delays in grid connection, and lack of public acceptance. Curtailment regulations and current management systems make it difficult to integrate large amounts of wind power into the renewables energy mix.[47] Wind power is also subject to intermittency. It becomes unviable for consistent use when capacity reaches a certain level which, together with low power density, can limit its widespread application. In addition, skeptics of wind energy raise concerns about its repercussions on human health, including possible auditory and behavioral effects, and its possible interference with other infrastructure. However, health warnings and other hazards related to wind turbines largely remain unsubstantiated and the problems of variable output may be addressed, for example, by widespread geographical output from wind farms, such as those in the North Sea.

Financially, wind energy is often capable of competing with traditional sources without state subsidies, and in some cases, has achieved grid parity. In 2016, onshore wind was already the most cost-effective option for new grid-based power in many markets, including Brazil, Canada, Chile, Mexico, Morocco, South Africa, Turkey, China, Europe, the United States and parts of Australia.[48] Still, wind energy needs a quantum leap in technological development to overcome intermittency issues in order to truly compete with fossil fuels.

Both wind power's successes and drawbacks have geopolitical implications. While companies such as General Electric in the United States are developing new turbine technologies that are designed for use in low-wind areas, broader application of wind energy technologies will ultimately favor the stakeholders that have access to the geographical spaces where wind conditions are optimal. This raises two separate issues. First, wind energy will benefit only certain countries, which, like the geographic spread of fossil resources, could lead to perceptions of inequity and exploitation in the long run. Second, offshore wind energy in particular could unleash disputes over international water jurisdictions and their use, despite successful examples of cross-border transmission in Europe.

Solar power has the highest theoretical power generation capacity of all renewables.[49] It is only limited in principle by the sun's lifetime. It has generated interest throughout history. In 1931, shortly before he died, Thomas Edison told his friends Henry Ford and Harvey Firestone: "I'd put my money on the sun and solar energy. What a source of power! I hope we don't have to wait 'til oil and coal run out before we tackle that."[50] Despite this early enthusiasm, current solar power technologies still face a number of challenges, making it difficult to harness extensive solar output efficiently. There are two main types of solar energy: Photovoltaic (PV) and Concentrating Solar Thermal Power (CSP) technologies.[51] While both remain relatively costly methods of generating power in comparison to fossil fuels and other renewables, the cost of PV equipment has dropped substantially in recent years. Solar PV module prices have declined around 80% since 2007 (from approximately US$4 per watt in 2007 to approximately US$1.8 per watt in 2015).[52] In the Mediterranean and other climates with high levels of solar irradiation, PV is rapidly approaching retail grid parity, meaning that the cost of PV-generated electricity is nearly the same as power obtained from conventional fuels. The cost is expected to be further reduced as new technologies are approaching commercialization, such as perovskite cells (cells that include perovskite (crystal) structured compounds that are simple to manufacture and relatively inexpensive to produce).[53] Despite PV's popularity, CSP has a few advantages: dispatchability and generating electricity while the sun is down. Significant installed CSP capacity is found in the United States and in Spain. Israel, Morocco, and South Africa are also taking steps to apply the technology. China brought online its first CSP facility, Shouhang Dunhuang, in 2016.[54] While there has been continuous improvement in the conversion efficiency of PV cells, concentrated photovoltaics (CPV)[55] may hold the key in enabling rapid increases in solar energy efficiency, recently reaching 46% for solar cells. The advantage of CPV is its ability to be easily integrated into existing electric utility grids.

With more widespread use of solar power, the political geography of electric power could directly and indirectly affect geo-economic and geopolitical dynamics between states. Solar exposure could become a valuable resource for less developed countries. Solar energy technologies are widespread and can provide geopolitical advantages to countries that have large amounts of solar irradiation. However, for countries to employ solar power as a geopolitical tool, they will need to make extensive investments. Advanced economies are more likely to achieve technological advances in solar power because they have relatively superior financing capabilities.

Biomass energy refers to living and non-living biological materials such as plant matter, abiotic trees and branches, yard clippings, and wood chips that can be used to fuel industrial production or generate electricity.[56]

Biofuels have long been touted as a feasible energy source.[57] Rudolf Diesel, the inventor of the diesel engine, indicated in 1893: "The use of plant oil as fuel may seem insignificant today. But such products can in time become just as important as kerosene and these coal-tar-products of today."[58] The technology itself is mature and the fuels can be used as direct replacements for fossil fuels. While production has increased steadily overall, fluctuations in producing countries' climates, harvest conditions, and exogenous economic factors, such as food prices and fossil fuel prices, can impede the sector's growth. The bioenergy share in total global primary energy consumption has remained relatively steady from 2005 to 2017 at around 10.5%, despite a 21% increase in overall global energy demand over the past 10 years.[59]

While many bioenergy technologies are well established and fully commercial, biomass energy suffers from numerous supply and application challenges.[60] At present, it can replace only a small portion of fossil fuels. It is used in transportation by being added to petrol at no greater than 10%

of the fuel mix and diesel at no greater than 20%.[61] Transportation, plant construction, and high maintenance costs are also limiting factors.

In addition, the full production cycle and use of biofuels raise questions about their environmental impact and effect on deforestation, food prices, water, and other essential resources. For example, the production of ethanol and other cereal-based fuels directly competes with, and reduces, the supply of commodities like corn. Moreover, regulatory regimes driving biofuels production in various countries more closely resemble subsidy programs rather than innovative incubators aimed at scaling the technology. The spill-over of biofuels into a number of sectors such as food, farming, and the environment are complicating policymaking, and restricting biofuels' development as an industry.

Biofuels can offer geopolitical and energy security advantages to states that perceive themselves as dependent on energy from hostile countries or aspiring rivals. Even though their production and export has already led to tensions, as in the case of the U.S.-Brazil bioethanol trade dispute,[62] biofuels can be a direct source of energy security and add to the diversification of the energy mix. Biofuels can therefore be both a practical consideration and a policy option that can enhance geopolitical power.

The pursuit of geothermal energy[63] illustrates the considerations and challenges of modern technological development. Deep-underground geothermal energy capacity is still in the early stages of development, despite first being proven on a commercial scale more than a century ago. The construction and maintenance of a geothermal plant requires heavy capital investment and inflexible siting primarily concentrated on geological plate boundaries. Currently, the United States is a leading producer of geothermal power, though there is large growth potential in East Africa, Central America, and Asia.

Natural conditions, such as steam, hot water, and reservoir productivity, influence the number of wells that must be drilled for a given plant capacity. Geothermal energy is more costly than fossil fuels and most other renewables because suitable locations are usually far from energy markets, which increases the cost of transmission.

As such, geothermal energy has not yet reached a stage of technological development that enables it to compete with fossil fuels or even other renewables. Such a prospect appears unlikely in the short or medium term. Additionally, geothermal energy development can lead to possible tectonic movements, resonance amplifications, and damage to ecological systems, raising costs and externalities.

However, extensive research and development efforts are being undertaken to make geothermal production commercially competitive. The government-funded FORGE initiative in the United States,[64] for instance, focused on developing and testing technologies for Enhanced Geothermal Systems (ESG), and geothermal systems research was undertaken in the UK in regions such as Cornwall, which were until recently deemed unfeasible for development.[65] In contrast to deep-underground geothermal, near-surface geothermal involving heat exchange is a widely used technology. Iceland obtains almost all its heating from near-surface geothermal systems.

(3) *Tidal, wave, hydrogen, nuclear fusion, Earth's magnetic field, and solar-from-orbit: experimental precursors of upcoming linear advancements.*

Potential benefits from the alternative energy megatrend are expanded by the prospect for truly "alternative," or more far-fetched, energy sources. Options that currently appear unviable, such as tidal, wave, hydrogen, Earth's magnetic field, and solar-from-orbit, may be developed during the megatrend's evolution and could reshape global energy security balances. For these technologies to contribute to energy security, their theoretical capabilities would need to be converted into practical applications.

Tidal power comes from the relative motions of Earth and the Moon, and of Earth within the solar system. Tides are more predictable than wind, which suffers from intermittencies, and solar energy, which fluctuates depending on irradiation levels and weather. The earliest applications date from the Middle Ages and some sources suggest it was used as early as in the Roman era. In the words of author, inventor, and futurist Arthur C. Clarke: "How inappropriate to call this planet 'Earth,' when clearly it is 'Ocean.'"[66] Tidal energy can be generated in three ways: by tidal streams, barrages (low dams), and tidal lagoons.[67] Power created through tidal stream generators is generally more environmentally friendly and causes less impact upon established ecosystems. Akin to a wind turbine, many tidal stream generators rotate underwater and are driven by the swiftly moving dense water.

There is growing recognition that tidal power may be viable, and numerous projects have been designed to feed into national electricity grids, increasing their widespread utility and commercial application. Several pilot and demonstration projects around the world, including in Spain, Sweden, the United States, the Republic of Korea, and China, are under way.[68] Tidal power also has disadvantages. There has been limited testing of the technology and many questions relating to its use remain unanswered.

Obstacles primarily involve particularly high start-up costs and the need for energy storage technologies that match the timing of tides. Furthermore, there is uncertainty regarding the efficiency and environmental impact of tidal power's large-scale deployment.

Wave generation technologies capture and transport energy generated by ocean surface waves. This energy is used for electricity generation, desalination of water, and pumping water into reservoirs. Wave energy is difficult to harness because the ocean and wave directions are unpredictable. Wave energy is therefore rarely generated on a practical scale since the technology and its infrastructure are at a very early stage of development and the costs of technology are high.[69] However, a number of projects are exploring building systems that are survivable and serviceable such as the large commercial wave energy facility being constructed in Sweden.[70]

The advantages that tidal and wave technologies could convey to specific stakeholders are difficult to ascertain. Since they are not available to all countries and actors, these technologies could lead to confrontations over access, particularly in territories and seas in which borders are disputed.

At first glance, hydrogen is an energy panacea with its high energy content and minimal pollution.[71] This resource, however, is an anomalous renewable. It is not a primary source of energy, but rather an energy vector because it is obtained using energy from another source. There is no free hydrogen in Earth's atmosphere or anywhere else on the planet—it needs to be extracted, usually from water or hydrocarbons. Although it is difficult to predict their long-term development, hydrogen fuel cells are deemed a promising technology. They could furnish heat and electricity for buildings and power electric motors that propel vehicles.[72] Despite its potential, hydrogen remains a costly and difficult-to-implement technology. Yet, the viable application of hydrogen technology could modify current geopolitical calculations.

Producing vast amounts of energy from nuclear fusion has been a long-held dream of physicists. The prospect of fusion emerged following World War II when physicists began to reproduce the reaction that occurs in the sun and stars. Fusion reactions normally combine two isotopes of hydrogen—deuterium and tritium. When combined under high pressure and temperature, they fuse together to become plasma. During this reaction, neutrons and energy are released. Nuclear fusion seeks to capture this energy and produce electricity through conventional methods (e.g., steam).

Many experimental devices around the world can produce fusion for a short period of time, but these reactors require the use of far more energy

than they generate. To demonstrate the viability of this form of energy production on a vast scale, several countries have undertaken the International
Thermonuclear Experimental Reactor (ITER) project. The ITER partners
have built an experimental fusion reactor in Cadarache in southern France. It
is currently the world's largest scientific partnership with the aim of demonstrating the scientific and technological feasibility of fusion as an energy
source.[73] The cost of the project is currently estimated at 20 billion euros.[74]

The European Fusion Development Agreement, the agency responsible for the EU's contribution of 45% to ITER,[75] published the EU's roadmap
toward the realization of fusion energy, though it recognizes that sweeping
efforts still have to be carried out in order to make fusion reactors viable.[76]
In addition, China is developing its own fusion device commonly known as
"artificial sun," which will be an important testing device during the development of ITER. Given that its fuel and application are inexhaustible, clean,
and secure, fusion energy could play an important role in the future energy
mix. However, along with technical and political challenges, it will also face
competition from other, more cost-effective renewables.[77]

Power generation using Earth's magnetic field is an experimental technology which generates electricity by using Earth's magnetic field through
electrodynamic tethers or similar devices.[78] It is currently only at a theoretical stage and there are no known efforts to implement it. Its geopolitical
impact is therefore difficult to predict.

Another example of a revolutionary energy source is orbital power.
Scientists are currently conducting experiments using satellites to beam
solar energy down to Earth as a radio frequency. These satellites, which are
equipped with photovoltaic panels, could greatly transform global security
realities. In the absence of a filtering atmosphere, the PV panels have longer
direct exposure to sunlight, significantly increasing their energy absorption
capacity.[79]

Other innovative technologies include "Atmospheric Vortex Engines"
that generate electricity from the troposphere and nanotech-enabled
solar panels. There are also far-fetched theories regarding Helium-3 (He3)
mining on the moon. While most of these experiments may not become
viable technologies, "alternatives" can nevertheless generate non-linear
leaps. An outstanding example of this is the effort by American scientists at
the Lawrence Berkeley National Laboratory to develop a virus-based piezoelectric generator.[80]

The path toward practical deployment of these visionary technologies
has yet to come into full focus. Experimental technologies like geothermal,

tidal, and wave energy remain largely unviable and limited mostly to pilot projects. Options such as hydrogen cells, magnetic field generation, and solar-from-orbit need even more investment and time for their feasibility to be determined.

These technologies of the future hold undetected potential to transform human life. The development and large-scale deployment of alternative technologies could help form new civilization paradigms, along the lines of Freeman Dyson's civilization "Types," with far-reaching implications for global security.[81]

The primary renewables technologies currently in use are relatively insulated from competition and their development appears restricted to a linear progression. However, the drivers of the alternative energy megatrend are acting as a catalyst for significant techno-economic, and sociopolitical changes that endow them with the potential for non-linear advances.

2. The trend's emerging identity as a factor in the Grand Energy Game: the mutually reinforcing and converging drivers behind the trend.

To understand why alternative energy developments represent a modern socio-political, techno-economic, and ideological megatrend, it is important to examine the driving forces that propel them. These driving forces include the increasing global energy demand as a material force that substantiates the megatrend, as well as a number of other critical drivers: growing environmental concerns, pursuit of economic growth, modern technological advances, the impact of energy on defense, society's changing ethical imperatives, the exploration of new paths toward empowerment, and the growing worldwide framework of associated policies and regulations.[82]

These driving forces are the essence of this trend; they actually constitute the alternative energy trend itself.[83] Their interactions shape the trend and their convergence makes it more than the sum of different, disparate parts. These drivers are a series of converging quantitative and qualitative transitions that accrue gradually and are often imperceptible over time. Collectively, these evolving forces find an expression in the visions, policies, and societal responses that define the trend and establish its new identity.

This identity is particularly relevant to the alternative energy megatrend's security trajectory. In a universally securitized world, the broad array of drivers propelling the trend act as the key focal points for its significance in terms of security. Through the securitization of these drivers, the megatrend assumes a meta-securitization with a connotation greater than the sum of its parts.[84] The megatrend and its components form a gestalt, and are in a symbiotic, mutually reinforcing relationship.

The megatrend's meta-securitization has vast and powerful potential. When the megatrend's drivers converge, they create the alternative energy phenomenon's own far-reaching security impact. The contradiction of immediate and long-term considerations is particularly pertinent, as the urgent is often dictated by societal pressure on policymakers. As a result, the process by which actors evaluate and deal with threats is distorted due to internal political pressures and considerations, potentially resulting in counter-productive and deficient actions in the longer term. This meta-securitization, however, enables the analysis of the 21st century security complexities that alternative energy generates.

(1) The insatiable demand for energy: coalescence of demand-supply calculations into a future energy vision.

Undoubtedly, a leading driver of the alternative energy trend is increasing global energy demand. Energy security approaches, such as independence, diversification, and interdependence, focus on the search for new reliable local alternatives to fossil fuels. Alternative energy developments have become an expression of the need to find options beyond carbon-emitting fossil fuels.

They are, more or less, the realization of futurist ambitions for uninterrupted affordable and controllable energy, a hedge against price fluctuations, manipulations, and restrictions of supply. The integration of renewables into energy security policies and strategies has been met with widespread support. Within the EU, for example, Europeans overwhelmingly support the enhanced use of renewable energies in order to reduce current energy dependency and strengthen the economy.[85] In the United States, the polls show that "across the political spectrum, large majorities support expansion of solar panel and wind turbine farms."[86]

The current and future uptake of renewables correlates with the fluctuating demand and supply of fossil fuels, and to an extent, nuclear energy. Of concern for actors is the ability to ensure sufficient supplies to meet domestic demand, which prompts calls for energy independence, supply diversification, and energy interdependence. Energy shocks, like supply disruptions or restrictions, cause price fluctuations and supply misallocations that are regarded as a failure of the current energy paradigm.

Naturally, when demand for fossil energy outstrips supply, states seek ways of redressing the balance and avoiding dependence on external

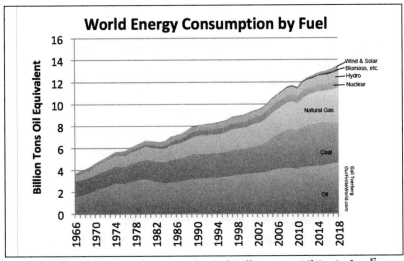

Figure 1: Global Energy Consumption by Fuel, Billion Tons Oil Equivalent[87]

sources. They also endeavor to expand the array of suppliers, and re-focus on the search for new resources. When there is oversupply of fossil energy, the situation is reversed. For example, many view the decrease in oil prices following the resolution of the 1973 oil crisis and 1979 OPEC oil embargo as the key factor that slowed the development of renewable energy in the 20th century.[88] At the same time, the impact of these crises stressed the need for shock-resistant energy policies and less dependence on fossil fuels.

It is perceived that a shift away from fossil-based energy to alternatives would also prevent some actors from manipulating access to energy. Support for their development can "help insulate alternative liquid fuels from OPEC market manipulation designed to cripple oil's competitors."[89]

In that context, oil and gas dependence have cast alternative energy as the dominant means of protection from energy manipulation by hostile actors, and thereby as the preeminent local solution to global problems.

Of particular significance is the value ascribed to renewables as an energy security solution. Doomsday scenarios, such as the prediction that energy demand could double by 2030, have in turn provoked gloomy projections of scarcity.[90] These forecasts might foster a long-term commitment to alternative energy. However, doomsday scenarios have existed for some time only to be averted by new technologies, sources of energy, and approaches to energy efficiency.[91] The limitations and aspirations embodied in renewable energy are a key component of the trend.

(2) The expansion of dominant environmental concerns: the imperatives for a "new habitat" here and now.
The alternative energy megatrend is driven by growing aspirations to protect the environment and human habitat.[92] Extensive studies that point to the immediacy of man-made environmental threats are transforming alternative energy into a major instrument for mitigating threats such as climate change. President Richard Nixon's establishment of the U.S. Environmental Protection Agency marks a major milestone on the road to greater government involvement in energy affairs.[93] The global environmental summits, although their practical outcomes may be limited, are steadily promoting worldwide policies to mitigate climate change risks. Public and political pressure to halt climate change sooner persists and influences the development of policies that bolster renewable energy.

Beyond environmental security, alternative energy is becoming a focal point of demands for a new eco-system which reconciles human existence and wellbeing with nature. Renewables are not simply expected to clean up the world we live in; their use is seen by some to presage a reconstitution of the global habitat in a new, green, and unquestionably beneficial manner. A prominent example of this mindset is the "smart cities" concept aligning economic viability, environmental sustainability, and high quality of life based on the application of new technologies and a participatory public administration model.[94]

Overall, a broadening "green agenda" is accelerating support for renewable energy. Alternative energy might yield advantages beyond a cleaner environment, including improved quality of public health and efficient use of resources, thus becoming the solution of choice for proponents of sustainable development models.

Advances in renewable energy technologies also allow states to put forward claims of political and technological leadership under the banner of a new "green economy." Environmental considerations are blended with foreign policy and loftier goals, such as human wellbeing and civil liberties. A range of actors see alternative energy as capable of moving the world toward a greener and more prosperous stage, prompting almost clichéd comparisons to "Archimedes lever."[95]

(3) The economic growth dictum: alternative energy as a stabilizer against economic risks.
Another critical driver of the alternative energy megatrend is the imperative for economic stability and growth. Economic security is a dominant

consideration in human endeavors. It entails the pursuit of stable growth, economic diversity and independence, job creation, and resilience to volatility and economic shocks. It also includes predatory economic behavior, economic power projection and cooperation.

Alternative energy is seen as capable of contributing to current and future economic growth as its technologies have the potential to produce gradual capacity improvements and cost reductions with beneficial implications for local, regional, and global economies. Renewables offer new options for economic diversification and can act as a springboard for the development of new industries. As public goods, renewables are relatively abundant and viewed as immune from price and supply volatility that plagues other industries and commodities. Introducing renewable energy technologies could offer new ways of creating wealth and boosting economic development.

Alternative energy is increasingly associated with the capacity to address problems of cyclicality. For instance, renewables are expected to reduce the volatility of national output and price levels by, according to Lord Peter Truscott, "opening up markets to competition and interconnection, thereby promoting investment in power generating capacity and transmission networks, whilst at the same time allowing for greater solidarity...in the event of supply disruptions."[96]

Ultimately, the alternative energy megatrend's projected outcomes allow economies to produce new competitive advantages, prompting policymakers to embrace the trend's promised outcomes. This is particularly important for post-industrial developed economies, where technological transformation furnishes one of the few options beyond service-oriented growth.

(4) The global technological revolution: a precondition and challenge.

The new technological capabilities arising during the global technological revolution are not only drivers, but also preconditions of the alternative energy megatrend. The ongoing Fourth Industrial Revolution is bringing together physical and digital technologies to create cyber-physical systems where data collected from physical systems is used to drive intelligent action back in the physical world.[97] Artificial intelligence, cognitive technologies, the Internet of Things, 3D printing, blockchain, mobile devices, and other breakthrough technologies[98] are transforming manufacturing and logistics, reshaping markets, changing business models, regulations, and lifestyles. Nevertheless, in the energy sector, it is undeniable that "Artificial intelligence has a huge potential for the drastic modernization of...the energy sector."[99]

The advances in connectivity, intelligence, and flexible automation will propel the alternative energy megatrend by providing solutions which will make generation and distribution of energy from renewable sources technically feasible and commercially viable—lowering capital expenditures and operating and maintenance costs as well as supporting sustainable grid integration of decentralized renewable power generation units. A broad array of new technologies—battery storage, micro-grids, analytics software, and intelligent substations—are expected to be integrated into the "retailized" power grid, while new home and office electric power installations may become "gateway hubs," providing not just energy, but security and telecommunications links.[100]

Technological advancements in alternative energy fit seamlessly within the technological revolution: they are subjected to systematic observation, measurement, and experimentation. As new horizons open up in the course of this revolution, alternative energy is achieving a level of acceptance that is successfully withstanding the initial disbelief and resistance that is usual "when a new invention is first propounded," where "in the beginning every man objects, and the poor inventor runs the gauntloop of all petulant wits."[101]

The ongoing, yet relatively quiet global technological revolution is establishing the framework of knowledge, capabilities, and needs for the alternative energy megatrend. In other words, the global technological revolution is providing a foundation that supports the megatrend's ongoing evolution. Without this knowledge base, many of the inventions necessary for the commercialization and wide-scale use of alternatives—smart grids, energy storage, new materials, and physiochemical applications—would not only be impossible, but also inconceivable.

Further, renewables are entrenched in the positive connotations of the very "idea of progress"[102] since they are viewed as one of the precursors of the next technological breakthrough. Alternative energy developments therefore acquire momentum even when they merely advance technological understanding and lack economic justification. Advances in alternative energy developments are therefore labelled as "progressive" and "beneficial," regardless of whether they are embraced by broader society.

Technological advancements are not limited to civilian applications; the military is both a major consumer and source of technological developments. In this regard, the exchange between military and civilian applications is increasing the pace of technological developments. Technology is a significant factor in security and is "beginning to transform the cultural and political codes of security—civil and military."[103] From this perspective, alternative energy benefits from a long line of previous advances and disciplines that have found practical applications.

Alternative energy developments are tied to the expectation of rapid growth associated with the modern technological revolution. This understanding of technological progress has underpinned global advances over the last 700 years. The resulting improvements in human wellbeing are uncontested. Malthus,[104] for example, would be disturbed by the fact that Earth's resources are managing to support a population that exceeds seven billion. Alternative energy technologies, wrapped up in this expectation of rapid change, are thus seen as reshaping society.[105] The pursuit of new renewable energy technologies can have outcomes with widespread repercussions not limited just to the energy sector. Renewable technologies are thus supported by expectations of technological leaps and non-linear advances.

The techno-scientific essence of the alternative energy megatrend has added to its socio-political momentum, seemingly providing the missing piece in its make-up. The technological advances of the 21st century appear to be answering Auguste Comte's contention that "now that the human mind has founded celestial physics, terrestrial physics (mechanical and chemical), and organic physics (vegetable and animal), it only remains to complete the system of observational sciences by the foundation of social physics."[106] Adding alternative energy developments to advances in biotechnology, nanotechnology, materials technology, and information technology bolsters the ability of technology to act as a catalyst for social change.[107]

As a factor that affects political and economic outcomes, technology goes beyond the ability to create goods, move objects and people across distances, or provide cures for diseases. It spurs a broader dissemination of knowledge that in turn generates new visions and ideas of what can be achieved, creating new hopes, aspirations, and promises.

(5) The quest for new military capabilities: reshaping strategic and tactical approaches and practices in line with the emerging security context.

Another significant driver is the integration of renewables into the 21st century defense sector. This integration is happening against the backdrop of the new Great Power Competition and the Fourth Industrial Revolution. Indeed, "Artificial intelligence, quantum computing, autonomy [] are the technologies that are going to define how our societies are structured, how our militaries are structured."[108]

The defense sector's continuous search for new energy solutions entails the pursuit of operational advantages, cost savings, and efficiency improvements. It is motivated by strategic considerations, the need to free resources, and the need to alleviate the burden of protecting fossil fuel infrastructure and supply lines in operational theatres.

New geopolitical changes and technological solutions are prompting a transformation in the defense sector. New technological capabilities are becoming integrated into existing military concepts and planning, in turn leading to a transition to a new level of military organization, strategy, and tactics. The alternative energy megatrend reflects and influences the parameters of inter-state competition and protection of vital national interests, reshaping defense approaches and practices.

The U.S. and other defense establishments are investigating the future benefits of alternative energy. The unforeseen military capabilities that alternative energy might deliver could be far greater than a mere replacement of fossil fuels, and could offer the means to attain a new defense paradigm. Modern military roles and missions that face asymmetric violence, unpredictability, frozen conflicts, and failed states[109] are further contributing to the imperative to integrate renewables development into the global security architecture.

Beyond direct defense benefits, the defense community is expected to serve as a source of technological advances, adding momentum to the spread of renewables. In the early 20th century, the combination of the internal combustion engine and the machine gun resulted in the invention of armored vehicles and aircraft that revolutionized warfare. In the same manner, alternative energy's role in defense-led advances can grow considerably and generate mass-market applications that could propel alternatives to new heights. Yet just as the military application of aircraft technologies took some time to materialize at the start of World War I, so too will the application of renewables in military operations.

(6) The new empowerment for the new times: state, community, and individual aspirations.

Renewables promise new powers for individuals, communities, states, and non-governmental entities as they seek to resolve pressing challenges. They point to the possibility of independence from the outside world, and the infrastructure and environment that surround us. For state and non-state actors, renewable energy grants the ability to transform balances and provide new abilities to promote their cause.

The trend promises state actors new levels of energy independence, geopolitical positioning, power-projection capabilities, insurance against volatility and shocks, and, more broadly, opportunities for assuming new stances in their strategies and policies. As "the political aspirations and projects of geopolitical agents are won and lost within a structure of geographic scales,"[110] alternative energy can help states leverage power, endowing them with greater capabilities.

Alternative energy developments can also play a role in empowering civil society in the global policymaking process. Renewables enable society to challenge states and influence domestic and foreign agendas. Momentum is even growing behind alternative energy as a symbol of collective empowerment with a capacity to overcome obstacles and achieve social change in many areas of global concern. This has led to an alignment of the technological community and environmental movements, such as Greenpeace and Friends of the Earth, behind the development of renewables. This is an unprecedented feat given the actors' sometimes mutually exclusive positions on biotech and other technological developments.

The megatrend also empowers communities to be independent and develop sustainably in line with a new "green agenda." There are concerns about the fate of global common resources prompting groups and communities to seek ways of contributing to environmental safety and security. Renewables are an easy "do-it-yourself" option for being more environmentally conscious at home and work, making previously contentious policies more acceptable. For instance, solar panels can easily be installed on residential and commercial buildings, enabling consumers to control their energy source and potentially receive a financial benefit from the surplus delivered back to the central utility grid.

The megatrend is propelled by individuals' quest for new, "natural" ways of achieving prosperity, self-reliance, and self-governance. As science and technological development becomes increasingly participatory, it becomes an effective tool for individual influence on politics and policymaking. Renewables have particularly empowered individuals to participate in policy debates in the areas of environmental security and health, economic security, and, increasingly, energy security. Although still limited, the broadening of constituencies that participate in the scientific development process has resulted in their accrual of power and influence.

In effect, the rise of the alternative energy megatrend reflects a developing ecosphere of socio-material factors[111] that are forming specific new societal structures and power relations among actors, institutions, and individuals. This 21st century ecosphere is subjected to strategic manipulations. In the process of these manipulations, modern phenomena, such as the alternative energy megatrend, are engendered and transformed to serve new purposes. These transformations demonstrate the emerging ability of actors to influence greater society, reversing the historical top-down process of policymaking in exchange for a society shaped by grassroots efforts.

(7) The ethical imperative: the moral impetus driving the trend as a "morally superior" form of energy.

Beside pragmatic calculations, the alternative energy megatrend is provided with added momentum by increasingly powerful moral imperatives in society. Alternative energy embodies an inherent "goodness" and "moral superiority" by establishing a harmonious relationship between humanity and nature. As such, history has witnessed an evolution in ethics associated with energy production and consumption—a moral position that is affecting behavior and social order.

Renewables are caught in an almost Manichean vision of good and evil[112] that interpolates the distinct divisions of this age-old contest into societal interpretations of the megatrend. For many segments of society, renewables embody a force for good, in the unwavering morality of "ultimate good" and "ultimate evil" rooted in Judeo-Christian principles.

Alternative energy presents itself as "intrinsically good;" a path to a good life and good society. Advocates of renewables argue that "renewables [are] cheaper, safer, and an altogether more sensible energy choice...."[113] based on an ethical response to climate change and sustainability challenges. The trend is thus positioned by members of society, the mass media, and even by some states as morally superior to other sources of energy.

The moral superiority ascribed to alternative energy permits and sometimes prompts new policy choices. This phenomena is best ontologically captured in the following: "though man (or the state) is initially motivated into action through the dynamism of interests (both material and ideal), it is his mental construct or 'image' of the external world which determines the nature or direction of this movement."[114] In this binary framework, those that deny the imminence of climate change and other environmental threats are included in the "evil" camp.

However, viewed more closely, the moral values attached to alternative energy developments have inherent inconsistencies. This is especially true regarding the costs associated with the deployment of new technologies. Because "energy is considered a commodity which is indispensably necessary for the support of life," one of the largest ethical issues is the impact alternative energy initiatives have on the poor.[115] Given current market realities, adoption of renewables is highly dependent on the financial resources that can be spared—once again making prosperity the realm of the rich, and unobtainable by the poor. This reflects a gap in the alternative energy trend between an optimal system and what is ideal for humans, "a bridge of excuses between the system and the individual, [which] spans the abyss between the aims of the system and the aims of life."[116]

In addition, renewables have unaddressed vulnerabilities and practical problems. For example, the rapid development of biofuels presents its own ethical conundrums. Increasing the proportion of biofuels in the energy mix has resulted in deforestation and rising food prices as crops envisioned for food consumption have been diverted to biofuel production. Solar and wind farms present ethical issues related to land use.

Alternative energy technologies form a reality that may not be fully tangible in the same space and time as the observer, but regardless are influential and actionable to such a degree that "the framework of former ethics can no longer contain them."[117] In a sense, as society increasingly ascribes ethical values to the political and economic sphere, the alternative energy technologies offer policy options that fall firmly in the moral high ground, or the "right side of history."

(8) The policies and regulations: integrating the drivers into a trend and transforming them into a phenomenon vastly surpassing its own drivers.

The crucial set of factors that not only propels the megatrend but also integrates all of its drivers is the coalescing domestic and international regulatory frameworks. To sufficiently promote the megatrend, these frameworks need to reflect three unavoidable 21st century realities. First, humanity is dependent on energy. Second, we are in the midst of the Fourth Industrial Revolution which will transform the way humanity interacts with energy. Third, these exponential technologies will disrupt individuals, businesses, governments, and societies in ways we can barely imagine today.

Policymakers are often driven by discreet near-term imperatives such as the pollution imperative, the technology competition/profit imperative, and the climate change imperative. That leaves an important question:

are national and global governance bodies able to create the holistic forward-thinking policies to manage the technological disruption that will characterize the energy landscape of the future? This encompasses the minutiae of creating new regulatory paradigms, managing the positive and negative impacts on labor markets, upgrading infrastructure, and broader challenges such as effectively managing the vast geopolitical and security implications.

Proactive government policies to clarify an emerging technology's regulatory environment can facilitate a new advancement's development or implementation as well as identify and persistently remove the roadblocks in front of human creativity and entrepreneurship. Energy policies dedicated specifically to renewables remain relatively rare, with the majority primarily focused on fossil fuels. However, removal of fossil fuel subsidies, for example, may not be prompted by, but will inevitably affect, renewables. Such policies are often a compilation of unrelated measures, and sometimes pursue contrary goals. Nonetheless, this indirect framework is a backdrop and unifier for the drivers explored above.

National laws and regulations directly spur alternative energy developments. Some policies directly incentivize renewables, while others offset competitive advantages of other forms of energy.[118] The alternative energy megatrend is thus path-dependent and institutionally situated by the processes of decision-making and policy implementation. Although policies guide development, they can sometimes backfire.[119] There is a growing call to harmonize domestic policies under international frameworks to hasten the alternative energy trend.

As Henry Kissinger and George Shultz argued, "[c]limate change and energy equally demand a cooperative global approach. We must not be diverted from these tasks by an avoidable policy of confrontation."[120] The emerging regulatory infrastructure can be seen in international institutions, practices, and organizations that have gradually established themselves as important producers of "soft law," or so-called secondary international law regimes, which are non-binding and focus on recommendations, guidelines, and standards.[121] Adopted in 2015, the UN's Global Sustainable Development Goals are a step towards synchronization of various states policies into an overarching international framework.[122] International trade in renewable energy is currently governed by existing international law and the rules of the World Trade Organization.[123] However, aligning domestic policies and international frameworks remains a challenging task since states are intrinsically linked to the particular socio-cultural context from which they emerged.

The convergence of alternative energy-related commitments, initiatives, and regulations into a global regulatory framework could result in a set of fiscal mechanisms, augmented by restrictive measures on the energy industry. Such regulatory policies, as Richard Haass has posited, "...will be the principal means of discouraging demand and encouraging the development of alternative energy sources and technologies."[124] They carry an implicit intent to create a market niche for renewables through cap-and-trade and carbon offset measures, as well as by providing greater access to renewables financing.[125]

In sum, the alternative energy megatrend is represented by, and goes beyond, its converging and mutually reinforcing drivers. In their interaction, they are not stand-alone events or phenomena, but are bundled together by ideas, notions, and visions that result in pragmatic and moral choices. These drivers are reinforced and channeled by a framework of local, regional, and international regulations. When combined, the drivers form the identity of the alternative energy megatrend.

(9) The ever-continuing social construction of the megatrend: impact, invention, and reinvention.

The alternative energy megatrend is a typical socially constructed phenomenon.[126] It is a consequence of the convergence of knowledge and actions by society, which in isolation could not instigate the creation of such a phenomenon, but together provide it with ongoing momentum and tangible presence. This does not preclude the megatrend's ability to exert influence on society, as "any stable pattern of rules, institutions and unintended consequences gives society a structure, recognizable as such to any observer."[127]

Human environments are shaped by human interaction, not just with nature but within and between individuals, social groups, and communities. The interaction between elements of society is a two-way process. In the same way that social relations construct people as individuals, individuals acting in concert modify the world in which they live. In this context, there is no distinction between natural and socially constructed objects— the reality within which we operate is the same product of form given to it.

In the words of Aristotle, "having form, the things of the world produce other things by giving form to them."[128] This interaction is characterized by individual choices being made in pursuit of a specific goal, and the effect that these choices have, whether intended or unintended. Alternative energy developments are no exception—they are formed by the interaction between individuals and the environment. They reveal societal priorities, which materialize into future organizational approaches and social institutions.

The perception of the alternative energy megatrend is determined by both systemic and intrinsic factors. Systemic factors include overall technological development, along with infrastructure compatibility and flexibility. Intrinsic factors include the readiness to be deployed, cost, and resource sufficiency. These factors are all formed by an interactive process between society and the technology itself.

The attitudes and ideas behind the alternative energy megatrend reflect efforts to address and securitize threats to human wellbeing and standards of living. These ideas affect relations within and between communities and change the direction of human efforts—from neighborhood movements to political parties, and from specific personal choices to actions by states or groups of states.[129] The alternative energy megatrend is also underwriting renewed approaches toward global governance.

The alternative energy megatrend's overt and subtle impacts can be equated with a societal Rorschach test—a reaffirmation of diverse self-interests and a litmus test for specific actions. The megatrend is judged on a cost-benefit basis that determines its acceptance or negation by different audiences with different foci—environmental, economic, energy, defense, and political. Within the reality and promise of renewables, individuals, state and non-state actors identify their own needs, see what they want to see, and associate with the aspects of the megatrend that are closest to their visions and ideas.

III. A very brief history of alternative energy's future—contemporary constructions charting alternative energy's progress.

What are now commonly referred to as alternative sources of energy have, in fact, been primary energy sources throughout the history of human civilization. Historical examples of alternative energy reveal prior transformations in societal customs, practices, and knowledge and provide insight into possible influences on the megatrend's future trajectory.

While knowing the past is not always a guarantee that its lessons are learned, history provides a view of the patterns of human behavior that are likely to dictate future actions. One of the most important and instructive lessons is the way humanity tends to discover and invent its own past.

1. The historicity: how the modern construction of alternative energy, its past and future have been shaped.

The first observation is that renewable energy sources are nothing new, though they have only recently, in historical terms, been recast as an "alternative" to fossil fuels. In fact, there was no record of a purposeful human endeavor to develop alternatives to fossil-based energy until the middle of the 20th century, when societies actively started pursuing alternative energy as part of a general energy mix that would enable them to sustain their rapidly industrializing economies without excessive dependency on fossil fuels. Recent alternative energy developments are viewed in light of their application as a complement, or antidote, to fossil fuels.

The history of renewable energy is "reconstructed" in that it is comprised of selective legends, facts, and conjecture that paint an optimistic picture of humanity's ability to overcome nature's challenges, in which it both masters and lives in harmony with the environment. It spans heroic deeds and scientific discoveries—from the myth of Prometheus' fire to the use of hydropower in Greece over 2,000 years ago, and from Socrates' advocacy of passive solar design to the development and use of the solar furnace by French chemist Antoine Lavoisier in 1774.

The past examples of alternative energy use demonstrate at least that, while game-changing inventions with far-reaching applications are few and far between, once such technologies become available, they enter daily use and become customary. Throughout history the introduction of a few inventive renewable energy technologies has had far-reaching applications. This selective history creates a modern perception of alternative energy and inspires its conception as a new "Golden Age" in energy use where nature is not only harnessed but a new pattern of co-existence between humanity and its habitat is achieved. Starting from a world lit by fire, alternative energy's ancient roots stake their claim to serve humanity well in times to come.

This reconstruction of alternative energy, defined as the selective extraction of experiments, applications, and achievements, has created a unique historicity. This historicity has been constructed with the hindsight of contemporary understanding, whereby historical occurrences and achievements provide a key understanding of alternative energy's contemporary presence and the means to define the future of the megatrend.[130] Such a reconstruction endows renewables' modern evolution with a significance that is more than the sum of its historical parts. In other words, despite being nothing new, when understood from the perspective provided by this reconstructed past, alternative energy assumes a grander scope and significance.

The emergence of the alternative energy megatrend does not stem from a single breakthrough or discovery, but from precisely this changing perspective about the significance of energy for the security and future development of humanity. The megatrend's history encapsulates modern concerns about resource depletion and environmental degradation, positioning renewables as a tangible and practical complement to the energy mix, a viable, large-scale option beyond fossil fuels, and a valid path toward future human development. In essence, the modern understanding of alternative energy's past informs its future.

2. The "Golden Age" redux: envisaging alternative energy's "glorious past" from antiquity to the Age of Enlightenment.

Modern societal visions about the development of alternative energy have spurred a desire to trace renewables to the deep roots of human civilization. Moreover, these snippets of historical fact, conjecture, and reinterpretation are recast as a reflection of a seeming longing by humanity to return to a "Golden Age" where the interaction between humans and nature did not hold the connotations of exploitation and despoliation with which modern resource use is often associated.

These examples from the Classical era, the Middle Ages, and through the Age of Enlightenment can in no way be construed to prove that modern renewables have a long and established history. Rather, these examples are drawn up as a means of associating today's alternative energy technologies and their use with a potential return to a glorious past without giving up the technological advantages incurred in the interim.

The modern sense of the historical longevity and widespread utility of renewables across sectors in society underpins today's confidence in their future application. The use of renewables dates all the way back to antiquity. Hydropower, solar, wind, and biofuel technologies represented the dominant source of energy in ancient Persia, Greece, and Rome. These resources were used by empires as far flung as China, the Mayans, and the Aztecs.

In the 6th century BC, Cyrus the Great of Persia had an ingenious system of underground aqueducts designed to bring run-off water from the snow melts into the heart of Persia for irrigation, enabling the creation of the legendary Persian Gardens. Archaeological evidence suggests that windmills were used to irrigate these same gardens in the 7th century AD.[131] Indeed, water was used as a source of energy as early as 200 BC in order to power food production and manufacturing.

Harnessing the sun's power also dates back to antiquity: the Chinese, Greeks, and Romans experimented with curved mirrors to concentrate the sun's rays. There are fascinating—though still insufficiently proven—instances of their attempted military use by Archimedes in the Siege of Syracuse.[132] The ancient Greek and Roman civilizations also employed passive solar design in their homes, using glass to trap solar heat.[133]

These snapshots of the past demonstrate renewables' ability to serve humanity effectively on a long-term basis, by fulfilling a range of purposes including economic and military roles. Renewables were widely accepted as complements for human and animal labor and shaped the human imperative to master nature in pursuit of independence from the elements and the environment. Modern alternative energy sources are endowed with an aura akin to this ancient pursuit of new forms of independence and paths to advancement.

The use of renewables throughout the Middle Ages provides a sense of empowerment arising from the application of technology. The precursors of today's alternative energy megatrend augmented humanity's power to change its environment from the upheavals surrounding the turn of the first millennium. The use of renewables freed populations to pursue new activities and removed constraints that had locked people into a daily life of drudgery.

Water and wind power were applied toward a wide range of economic activities, including the use of waterwheels in mills to crush grain, weave cloth, tan leather, smelt iron, and saw wood. Ingenious uses of wind and the continued refinement of sails allowed a succession of European countries to dominate sea-lanes worldwide, opening global trade routes. Renewables' broadening utilization through the Middle Ages informs today's perception of their reliability and transformative potential. In the medieval era, alternative energy proved its capacity to reshape societies by engendering new ways of powering human activity.

During the Age of Enlightenment, renewable energy joined forces with the scientific revolution, which, equipped with rationality and reason, transformed the societal landscape.[134] The Enlightenment conferred scientific advances which demonstrated science's emerging role in improving humanity. With the Enlightenment's intense pursuit of knowledge, exploitation of energy firmly began to incorporate scientific precision while also encompassing technological and economic paradigms. In fact, the scientific method, a chief accomplishment of the era, reshaped humanity's ontological orientation toward the natural environment, empowering civilizations to pursue new achievements.

Europe's advancements were particularly significant. As the epicenter of the Enlightenment, Europe had an advantage in the use of energy for power projection. This power directly impacted the formation of the modern global world order.[135] Modern imagery of alternative energy as an empowering enabler and solution to societal ills stems from this era, and the technological progress made in the field illustrates the transformational potential of alternative energy today.

However, before it started using fossil fuels, humanity had confronted the same problems that mankind faces today in applying alternatives: systemic limitations in flexibility, mobility, location, and infrastructure. How the alternative energy megatrend evolves, and whether it will prove long lasting, will be determined by how renewables integrate themselves in humanity's energy-intensive culture.

3. The re-conceptualization: the juxtaposition with fossil fuels enabling the envisioning of practical alternative energy applications from the Industrial Revolution to the latter half of the 20th century.

Renewables became a true alternative source of energy only after fossil fuels became the dominant energy source for humanity. The re-conceptualization of renewable energy developments as a distinct trend took place after the Industrial Revolution and intensified over the course of the early 20th century, with their perceived significance increasing after the end of World War II.[136] In the course of this re-conceptualization, renewable sources of energy gradually emerged as a technological development balanced against fossil fuels—coal, and subsequently oil and gas. Renewables acquired the aura of a novel development only after they could be put in juxtaposition with, and become alternatives to, fossil-based energy. Thus, alternative energy could only emerge when it became an option comparable with a proven source of energy.

The capacity for alternative energy to meet the expanding consumption needs of intensifying industrial and economic activity became evident during the Industrial Age. Developments in water and wind power during the early phases of industrialization inspired experimentation. They were fostered by deep-rooted innovative traditions that were at the heart of the Industrial Revolution and stemmed from new developments in physics, chemistry, and engineering. Renewables were a major source of energy throughout most of the Industrial Revolution and remained part of the energy mix even after coal became the preferred source of energy. For example, by the late 1830s, alcohol blends had replaced increasingly expensive whale oil as a source of light and heat,[137] as well as other forms of fuel.[138] The first hydrogen fuel cell was developed to generate electricity in 1838.[139] In 1892, the world's first geothermal district heating system was built in Boise, Idaho.[140] Even before the use of oil became widespread, scientists like Augustin Mouchot were seeking ways to harness solar power to generate heat.

Nonetheless, the advent of coal, oil, and gas as the main energy sources during the Industrial era dislodged solar, wind, water, and biomass and consigned them to the category of "alternatives." But the emergence of fossil fuels as the dominant form of energy did not mean that renewables were entirely discarded. Renewable energy use reflected an ongoing desire to achieve political solutions that were sometimes emotionally driven, a goal that often ran counter to the reality of concurrent financial commitments and cost factors that were disproportionate to short- or medium-term

Figure 2: Engraving of Mouchot's Solar Power Collector at the Universal Exposition in Paris in 1878[141]

benefits. In a way, renewable energy assumed the role of a technical means for achieving social ends.

The history of alternative energy in the Industrial era offers insight into the evolution of Post-Industrial culture. The era of industrialization, with the advent of economies of scale, marked a transition in economic approaches that spread from Europe to the rest of the world and encouraged new practical applications and means of energy use.

During the re-conceptualization process, renewables became more than novel experiments and expressions of humanity's pursuit of new knowledge. In the 20th century, they represented an intentional endeavor to develop new methods for harvesting energy and challenging the dominance of coal, oil, and gas. In this process, renewables were associated with new capabilities in the eyes of both policymakers and society, expanding humanity's energy options to include sunlight or wind. Renewable energy was repositioned as a viable and practical solution to energy needs, and as a development path that does not rely on depleting fossil fuels. This re-conceptualization can be notionally divided into two distinct periods: pre- and post-World War II.

Despite fossil fuels' dominance of the energy mix before World War II, interest in renewables persisted. The first electric cars were developed in the 1880s and Henry Ford's Model T was initially designed to run on a mix of ethanol and gasoline.[142] In one of the first examples of biofuel use, "at the Paris exposition of 1900, a Diesel engine, built by the French Otto Company, ran wholly on peanut oil."[143] By 1938, one alcohol plant in the U.S. state of Kansas was producing 18 million gallons of ethanol as fuel for transportation, following President Theodore Roosevelt's lifting of the spirit tax in 1906.[144] The first geothermal power plant was built in California in 1922.[145]

New applications and, more importantly, new directions of thinking about energy use increased the prospects of powering human development beyond fossil fuels. The increasingly evident transformative potential of alternative energy thus offered a modern version of the age-old vision that nature is both perfectible and exploitable.

Post-World War II energy alternatives to fossil fuels became increasingly subjected to policy considerations as they became practical energy solutions for fueling development. The forces that prompted a greater focus on renewables included the growing need of industrialized economies to expand their energy options, the intensification of the defense sector's energy needs, the emergence of new technological requirements and intensity of technology use, and a rise in the price of fossil-based energy sources.

The introduction of nuclear energy as a by-product of military advances after World War II provided a vivid demonstration of the breakthrough impact of technological developments in the energy field. The war also gave rise to a range of new practical applications. For example, in 1958 the United States powered one of its satellites with solar energy for the first time.[146] During the Carter administration, even the White House installed solar panels.[147] These technological achievements prompted their gradual acceptance by society and policymakers alike as a viable unified energy option. This acceptance was a testament to the human capacity to believe and to adapt, which throughout history has created seeds that eventually become reality.

In the latter half of the 20th century, despite the lack of a strong commercialization potential, interest in alternative energy technologies increased due to global energy supply concerns after the oil shocks of the '70s. Endeavors to reduce U.S. and European hydrocarbon reliance featured renewables. By 1973, Dr. Henry Kissinger called for "a massive effort to provide producers with an incentive to increase their supply, to encourage consumers to use existing supplies more rationally, and to develop alternative energy sources."[148] The 1970s oil crisis could have provided the momentum to foster the development of the alternative energy sector, but as the price of oil diminished in subsequent years, fossil fuels became affordable again and the pressure on policymakers to find alternatives dissipated.

Technology's rising prominence also has influenced policy decisions, reflecting the notion advanced by Jacques Ellul that "the conjunction of state and [technology] is not a neutral fact."[149] In this view, investing in new alternative energy technologies becomes an issue of political will rather than of scientific ability.[150] While the practicality of renewables as a dominant fuel has fluctuated in the public's mind, ebbing and flowing according to the supply and demand of fossil fuels, the image of a society empowered by renewable sources of energy has meant that renewables have not lost their public appeal.

4. The transformation: the post-Cold War paradigm shift in the context of globalization and the global technological revolution.

Renewables were rebranded as an alternative to fossil fuels during the 20th century. Society perceived renewable energy developments through the lens of modern socio-material environments,[151] and they increasingly became associated with an ideal future. In effect, the re-conceptualization was not so much tangible, but rather a transformation of how renewables were perceived and accepted by society.

The post-Cold War paradigm shift played a critical role in the transformation of renewables, which changed numerous conditions related to global politics, social order, and the political economy.[152] This paradigm shift grew global demand for energy, freed a wide range of resources that were previously relegated to the bipolar standoff of the Cold War, and introduced new actors capable of exerting their influence in pursuit of new forms of power. Moreover, it enabled the emergence of new societal attitudes and changed political, economic, and cultural practices.

The post-Cold War paradigm shift created a critical mass that altered societal understanding and visions of how humanity should interact with nature and use energy. It was the outcome of a prolonged and sustained accumulation of diverse aspirations, approaches, and methods—"a process of generating and exploiting knowledge so deeply engraved into our society that all its citizens are profoundly affected."[153] This unique confluence of factors created a situation similar to what Ludwig von Mises described on the eve of the Age of Enlightenment, where "only in the climate of huge capital accumulation could experimentalization develop from a pastime of geniuses like Archimedes and Leonardo da Vinci into a well-organized systematic pursuit of knowledge."[154] The new and rapidly increasing demands, mounting techno-scientific knowledge, and novel forms of socio-political interactions and power manifestations further focused attention on alternative energy developments.

The post-Cold War paradigm shift also freed military and economic resources, making them available for investment and consumption elsewhere. Significantly, the growing global demand for energy could no longer be addressed through the prism of Cold War polarity. It now became a primary concern for a growing number of state and non-state actors alike, as well as for global civil society. The post-Cold War era move from a bipolar to unipolar to multi-centric world introduced unprecedented societal demands for energy, giving rise to the conditions that form the megatrend. The massive demographic shift and migration that occurred at the end of the 20th and beginning of the 21st century also contributed to the rise of global energy demand and to new patterns of energy supply and utilization.[155]

In the post-Cold War era, globalization played an extraordinary role in defining the conditions of the new international system. Globalization modified alternative energy's propagation by impacting human populations and their environment, and triggering resource-related demographic, eco-logical, and technological changes.[156] Globalization is also viewed critically as a predominantly Western "model of development."[157]

Globalization ensured that the demands prompting the need for an alternative energy transformation were disseminated across the world. It provided the channels through which the megatrend spread and reinforced the acceptance of renewables.[158]

As globalization makes the world smaller, and its processes "speed up the flow of history,"[159] it forces changes in policies and traditional power structures. It has endowed the alternative energy megatrend with a new meta-geography, or "spatial structures through which people order their knowledge of the world."[160] The compression of geopolitical space combined with the hastening of geopolitical time has increased interdependence among state and non-state actors.[161] It has ensured that localized political events engender worldwide concern, and that territorial boundaries are no longer a barrier to political influence. It has also led to new rules, practices, and institutions through which power is projected and received, trans-forming the policies, strategies, and stances that imbue alternative energy developments with a redefined identity.

The ongoing global technological revolution[162] allows renewables to achieve new levels of acceptability and viability. Today, technology is increasingly instrumental in the formation and shaping of human values,[163] thus furnishing another important set of conditions for the transformation of alternative energy developments into a modern trend.

The evolution of the alternative energy megatrend has also been impacted by the rise of new actors of consequence on the global scene that have exerted new forms of power. This "geopolitical transition"[164] created new economic powerhouses and political power centers that interacted according to shifting patterns of organizations, international relations, pol-icies, and regulations, along with new ideological constructs, intellectual assumptions, modes of rationale, and logic.[165]

The end of the Cold War saw the rise of hegemonic U.S. power in global affairs. Now, other nations such as China influence global relations. Although the United States remains dominant in military and economic affairs, it no longer exerts absolute dominance, in part because the logisti-cal costs outweigh its benefits. Meanwhile, an increasing number of actors are on the threshold of acquiring and projecting greater geopolitical power. In this context, alternative energy, as a local solution to global problems, takes on an increased level of importance for actors wishing to enhance their power endowments. Moreover, the growing number of power centers that affect cross-border agendas has coalesced into a network that propagates and accelerates the alternative energy trend, channeling and directing the intent, strategies, and actions of actors that influence its evolution. The emergence of the alternative energy megatrend can be considered the result of a series of profound changes in global affairs from the Cold War to Post-Cold War eras in which new rules and opportunities to wield influence emerged.

5. Achieving the impossible: The impact of the Fourth Industrial Revolution and Artificial Intelligence on the alternative energy megatrend.

The Fourth Industrial Revolution is characterized by an unprecedented rate of technological change. This exponential change impacts our physical and digital worlds and creates fundamental shifts in the industrial paradigm. It encompasses ultra-automatized production, and the growing role of robotics and artificial intelligence in economics, business, politics, management and private life. What we now call "AI" is going to be the central driver of future changes.

Massive machine-type communications will aid in the development of the "Internet of Things," the network of interconnected devices embedded in everyday objects that share data, as well as smart devices, sensors and industrial equipment that use mobile networks. 5G mobile communications will hold together many of the technological innovations that will define the world in the decade to come. It will provide services across all key disruptive technologies, including alternative energy technologies. The ability to develop, control and access 5G technologies could play a critical role in the Great Power Competition.

Unlocking the full potential of today's alternative energy technologies largely rests on energy storage solutions and advancement in the digital grid.[166] An energy storage revolution will have tremendous implications across the electricity value chain because energy storage can replace peaking plants, alter future transmission and distribution investments, restructure power markets and help digitize the electricity ecosystem.

The Fourth Industrial Revolution is also transforming the digital grid architecture. Technological advances in the energy grid such as visibility at the grid edge; integration of sensors and data analytics for distributed generation; smart contracts for energy management; flexible demand; and intelligent control systems will propel the alternative energy megatrend.

The changes engendered by the Fourth Industrial Revolution are propelling the possibilities of alternative energy. Bold ideas and technologies that even a decade ago were the realm of science fiction are now a reality. The synergies between the Fourth Industrial Revolution and alternative energy require that societies reimagine the relationships between the land, energy, infrastructure, technologies and global-local economies. Exponential solutions in the field of alternative energy are already altering humanities' relationship with energy.[167]

The momentum of the Fourth Industrial Revolution facilitates the megatrend's ability to generate intersecting vulnerabilities and cascading consequences. Furthermore, the forces unleashed by the Fourth Industrial Revolution and its unaddressed impacts on inequality, energy security, economic security, and defense reinforces the need to find a way to govern the new technological world order. The question of how it will be governed and how the Grand Energy Game will unfold remain elusive and current political trends towards nationalism, protectionism, and zero-sum relations does not bode well for its impacts on global security. As Lionel Barber aptly put it when asked if we now understand this new world that we are dealing with, "we haven't even begun to see what machine learning and artificial intelligence is going to do...[there is] more disruption to come...[however]...the human mind cannot be replicated."[168]

6. The delayed arrival of the future: assuring the marvelous prospects of alternative energy.

There is a relative impatience with the alternative energy phenomenon. This has been prompted by expectations of greater technological advancements, which have already been demonstrated by renewables. This urgency will not go away, as the heightened societal anticipation of technological advances today is creating a persistent sense that alternative energy developments have lagged behind their rightful position.[169]

At the height of the Industrial Revolution, technological progress and thirst for innovation inspired imagination and vision of the likes of Jules Verne. Similarly, alternative energy's potential has captured modern-day public imagination. That said, counter to Alvin Toffler's view of technological advancements as a development that exceeds societal expectations, the alternative energy megatrend does not represent a "premature arrival of the future."[170] Rather, the anticipation of the delayed arrival of alternative energy's future is actually making this future more assured by fostering the achievement of a certain level of "preparedness" for the upcoming progress.

This is exemplified by the vision of Arthur Clarke's *2001: A Space Odyssey*, and many other futuristic and science fiction ideas.

The intensity and urgency that underpin support for renewables reinforce this impatience with the seeming postponement of the promised energy future, creating societal pressure that suggests, and sometimes dictates, the actions of policymakers. Reminiscent of the literary rendering of the intensity of popular support for Galileo's confrontation with the medieval church in the 17th century,[171] a number of external and intrinsic societal factors and global socio-political changes have propelled and shaped renewable energy developments, or, rather, their expected impacts.

Modern audiences and constituencies are no longer passive spectators; they participate and interact, assuming the role of active agents in the creation of the reality projected by the megatrend. Idealized visions of alternative energy are factored into expectations before the technologies have even been invented, let alone applied. The post-WWII generations in the West are perhaps the ones most surprised, or even disappointed, with the current state of technological affairs—there are no *Back to the Future Part II*-style fusion-powered flying cars, or *The Jetsons*-esque personal jet-packs and robot maids.

To conclude, specific 21st century circumstances and conditions have transformed the contemporary perspective of alternative energy, creating the foundations of a modern megatrend. It represents a conceptual rebirth, akin to Ovid's *Metamorphoses,* stories of bodies changed into new forms.[172] This phenomenon has been enabled by a reconstruction of its history and a set of modern conditions that provided for its critical mass. The transformation of this critical mass has been catalyzed by globalization, the emergence of the multi-centric world system, and the ongoing global technological revolution. It is this linkage to real-world affairs that prompts the megatrend's claim to longevity.

The alternative energy megatrend is driven by events and processes that inform and underpin everyday life and are often socially constructed, giving rise to the consensus theory of truth, where what is "true" is what is perceived by the respective community—the family, the hamlet, the town, the city, the country, or global society.[173] It includes a number of practical imperatives that propel it and is itself shaped by societal notions, visions, and idea constructs.[174] The evolution of global affairs and societal attitudes has resulted in driving forces that comprise the megatrend. These drivers, such as new economic powerhouses and increased demand for energy, created the modern perception of alternative energy and, thus, the megatrend itself.

In conclusion: How have alternative energy developments in the 21st century evolved into a socio-political, techno-economic, and ideological megatrend in a universally securitized world?

- Alternative energy developments are a global phenomenon that constitutes a 21st century megatrend. Renewable sources of energy such as solar, wind, biofuels, hydro, geothermal, tidal, and wave have undergone a process of transformation that promises to provide practical answers to energy supply and demand issues and charts the future path of human energy use and overall interaction with nature.

- The transformation of renewables has been facilitated by the process of globalization propelled by the ongoing technological revolution and turbulent 21st century multi-centric world system. They were further propelled by the dynamic of the international system in flux and the emergence of a post-Cold War global rivalry. The emergence of the megatrend is also a response to the changing view of the availability, accessibility, and security of supply of traditional energy sources, as well as the shocks stemming from fluctuating energy prices. Beyond bottom-line energy supply and demand imperatives, the alternative energy megatrend has been invigorated by symbolic moral values and modern ideologies. These values have reinforced modern societal perception and quasi-ideological visions related to energy use in the upcoming world.

- The emergence of the alternative energy megatrend is promoted by a retrospective rationalization of alternative energy's history. In other words, its history is reimagined and rearranged. The interpretation of the history of alternative energy reflects contemporary perceptions and serves as a prism through which to view the present and future of the trend. The reconstruction of renewables' history runs parallel with modern post-industrial culture, linking modes of human energy consumption with a return to the morality and traditions of the past, promising a new "Golden Age," as well as other benefits.

- This socio-political, techno-economic, and ideological phenomenon is a modern megatrend with distinct features. Most dominant among them are: innovative responses to 21st century geopolitical, social, and economic challenges; a broad geographical footprint; an expanding socio-political and techno-economic impact; and a projected longevity. The megatrend has already achieved a global scope and, although the use of alternative energy is still negligible when compared to the use of fossil fuels, it has pronounced political, economic, and socio-cultural implications.

- The drivers that propel the alternative energy megatrend highlight a growing spectrum of energy, consumption, environmental, military, technological, and political imperatives, as well as a broad spectrum of ideological values. A leading driver of the alternative energy megatrend, and a material force that substantiates it, is the increasing global energy demand. Other critical drivers include: growing environmental concerns, pursuit of economic growth, modern technological advances, the impact of energy on defense, society's changing ethical imperatives, the exploration of new paths toward empowerment, and the growing worldwide framework of associated policies and regulations.

- The trend is endowed with added momentum by alternative energy's promise of empowerment of individuals, state actors, and non-state actors. These drivers mutually influence each other to form a global phenomenon, unified and reinforced by alternative energy's perceived claim to be a force for good in the age-old morality play between good and evil. The trend is also propelled by the evolving matrix of grandiose domestic and international plans, policies, and regulations that meld the drivers into a cohesive whole.

- The alternative energy megatrend is formed by the interaction between individuals and the environment in a profoundly and rapidly changing world. It has become an integral element of the Grand Energy Game. The attitudes and ideas behind the alternative energy megatrend reflect efforts to address and securitize threats to human wellbeing and standards of living. These ideas affect relations within and between communities and change the direction of human efforts—from neighborhood movements to political parties, and from specific personal choices to actions by states or groups of states. The alternative energy megatrend is also underwriting renewed approaches toward global governance that still need to live up to their promise.

PART 2

Geopolitics: Charting a Complex Megatrend in a Globally Securitized World Under the Gathering Storm of Old and New Great Power Rivalries

*"Men keep agreements when it is to the advantage
of neither to break them."*

Solon[1]

Does alternative energy play a role in modern geopolitics?[2] By most measures, its role is rather insignificant. However, the age of Great Power Competition is back.

In the midst of a resurgence in Great Power Competition, the megatrend offers a unique perspective on the pressures exerted on the geopolitical equilibrium. Of particular note are the forces and influences engendered by a 21st century multi-polar world system in flux, many of which can exacerbate tensions. The megatrend's imprint on international relations reflects the nature of geopolitics as a convergence of balance and dominance through power, expressed in the current state of disequilibrium.

The megatrend's drivers and the megatrend itself have extensive geopolitical connotations and implications. The megatrend underlines the increasing complexity of power balances and illustrates the current movement toward a punctuated, or interrupted, equilibrium.

47

I. The Equilibrium—plotting one more variable, the megatrend, on the geopolitical system in flux.

The alternative energy megatrend provides a revealing perspective on the international relations implications of modern phenomena[3] and on the reshaping of 21st century geopolitics. Charting its evolution demonstrates the complexities of the 21st century world system and tests the established geopolitical constructs of Core-Periphery, East-West, North-South, and top-down/bottom-up dynamics.

It also demonstrates that the megatrend's most outstanding geopolitical trait is its contribution to creating new spaces and interrelations on the contemporary energy map. This stems from the importance of resources and energy to modern international relations. As one more variable among other modern developments, the alternative energy megatrend offers new explanatory frameworks in light of the reshaping of 21st century geopolitics.

1. The megatrend: shedding a new light on the equilibrium.

Traditionally, the concept of the geopolitical equilibrium entails a balance of power, predominantly military, among actors that have assured their survival and secured their safety through alliances and partnerships with other actors and prevented domination by a single entity. By keeping each other in check, actors contribute to an equilibrium that is not fixed but rather entails continuous actions by these very actors to ensure that the geopolitical balance is maintained.

After the end of the Cold War, the notion of equilibrium underwent a transformation: power that could be exerted on actors widened in scope, while centers of power became more numerous.[4] Thus, the stability conveyed by or attributed to Cold War bipolarity and subsequent U.S. unipolar dominance is being gradually replaced by a multiplicity of power centers wielding power and influence across borders. Most prominent among these centers are the BRICS countries—China, Russia, India, Brazil, and South Africa—with China as a particularly active geopolitical actor that contributes the most dynamism to the international system and, therefore, has the most capability to change the status quo.

Technology is increasingly a dominant factor when assessing the geopolitical equilibrium from the perspective of the alternative energy megatrend. Exponential technological changes unleashed by the Fourth Industrial Revolution, including those propelling the megatrend, also impact the geopolitical landscape. With the growing spread of technology and the

48

increasing inability of actors' ability to control this spread, technological advantage can be obtained by almost any state and non-state actor. This permeability is generating new techno-civilizational ecosystems that blur the distinction between actors with geopolitical power projection capabilities and the rest.[5]

The new multi-centric world features a constantly shifting dynamic that tends to move away from rather than toward a status quo. The geopolitical equilibrium therefore does not accommodate statist comprehension but is rather a fluctuation of pressures, external conditions, and the ability of new emerging actors to exert power on the geopolitical stage.

The megatrend introduces unanticipated factors that change the actual and perceived power balances between actors, underscoring the fragility of any new geopolitical equilibrium. National power now flows in numerous directions along different international networks. The dynamic toward a new 21st century geopolitical equilibrium resembles a fluid tug-of-war between states as well as between states and non-state actors, which have at their disposal different forms of economic, political, and military power.

These forms of power can be charted along the traditional cleavages—core/periphery, East/West, North/South, and top/bottom—that are changing the path toward equilibrium. However, geopolitics itself is not static, and as a process it poses questions to its practitioners that prompt different answers under different circumstances. That is why the notional divisions of geopolitics, such as the core/periphery or North/South, are mutable and continuously adapt to the transformative nature of international relations.

The megatrend appears to display substantial transformative power by influencing the behavior of actors and adding lucidity to how the traditional cleavages are reshaped in the 21st century. With the dispersal of new geopolitical knowledge across both geopolitical cores and peripheries, the marginalization and disenfranchisement of previously peripheral groups comes to the forefront.

Although the North-South and East-West paradigms remain a key dimension of the world order, the momentum of Western universalism is gradually dissolving. This dissolution, which is rather chaotic and taking place in numerous areas, is spurred on by the broadening of the perception of national interests and security issues in an increasingly universally securitized world.

The fading of Westernization permits space for the pressure from broadening national security interests to bubble up at the surface and spill over onto global affairs. Furthermore, states are no longer the only entities with the ability to address security issues. Within this emerging geopolitical network, non-state actors[6] are increasingly capable of influencing the affairs of states, thus staking a claim to their own foreign policy agendas. This questions the rationale of top-down, government-dictated national security interests.

This trend has only amplified the chaotic nature of the international system, which is marked by the pursuit of power by states across national borders as they seek to ensure their survival under turbulent geopolitical dynamics. According to the realist school of thought, "The international system is anarchic. It is a self-help system. There is no higher authority that can constrain or channel the behavior of states."[7] This realization has profound implications for the many norms and regulations that are yet to be devised to regulate actors' behavior, including those related to the alternative energy megatrend.

New factors and phenomena impact geopolitics and are changing institutional arrangements in the modern world order. Each group in the emerging system has its own foreign policy positions that are often incongruous with the existing international framework. The disparity of power within current institutional frameworks has resulted in sometimes unrepresentative arrangements, and some actors, due to their lesser influence, perceive their interests are not properly understood or addressed.

For example, the decreasing relevance of the G7 (the group of the world's most powerful states) coupled with the emergence of the G20 (the top 19 economies and the EU) is but one manifestation of the changing contours of the world order, where the agenda of the West is not always predominant. Despite institutional imbalances, actors will continue to seek a world configuration with an adequate level of cohesion and a tolerable level of disagreement. The resulting configuration will be guided by terms and conditions imposed by the dominant actors, with an eventual pattern that is accepted by the majority of the system's participants.

2. Core-Periphery dynamics: the megatrend as a counterweight between multiplying power centers.

The concept of a core and a periphery in geopolitics is a spatial metaphor that sets the tone for the relationship between the advanced, or economically mature, actors (the core) and the less developed states (the periphery).[8] Beyond the static and narrow exploitative sense, this dichotomy provides a useful reflection of the relationships between unequal actors—whether politically, militarily, or economically. The core is deemed to dominate the periphery in economic relations, military postures, and diplomatic interactions with third-party entities. It also channels and monopolizes the periphery's economic and political relations with the outside world. Implicit in this framework, therefore, is the marginalization of the periphery.

Core-periphery relations have determined the geopolitical equilibrium since ancient times. Examples of a central dominant core exerting influence over lesser and weaker peripheries include the Roman hegemony in the Mediterranean between the 1st century BC and the 3rd century AD, as well as the Chinese dominance of Asia, beginning with the Qin's unification of the Middle Kingdom in the 3rd century BC.[9]

These associations went beyond the practice of hegemonic dominance, however, and incorporated relations between developmental pacesetters and less developed trend-takers in various fields: military power, agriculture, trade, metalwork, and culture. Core-periphery relationships were used to justify actions that shaped regional developments, whether to underscore the dominance of Europe from the 16th through the 19th centuries or to explain the relationships of the former republics of the Soviet Union with Moscow.

These dichotomies between developed centers and developing perimeters have not always been based on military dominance. Examples of non-military dominance include Byzantium's relationships with its neighboring civilizations and the U.S. bonds with its United States-Mexico-Canada Agreement (USMCA) partners Mexico and Canada,[10] as well as with developing countries such as Colombia, Peru, Costa Rica, and Morocco, with which Washington has signed free trade agreements.

Core-periphery relations have historically been maintained through the harmony of interest between the centers in the core and the centers in the periphery. As long as the ruling elites in the periphery country are aligned with those of the core country, the harmony is maintained. In effect, a transmission mechanism is developed; interests from the core country's center are imposed on the periphery country's center, which then spread throughout the periphery. This direct link allows for the centers of both the core and periphery to share their visions and intentions with the other. The core-periphery interactions, according to Johan Galtung, are vertical.[11]

Exchanges take place between the core and the periphery, and both profit by obtaining benefits such as exports of raw materials, preferential trade terms, or exports of consumer goods. Within these vertical relations, if the value that the core extracted was greater than the value reaped by the periphery, a colonial relationship—political or economic—was forged. In this manner, core-periphery relations are a structure of dominance whereby the centers of both the core and the periphery are increasingly interdependent, while the peripheries of both are not. The links between the elites of the core and the elites of the periphery are stronger than the core's links with the rest of the periphery.

Within the core and the periphery, transitional processes have also resulted in the emergence of what Immanuel Wallerstein calls "*semi-peripheries.*"[12] These semi-peripheries are undergoing relative decline within what are considered core regions (for example, Greece in Europe) and are further impacted by a rise in the development of the periphery (such as the United Arab Emirates, Colombia, or Chile). With different interests aligning with both the core and periphery, semi-peripheries act as a buffer; these nations (e.g., Mexico, Brazil, South Africa, South Korea, etc.) provide the glue between the polarities of historically core and peripheral states. The international system thus features a three-part structure with the semi-peripheries representing a middle layer that allows the system to maintain cohesion despite pressure from the periphery and exploitation by the core.

The distinction between core and periphery was clearly defined during many historical periods, including the Cold War. This distinction is becoming increasingly difficult to discern in the post-Cold War setting of the multi-centric system. This is largely due to the proliferation of non-state actors and the emergence of new types of power dynamics characterizing interactions between geopolitical entities. In the 21st century, core-periphery relations are shaped by political, economic, and military power balances and arrangements between actors that are grouped within shifting and multiplying geographical spheres of geopolitical influence. In this manner, there is a division between core and peripheral countries, as well as a center-periphery division within countries.

It remains the case that the societies of the periphery are less able to affect those of Western Europe or North America than vice versa. However, the new reality of the multi-centric world system is that even when Western influence—whether multilateral through the institutional channels of the International Monetary Fund (IMF), the World Bank, or the G7, or unilateral through particular government initiatives—is being disseminated, its adoption is increasingly subject to localized adaptation.

In the multi-centric world system, the core-periphery relationship is moving away from the traditional development-based distinction with an increasing number of states demonstrating the ability to act as a geopolitical core in specific contexts. This has led to the emergence of multiple unstable cores. Peripheral countries increasingly have the capacity to attach themselves to different cores under different conditions. Some Eastern European, Central Asian, and South East Asian countries, for example, have established linkages and even dependencies with different actors in different areas—economic, military, political, trade, and technology. This situation is exacerbated by the rising volatility of power capabilities by some cores, e.g., Russia's influence on former Soviet republics and the Council for Mutual Economic Assistance (COMECON) states. Indeed, transplanting the 20th century near-colonial pattern of domination through modernization is now less viable under the conditions of the multi-centric world.

In the context of the alternative energy megatrend, the core-periphery relationship goes beyond the traditional dynamic between underdeveloped periphery and developed core. The megatrend provides a means to describe the new multi-centric or multi-core "geometry" of geopolitics. The designation of core or periphery is increasingly influenced by a range of new socio-political and socio-economic factors. The alternative energy megatrend could be one such factor since its spatial situation does not preclude global applications. Also, it is not yet structurally dominated by specific actors in the core, semi-periphery, or the periphery, enabling and empowering actors to change the side of the divide they find themselves in.

The megatrend reflects the new balance of power between cores and peripheries where levels of power and dominance fluctuate thereby preventing domination by a single entity. New ways of projecting power can endow peripheral actors with both perceived and actual capabilities that will help them avoid or mitigate the burdening core-periphery dynamics.

The alternative energy megatrend points to the emergence of new cores, as well as to the transition of peripheries into cores and vice versa. This significantly reshapes and blurs traditional core-periphery relationships and spheres of influence. Certain core-periphery cleavages in the 21st century are still a product of the Western-centric dominance over techno-economic developments that has existed since the advent of the Industrial Revolution. The overwhelming techno-economic dominance of Europe, and later of the United States, was based on the premise that Western modernization was the route to universal capitalism and economic well-being; however, Western modernization is increasingly challenged by the diversity, cultural distinction, and economic power of the periphery. Moreover, many countries in the semi-periphery and periphery have developed their economies with state-directed and nationalist capitalist models and stand in strong contrast to free market principles characterizing Western economies.

Despite these changes, the notion of a geopolitical core and periphery remains useful in representing the bonds of dominance and power in international relations.[13] After all, inside-outside cleavages remain as complex and as heterogeneous in the 21st century as they were in the 20th. The difference is that the external influences that were traditionally subject to national security considerations are more ubiquitous in a globalized world. Moreover, the influence of the core over the periphery is continuously mutating, resulting in different social, economic, and political processes that highlight new areas of confrontation, including pressure on the core from the periphery in its upward development. The changing nature of relations between core and peripheral actors contributes to the reshaping of future security risks.

The emergence of multiple centers of power in the post-Cold War era has made the achievement of dominance by any one given actor unpredictable. It has raised new questions about the accuracy of traditional conceptions of the geographic distribution of power. The incorporation of the megatrend in security considerations and geopolitical processes and dynamics will add additional layers of complexity to power dynamics among states and between state and non-state actors operating in today's multi-centric world system.

3. East-West rivalries: how the megatrend is reshaping past Western hegemony along new lines of contention and cooperation.

Traditionally, East-West cleavages have shaped the flow of global political power and influence between geographically situated civilizational and cultural focal points. The notion of the East-West divide is a geopolitical code that assumes a level of opposition and competition in foreign policy formulation.

While the dichotomy between East and West is primarily a sociological construct describing the distinctions between Western and Eastern cultures (with Australia for example being considered part of the "West"), this distinction provides a "geographical framing" within which "political elites and the public act in pursuit of their own identities and interests."[14] It also sets out clear lines of security confrontation and perspective, requiring each side of the divide to secure itself from the other.

East-West contentions have existed since antiquity. Great Western civilizations, such as Greece and Rome, existed alongside and competed with

Eastern ones, such as Persia, Pontus, and Parthia. The idea of the West that is substantively different from the East evolved over the succeeding centuries, in particular, during the period of the Crusades, the travels of exploration, and the subsequent colonial expansion of the Europe-centered West. The East-West cleavage after World War II broadened to encompass the bipolar division between the U.S.-led West and the Soviet-dominated East. The meta-narrative of the triumph of Western liberal capitalism, which established itself at the end of the 20th century following the Cold War, has now been subject to challenge. The social and geopolitical heterogeneities it had closed off at the end of the Cold War have now reappeared accompanied by a greater diversity of multicultural forms of knowledge that in turn engender a transition from conformism to rebellion against the status quo.[15]

The perceived East-West division of the 20th century between the West's liberal democracies and the more authoritarian states of the East is becoming blurred in the post-Cold War multi-centric international system. After World War II, the East, e.g., Japan, Singapore, Thailand, South Korea, and other countries, undertook the process of adopting and adapting Western liberalism and capitalism. The traditional understanding of the East-West rivalry has been further complicated with non-state actors' and civil society's emergence as a more potent and autonomous force. At the same time, while the imperatives that defined the West have lost some of their distinctiveness, in particular with regard to economic development and empowerment that traditionally embodied the success of the West, Western liberalism has yet to be truly challenged by a viable alternative.

Indeed, the modern notion of East-West rivalry is itself rooted in Western-based traditions that have dominated the world system for about five centuries. Some in the West are concerned over the potential loss of primacy and the passing of the leadership baton to countries once classified as being on the periphery of the world-system. For instance, President Obama's pivot to Asia could be seen as an existential concern over the West's waning influence as the East emerges and exerts newfound political power. Geopolitics has been Western-centric due to a tendency to assume the superiority of Western models. Although Eastern visions of realpolitik are emerging (China being the most prominent example), the theoretical drivers behind the exercise of geo-power are underwritten by and framed within a Western-centric tradition. Ironically, the fact that the East is pursuing the rivalry with the West within the still Western-oriented paradigm underlines that the West continues to dominate key geopolitical dynamics.

Today's East and West manage their relations in a careful way and recognize each other's economic and geopolitical advantages. The current East-West cleavage reflects a greater recognition of the differences and similarities in vital interests, and is not focused on military rivalries as much as economic ones. This recognition is however accompanied by suspicion about ideology and concerns about economic competition. The resulting process exerts influence over notionally unaligned regions, seemingly amassing points in a new round of the geopolitical game of power balances. To a certain extent, today's rising inequality in Western economies is playing a similar role to what the lack of economic development did to separate the East and West in the 20th century. In fact, anti-capitalist and anti-Western ideologies continue to proliferate and in some cases flourish. They may become even more powerful should the economic balance shift further toward the East. In addition, the cohesion of the West is weakening due to a number of countries actively pursuing policies that are either met with indifference or opposition by other Western states. The decision by Britain to leave the European Union is a prime example of the splintering cohesion.

The propagation and acceptance of non-Western models across the globe demonstrate the superiority of ideological, socio-economic, and cultural considerations in global affairs over other dynamics of state relations. The "ideological" cultures associated with the East and West are not restricted by geographical boundaries, and it is possible for individuals and groups to belong to different cultures simultaneously. In this manner, we have liberal, capitalist, Islamist, Christian, ecological, and technological cultures that span the globe. Within this framework, alternative energy has already become a pillar, if not of a culture, then at least of a global subculture that is expanding and incorporating elements of other cultures. Both the traditional (geographically determined cultures) and the new ideological cultures have acquired a position of influence impacting geopolitics.

The rise of the East following the Cold War has emboldened and bolstered the ambition of new emerging powers to act as global and regional leaders. As rising powers, China and India will be increasingly expected to play a role in defining the global order and offer solutions to the world's pressing social, political, and economic challenges. In the case of alternative energy technologies, sometimes viewed as a public good, the market-dominating Western powers will be under pressure from civil society and emerging leaders like China and India to share renewables' benefits with the rest of the world. This pressure from the emerging East on the West is exemplified by China and India's strengthened commitment to alternative energy development. The ability of these actors to challenge the previous hegemons and their ambition to drive the global environmental agenda was expressly demonstrated after President Trump's declared withdrawal of the United States from the Paris Climate Agreement.[16]

Despite the potential for conflict, the alternative energy megatrend could also yield a new form of East-West cooperation.[17] While projections of the megatrend's future provide a new understanding of the rivalries that emerge in East-West relations, they also indicate common points that will serve as a platform for cooperation. Traditional dichotomy between the East and the West also proves operational in exploring evolving relationships within the alternative energy value-chain which includes the U.S. or European-based research institutions and OEMs producing wind turbines from China. Cultural differences and competing value systems do not prevent the West and the East from pursuing common goals in global environmental initiatives notwithstanding the challenging nature of the endeavor. The megatrend demonstrates the possibility of the coordinated action based on very different understandings. As noted by an observer, "In the West, eco-cities are supposed to save the world; in China they are simply meant to provide a decent quality of urban environment."[18] Still, eco-cities in all occasions bring value, though the motivation behind the projects might widely differ. At the same time, East-West relations may often be accompanied by ideology-based lack of trust and concerns about economic competition.

4. The North-South divide: the megatrend's projected iterations altering divisions and alignments.

The dynamics between the global North and the global South, like other geopolitical divisions, can be seen through envisioning the future of the alternative energy megatrend. The megatrend's outcomes hold the promise to reduce past tensions and create new areas of contention, thus revealing the framework of the new order.[19]

The North-South division evolved from the alignment of states based on the U.S.-USSR bipolar power struggle during the Cold War. The United States and its allies were considered members of the First World, while Russia and other nations under the influence of the Soviet Union were Second World actors. First and Second World states dominated the global arena and exerted influence on the periphery, or so-called Third World states. The periphery, by default, comprised all other actors not wielding influence during the bipolar power struggle.[20] These states, primarily in

Africa and Asia, were largely underdeveloped and were perceived as having limited geopolitical significance.

After the end of the Cold War, the developed market economy countries of the First World became the global North, and the remaining, lesser developed countries became the global South. This designation is becoming increasingly complex and in certain cases regionalized,[21] because of the growing inequality within regions and emerging market economies advancing out of the South. The differences in power capabilities between the North and the South are becoming less easy to discern today than they were at the height of the Cold War. New players are emerging from the South that are capable of exerting significant influence on international relations as previous balances no longer hold. These new players also demonstrate increasingly sufficient capabilities to pursue the development of alternative energy resources and technologies without having to rely on the North.

As such, the modern North-South relationship provides a backdrop upon which to view the continuously shifting power balance between the developed and developing world. Together with the developed North, the entities of the South have entered into a new maelstrom in which norms, practices, and institutions are reconstituted, essentially introducing a new world order. This process is not going to be smooth, and the mutable geopolitical divisions between North and South will continue a dynamic of constant changes. This constant dynamic will reflect the changing context of the North-South divide, considering the amassed capabilities of countries in the South and likely resistance of entities in the North to accommodate the shifts in power. Nor will it necessarily prove utterly anarchic, considering the constructivist legacy and approach undertaken by major powers over the course of centuries to regulate the otherwise "self-help" international system. In addition, this divide provides an important framework for assessing comparative power between the actors in the global political economy and the manner in which these actors might approach and be impacted by the alternative energy megatrend.

Given the distribution of financial resources invested in alternative energy by region, it would be easy to suggest that the megatrend presents the traditional North-South divide as a still relevant dimension of the world order: the map of global new investment in renewable energy closely follows the lines of this framework. However, with North-South divide still in place, the megatrend opens new venues for cooperation between individual states of the North and the South. This provides the opportunity for expanding the territory of the islands of development and, in the long-term perspective, for bridging the prosperity gap. At the same time, the process will have its ups and downs as the divides within the South may evolve and thus cause new tensions and conflicts.

Under the megatrend, the complex dynamics within the former Third World become even more obvious with China, India, and Brazil ambitiously investing in renewable energy, considering it as a means of energy security as well as of technological advancement and promotion of national interests. Challenging established global leaders, these countries make a strong application for taking part in global rule-setting mechanisms. They also claim regional leadership by turning themselves into knowledge and technology hubs, transmitting and localizing renewable energy solutions and applications, which in turn can strengthen their positions.

The megatrend could contribute to the emergence of new sources of tension over perceived iniquities that could exacerbate North-South divisions. The divisions between North and South are closely associated with the inequality attributed to free market capitalism with the South considering the exploitation of its resources to have been predominantly for the benefit of the North. These perceived iniquities underpin the premise that the South deserves compensation from the North for the vicissitudes imposed on the South by the North-determined world system. The perceived plight of the South has resulted in the pursuit of alternative models that go beyond the free market model of the North. At present, the use of modern renewables is expensive and often regarded as a luxury of the "green leafy suburbs" of the North. While global green free trade is gaining traction in both the North and the South, calls for alternative energy technologies to be made available for less than market value to developing countries have largely been rebuffed. Efforts to reduce the inequality between North and South through some form of distributive justice have not been successful. Moreover, there is no consensus on what such distributive justice would entail.

The alternative energy megatrend's evolution offers a new perspective on the geopolitical and security divisions between North and South. The countries of the South in particular will likely continue to perceive global issues, including the protection of the habitat and alternative energy developments, as being managed by the North on the basis of fear tactics. Countries in the South could demand and possibly extract concessions from OECD countries due largely to the latter group's purported historical responsibility in causing adverse environmental effects.[22] In this regard,

North-South disputes over renewable resources could become frequent, incorporating issues as diverse as economic development, energy security, and the environment.

5. Top-down build-up and bottom-up pressures: changes in state–society relations.

Divergent top-down and bottom-up socio-political pressures arise when the guiding hand of the state meets the upward influence of society. This tension is reflected in the evolution of the alternative energy megatrend. As a socially constructed phenomenon with broad applications, the megatrend sits at the intersection between state-led and grassroots initiatives. Thus, it can have widespread impact on both spheres and, in effect, the global order. In addition, the top-down and bottom-up pressures influence the megatrend by transforming the "innovative interactions in the geopolitical sphere" and linking them with a new "formation, reproduction and diffusion of changes leading to a new quality of political relations."[23]

Alternative energy developments are currently dominated by the top-down influence of governments. The state is predominant in encouraging or inhibiting the development, deployment, and use of alternative energy.[24] Government's central role not only is essential in promoting alternative energy, but also often represents the only current option for its development at this stage and in the foreseeable future. This state role is characterized by a hierarchy structured to flow from overarching governmental institutions to the subunits of society and markets. It reflects the state-led international system, which is dominated by the core states with a gradual diffusion of power to the periphery. Today, however, there is increasing pressure from society and non-state actors on the state and international system, which is affecting this traditional order.[25]

The state's growing presence in the deployment of alternative energy technologies has prompted calls for global governance structures. These calls have already been answered through new approaches to climate change governance and more positive notions of the potential for global "green" capitalism.

The complex interactions between top-down and bottom-up pressures on the alternative energy megatrend demonstrate how the inherent contradictions of the democratic process result in divergent and sometimes chaotic actions by politicians, and how state policies may lead to developmental dead-ends or even stymie the development of alternative energy technologies.

Despite the predominant role of the state in dealing with the world's most pressing transnational challenges, numerous societal groups and grassroots movements have emerged, exerting a considerable influence on state policies. These groups and movements are seeking to address a wide range of issues, such as environmental threats, poverty, human suffering, underdevelopment, and regional hardships. The acceleration of socio-political processes in the 21st century has created conditions in which grassroots pressures increasingly affect state policies. This represents a fundamental transition of power from states to non-state actors, and an inability of states to wholly reverse the shift of power back into the hands of the elite.[26]

Bottom-up pressures that permeate from society's base sometimes lead to policies geared more toward domestic politics and short-term public posturing rather than strategic and long-term solutions. For example, bottom-up political pressure contributed to extensive wind power developments in Scotland that later had to be curtailed, as well as ill-considered solar and wind installations in the Philippines. These undesirable results have slowed the flood of political declarations supporting renewables.

However, the alternative energy megatrend offers society a tool to articulate its needs and transform this articulation into political pressure to shape governments' short-term plans and long-term strategic postures. It could also influence new forms of interaction between civil society and governments, both on matters directly related to alternative energy and on broader issues of human security, development, and freedom. These novel forms of interaction will be explored in detail later in this chapter.

An alternative energy agenda is thus emerging that circumvents the traditions and approaches that have governed international relations over the last fifty years. This agenda could skew how human development unfolds. From the perspective of traditional capitalists, this promotion of perceived social good is at the expense of practical and profitable commercial sector growth. On the other hand, the environmental movement today proposes the triple bottom line, in which social and environmental values reinforce, rather than stymie, economic development. This formula currently finds rather wide acceptance within the corporate world. An impressive number of companies has joined UN Global Compact,[27] assuming obligations to promote "sustainable development," which implies "speeding up world growth while respecting the environmental constraints"[28] with renewable energy high on the agenda. Having accepted the rules of the "sustainability game" under pressure from environmental and social activism, business then puts pressure on governments in order to ensure sound business cases for renewable energy undertakings. One example may be a campaign launched by "RE100" companies[29] calling for supportive EU policy to enable more businesses to make large-scale investments in renewable power.[30]

Nevertheless, the increase in bottom-up societal pressure on political decision-making has given rise to the notion of a global civil society. This concept challenges the relatively unjustified notion that territorial boundaries delineate the existing social order or contract. Instead, human conduct is dictated not only by a citizen's implicit and explicit obligations to the state, but also by moral considerations that surpass the borders of sovereign states. With regard to the alternative energy megatrend, this has generated societal tensions, particularly in the context of environmental damage whereby who is responsible and should bear the burden of its mitigation is a point of extreme contention.

Where these top-down and bottom-up pressures meet, a whirlpool of influences is generated that affects the direction of the alternative energy megatrend and, more broadly, the rules that govern international relations. Indeed, societal influences have come to play a major role in shaping the megatrend, both undermining and contributing to geopolitical power wielded by states as they consider incorporating renewables in their environmental, energy, and defense policies.

In sum, the alternative energy megatrend has already established a foothold in the relations between the state and society, exhibiting the capacity to influence domestic policies and state relations. Alternative energy developments bring to light the pervasiveness of clashing top-down and bottom-up influences in modern society. These influences are introducing new factors in the interplay between geography and political power and altering the balance of power among states, as well as between state and non-state actors. The alternative energy megatrend illustrates how interactions between governments and societies are changing and how this change could modify global security considerations.

Inherent in this scene are future security threats that will necessitate securitization. The geopolitical meaning of security approaches and actions provides a physical link between securitization measures and the speech act of securitization, in the form of geopolitical interactions. These interactions determine the manner in which objects of securitization, whether national defense or the environment, are prioritized within the global order.

When viewed through the prism of geopolitics, securitization acts are therefore a part of a steadily evolving system of rules that govern actors' conduct. These measures are in large part proposed by the current hegemons of the world system and accepted to one extent or another by the other actors within that system.

II. The resources—rethinking the political topography of energy.

In addition to highlighting the complexities of 21st century geopolitical interactions, the alternative energy megatrend's evolution points to the emergence of a new global political geography.

This new geography of resources is predicated on the development of new technologies. Exponential technological change unleashed by the Fourth Industrial Revolution will undoubtedly change the energy resource landscape as valuable resources in a low-carbon world will be different.

Moreover, many renewables, unlike fossil fuels, are dependent on flows, rather than exhaustible stock, with widespread locations of the resources.[31] Alternative energy, although still geographically situated, could be propelled by technological advances to become "de-territorialized," changing the geopolitical context. The potential geopolitical ramifications lie in the fact that agents pursue very particular political ends based on the spatial distribution and fluidity of resources that they can utilize.

Renewable technologies could introduce new resource-based geopolitical concepts, approaches, and value judgments to international relations. This is true for both established technologies, such as solar, wind, and hydropower, as well as those at a more experimental stage, such as geothermal, tidal, and space. This new resource geography could prove to be a geopolitical stabilizer in some instances, while in others it could contribute to new forms of friction and conflict. Thus, assessing the geopolitical impacts derived from the evolution of the megatrend will require rigorous geospatial analysis.

The alternative energy megatrend is accompanied by influences that reshape the map of energy resources, production, and distribution. From conflicts over the Nile, Indus, Yangtze, and Tigris/Euphrates valleys to modern Angola's oil and diamonds, the use of force by opposing groups seeking control over natural resources is nothing new. Today, however, the competition is entering a new phase, reshaped by new capabilities and geographical distribution of capabilities and power. Such a new geography of alternative energy resources reinforces the fluidity of the power and influence transmitted over the global networks of stakeholders, giving rise to new security ramifications.

Tensions generated within the new geopolitical landscape can lead to charges of regulatory discrimination, protectionism, and disruptions of trade flows. Like oil, alternative energy could generate a confluence of energy and conflict shaped by the emergence of new forms of "governable space," including intellectual property.[32] The new energy map that emerges reflects how changing values assigned to resources affect geopolitical and geo-economic calculations and thereby exacerbate the perception that other actors can affect a nation's security.

Approaches to addressing energy threats continue to be framed within the prevalent zero-sum perception of an ongoing international struggle between energy-dependent and energy-rich states. Control over energy resources is part of the security landscape and is recognized as a destabilizing factor both domestically and internationally. This has already raised questions about the geopolitical connotations of non-traditional oil and gas resources (shale gas, tar sands, etc.) that are transforming previous energy importers into potential net energy exporters. As energy restrictions threaten the survival of states, societal groups, and individuals, a redrawing of the energy map repositions actors within the global order, revamping states' distinct security priorities.

Historically, the distribution of resources has been managed within a framework of international cooperation. States' actions within the geopolitical realm, and the manner in which resources were shared in particular, have been determined by human rationale and desires, which dictate the configuration of what the English School of geopolitical thinking terms "the society of states."[33] The conduct of this society of states is subject to a set of rules and practices that are constantly evolving and are acknowledged by these states' ruling elites as well as their broader societal constituencies. Resolving new energy conflicts could result in actions to enforce access to new resources and technologies, conduct that may stand in opposition to the society of states and further strain the international order.[34]

Like with fossil fuels, some countries will be better positioned to take advantage of these resources based on their geological or technological endowments. Renewables could introduce new "energy resource regions" that transform the geopolitical map by bestowing new potential upon areas that were previously lacking energy. The developing world may use this potential to accelerate growth and strengthen its political stand as it possesses a wealth of underdeveloped (and largely unmapped) renewable sources.

As the scope for renewable power generation grows, it will likely be accompanied by geopolitical leveraging. Indeed, the changing global energy map will likely bring about new power centers, impacting the geopolitical equilibrium. However, as discussed in later chapters, the extent of this geopolitical transformation and the list of its beneficiaries will be contingent on addressing a number of challenges and vulnerabilities.

1. Solar: generating power potential for the South and beyond.

Solar energy is a resource that can greatly affect the geopolitical map by transforming the power endowments of certain countries with particular implications for the divisions between the global North and the global South. With the installed capacity for solar-powered electricity producing 1% of all electricity used globally,[35] solar power currently remains a localized development; however, the geographical distribution of solar resources points to possible regional trends involving countries in the "solar belts" including the U.S. Southwest, Tibetan Plateau, Sahel, and Middle East. Large areas of Africa and Australia also have world-class solar resources. Despite its limited uses presently, many believe that solar power will become the largest source of renewable energy.[36]

The last decade saw rapid, yet uneven, growth in solar PV capacity with Asia ahead of all other markets, accounting for about two-thirds of global additions. The top five markets—China, the United States, Japan, India, and the United Kingdom—accounted for about 85% of additions; others in the top 10 were Germany, the Republic of Korea, Australia, the Philippines, and Chile. The leaders for solar PV capacity per inhabitant were Germany, Japan, Italy, Belgium, and Australia.[37] Evidently, the boundaries of today's leading solar PV power capacity holders do not entirely coincide with those possessing the most impressive solar energy resource potential. This highlights the importance of "extra-geographic" drivers for wide scale and effective utilization of solar power potential, including financing, clear policies, sound legal frameworks, and developed transmission infrastructure. Lack of these drivers hampers the rate of solar power solutions in the regions rich in these resources like Africa and the Middle East.

In this context, the pursuit of power endowments through the development of solar energy resources will inevitably influence relations between the actors in this sector. These new dynamics will raise questions about the validity of solar power targets and sustainability of supporting projects as well as about the vulnerability of solar power generation and distribution to asymmetric threats, such as sabotage, terrorism, and organized crime.

Overall, the expectation of widespread solar power generation is modifying power relations between actors, which redefines supply-demand relations with implications for the world order. A North-South distribution of resources raises concerns about energy security for consuming countries, much along the lines of current concerns about fossil fuel supplies. In addition, it is still a matter of debate whether solar energy in the global South will help to elevate impoverished countries and place them in positions of newfound geopolitical power, or rather, reinforce existing "resource-curse" relationships, in which resource-rich countries experience greater poverty than importing developed countries.

2. Wind: game-changing potential?

For some, wind energy could be a game-changer that endows its bearers with new power. Various wind resource assessments performed across the world to date state that wind energy is abundant, is widely distributed, and may serve as a key ingredient in the future energy mix for unlimited time. Thus, researchers at Stanford University's Global Climate and Energy Project estimated that even if only 20% of this power could be captured the world's wind resources could generate more than enough power to satisfy 100% of the world's energy demand of the year 2000 seven times over.[38] Among the areas with the greatest wind power potential are North America, northern Europe, the southern tip of South America, the Australian island of Tasmania, north and northwest Africa, Mongolia, and Sri Lanka.[39] When the wind power map is charted in more detail, more advantageous areas will likely be identified.

Global wind power generation steadily grows, reaching around 7% of total global power generation capacity.[40] Although the wind power map is currently dominated by China, the United States, and the EU, India has joined the ranks of the top five wind power-producing countries in the world. New markets continue to open elsewhere in Asia and across Africa, Latin America, and the Middle East.[41] By total wind power capacity per inhabitant, the leading countries tend to concentrate in Europe: Denmark, Sweden, Germany, Ireland, and Portugal.[42]

Harvesting energy from the wind is a widely disseminated technology that has two major applications—onshore and offshore. Mass deployment of onshore wind energy in China has begun to shift the center of gravity for wind energy markets from Europe to Asia, exerting pressure on the East-West dynamic. Offshore harvesting is more challenging and costly but is developing strongly, especially in Europe. Like other renewables, wind energy can remove dependencies and furnish power to populations that feel left out of the benefits of globalization, resulting in "re-globalization from the bottom up."[43]

At the same time, wind power, like other renewable energy technologies, has not yet been sufficiently tested for safety and side effects and could spark imbalances and even tensions on a localized and regional scale. Should mass deployment of wind farms result in shifts in weather patterns and generate climate shocks, the impact of such endeavors could trigger tensions between municipalities and even states. Future reliance on wind power could generate friction over the use of "monsoon alleys" and other regions with high wind capacity.

3. Biofuels: national interest-driven competitive advantages.

Biofuels are among the most contentious of alternative energy sources from a geopolitical perspective, in particular due to their impact on other essential resources. Biofuel production depends on the ability to grow crops such as corn, cereals, beet, and sugar cane.

Sub-Saharan Africa seems to have the greatest bioenergy potential, closely followed by South America and Russia. The EU and U.S. are in the middle and could become potential biofuel importers. East Asia and China have a clear potential; Japan is in a less comfortable position. Southeast Asia and India in particular have a clear potential, but this is not in proportion to their rapidly growing populations. Australia and the islands in the Pacific Ocean will probably become major exporters, possibly six times more than their domestic consumption.[44] Current production of a number of crops suitable for biofuels production is led by the United States and Brazil with opportunities for other potentially strong players still to be uncovered.[45]

Biomass energy can be a source of empowerment for developing countries that enjoy these geographical advantages. Countries with the right conditions for the production of these crops tend to endow biofuel production with a political and geopolitical value that goes beyond its immediate utility as an energy source, as Brazil's rapidly growing biofuel sector and related industries have clearly demonstrated. Biofuels can also be a source of domestic and regional tension. One example may be a fierce competition between the United States and Brazil for a control over and more importantly access to markets.[46] The biofuels' perceived advantages are undermined by their environmental side effects, as well as by the conflicting interests biofuels production can engender for state actors. For instance, biofuels production can lead to regional shortages, food price increases, and medium to long-term resource imbalances due to its adverse effect on scarce resources, particularly water, land, and certain crops. It can cause economic disputes between countries and distort economic balances because of its high costs and concomitant requirements for extensive subsidies. Just as in the case of fossil fuels, the prospects for conflicts over biofuels production will increase exponentially in disputed areas, especially in Africa and Asia.

4. Hydropower: proven performance with limited scope for future expansion.

Hydropower is the one renewable energy source that is an established mainstay of the energy mix and wholly dependent upon geography and water supply. Currently, hydropower is the leading renewable source for electricity generation globally and the dominant renewable energy source, accounting for 71% of all renewable electricity.[47] Hydropower potential and present-day deployment show large spatial heterogeneity with undeveloped capacity ranging from 50% in Europe to 90% in Africa.[48]

The list of key hydropower capacity holders is led by China and the United States. The most significant new development is concentrated in China, Latin America, and Africa.[50, 51]

Hydropower generation is a mature and price-competitive technology. However, the hydropower capacity expansion in the developed world is sometimes restrained due to environmental concerns. Significant potential remaining in the developing world is mostly undeveloped as the potential for hydropower capacity expansion is undermined by financial constraints as well as by institutional challenges such as a lack of dam safety enforcement and compliance, a lack of training needed to operate and maintain facilities, limited access to technical support, and potential environmental impact.[52]

Figure 3: Global Gross Hydropower Potential Distribution[49]

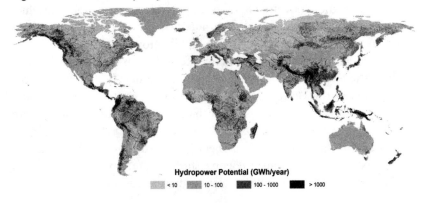

Hydropower Potential (GWh/year)

< 10   10 - 100   100 - 1000   > 1000

Hydropower's geopolitical significance lies predominantly in issues of control and access to resources. Its development can threaten environmental and economic security and contribute to conflicts.[53] Indeed, access to hydro energy is already exacerbating existing tensions and generating new disputes as countries interfere with their neighbors' access to water. This has raised concerns that, in the context of the megatrend, disputes over access to water could have a greater immediacy than other sources of conflict.[54] Likewise, its expansion could produce localized and regionalized environmental security concerns, making it a practical source of tension between actors, such as states, companies, environmental protection organizations, and biodiversity groups. Hydropower development could also generate resource conflicts that bring about diminished living standards, and threaten global security balances.[55]

5. Geothermal and tidal sources: holding promise for many but still at the experimental stage.

Tidal and geothermal sources have not produced a significant impact on geopolitical relations in their current stages of development because they are highly dependent on specific technological, geographical, geological, and climate conditions.[56] However, like other renewables, should they be deployed on a massive scale, they could dramatically bolster certain actors' powers and create new energy exporters. The resulting power imbalances could reshape relationships between allies or remove the need for concessions to previous energy suppliers. The future impact of geothermal and tidal power is difficult to quantify, and this uncertainty can generate security and geopolitical risks. These resources present a complex geographical picture. At present, the global geothermal power operating capacity is spread across 24 countries, and there are projects under development in 82 countries.[57] Turkey and Indonesia are leading the way in new installations. Kenya is the largest producer in Africa, and interest in the region is growing. For example, Rwanda is undertaking exploration studies of its geothermal reserves.[58]

Geothermal energy presents concerns due to its potential for seismic events associated with its generation that could lead to natural disasters and conflict. Although the areas with the highest underground temperatures feature active or geologically young volcanoes, geothermal energy can be found almost anywhere.

The availability of tidal energy is more difficult to predict due to limited locations with high enough tidal ranges and/or flow velocities. To date,

Figure 4: Global Geothermal Power Potential[59]

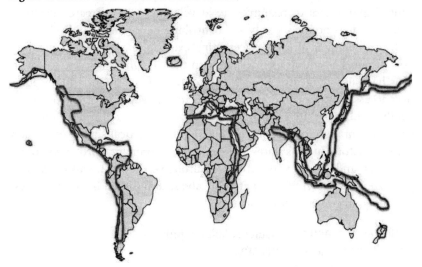

investments in ocean energy are primarily found in the Republic of Korea, the United Kingdom, the United States, France, Canada, and China.[60] The technologies required to tap into and generate power from these resources have not been sufficiently scaled up to enable an accurate appraisal of their geopolitical impact. In the short to medium term, state and non-state actors are unlikely to assign significant resources and give serious consideration to geothermal and tidal power production.

6. Space-based sources of energy: the new frontier.

The development of experimental energy technologies such as solar-from-space or magnetic space tethers still lies in the realm of the imagined rather than the practical. However, they could add new dimensions to the global energy map by turning space into a new resource region and by opening up near-Earth space to energy competition, thereby creating opportunities for new areas of potential instability. These technologies hold vast potential for actors with the technological resources necessary to achieve a breakthrough, as they would leapfrog other actors and become pioneers. Although the concept of solar power being generated and beamed down from space has long been pondered and quickly dismissed as too costly and impractical, the Japan Aerospace Exploration Agency's efforts to develop a space solar power system and the joint U.S.-Indian initiative to construct a space solar power array illustrate how the future of the alternative energy megatrend could transform political geography and global security.

However, developing these technologies carries risks that could be construed as security threats by other actors. In particular, energy from space impinges on the use of space as a resource, which to date has not received serious geopolitical consideration. In addition, these technologies could be easily diverted to serve a military purpose and influence global military balances. Overall, these technologies open the door to an array of new geopolitical and security considerations, centering on the use of space resources and the competition between states to tap them.

7. Rare earth elements: another area of potential conflict.

Many of the alternative energy technologies, like batteries to solar panels or magnets to wind turbines, require such materials as scandium, yttrium, and other minerals known as rare earth elements with unique chemical and physical characteristics. The rare earth elements' sustainable supplies are a challenging task as these elements are scarce with the reserves concentrated within a narrow group of regions and China being the leading supplier.[61] China's restriction of exports of rare earth elements to Japan, the United States, and the EU highlights the risk of greater conflict over these precious materials and showcases another alternative energy market niche where the major powers are already competing for leadership.

The limits on rare earth elements' supply may be also caused by internal tension in producing countries. These compounds are highly toxic when mined and processed, and have significant negative impact on soil and water, raising environmental concerns.

Looking for ways to mitigate the risks of supply disruptions, researchers are working on alternatives to these critical elements and on ways to effectively recycle them. However, for today there is no suitable substitute available to minimize the conflict potential of rare earth elements that are complementing the set of natural resources put into play by the alternative energy megatrend.

III. The old and some new actors—the cast of the Great Energy Play.

The progression of the alternative energy megatrend provides a view of how state and non-state actors are testing novel approaches and strategies for achieving new power capabilities. The megatrend also highlights how the emergence of a new geography of resources affects the relations between actors, with unexpected implications on the relationship between energy suppliers and consumers.[62]

Examining the megatrend offers insight into the future of geopolitical interactions. Particularly, it reveals how actors could be influenced, whether traditional ties could be altered, and how this would change the geopolitical architecture. Global phenomena like the alternative energy megatrend could prompt state actors to pursue new paths for enhanced geopolitical positioning.

At the same time, the megatrend provides a new angle on how non-state actors, including intergovernmental institutions, NGOs, multinational corporations, and even organized crime and terrorist organizations, are increasing their geopolitical influence. As Jeff Bezos has stated, the climate change threat "[is] going to take collective action from big companies, small companies, nation states, global organizations and individuals."[63]

The changing visage of geopolitical actors spawns a revised understanding of the geopolitical themes that underscore actors' practices. The megatrend highlights in particular how the scope of geopolitical and securitization roles has expanded and how the roles that actors are assuming have transformed, with implications for the geopolitical equilibrium.

1. The dynamic and interconnected networks: fluid balances of multidimensional alliances and divisions.

Looking through the prism of the megatrend allows a better understanding of geopolitical dynamics, raising questions such as who influences geopolitics and how, what are the rules, how are the rules applied, and how do actors follow the rules. In traditional geopolitical parlance, participants in geopolitical interactions are considered to be the "agents of statecraft." Through the end of the 20th century, such agents were overwhelmingly states since they were the only entities capable of projecting significant power on the geopolitical stage. Classic geopolitics sought to explain and predict states' strategic behavior. States were regarded as sovereign actors that dealt with clearly defined foreign and domestic issues, with interstate relations perceived as a contest for and between different territories and their associated resources. States' interactions in the global field entailed the imposition of order on the space, resources, and population of a given territory through the wielding of geopolitical power.

The alternative energy megatrend's drivers elicit different responses and hold disparate meanings for various actors. For some, these developments represent an answer to key questions of survival, such as environmental and energy security challenges. For others, they portray a risky venture with an uncertain outcome and embody a range of vulnerabilities and threats. The alternative energy megatrend holds the promise of solving many of Earth's environmental ills.

It also presents states with a difficult geopolitical choice: whether or not to pursue relatively risky alternative energy developments in light of the impact of this decision on their relations with other states. For state actors in particular, such choices represent reprises of the classic prisoner's dilemma;[64] their resulting interactions and mutual influence would be as much instinctive as deliberate. To win this game states must exhibit resilience, which has been defined by Adrienne Arsht as the ability "to bounce back after a jarring incident and adapt to the new normal."[65]

(1) The changing power endowments of 21st century actors.

Alternative energy developments are a force whose geopolitical meaning changes depending on the strategies that rely on them. In some instances, they contribute to the emergence of new powers; in others they reduce the sway actors previously held.[66] The megatrend reflects the changing power endowments of a proliferating number of 21st century actors that have the ability to enact securitization. The growing number and shifting power endowments of developed and developing countries, as well as other international actors, enable the debutants in the reprise of the Great Game to move toward new positions on the geopolitical stage. These stakeholders will not only help determine new strategic balances but also modify foreign relations' rules of conduct and established practices. By implementing policies that affect the megatrend directly or indirectly, actors will exert their newfound power to influence others.

The alternative energy megatrend reveals the weakening of traditional ties and the reshaping of geopolitical interactions in unexpected ways. Relationships between actors are determined by power and interests, which balance out within hierarchical institutional formations. The megatrend encapsulates the growing number of factors that will upend those balances and add new twists to states' traditional approaches of viewing and dealing with the world.

(2) Upending the balances.

The megatrend points to a new path toward unification, ignoring geographical boundaries and providing options for ungoverned peripheral regions that threaten power centers and the geopolitical equilibrium. In addition, those who view themselves as losers in the alternative energy race could redirect their attention toward forming new types of regional energy unions that could lead to imbalances.

The megatrend's evolution reflects changing stakeholders' value judgments about their and others' power projection capabilities. Equilibrium is continuously undermined by shifting values and perceived interests that result in new power drifts, for example from West to East, leading to realignments and tensions in the global balance of power. The notion that competition for resources is consequently the source of many conflicts applies to the alternative energy megatrend as well.[67] The megatrend could lead actors to pursue new expressions of geo-economic power that they would enforce through regulatory discrimination, protectionism, and disruptions of trade flows. Accelerating this transition could prompt major powers to play one-upmanship with each other, resulting in unprecedented economic shifts that could be described as a global gold rush—a race for resources between players with competing priorities.

The megatrend's consequences could open up new areas for international disputes due to actors' changing power endowments and geopolitical goals. By redefining the mutual interests that served as the basis for alliances, the megatrend could play a role in opening up new rifts between historical allies, such as the U.S. and EU;[68] the U.S./EU and Russia;[69] the West and the Middle East; Japan, China, and the Republic of Korea; and India, China, and Pakistan.[70] Indeed, the new power endowments offered by the alternative energy megatrend can present a rationale for forging new alliances. This could alter the balance of power between developed and developing countries by furnishing new sources of soft power for rapidly developing economies. The evolving conditions of the post-Cold War paradigm shift could reinforce the megatrend's effect on energy balances. The transformation of energy dependencies could be a source of tension on a global scale.

The megatrend thus makes evident the increased fluidity and mutability of alliances, which could ignite local and regional tensions, paving the way for regional destabilization. The loss in revenue from Western energy purchases could spark turmoil in countries that export fossil fuels, or even create upheaval across whole regions. Such a development would require additional policy commitments from developed countries as part of an overall stability mandate. Alternative energy development, therefore, could contribute to strife and even the collapse of states with an abundance of fossil fuel resources, particularly those dependent on the extractable rent from these resources.[71] In addition, alternative energy suppliers might eventually conduct themselves in a manner similar to Organization of the Petroleum Exporting Countries (OPEC) member states, forcing energy consumers to adopt new foreign policy stances.[72] The outcome of such alterations in the demand-supply relationship could breed new forms of tension.

Intensifying regionalism in the multi-centric world can be associated with new forms of conflict prompted by modern trends.[73] Formal and informal pacts, such as the BRICS and the U.S.-EU Transatlantic Trade and Investment Partnership (TTIP), can be seen as a response to the new security and economic concerns of the 21st century. Regionalization corresponds not just to geography but along other demarcations, e.g., geographical such as the EU, institutional such as the World Trade Organization or the International Monetary Fund, and civil society such as the environmental or human rights movements. This post-Cold War rise of regionalism has been accompanied by a gradual erosion of the power and influence of the nation-state.

(3) Modifying the actor's geopolitical stances.

The alternative energy megatrend contributes to this recasting of actors into a new global institutional framework. Rebalancing, driven by renewables development, could change the geopolitical stance of emerging economies in particular. States' shifting priorities could further exacerbate perceptions of inequality, leading to realignments in the understanding of global balances.[74] Among the BRICS countries, for example, China and India's need to secure access to the energy supplies will enhance their global presence while Russia will struggle to secure co-dependency with Europe. The emerging common interests among rapidly developing economies, particularly in Asia, in dealing with energy security and climate change could bring about new waves of cooperation from regional centers of power. Of course, it could also result in competition between these rising powers and the current provider of security in the global commons, the United States.

The uneven evolution of power endowments can lead to an unstable framework of state and non-state actors that may apply, in an unprecedented manner, the codes that have governed international relations with respective security repercussions. These geopolitical agents are assuming new roles with international organizations, multinationals, NGOs, and other non-state actors finding new ways of pursuing untested geopolitical ambitions. By charting the megatrend's trajectory, it is possible to prognosticate the impact of evolving power endowments.

2. State actors: emerging postures and the pursuit of untested options.

Despite the rising power of global society, states remain the primary geopolitical forces and securitization actors. States will help determine the megatrend's direction, even when the wider diffusion and application of alternative energy technology changes the characteristics and conduct of the states on each side of the energy consumer-supplier equation. The state will remain the key securitization actor due to having the innate capacity to reach audiences not only through visual and auditory mechanisms but also through regulation and the traditional tools of government. Moreover, audiences are more amenable to states' imposition of limitations or restrictions and even expect states to be the main instigators of such actions.

As geopolitical agents, states exercise power when they endeavor to achieve specific goals or change other agents' views or stances. The classical view states that only military force or diplomacy enables the projection of power.[75] Exerting geopolitical power often entails explicit or implicit bargaining over a wide array of resources. It also involves gambling on the future outcomes of specific resource rivalries and the manner in which certain resources will be utilized. These resources can be tangible (financing, mineral resources, infrastructure access, etc.) or knowledge based (cultural leadership, market niches, technological advances, defense postures, etc.). Regardless of the nature of the resource that is the object of the negotiations, the structure of power exchanges is apparently a zero-sum exercise: One party loses something in order to gain something else. But this view is too simplistic. With the introduction of new resource capabilities, these exchanges are not zero-sum, as they can benefit a wide array of actors tied to or constituting the states in conflict: neighboring countries, political allies, international corporations based within a given territory, and NGOs.

(1) Power projection tactics.

The alternative energy megatrend can contribute to a number of strategies for states seeking to develop new powers. The new forms of power sought by actors can change the paradigm of global politics that is still perceived as a zero-sum game. They can offer new avenues to states that emerged as powers after the end of the Cold War to further integrate into the global economy following the loss of patronage they received from one of the competing superpowers. The ways to achieve this may include:

- *Gaining leeway.* Current net consumers seek to achieve energy security through energy independence and diversification. Integrating alternative energy into their policies marks a stepping stone toward a new international dynamic that incorporates common approaches and strategies vis-à-vis current and new suppliers. It grants actors the ability to wield greater influence on energy prices and markets, in some cases transforming energy consumers into energy suppliers. Examples include the EU's development of solar power generation in Africa,[76] the biofuels revolution in Brazil, and Denmark's reliance on wind power.

- *Hedging energy bets.* OPEC and other states' national oil and gas companies can buy stakes in their customers' future by becoming more active in alternative energy development. Some fossil fuel suppliers develop long-term national renewable energy programs and invest in alternatives, considering their potential economic and geopolitical dividends.[77] The trend's propagation could force countries to diversify their oil and gas-dominated industries to strengthen their economies. Conversely, the trend could also lead to regional failures, altering the interdependence between developed and developing economies, as well as traditional suppliers and consumers.

- *A shift from stakeholders to shareholders.* Alternative energy technologies allow state actors to move beyond their role as stakeholders toward formalizing their position as minority shareholders in the emerging security equilibrium—a shift that grants actors more control in an unstable world. This is particularly apt for emerging countries, which use environmental initiatives to increase internal security and international standing. An indicative example may be China, which has demonstrated support of the global regulations aimed at mitigating climate change and its ambition of becoming an emerging global clean energy leader. The multi-centric world reinforces a sense of vulnerability, motivating actors to internalize decisions that affect national interests. This ultimately could instigate a reprise of certain elements of the balance of power games of the 19th and early 20th centuries, a process clearly demonstrated by the diverging reactions of developed and emerging economies to the global governance mechanisms proposed by the G20.[78]

- *Building on LDC's potential for growth.* Least-developed countries (LDCs) view alternative energy as a means of alleviating energy cost burdens and achieving economic growth and social development. Fostering renewable energy expansion could prove costly, but developed countries' transfer of technologies and know-how for free or for a nominal cost could spur LDC's economic and social growth and reduce the cost of addressing security risks that could otherwise arise. Like other forms of technology transfer, offering new alternative energy capabilities to developing countries may also help to create ties that the technology providers deem beneficial.[79] This growth could produce savings for developed countries, justifying foreign aid budgets to domestic audiences. The evolution of a normative framework will increase bottom-up pressures on technologically advanced states to render development support to LDCs in the form of alternative energy know-how, irrespective of whether or not developed economies are capable of facilitating such transfers. This pressure would further influence local regimes to be more responsive to the needs of their citizenry. In the post-Cold War paradigm shift, the global political awakening posited by former U.S. National Security Advisor Zbigniew Brzezinski encompasses a broad spectrum of concerns, with environmental security assuming a prominent place. The global environmental movement and the state actions it has spurred are proof of this awakening.

(2) *The alternative energy megatrend increasing the pressures on policymaking.*

Powerful constituencies have developed with vested interests in maintaining a high level of funding for renewables. Even the public at large in developed countries expects politicians to pursue development of renewables to prevent or mitigate climate change and increase energy independence.

The alternative energy megatrend reveals how traditionally state-driven policymaking is increasingly subject to societal influence, which challenges the notion of sovereignty.[80] As noted by prominent 20th century political theorist Hans Morgenthau, the increasing influence of non-state actors generates pressures that reduce "the supreme legal authority of the nation to give and enforce the law within a certain territory and, in consequence, independence from the authority of any other nation and equality with it under international law."[81]

In this context, charting the security trajectory of the alternative energy megatrend provides a deeper understanding of the manner in which states are pursuing power and projecting it beyond their borders. The way geopolitical agents can influence the processes of international politics and relations is equated with their political power; however, the state-centric view of the world system no longer fully reflects reality. While states remain major actors, they no longer enjoy complete freedom of action.

3. Non-state actors: deriving new powers and moving toward the spotlight.

Within the projected evolution of the alternative energy megatrend, a new geography of control is coming to the fore that underscores the changing balances between state and non-state actors. The growing influence of non-state actors is a defining feature of today's global environment, and it characterizes the momentum behind the alternative energy megatrend. Of particular importance is the increasing frequency of non-state actors enacting securitization. Many non-state actors are putting alternative energy issues at the top of their agendas, adding another layer of complexity to the security landscape of the modern multi-centric world.

Globalization has contributed to the diffusion of geopolitical and securitization power to non-state actors, often raising questions about what constitutes sovereignty. By impacting numerous localities, societal groups, and political actors unconcerned with territoriality or political power, globalization reduces sovereign power and imposes new conditions for economic activity, political practices, and customs. These new conditions make it increasingly difficult for state actors to dominate the economic and political agendas both beyond and within their borders. The arsenal of instruments available to states is narrowing, and solutions to a number of local, regional, and international problems increasingly depend on cooperation between states and with non-state actors.

Coupled with the ongoing diffusion of sovereignty, the new energy resource geography enables non-state actors to acquire a legitimacy comparable to that of states in pursuit of new ambitions. The megatrend's projected evolution provides additional evidence of the growing disparity between traditional geography, reinforcing an ideological discourse about the evolution of the strategic importance of space[82] and the geography of politics.[83] The megatrend's driving forces also endow old and new actors with new geopolitical attributes, invigorating new alliances, intensifying divides, and revamping modern geopolitics. Of particular significance is the increasing ability of non-state actors to establish cross-border institutions and rules.[84] In this manner, it parallels and sometimes displaces the role that states play in global environmental and other issues.

(1) Non-state actors: a diverse world of assorted initiatives and inspired approaches.

There is an extensive and continuously broadening range of non-state actors that can exert tangible geopolitical and security influence. Major international corporations, ideological movements, NGOs, religious groups, and other agents are increasingly acting on their constituencies' behalf and formulating their interactions with other state and non-state agents. Foreign policy is thus no longer aimed chiefly at ensuring territorial integrity and the preservation of political and cultural institutions. There are now a number of non-state actors with security concerns other than state preservation. These actors can influence foreign policy to suit their ends. This is most evident with non-state actors that exercise power through violence. The various types of non-state actors bring different elements to the mix.

- *Intergovernmental institutions.* International intergovernmental organizations represent states' interests and recognize the sovereignty of nations. However, they increasingly wield power beyond what they are endowed with by the states they represent. In particular, they have assumed a new level of influence by helping to set global guidance norms and regimes, maintaining the momentum toward energy rebalancing and connecting the domestic and international politics that influence state action.[85] They also have taken on some aspects of the sovereignty of states they represent. Further iterations of the megatrend will determine whether this transfer of sovereignty harms states' interests or instead allows for an evolution beyond a zero-sum game, as is their intention.

- *NGOs.* The increasing number of NGOs is matched by their growing ability to influence the conduct of states on a range of concerns, including those affecting and affected by the alternative energy megatrend.[86] Their enhanced roles have accelerated the convergence of state and non-state actors' agendas, which has embedded NGOs in the policymaking process as advisors, critics, and even leaders. By focusing on alternative energy development, NGOs are poised to affect global regulatory mechanisms. They are even capable of creating a transnational governance framework. The propagation of a "green creed" by non-state actors worldwide is not only fulfilling their goal of addressing climate change and other environmental threats but also circumventing traditional development processes. NGOs represent the subjective reality of the alternative energy megatrend, in which global civil society has become empowered and strengthened by the need to solve transnational problems. It is also important to note, however, that NGOs could include actors that will resist and even undermine the emerging agenda of the alternative energy megatrend, such as the fossil fuel lobby.

- *Multinationals.* Major international corporations are taking on dual roles in the multi-centric world order with a clear agenda: profit and advancement based on control and the ability to wield power. They have been firmly entrenched within intergovernmental relations for decades. This has enabled them to become insiders with influence on the international policy and strategy-making process, putting them in a position to actually direct it and take on functions traditionally performed by states. Numerous multinationals, for example, are part of climate change negotiations. They are exerting influence on the adoption of the legislative and policy frameworks in both developed and developing countries, regardless of whether such countries are suppliers or consumers of fossil fuels. They also play a role in technology transfers. Multinationals have started to take advantage of the potential the megatrend offers to gain access to new markets, intensifying their role in the public-private interactions that underwrite current alternative energy development worldwide. Moreover, multinationals have demonstrated an ability to alter global strategies and security considerations tied to the alternative energy megatrend. States also indirectly or directly rely on sovereign wealth funds, which often resemble multinationals in their conduct and strategies.

- *Malevolent groups, organized crime, and terrorist organizations.* This distinct grouping is endowed with its own, albeit relatively small, significance in the multi-centric world order. These non-state actors have shown they can influence the framework of international relations in a dramatic fashion. This influence is made particularly evident by the set of wars and conflicts described as The War on

Terror or simply The Long War, involving the major world powers and non-state actors espousing radical interpretations of ideologies and religions.[87] The War on Terror provides a stark example of the scope of the challenges that non-state actors can pose to both major state powers—the U.S., EU, Russia, China, and India—and the world system in general. Given the potential military implications of the alternative energy megatrend, terrorist groups could seek to employ alternative energy sources as weapons of mass destruction or utilize conventional military means to disrupt, subvert, and inflict damage on the alternative energy infrastructure.[88] Infecting or diverting water streams, sabotaging power installations or transmission facilities, and destroying critical infrastructure in both developing and developed countries are some of the targets for terrorist groups. While their impact on the megatrend's geopolitics is relatively insignificant, their actions drastically increase the cost of doing business and add complexity to the megatrend's security significance.

(2) Shifting relationship paradigms.

The megatrend also helps reshape relations between state and non-state actors by furnishing non-state actors with new platforms, and legitimizing their more prominent role in the stabilization of the global order.[89] With the diffusion of state power, conflicts between state and non-state actors have risen. As concentrated power in the core fades and spreads to the periphery, instinctive tensions between grassroots civil society and elite power come to the fore. This tension is embodied in the archetypal contradictions between the state and individual, as well as the establishment and civil society.[90] Government apparatuses are unable to wield complete control over a range of individuals and agents within their own territory, and "institutions such as the press, research institutes, and lobbies have been absorbed into the structure of modern governance. While government may be losing power over individual policies, it is gaining more as coordinator, intervener in, and ultimate legitimator of the activities of the many informal agents that make up the modern state."[91]

Alternative energy developments do not in and of themselves change actors' overall strategies and policies. Rather they modify actors' attitudes, values, and expectations, which subsequently steer them in a new direction. The projected evolution of renewable resources highlights the forces that could allow state and non-state actors to play new roles in a new geopolitical balance. The road to this new balance is likely to be rocky, due to the propensity for new alliances and the destruction of existing ones that is part of geopolitical restructuring. The relationship paradigms that underpin the megatrend's progression often lie beneath the surface: They can sweep smaller players in unforeseen directions, creating whirlpools around power centers and irrevocably altering the arenas within which both state and non-state actors operate.

In the immediate term, non-state actors are acquiring an enhanced role in promoting the alternative energy megatrend. This stands in stark contrast to traditional approaches, which granted non-state actors no place in ensuring global security. In the wake of the post-Cold War paradigm shift, however, non-state actors have achieved a greater significance in international relations.[92] As many are not affiliated with a particular state, they are essentially free from association with a given sovereign and capable of challenging states' ability to perform their usual functions.

Non-state actors can also impact global security balances. The continued development of a variety of military and civilian technologies and their proliferation has greatly increased the ability of non-state actors to present a military threat to states. The Westphalian order, dominated by states, is gradually giving way to a world dominated by international institutions, private sector associations, and social movements, which have developed platforms to address issues of global development, security, and politics that were previously the exclusive purview of states.

In conclusion: The megatrend reveals 21st century security complexities that are rapidly reshaping geopolitical divisions and stances in the age of new Great Power Competition.

- The alternative energy megatrend's security trajectory highlights certain essential elements of the current geopolitical disequilibrium. It poses new and important questions about the factors that influence the movement toward the future global equilibrium, in particular in the context of emerging global geopolitical rivalry. The megatrend's projected evolution demonstrates how the new abilities of actors to exert influence and project power across borders can further skew geospatial and geopolitical balances. The megatrend might lead to unforeseen geopolitical divides based on the new global resource map, ultimately leading to tensions over energy-related spaces and geography.

- The megatrend provides a new perspective on the 21st century geo-political dynamics including: a shifting relationship between the core and the periphery; the potential for both new forms of East-West cooperation and the persistence of East-West divides and tensions; and the probability that new geopolitical and security divisions between North and South will be reshaped by the pursuit of new forms of power and leverage, with energy being a contributing factor. Where top-down and bottom-up pressures meet, a whirlpool of influences is generated that affects the direction of modern develop-ments, such as the alternative energy megatrend. As the intensifying uncertainty of international relations is translated into an increasing number of conflicts, it can be anticipated that the power of emerging actors will be tangible.

- The alternative energy megatrend's impact on a new geography of resources and its broader implications is not just determined by the energy supply-demand equation. It also influences geopolitical dynamics and stability. It can contribute to both the alleviation of existing rivalries and conflicts or create new rivalries and tensions, depending on the direction in which the trend evolves and how it is incorporated into actors' strategies. In addition, the very idea of resource scarcity might need rethinking.

- The future impact of alternative energy on the resource map will depend to a large extent on the development of the different tech-nologies and resources that underpin the megatrend. That means that the upcoming iterations of the alternative energy megatrend are a direct result of the ongoing global technological revolution and in particular the role of artificial intelligence. All this spells a new itera-tion of the Grand Energy Game.

- The alternative energy megatrend demonstrates how a growing number of actors are assuming new roles and how existing actors are donning new geopolitical guises. The megatrend reveals the expanding cast of state and non-state actors increasingly capable of shaping the geopolitical agenda. New sought-after power endow-ments can present a rationale for realigning international relations in general and geopolitical alliances in particular. In this context, the megatrend introduces a range of novel parameters that change the process of ordering space, territory, and resources. It also modifies the geopolitical codes that determine the balance of power between geopolitical agents. Moreover, the megatrend reveals how policymaking is increasingly subject to influence by non-state actors, which presents new challenges to the notion of sovereignty closely guarded by states that are no longer able to fully control cross-border interactions.

- Analyzing the geopolitical equilibrium through the prism of the megatrend highlights how growing 21st century geopolitical complexities and security threats require new frameworks of analysis. The megatrend helps discern related dynamics as it contributes to the generation of new spaces and the revamping of areas of strategic competition. It also alters the role of actors, questioning the viability of traditional sovereignty.

- Viewed through the prism of the megatrend, the world system will remain one of competition but with an increasing fluidity of relations, where alliances will be less stable and where the imperatives toward utilizing stronger measures to securitize issues will be more pronounced. This anarchical nature of forthcoming global geopolitics will likely raise questions about the spatial locations of power and the new types of power projection used as a tool by actors to achieve security. At the same time, certain forms of power will crystallize as an integral part of the new Great Power Competition.

PART 3

The Alternative Energy Megatrend's Trajectory Across the Transforming Energy, Defense, Environmental, and Economic Security Domains

*"If you add a little to a little, and then do it again,
soon that little shall be much."*

Hesiod[1]

Although the future remains unpredictable, the alternative energy megatrend clearly constitutes a movement and is an agent of global change. It will transform itself as much as it transforms all that surrounds it. Such a transformation will produce a range of security implications that encompass specific security domains including energy, defense, environmental, and economic.

The megatrend's security trajectory across institutional domains provides a view of how different security aspects have intermeshed in the modern world system in flux, where converging explicit and implicit security parameters interact and are mutually influencing. The megatrend's developments point to the emergence of new power projection capabilities and new tools that actors could deploy. It also points at a number of new security vulnerabilities stemming from the development of the megatrend.

I. The modern age of energy security—factoring in the alternative energy megatrend.

Energy has long played a significant role in the security of states, communities, and individuals. The contemporary concept of energy security is constantly evolving and increasingly integrated into states' broader national security considerations. Even minute changes in energy security balances can bring about extensive repercussions in other security areas. This chapter examines how the notion of energy security is evolving against the backdrop of 21st century challenges and how developments in alternative energy impact energy security.

Despite the growth of renewables, the anticipated rise in global energy consumption during the second decade of the 21st century is projected to be met with fossil fuels. The scenarios by different institutions may differ in details, however they are mostly in agreement both in forecasting the renewables market growth and in expecting the developments to take substantial time.[2] The ability of the megatrend to revamp the energy mix, therefore, remains to be seen.

Paradoxically, the relatively modest presence of alternative energy in the current energy mix has given rise to substantial energy security implications, and poses significant questions about the pace of technological advancements in the context of the global technological revolution.

Below is discussed the future of the megatrend's perceived potency in further influencing geopolitical attitudes and practices, including energy imperialism and resource nationalism, and forming notions like "energy superpower." The section also takes a deeper look at the new geopolitical tools the megatrend brings to the table.

1. The broadening scope of energy security: new approaches to securing energy and new threats to stability.

For most of the 20th century, actors grappled with the energy security challenges associated with disruption and manipulation of fossil fuel supplies, predominantly from the Middle East. Toward the end of the century, the geographic focus expanded to include other regions, such as Latin America and Russia. Energy as an object of securitization has been a part of states' general concerns as societies have grown increasingly energy dependent. Energy has gradually assumed a place of its own as a factor in the survival of states, separate from other resources. In addition, energy security has grown in stature in national security agendas due to the perceived limitation of fossil fuels. Depletion, supply and demand volatility, and the capacity of actors to restrict access to conventional fuels has turned lack of access to energy supplies into an existential threat that is prompting a range of securitization efforts and a revision of traditional approaches.

(1) *Adding new dimensions to energy security.*

The primary energy security consideration of states rests on the notion of maintaining the ability to obtain secure supplies of energy at reasonable prices.[3] Geopolitical agents have thus projected their power in energy-rich regions to ensure a reliable supply on acceptable terms. Clearly, the measures to address fossil fuel security have reflected the view that a relative scarcity of energy resources is contributing to energy insecurity and, by implication, undermining national security.[4] These energy security approaches have gradually become accepted and institutionalized amongst consumer countries in institutions such as the International Energy Agency.

The persistent significance of control over energy resources for the survival of the state has led to varied positions on how to deal with conflicts resulting from competition over access to energy resources. The realist tradition posits energy security as a zero-sum game of mutual vulnerability between exporters and importers. Modern energy security strategies aim for a more nuanced form of energy security, beyond energy independence and energy system resilience.

In the age of global economic interconnectedness, energy security approaches have increasingly become reliant on the concept and practice of energy interdependence,[5] which reinforces the realization that there is no such thing as "absolute energy security." The notion of energy interdependence is still a matter of debate among actors. Perceptions are determined by actors' particular strategic interests, resource endowments, population distribution, and economic make-up, as well as domestic energy-specific factors like energy affordability and price volatility. Nonetheless, energy supply vulnerability and the geographical distribution of energy resources have bound suppliers and consumers in a global network of interdependence.

Approaches toward energy security are thus focusing on the need to facilitate market liberalization and mutual interdependence, as well as the traditional aspirations to diversify energy supplies, and accumulate and properly manage strategic reserves of energy resources. The prominence of the concept of energy interdependence also applies to the ongoing pursuit of technological advances intended to enhance both the sustainability of energy supply and the diversification of options.

In a universally securitized world, the notion of energy security is expanding to include not just threats to energy supply and consumption but also wider threats that result from existing energy practices. Other factors also explicitly or implicitly drive energy security calculations and could shape the energy landscape during the 21st century. These factors include the emerging global regulatory framework for greenhouse gas emissions, international public pressure to tackle resource depletion and environmental sustainability, and the unrelenting pace of technological development. Taking these factors into account, the impact of the alternative energy megatrend highlights a spectrum of possible effects on global energy security, despite the current focus on oil and gas as the primary sources of energy.

The governance of energy use has expanded to include the broader impact of energy on habitats and ecosystems. From this perspective, energy-related damage to the environment has been likened to "a gigantic uncontrolled experiment on earth."[6] Pressure is increasingly exerted onto states—particularly by global civil society—to ensure that they maintain an acceptable standard of energy security. In many cases, this means ensuring the availability of affordable and diversified energy supplies, including from alternative energy sources, which can sustain economic growth and minimize damage to the environment.

Securitization also involves energy relations and dependencies that bear obvious geopolitical implications. Energy security plays an increasingly significant role in the diffuse relations between the geopolitical power cores and the peripheries that make up the modern world system. The alternative energy megatrend also provides a new analytical perspective on how threats to the global energy system can be securitized in a way that addresses their impact on other national security interests. A securitization act in the energy field can have a spill-over effect into other realms. Generally, threats stemming from energy dependency are strongly correlated to geographical proximity. Thus, geo-spatial energy security complexes spring up. Within these complexes, the interdependent relationship between supplier and consumer is, in effect, marked by contention. The many public and private agents active in the field further complicate this situation, adding to the already rich complexity of energy security that shapes actors' securitization policies.

The energy security impact of renewables will likely coalesce around two main focal points. Alternative energy can wield a stabilizing influence over the global energy system by broadening choices, reducing barriers to access, and buffering/reducing price shocks. However, despite alternative energy's propensity for introducing new resources, options, and ambitions for different actors, it could also prove to be disruptive as it disturbs the status quo of the global energy system. The breadth of alternative energy's impact on energy security, to a large extent, will be determined by fluctuations in fossil fuel demand and supply. It also will rest on the societal notions and understanding that determine the acceptability, attractiveness, and viability of other energy sources, such as traditional and non-traditional fossil fuels and nuclear power.

(2) *The technological revolution's impact on energy security: adding momentum to new approaches.*

The global technological revolution is adding momentum to alternative energy developments and bolstering expectations for their contribution to energy security strategies which are to ensure supply of reliable and affordable power without contributing to climate change. The exponential advancement of nanotechnology, automation, artificial intelligence, bioengineering, and the Internet of Things within the Fourth Industrial Revolution adds new elements to the very notion of energy security. Beyond the availability of natural resources, access to technologies that propel distributed energy storage technologies, 5G communications networks, the ability to bioengineer materials such as lithium for batteries, and the creation of smart utility and electricity networks are becoming as indispensable as having access to oil, gas, sun, or wind.

The ongoing global technological revolution is providing opportunities for the development of new energy-related capabilities and allowing actors to seek new energy security approaches. Technological advancements bolster expectations of change—in this case, a transition to a new energy mix. This revolution entails a series of interrelated radical breakthroughs that in turn foster even greater developmental momentum, or "the processes of diffusion of each technological revolution and its techno-economic paradigm—together with their assimilation by the economy and society as well as the resulting increases in productivity and expansion—constitute successive great surges of development."[7] The momentum thus driving the alternative energy megatrend can lead to a new dynamic pace of overall development with socio-political and techno-economic effects well beyond the confines of energy security. This allows the megatrend, like other global phenomena, to achieve a greater, and even a disproportionate, impact on economic inputs and outputs, political decisions, and societal order. In this way, the momentum of the technological revolution facilitates the megatrend's ability to generate vulnerabilities, transform economic relations, induce burdensome and disruptive rivalries, and affect the existing energy supply-demand relations and the geopolitical balances they sustain.

The greater technological capabilities and options they provide are increasingly directing the evolution of the energy mix toward sustainability and diversification of energy sources, with new endeavors being undertaken across the board.[8] For example, alternative sources of energy are being integrated into national electricity grids, bringing closer the establishment of truly smart grids.

Within the evolution of a new technological paradigm in the 21st century, there is a growing anticipation that an energy shift away from conventional fossil fuel sources is actually under way. Prompted by diverse considerations, such as energy price increases, depletion of fossil fuels, rising emissions, and concerns over global warming, political positions and societal views have converged to produce energy policies that increasingly look beyond fossil fuels as the main sources of energy. This transition has affected different industries, often leading to new strategies for different sectors—from auto manufacturers to oil companies.

The inherently disorderly nature of technological progress could result in a number of new security vulnerabilities stemming from the development of the megatrend. The technologies of the Fourth Industrial Revolution are instrumental for realizing intelligent grids and interconnected assets. At the same time, these technologies introduce new threats such as the possibility of cyberattacks. The increasing interconnectivity and proximity of energy systems means that conflicts can have ripple effects on energy markets and prices. New technologies, such as batteries and grid-embedded generation, are making the cybersecurity of grid systems more vulnerable. Global inexperience in handling large-scale cyberattacks, combined with the greater capabilities of state and non-state actors, has increased the likelihood that future wars and attacks will have a larger cyber component.

Alternative energy's unanticipated technological advances could radically overhaul current techno-economic sectors, such as transportation and construction. The technological revolution also creates new and sometimes unexpected drivers for energy demand growth that can also push forward renewable energy production. For example, in 2018, Morgan Stanley analysts noted that the energy needed to create cryptocurrencies could rival the entire electricity consumption of Argentina, contributing to global energy demand growth by up to 0.6%. This may fuel new renewable energy efforts, primarily in those countries most involved with cryptocurrency mining.[9] Indeed, in our increasingly globalized civilization, technological development engenders power, but powering technology requires energy.

2. The viability of alternative energy technologies: the challenges to be addressed to ensure the alternative energy megatrend's future energy security relevance.

As both a driver and a precondition of the alternative energy megatrend, the technological revolution sets the tone and expectations of how the megatrend and its underlying technologies will progress—both linearly as well as non-linearly. However, not only is transforming a technology from promising into a game-changer a difficult endeavor, but also the technological influences on the megatrend could have adverse repercussions on markets and economic relations. These could lead to different forms of economic, technological, and socio-political externalities that will affect the megatrend's future.

As current renewable technologies cannot yet respond adequately to energy demand levels, there is a sense of urgency surrounding their development.[10] This urgency to meet energy demand requirements does not take into consideration the fact that the testing and assessment of alternative energy technologies remains inadequate, blocking their development and deployment. For example, the full life cycle of renewables—from production to disposal—and the application of some technologies on an industrial scale are largely unexamined and not comprehensively tested. Such testing is contingent upon achievement and enforcement of multilateral agreements regulating cross-border applications of alternative energy, such as those envisioned by the Desertec project in the Sahara Desert.

Alternative energy systems face significant technological limitations that obstruct their development and ability to complement traditional fossil fuels. These include intermittency, transmission, storage capacity, and infrastructure vulnerabilities. The alternative energy megatrend's impact will likely be determined by current technologies' shortcomings and how these challenges are addressed. Indeed, technological weaknesses can create opportunities for advances that facilitate non-linear breakthroughs. In short, negatives become positives, roadblocks become open gates, and the path to the future beckons.

(1) Intermittency impediments: in search of timely delivery.

Intermittency is one of the most significant challenges to the wider integration of renewables. Because solar and wind technologies in particular are intermittent, their utilization is plagued by fluctuations in power generation that are not suitable as base load energy during peak demand periods.[11]

Managing intermittency adds to the costs of deploying already costly energy alternatives. Even now, substantial fossil fuel reserves must be maintained to stabilize energy supply, largely defeating the purpose of investing in alternative energy. In addition, situations can arise in which overcapacity can be dangerous to the grid. Conventional infrastructure must still be built to provide supply stability. This entails building back-up natural gas generators, as nuclear or coal plants cannot be fired up at a moment's notice. Additionally, costly infrastructure is necessary to connect regions with lower intermittency (such as windy or sunny deserts or plains) to the major grids.

The intermittency problem is not insurmountable. Electricity grids are capable of adapting to variable loads from gas, hydro, nuclear, and coal plants. In the case of wind, intermittency can be dealt with for levels below 20–25% of grid capacity. Intermittency poses greater complications when wind power becomes a larger part of the overall energy supply of a given grid, because variable wind strength can require back-up generation in down times and result in wasted energy when wind is strong. Addressing this issue calls for a comprehensive approach to developing new forms of energy storage and use. It also reveals the need to equip grids with the ability to redirect energy on demand.[12]

(2) Transmission shortfalls: improving the current grid.

A lack of adequate transmission infrastructure poses a substantial challenge for the widespread applicability of alternative energy. Electricity grids will be impacted by the mass deployment of alternative energy technologies. For example, plug-in hybrid electric and electric vehicles necessitate a new dimension of grid management with corresponding investment and expenditure for large-scale wind and solar-thermal electricity.[13] The disparity of sources of energy also raises the issue of integrating the energy produced into regional and international transmission systems.[14] However, changes are afoot, as evidenced by the consistent decrease in solar power costs.[15]

The predominant consensus is that alternative energy will require sophisticated infrastructure to allow its integration into the global energy transmission system—a so-called "smart grid."[16] Smart grid infrastructure, along with enhanced energy storage and discharge options, would reduce the variability in renewable power sources. Smart grid technologies and practices as well as integration into existing networks are thus key to the fulfillment of energy policy and technology goals. Some of these goals include improving consumer efficiency, an expanded role for new technologies and fuels in modern infrastructures, and furnishing greater security for electricity supplies.[17]

(3) Storage capacity restrictions: needing more power...greater density.

Storage capacity restrictions are also an impediment to alternative energy deployment. Energy storage will likely play a critical role in determining the feasibility of renewables and the alternative energy megatrend's impact. Various energy storage technologies, capturing energy during periods of high electricity supply and surrendering stored energy when demand is high, provide backup power, load leveling, frequency regulation, voltage support, and grid stabilization, and they contribute to emergency preparedness.[18] However, higher levels of grid-connected variable renewable energy will require a major increase in power system flexibility.[19] The characteristics of existing technologies do not enable non-fossil energy to be stored and used over time efficiently enough. In fact, storage is the most compelling hurdle. Advances in electric storage and renewable energy are key areas that have the potential to dictate the pace and the scale of the energy transition.

Today, most electric energy storage capacity is provided by pumped storage, the oldest and most mature electricity storage option developed for hydropower, while all other technologies are undergoing development and transition.[20] If additional research and investment increase the pace of development, alternative energy technologies could replace fossil fuels sooner than anticipated by even optimistic scenarios. Conversely, slower development of storage capacities will delay their practical viability. Currently, the problem of unresolved storage puts continuous power generation and energy transmission under great pressure.

(4) Imperfect infrastructure: adapting new applications and demands of energy efficiency.

Security vulnerabilities associated with the drive to develop alternative energy infrastructure (power plants, transmission lines, pipelines) are another obstacle to alternative energy deployment. Alternative energy installations are harder to monitor and secure as they tend to be scattered and located in outlying areas. Securing the new infrastructure and supply chain and defending it against terrorism and sabotage, particularly in certain developing countries, remains an issue of concern for both suppliers and consumers. Alternative energy-based decentralized systems offer certain benefits for securing infrastructure. In the United States, an additional security complication is the fact that 80% of the energy sector is owned by the private sector, which has less capacity to secure infrastructure than the state.[21]

Like other energy facilities, alternative energy infrastructure remains highly vulnerable to physical attacks and sabotage. As transmission systems and grids get "smarter," so too increases the ability to inflict significant damage. A successful attack could disrupt an entire economy. Energy infrastructures are especially attractive and vulnerable targets to terrorists because they can cause highly visible, rapid, and significant economic loss, disruption, and perhaps loss of life. Likewise, the transition to smart grids will require new security arrangements. "Smart" implies a move away from centralized generation and control to two-way communications between the utility and end users, tying in decentralized renewable energy sources along with other distributed generation sources, currently dominated by fossil fuels. However, unless security is part of the design criteria, the smart grid will not live up to its name; increased communications will be accompanied by increased cyber vulnerabilities.[22]

Information and communications systems that control and monitor energy infrastructure are particularly vulnerable to cyber-attacks and intrusions. Alternative energy infrastructure's dependence on data requires careful consideration of data packaging, collation, and interpretation, as well as protection from data-related threats. There is also a need to contend with security threats that could arise due to technical failures, such as power outages (blackouts and brownouts) caused by grid or power plant malfunction.

Preventing such events requires extensive, time-consuming, and costly adaptation, and improvements in logistics infrastructure. In the United States, for example, further grid expansion has been depicted as a national security imperative since transmission capabilities are an important consideration for energy security. Solar and wind farms, however, are not currently considered critical components of national energy infrastructure in the United States. They are trumped in security prioritization by nuclear energy sites, large hydropower plants, refineries, pipelines, and key pieces of the national grid.

The deployment of alternative energy technologies could be accelerated by addressing technological compatibility issues. Of particular importance would be ensuring the compatibility of off-grid generation and grid requirements (such as AC/DC power supply), as well as the compatibility of biofuels with the vehicle technologies used. Without compatibility, the effectiveness of renewable sources will be diminished, which will generate shortages and mismatches that could create new energy security risks.

Despite the issues concerning alternative energy's viability and practical deployment, state and non-state actors remain committed to renewables' development. These actors are increasingly aware that, within a few decades, changes in policy and behavioral patterns beyond energy consumption and utilization will be warranted in order to accommodate the security implications of resource depletion and the shift away from fossil fuels. Rapid technological progress and the increased application of alternative energy are coaxing stakeholders to bet on further paybacks.

Some states might possess technologies that enable them to generate energy from local or regional sources, or have a significant amount of materials and resources that are suddenly in high demand. In addition, a growing focus on energy efficiency could produce significant breakthroughs that diminish the intensity of energy use. The new societal perceptions that reinforce the impact of technological developments and of the megatrend in particular, in a sense, bring to mind the remark of Bertie Wooster about his Uncle George, who "discovered that alcohol was a food well in advance of medical thought."[23] In essence, the megatrend is shaped by societal perceptions of it long before technological developments are defined or realized; society thus imagines and in so doing creates the megatrend's future.

3. The megatrend as an attitude modifier: offering a new slant on socio-political perceptions, attitudes, and energy relations.

Energy is one of several factors that contributes to the association of power and knowledge that forms the global political order. While alternative energy resources cannot yet be employed as a practical tool to project geopolitical leverage, their development highlights the new foreign policy connotations that could appear as a result of significant advances in their deployment. More importantly, the megatrend's projected influence presents an example of how modern phenomena can modify socio-political stances, perceptions, and attitudes.

Energy resources and competition over them have helped generate successive attitudinal build-ups among geopolitical actors. The notions of energy imperialism and nationalism are among the most dominant socio-political and socio-cultural ideas influencing these attitudes. Through the prism of the alternative energy megatrend, it is also possible to shed light on how energy security considerations are impacted by anti-American and anti-Western stances. Geopolitical attitudes and ideologies are often shaped as an expression of a perceived imbalance or inequality between actors who want to maintain their advantages and those who seek to acquire them. This type of assessment reveals the extent to which the megatrend is increasingly becoming integrated into existing geopolitical perceptions and engendering new dynamics based on energy.

(1) Energy imperialism: reshaping the ties that bind consumers to producers.

The trajectory of the alternative energy megatrend can shed new light on the geopolitical notion of energy imperialism.[24] This notion, which is gradually evolving to become more about influence rather than control between the major powers and their spheres of interest, focuses particularly on areas where resources such as energy are a point of contention. The advent of the megatrend could prove to be a pivotal point that transforms the notion of energy imperialism, by removing the limitations geography imposes on resource use. This alters the inherent ownership conveyed by the spatial disposition of resources and, more importantly, helps remove areas of contention that underpin the evolving notion of energy imperialism.

Energy as a natural resource has historically been at the heart of imperialism and is one of the cornerstones of the process of legitimization and reordering of power on a global scale. Relations between states have often been determined by control and access to energy resources, in particular over fossil fuels. This reflects the predominantly Western approach of seeing the world in terms of binary oppositions that establish a relationship of dominance, informed by the divergent views of energy consumers and energy suppliers. Broadening the notion, consumer countries may also exert their control through directly investing in and exploiting the target country's natural resources. Energy imperialism can thus also be a perception resulting from the sovereign wealth funds of certain countries investing in other states' resources.

The notion of energy imperialism is inherently confrontational and contributes to geopolitical tensions. The views of developing energy-exporting countries are fueled by an inherent sense of inequity. Resource-rich states often have a strong perception of being exploited, particularly when their commodities are exported at lower than market costs. At the same time, energy consumers often believe that energy-exporting countries are manipulating resources to an extent that is detrimental to others. Consumer states perceive energy as a necessity that should not be unreasonably withheld, while producers value it beyond its intrinsic qualities as a commodity.

This underscores a converged perception of inequity between producers and consumers—both see the geopolitical power inherent in energy as a zero-sum game, where the winners' gains are the others' losses. Energy suppliers often regard consumers' efforts to control energy sources as energy imperialism, which can be offset by alleviating the need for control of conventional energy resources through egalitarian trade mechanisms.

The alternative energy megatrend could directly impact the dichotomy between geopolitical balances and strategic goals for energy consumers and producers that results in perceptions of energy imperialism. The anticipated evolution of the megatrend could play a role in altering the imperatives and perhaps eliminating consumer states' drive to achieve economic and political hegemony over supplier states. In this manner, alternative energy developments could reshape traditional geopolitical attitudes, leading to a gradual erosion of the need to exercise geopolitical pressure over traditional energy suppliers. Thus, it could lead to a reevaluation by suppliers of their relationships with energy consumers. For example, suppliers will need to decide whether to remain open and maintain revenue flows or generate geopolitical leverage by curtailing and manipulating access to their resources. Alternative energy, then, could add to existing "structurally-induced temptations" for "imperialist-like" domination[25] of consumers over suppliers. Just like other technologies, alternative energy can become a tool of dominance over those lacking an industrial and knowledge base. Such tools can then be used as a form of exchange that maintains the desired status quo—if the balance is broken, the relevant technological support can be withdrawn.

The megatrend also highlights the inherent danger of new areas of perceived imperialist dominance. For example, the growing importance of certain renewables, such as biofuels and solar power, could generate new imperatives for cross-border political control. Energy imperialism is also playing a bigger role in the agendas of some malevolent non-state actors, who integrate it into their ideology as a motivating cause and justification of their activities.

(2) Resource nationalism: the megatrend's effect on fossil fuel suppliers' perceived leverage.

Resource nationalism is a term often applied in relation to the use of natural resource capabilities as foreign policy tools. Different nation-centric ideological and geopolitical underpinnings bolster imperatives to convert control over resources into geopolitical clout. These underpinnings have less to do with national identity, from the perspective of a given nation-state. They have more to do with national power and ambitions, and the ability to use resources to influence cross-border agendas. In pursuit of this type of nationalism, governments endeavor to influence other actors' strategies by controlling access to a given resource—particularly energy. Resource nationalism can take overt forms through unilateral cessation of supply, or more subtle forms of leverage through the economic power the resources convey.[26] This term is popularly applied when states pursue control over the use of their own natural resources and hence prioritize national political interests over established international industry and trade practices and investor relations. This type of resource nationalism has been practiced in the past by Venezuela,[27] Bolivia,[28] Ecuador,[29] and Argentina.[30] These countries' leaders are heavily influenced by political ideologies that call for national governments to take over their natural resources in order to free themselves from Western influence.

Even when ideological factors wane, resource nationalism may prove resilient and hamper efforts to move toward more open energy policies. For instance, the Mexican government, which had already opened up its energy sector to private investment after decades of state control,[31] made investors uneasy with its plans for new proceed-sharing regulations after a significant oil field discovery by an international consortium in 2017.[32]

Although mainly applied to resource-rich and exporting countries, broader forms of resource nationalism can be used by consumer countries seeking to increase their control over natural resources in other countries. From the perspective of those countries lacking natural resources and who believe in liberal trade, open investment climates, and international institutions, resource nationalism runs counter to the paradigms that govern the global market. It is therefore not surprising that such forms of nationalism have generated opposition predominantly from foreign investors, corporate communities, and these entities' home states. From the perspective of these investors, any use of economic tools for nation-centric political goals is viewed as "a pernicious doctrine, and its proponents as the political enemy."[33]

The potential for resource nationalism to generate conflict remains untested. Not all violent conflicts have a foundation in nationalism, but the two cataclysmic World Wars of the 20th century, and many other wars, contained overt elements of it. Like other forms of nationalism, it can prompt aggressive policymaking, reflecting the growing usage of economic strategies as ideological and political tools.

Charting the national security significance of the alternative energy megatrend's drivers reveals how modern trends and developments could mitigate supplier countries' efforts to manipulate energy reserves for their own political needs. In practice, broader deployment of renewables in the future could reduce tensions between states over fossil fuels, potentially taking global energy balances beyond their current zero-sum status. The megatrend can give rise to new ways of transforming, diminishing, or removing natural resource dependencies and the perceived or actual ability of exporters to restrict access to such resources.

Effects of the megatrend could play a contributing role in a new power play between energy suppliers, consumers, and, eventually, energy transit countries that will shape a new round in the Grand Energy Game. Advances in alternative energy technologies can also help redefine political geography, making it increasingly dynamic and generating a geopolitical map that Robert Kaplan suggests "will be an ever-mutating representation of chaos."[34] New geopolitical and geo-economic developments will be charted on this changing map, as determined by the currents of the megatrend's technological progress.

The alternative energy megatrend underscores the impact of the pursuit of energy independence by fossil fuel consumers on resource nationalism, and portends that renewables could repeat that impact. Overall, resource nationalism by supplier countries serves to reinforce energy independence imperatives by consumers. The goal of independence, in turn, further promotes the alternative energy megatrend.

The megatrend can, however, also serve as a platform for resource nationalism policies by alternative energy producers. New dependencies could arise in this context, as exemplified by plans to produce electricity from solar energy in North Africa and export much of it to Europe.

(3) Anti-American and anti-Western attitudes: highlighted overtones of the megatrend.

Alternative energy developments could influence and even contribute to changing anti-Western sentiment by energy-exporting countries. By reducing the geopolitical significance of fossil fuels, the megatrend can play a role in diminishing tensions between resource-rich countries that perceive Western involvement in their energy sector as exploitation that is detrimental to their national interests. It presents a new perspective on the traditional lines of confrontation between energy consumers and energy producers which could reshape anti-American and anti-Western attitudes, particularly among fossil fuel supplier countries. At the same time, the megatrend's promise can also prove to be a factor that exacerbates anti-Western attitudes in cases where technological dominance by the West is seen as deliberately withholding the benefits of renewable technologies from less developed countries. In essence, the megatrend could foster two distinct yet concurrent outcomes; it could both alleviate existing confrontational attitudes and contribute to the possible emergence of new tensions.

Some oil-rich parts of the world, such as the Middle East, North Africa, and Latin America, have long been sources of instability and have possessed hostility toward the West, and the United States, in particular. Such adversarial attitudes have flowed from the Iranian, Sudanese, and Syrian governments for decades. Anti-Western and anti-American feelings are also common in countries ruled by regimes friendly to the West, such as Algeria, Libya, Lebanon, Jordan, and even Morocco. Even the more moderate Islamic societies of Turkey and the former Soviet republics in Central Asia are not immune to such sentiments. In part, anti-American and anti-Western perceptions are a form of a domestic internalization of international concerns. With regard to energy, states view access to resources within their own territory as tied to their economic development and national security and feel threatened by Western and American power. These negative attitudes, whether spontaneous or fanned by governmental propaganda, are used for internal political purposes, as demonstrated in Iran for example.

Alternative energy developments could directly influence anti-American and broader anti-Western attitudes, in particular those sentiments that sometimes thrive in energy-exporting countries. Integrating the megatrend into global energy security calculations can reveal the extent of a possible reduction of tensions that link fossil fuels with anti-Western sentiments. The megatrend could also deprive current energy-rich authoritarian countries of their geopolitical leverage. Given the projected progress of renewables, the underlying causes for such attitudes may be alleviated or more easily deflected. However, lingering adversity toward the West by fossil fuel exporters in the Middle East, North Africa, and Latin America is unlikely to dissipate; in all likelihood, it will increase or assume new contours given the loss of revenues exporters will endure as one possible consequence of the megatrend's propagation.

Meanwhile, fossil fuel suppliers might consider themselves purposefully constrained by the West in the wake of a large-scale deployment of alternative energy technologies. Under another scenario, anti-American and anti-Western attitudes could be stoked if it is perceived that the West is limiting access to alternative energy sources or technologies in non-Western countries. This is a particularly viable outcome considering that many of these countries lack the technology to launch their own alternative energy development initiatives. This has fed concerns from some areas that the United States will touch off a wave of new imperialism linked to the alternative energy megatrend.[35]

The megatrend shows that modern phenomena can change dependences between actors, thus introducing new values into established geopolitical attitudes. The end of the Cold War and the disappearance or weakening of alternatives to Western liberal democracy (such as Communism, the non-aligned movement, or pan-Arabism) has strengthened fundamentalist Islamic and other terrorist organizations, which are driven by a mixture of materialistic, ideological, and religious values. Consider the Internet's development, which closely resembles the alternative energy megatrend: "Although it was created by the U.S. government during the Cold War, governments now struggle to restrict the Internet's technology and many of its uses."[36] Renewable energy development will also take on a life of its own as it evolves as a megatrend, influencing attitudes and actions between actors in unforeseen ways.

4. Energy securitization: a new means of projecting power?

Securitizing energy accessibility and supplies will alter actors' power projection abilities. When actors implement specific energy security mechanisms, they will inevitably affect others. For instance, if a consumer achieves energy independence, it will influence its suppliers and gain a competitive advantage over other consumers. The megatrend can therefore become a part of securitization mechanisms for one actor, and create security threats for others.

Factoring the alternative energy megatrend's progression into the energy security and international relations equation not only highlights the diverse ways in which actors can project new types of power but also unveils new paths toward imposing influence on others. Indeed, the alternative energy megatrend's drivers furnish both state and non-state actors with new tools for exercising political influence. In the context of universal securitization, it can be used as geopolitical leverage by changing threat perceptions. These new forms of geopolitical leverage, whether real or perceived, are then transformed into new forms of deterrence. Although alternative energy is unlikely to single-handedly alter deterrence strategies, renewables can address concerns about energy dependence and energy scarcity. The megatrend's anticipated developments may even endow state and non-state actors with new forms of so-called soft power.

(1) Alternative energy-derived geopolitical empowerment: new dimensions of "soft power"?

Alternative energy presents a new perspective on what factors could strengthen actors' capacity to leverage so-called "soft power." When Joseph Nye first introduced the term, he defined soft power as "the ability to get what you want through attraction rather than through coercion," or changing and inducing behavior in others through means other than military force. Various kinds of soft power are differentiated by the degree of directed effort applied toward influencing specific behavior.[37] A country can exert more soft power if its culture, values, and institutions evoke admiration and respect in other parts of the world, or if its diplomacy and standing in international institutions enable it to better build alliances and partnerships for collective action. Power based on cultural enchantment has consistent momentum, but lacks the immediate effectiveness of the type of soft power founded on economic power and natural resources. In this context, the megatrend can be a new factor that can shift power balances between actors, necessitating another look at what power is and, in particular, how phenomena like the megatrend contribute to new forms of geopolitical and geo-economic power.

Understanding what power is allows one to determine what aspects of the megatrend can generate it. This includes assessing the various forms that such power can embody, the institutional basis from which it springs, and the channel(s) through which it is disseminated. Power results from the association of the biological/human with the political. Geopolitical power resembles Susan Strange's "structural power" notion, which "confers the power to decide how things shall be done, the power to shape frameworks within which states relate to each other, relate to people, or relate to corporations." According to this concept, power is relative and based on which actor determines the structure of the relationship or of the world order. Strange writes, "The relative power of each party in a relationship is more, or less, if one party is also determining the surrounding structure of the relationship."[38] This type of power is gradually receding from states and becoming diffused along the networks of rising new power centers in the modern world system.

In terms of physics, energy itself represents power; it allows the performance of specific actions, work, or interactions that affect another object and change its state or behavior. Power, in turn, is the rate at which energy is applied, utilized, and converted into a utilitarian/functional outlet. In the case of geopolitics and geo-economics, energy resources provide a metric by which it is possible to ascertain an actor's ability to influence the behavior of others.

The megatrend's promise thus extends to its potential to play a role in creating new forms of geopolitical power for states. Energy resources have become an overriding parameter in global power politics due to their significance for the economic wellbeing and standards of living of any given society. Energy as a resource can exist even when it is not used. In the same manner, power, in particular geopolitical and geo-economic power, can be applied or held in abeyance in order to generate reactions, value judgments, suppress the emergence of outcomes, and transform preferences and ideas.

The alternative energy megatrend can also confer resource-based economic power that can be converted into geopolitical influence. Those holding advantages in alternative energy resources could use them as trade-offs in other areas. Yet the West is unlikely to easily transfer its technological know-how. It is even less likely to cede supremacy to emerging powers seeking to use renewables as a tool to impose their views.

Through the prism of the alternative energy megatrend, it is possible to perceive the direction of modified power projection capabilities by a growing number of actors. The global balance of power could be further reshaped if developed economies achieve advances in alternative energy development that enable them to export energy. This could lead to the creation of a "renewables OPEC," which in turn could generate new sources of tension. This does not suggest that emerging power centers will prove unable to master renewables technologies or find ways to court the West and gain access to these technologies. The ongoing economic growth of many economies in Asia, for example, will create opportunities for these countries to capitalize on their increasing technological capabilities to shape their alternative energy futures, while strengthening their bargaining position vis-à-vis the Western world.

(2) The deterrence factor: accruing the geopolitical tools and capacity to signal and dissuade.

Analyzing the propagation of the alternative energy megatrend provides a better understanding of how renewables can contribute to the development of new forms of deterrence. While approaches to deterrence have remained essentially the same since the end of World War II, the perception of its comparative benefits and detriments has changed. Henry Kissinger once noted that "deterrence depends, above all, on psychological criteria. It seeks to keep an opponent from a given course by posing unacceptable risk. For the purposes of deterrence, the opponents' calculations are decisive."[39]

In other words, "Deterrence is managing the expectations of consequences and is based on the ability to convince (the other party) that an attempt to gain his objective would cost more than it is worth and that the cost to the deterrer of applying the deterrent would be less than conceding the objective."[40] It seeks to transform the perception of weakness by specific actors into a state of perpetual threat in order to unify a state's population. These threats were often based on a history of wars associated with the establishment and survival of statehood.[41]

Deterrence targets and threats in the past were limited to narrow national security and defense assets that a state or an alliance used to deflect armed aggression by other states.[42] They have been consistently broadened to include an evaluation of perceived gains and losses from specific interactions between nations. Novel technologies, such as those upholding the alternative energy megatrend, modify the framework within which deterrence geopolitics functions today by speeding up and broadening the impact of actors' actions.

After the end of the Cold War, the strong connection between deterrence and economic, political, and military hegemony gradually diminished. Prevailing deterrence approaches, based on the bipolar balances that created them, have gradually weakened. New forms of deterrence have appeared that are sometimes equated with soft power. The scope of deterrence is no longer limited to demonstrating the capability to respond to aggression. It now encompasses a comprehensive approach to securitization and managing risks as a composite set of factors: "Risk is becoming the operative concept of Western security."[43] The new asymmetric threats that states and non-state actors contend with require a new calculation of the "finity of uncertainty and potential damage."[44]

With the end of the Cold War, energy has increased its potential as an effective political deterrence mechanism in relations between states. This role has gained in stature as energy security concerns have intensified. Technology itself is becoming an element of various deterrence factors and is even becoming a deterrent in its own right. Technological deterrence can be used as a tool to correct behavior—the most obvious example was the use of new nuclear applications that brought about an accelerated end to World War II in Asia. When combined with energy, technology's deterrence capability is multiplied. Specifically, for fossil fuel exporters, attempts to manipulate oil and gas supplies and prices can be countered with policies that focus on replacing fossil fuels with renewables.

Energy's role as a deterrent has already been demonstrated by fossil fuels.[45] The mutual leverage between energy consumers and suppliers is an instrument of national power for each actor. It allows "country A" to extract military, political, and economic advantages from its trading partners when "it is extremely difficult and onerous" for trading partners "to dispense entirely with the trade they conduct with A or to replace A as a market and as a source of supply with other countries."[46]

The future use of energy as a deterrent may, however, have unintended consequences. An actor using energy as deterrence may find itself shut out of the global energy market.[47] Energy can also be used as a balancing factor to preserve the status quo and enforce appropriate conduct. Deterrence can be achieved through development patterns that integrate net suppliers and net consumers of energy. In these patterns, "the 'have-nots' must either develop their own resource bases or build a mutually advantageous trading relationship with the 'haves.'"[48] The ability to withhold trading advantages can thus be used as an element of deterrence that prevents those that depend on trading relationships from undertaking a specific action or assuming a particular geopolitical position. Although this mutual dependence is presently evident with regard to fossil resources, alternative energy sources could also be subject to similar constraints, such as geography, industrial infrastructure, customs and practices, and economic power.

The alternative energy megatrend could also foster energy consumers' independence from fossil fuel suppliers. It could act as a deterrent against threats of oil and gas supply manipulation, thereby altering stances and affecting conduct. These and other projected energy-related dynamics can generate conditions and forms of resource diplomacy that can serve as a deterrent.

As alternative energy developments spread, the challenges facing the "have-nots" are also manifesting into breakaway strategies, enabling states to go their own way. In response, fossil fuel producers may seek to deter or dissuade state and non-state actors from pursuing the development of alternative energy sources,[49] by seeking to obtain energy-related leverage. The megatrend enables actors to project assurances of enforceable penalties that can thus alter balance of power calculations and discourage manipulations of energy supplies and markets.

The megatrend's trajectory therefore reveals new approaches for dealing with fixed and quantifiable threats and challenges. It also demonstrates its deterrent capacity that reflects a broader transformation of the practice and understanding of political deterrence in the post-Cold War period. Despite its role as a deterrent, however, alternative energy is neither the missing key for energy independence nor for perpetual peace. As observed, "the problem with deterrence is that it is ultimately a matter of comparative psychology: one can never know what will deter a potential enemy, only what would deter oneself."[50]

(3) Adding geopolitical leverage: one more "bargaining chip" on the table, or something more?

The benefits which the alternative energy megatrend promises may also provide actors with an additional bargaining chip when it comes to national, regional, and global negotiations. The transformative potential of the megatrend can be converted into new forms of leverage that would endow actors with added capabilities to influence others, beyond the ability to deter. Unlike deterrence, leverage has an all-encompassing nature, whereby actors are provided with more freedom to act outside the framework of international standards and rules imposed by hegemons. Leverage can be any form of power—economic or political—exercised coercively.[51] Energy resources can convey different types of leverage—be it punitive economic power or the ability to respond to others' geopolitical or geo-economic actions.

Access to new technologies, along with their development and regulation, might become new drivers of geopolitical leverage. Factors including geography, existing infrastructure, labor market flexibility, demographics, education systems, and capital mobility could determine which countries are best situated to take advantage of emerging technologies, including those technologies that propel the alternative energy megatrend.

For developed economies, the megatrend can contribute to leverage through the ability to guide techno-economic development and market operations, in essence having the ability to withhold advantages from others in exchange for imposing their geopolitical will. For developing and emerging economies, breakthrough advances in renewables can provide both an ability to compete on par with developed countries and an additional economic resource for use in geopolitical bargaining. Thus, leverage allows actors not only to offer an equivalent response to putative threats, but also to actively engage in influencing others' conduct.

In geopolitics, leverage is often equated with the susceptibility and vulnerability to external pressure that can influence the behavior of specific actors. Energy generation conveys leverage not only through the economic power from the revenue it generates, but also from the ability to deny or grant access to it. For example, pipelines and energy infrastructure can be used to provide options that are independent of specific suppliers or consumers. It is "important both for producing countries and for ultimate consumers to have a diverse option, an array of supply lines," which can be used as a source of leverage.[52] Alternative energy technologies can be another option, offered to recalcitrant actors as an inducement to change their behavior. This leverage can also take the form of punitive economic mechanisms, such as embargoes that dry up energy revenue and its accompanying advantages.

The ability to generate new leverage in geopolitical negotiations is still challenging due to the uncertain nature of mutual logic and value judgments that govern bargaining processes. The modern multi-centric world is increasingly bucking the post-modern trend of a system based on consensus. In such a system, everybody plays by the rules and "politics will never be anything but the art of the possible."[53] In this context, legitimacy and universal acceptability are continuously sought but less relevant for geopolitical agents. Instead, particular focal points—cultural, ethnic, religious, economic, and political—are becoming more widespread, signaling the break from older traditions of social development and political interaction. The increasing differences, plurality, fragmentation, de-territorialization tendencies, and global-local transformations are yet to be fully understood and incorporated in agents' strategies and actions. The question of power and spatiality remains unresolved, providing a hint of the upcoming vicissitudes of the post-Cold War world's uncertain geopolitical interactions.

Generating geopolitical leverage is a major driver for the United States and other developed economies, furthering the process of modernization and technological advancement of energy alternatives. Alternative energy can alleviate energy dependencies and the concomitant need for strategic commitments by creating new bargaining options. As retired U.S. General and former National Security Advisor James L. Jones pointed out, diversifying the energy portfolio, such as by developing alternative energy, could prove advantageous: "To achieve energy security in the long run, our energy markets need to achieve a greater level of flexibility."[54]

The alternative energy megatrend might also generate new geopolitical leverage for developing countries, which in turn could upset the global equilibrium and create new security concerns. The possibility of using renewables to gain advantage will inevitably lead to the question, as posed by the 11th NATO Secretary General Jaap de Hoop Scheffer,[55] "should some alternative energy producers wield greater geopolitical influence in shaping the new global security order?"[56]

Renewables can also enable developing countries to obtain new sources of funding and technological transfers. For example, the least developed countries (LDCs) are becoming increasingly vociferous in demanding their own place at the negotiating table. They request more technology transfers and financial aid from developed countries. Distinguishing between withholding foreign aid and restricting the spread of alternative energy technologies perceived to be of global benefit will become increasingly difficult. Developed economies will be put in the fraught situation of being seen as selfish or aloof.

The geopolitical leverage of alternative energy developments will largely depend on the interaction between the perceived alternative energy winners and those left behind. Altered global balances could bring about a convergence of socio-economic and socio-political tensions that could change assumptions about the use of force and result in resource conflicts. As these balances shift, "the exploitation of nature represents a source of power and conflicts that should not be ignored."[57] The upcoming energy security threats that the megatrend highlights indicate that future conflicts over resources are "the ones we must act now to avoid."[58]

Abundant and affordable renewable energy can provide leverage for fossil fuel-consuming countries by enabling them to mitigate against adverse actions by suppliers. Renewable resources, therefore, may be politically useful both in what they will furnish to the actors that have them and when being offered to those that do not. In effect, renewables provide leverage that can be used, in the words of George F. Kennan, for the "adroit and vigilant application of counter force at a series of constantly shifting geographical and political points."[59] The developed West could use alternative energy technology as both a carrot and a stick in its foreign policy.

In sum, the renewables megatrend suggests that countries will seek novel approaches to develop additional bargaining power, and future alternative energy developments could offer the capability of mitigating energy security threats and dependencies. Technological development will either prove a "universal deterrent" or lead to more destructive and violent conflicts between states.[60]

5. Nuclear power: charting a possible roadmap for the future of the alternative energy megatrend.

Nuclear power is currently the sole practical alternative to fossil fuels that has become an established, functional, and indispensable element of the current energy equilibrium.[61] Renewables are also an alternative to the already established nuclear alternative to fossil fuels. In this light, it is a special case whereby developments in the field of nuclear energy could chart a course for the future of the alternative energy megatrend itself and its security trajectory. Against the backdrop of a post-proliferation world, nuclear power is also a special case because the advantages it offers as a source of energy can also be translated into geopolitical leverage via its weaponization.

Nuclear development has already influenced the visions and some of the practices permeating the alternative energy megatrend, and it can be a techno-economic model for the developments that underlie the megatrend itself. It is characterized by the same need for extensive government intervention, and the invisible hand of the market has touched relatively lightly upon nuclear energy. Furthermore, social attitudes and political perception affect the development and deployment of nuclear technologies, which could be an indicator as to how global society will come to influence the renewables megatrend. At the same time, the curtailment of nuclear energy diffusion could reinforce the development of renewable technologies and provide added momentum for the megatrend.

(1) Nuclear power: a possible template for alternative energy developments.

Nuclear power is a unique source of energy—a non-fossil-based fuel that matches the density of oil, gas, and coal and has proven its effectiveness over half a century of use. Nuclear power clearly demonstrates the significance of the unanticipated consequences of technological advancement. Not unlike the transformation of military radar technology into the household microwave, nuclear power generation for civil use grew out of weapons research undertaken in the labs of the Manhattan Project, which were set up to produce a deployable nuclear weapon. What was initially conceived as a method of mass destruction has become a viable tool for power generation.[62] In fact, nuclear energy has contributed significantly to world energy needs for more than 40 years, with hydro the only other significant non-fossil fuel energy contributor.[63] Today nuclear power represents about 10.5% of total global electricity generation.[64]

There are broader advantages that can be associated with the role of nuclear technology as a non-fossil source of power. It is currently the only energy source that has an "environmentally acceptable" capacity to meet demand at a level on par with fossil fuels. Indeed, the quantity of toxic pollutants and waste generated from fossil fuel plants dwarfs the quantities from nuclear energy options.[65] Nuclear energy is essentially emissions-free, scalable, and comparatively energy efficient. While nuclear energy is not a true "public good," its inherent advantages—density,[66] accessibility, and established infrastructural linkages—make it an attractive proposition for states seeking to address energy security issues.

Nuclear power has been embraced by a number of developing and developed economies.[67] The "big five" nuclear-generating countries (by rank, the United States, France, China, Russia, and South Korea) generated 70% of the world's nuclear electricity in 2016. The United States and France accounted for 48% of global nuclear generation.[68]

While isolated incidents such as Three Mile Island, Chernobyl, and Fukushima give rise to adverse public opinion and consequent political responses, nuclear power generation retains an essential role in the global energy balance. Though, by 2016, the share of nuclear power in global electricity was stagnating at about 10.5% following years of decline from its peak in 1996, the volume of the world's nuclear generation is increasing.[69]

Although associated with high up-front capital costs, nuclear power generation is considered relatively cost-competitive, except where there is direct access to fossil fuels, in particular natural gas. Combined with its better record on emissions, nuclear power is a viable competitor to fossil fuels. However, there is evidence that alternative energy may be able to match these achievements.[70] Should a decrease in alternatives' prices become sustainable, the megatrend would be respectively strengthened, and its future more assured.

Nuclear energy technologies have gone through several developmental stages, and their dynamics provide a preview of the vagaries the alternative energy megatrend could experience. After cresting a wave of technological euphoria following World War II, nuclear power development faced increasing societal resistance after the attention-grabbing disasters of Three Mile Island and Chernobyl. Since the beginning of the 21st century, with these disasters becoming an increasingly distant memory, nuclear power experienced a renaissance in popular support, which largely continues today in spite of the safety concerns raised by Fukushima.

As is the case with renewables, nuclear power's greatest potential to transform the global energy landscape lies with currently unrealized technologies. As was already mentioned earlier in the book, one particular area that offers a broad spectrum of possibilities is the potential development of feasible nuclear fusion technology. The hope is that fusion power will provide a steady power supply that can meet peak demand, allowing the extraction of proportionally more power than is input for its generation. To date, realistic practical applications of fusion power have not been developed, and its potential remains theoretic.

The influence of nuclear power on renewables development will also be determined by how a shift away from fossil fuels will impact geopolitical, national, and global security considerations. Nuclear power could shed light on how the megatrend may develop, and highlight the trade-offs which decision-makers may have to face between security and technological advancement.

The acceptability and attractiveness of nuclear power is subject to different influences and changing trends, namely societal attitudes and political perception of such technologies. The alternative energy megatrend today is at the same crossroads that nuclear power was at by the end of the 20th century—agreed-upon potential coupled with a number of challenges.

Despite the similarities, the alternative energy megatrend as a whole, however, is not encumbered by the suspicion and fear that characterize societal attitudes toward nuclear energy. The nuclear model is not the only option available to the trend, but it does provide a tangible example of how policymakers could magnify alternatives' advantages and minimize the impact of their impediments.

(2) Anti-nuclear sentiments and non-proliferation efforts: alternative energy offered as a substitute for nuclear power.

The promise offered by nuclear power is a double-edged sword—one state's approach to energy security could easily become another's strategic vulnerability. Being the only current alternative to fossil fuels that has the energy density and capacity to meet energy demand, nuclear power opens up avenues for the pursuit of development and proliferation of weapons of mass destruction. It is in fact the potential drawbacks of nuclear power that may propel support for and accelerate the development of renewables, technologies, and applications that purport to have a relatively minor impact on the environment as well as few security concerns. Indeed, renewable energy technologies could be pursued as not only an alternative to fossil fuels but as an alternative to nuclear power.

Despite numerous academic and technical studies underscoring the strenuous safety standards that nuclear plants meet,[71] global society remains concerned about nuclear power due primarily to persistent doubts about its safety and transparency. As a feature of any large infrastructure system, technical failures are an ever-present possibility for nuclear power plants. While newer technologies have reduced the threat of technical malfunction or sabotage, risks still remain. Furthermore, nuclear power's positive track record clashes in part with the stances promoted by some governments, as exemplified by New Zealand's Nuclear Free Zone, Disarmament, and Arms Control Act of 1987, and Australia, Austria, and Ireland's "nuclear-free" policies. In some cases, political pressure on governments has led to reversals of policy, such as the German government's 2011 decision to go back to a phasing out of nuclear power generation in the country by 2022 rather than 2036.

Protest movements against nuclear power first emerged in the United States, then spread quickly to Europe and the rest of the world. Anti-nuclear campaigns became a feature of the social and political environment in the late 1970s. Fueled by the Three Mile Island accident and the Chernobyl disaster, the anti-nuclear power movement mobilized political and economic forces that set back nuclear technological development for many years. Although there have been few serious plant-safety incidents, safety concerns again came to the fore with the 2011 Fukushima nuclear plant accident. In the aftermath of the Fukushima accident, a number of states, seeking to allay public fears, took a tough stance on nuclear energy development. For example, Switzerland placed a moratorium on plans to replace its stock of reactors; China temporarily suspended approval of further nuclear projects until new safety rules were put in place; and Germany decided not to pursue nuclear development further and even to close seven reactors built before 1980. While opinions diverge, nuclear power remains unthinkable in a number of countries because of the strength of the actors organized against it.

Despite stringent safety regulations, guarded communications have also generated a perceived lack of transparency, which exacerbates the popular mistrust of the technology. Concerns also exist about the range of physical hazards and the environmental impact of nuclear power generation and waste disposal. Safety concerns, the perceived lack of transparency, and broader lack of approval for nuclear energy are already affecting the advancement of the alternative energy megatrend in several ways. Some markets that are turning away from nuclear power realize the need to fill the resulting vacuum in some way. A political decision to phase out nuclear energy or to cancel nuclear power plans could lead to the freeing of monetary resources for renewable energy development. From a technological perspective, some of the developed economies in Europe, such as Germany and Switzerland, can consider making the necessary financial outlays to develop a significant alternative energy capital base. For example, Germany's decision to phase out nuclear power initially boosted renewables, as Germany had the financial wherewithal to invest in extensive alternative energy-generating capacity. Despite the fact that only 8 reactors remained in operation in 2017 (of 18 reactors in 2011), Germany maintained its position as a net electricity exporter.[72]

The pursuit of renewable technologies as alternatives to nuclear power is also reinforced because nuclear power's development is occurring against the backdrop of a post-proliferation world. In the incipient post-proliferation world, more nations that are currently non-nuclear could be encouraged to develop nuclear options, increasing the likelihood of conversion of civil nuclear technology for military purposes.[73] In addition, in the post-Cold War conditions of uncertain alliances, the imperative on militaries to pursue advances in nuclear weapons development remains strong.[74] They are accompanied by continued interest by many countries to develop civilian nuclear programs.

Nuclear technology advances are further weakening the already strained non-proliferation regimes that are currently in place. This weakness is exacerbated by the perceived leverage that players possessing nuclear technologies can exert on emerging state and non-state actors, which increasingly positions nuclear technology as an advantage outweighing the concomitant risks. The efficacy of implementing non-proliferation regimes appears to be beyond the control of the international community. This is further complicated by the contradictory issues of jurisdiction, ineffective multilateral approaches, illicit proliferation rings, and the attractiveness of nuclear weapons for some non-state actors.[75]

Counter- and non-proliferation efforts could be reinforced by providing renewables as a viable replacement to nuclear power. As part of non-proliferation regimes, it may prove feasible for developed economies in particular to offer preferential terms for installing appropriate technologies, as well as assist in their grid integration, maintenance, and further development. In other words, traditional technology leaders could provide alternative energy technological transfers to countries suffering from energy and technology deficits in return for the latter's abstinence from pursuing nuclear energy development or nuclear weapons. Such an option would be taken or rejected on the basis of political decisions by host states that would not be limited to purely energy considerations. Economic links, national security considerations, geopolitical balances, and socio-political imperatives would also play a role. In that regard, nuclear energy can influence geopolitical decisions even by its absence, acting as a tangible option that is withheld or replaced.

However, it should be noted that the removal of nuclear power from the energy mix could actually be detrimental to alternative energy developments. Faced with expanded demand and reduced supply of power, some states could be forced to find quick, reliable, and inexpensive solutions, which, at present, can be found mainly in improved fossil fuel-generating facilities, such as natural gas plants or increased imports. In Europe, for example, dependence on Russian gas is felt to be an energy security vulnerability by a number of states.[76] The rationale for avoiding renewables in favor of fossil fuels when phasing out nuclear power differs for each region and country.[77]

Similarly, providing current alternative energy technologies to actors as encouragement to forego nuclear options may be rejected and seen as detrimental for both recipients and suppliers of such technologies. The rationale not to offer such options could be prompted by economic pressures, political tensions, or purely technological considerations. Not all technologies are at the disposal of governments to offer. More and more alternative energy technology patents are owned by private sector companies that will have different considerations and motives beyond stemming nuclear proliferation. Also, offering solar power capacity, for example, may not be very attractive for a country that is not exposed to much sunlight. As a proverbial dual-use technology, nuclear power poses challenges that also reflect the importance of corollary advantages, such as weapons sales, for some state actors.

In sum, an important difference is emerging between nuclear and renewable energy—the latter has a growing societal acceptability, which is seemingly proportionate to the mistrust of nuclear power. This acceptability does not discount the parallels between nuclear power developments and the megatrend. Indeed, it demonstrates how future development of both renewables and nuclear power can be impacted by public perception. Should renewable technologies encounter concerns about their potential dangers and outstanding environmental and safety issues, their future acceptability could be similarly tainted. Furthermore, the possibility for renewable energy sources being adopted as replacements for nuclear power is reinforced by nature of today's post-proliferation world.

(3) The question of the post-proliferation world: a potential weaponization of renewables through the looking glass of nuclear power's dual use.

Although it may not be possible to state with full certainty that the world has entered a stage of post-proliferation, it can be firmly stated that no one actor can control, halt, or reverse nuclear weapons proliferation. The conversion of civil nuclear power technology into weapons technologies is difficult to control, let alone stop, either as a technological development or as a desired strategic objective. The envisioned advent of the post-proliferation world is a part of the changes associated with the post-Cold War paradigm shift. This focus on non-proliferation also affects the alternative energy megatrend and its future, irrespective of the likelihood of alternative energy's weaponization.

As both a fuel and a weapon, nuclear energy has the greatest impact on renewables and illustrates their potential future. For one, the hazards of nuclear energy present today's renewables as a safe alternative. On the other hand, should technological advancements create military capabilities for renewable energy sources, there are obvious parallels with nuclear weapon proliferation. Nuclear energy's path could therefore provide a realistic template for renewables. Furthermore, the paradigm-changing role of the military in incentivizing nuclear technology development could be repeated for renewables if a potential for weaponization comes to light. The complexity of the security environment in a post-proliferation world requires more comprehensive policy solutions to address the spread of nuclear weapons capabilities. All of these security considerations would undoubtedly play a role in the process of adapting policies to fit with the evolving renewables megatrend.

II. 21st century national defense transformation—the influence of the alternative energy megatrend.

How does the alternative energy megatrend fit into profound defense transformation that is currently occurring worldwide? This transformation is prompted by a radical shift in the nature of defense threats and challenges, including widespread technological advances, increasingly asymmetrical operations, a greater need for expeditionary engagements, and a broadening defense mandate that goes beyond traditional national security considerations.

The defense sector is the agent that actors rely on to address the most prominent security threats to the survival of the state—those of violent conflict. In a universally securitized world, the domains of human activity exposed to security risks are growing and encroaching on one another, potentially engendering military conflict that could threaten a state's survival. To ensure their national security, actors adopt strategies to deal with a myriad of traditional and non-traditional security challenges, inducing the profound defense transformation.[78] When assessed through the lens of the alternative energy megatrend, the defense transformation represents an adaptation of security strategies and practices to the reality of the universally securitized world.

This book does not provide a comprehensive assessment of the defense transformation. Rather, it explores this phenomenon from the perspective of the alternative energy megatrend. Geared up by technological revolution, the megatrend is one of the harbingers of this transformation, factored as it already is in defense strategies, policies, and practices. Not only does it bear significance for the energy considerations of the military, but it also presents a unique security agenda in its own right.

This chapter examines potential defense implications from the wider integration of alternative energy solutions in defense establishments and militaries worldwide. It also explores the impact of the defense transformation on the alternative energy developments as well as the momentum and direction it imparts on the megatrend.

1. The expanding defense mandate: the perspective of the alternative energy megatrend.

A range of broader security considerations other than military are increasingly defining the defense sector's purview. Environmental security and resource scarcity, for instance, can serve as root causes of destabilizing trends. Inter-state rivalry over access to energy resources is perhaps one of the most obvious candidates to serve as potential casus belli in the coming decades. Although these broader challenges are often local in cause, the global scope of their effect introduces threats of grander scale to populations in different countries and regions. This requires the formulation of new securitization approaches. This is critical as most of the West's developed countries continue relying on their Cold War defense establishments despite the evolved threats and security requirements in the modern world.

Renewables' promised contribution to the reshaping of the global energy mix provides a new perspective from which to consider future risks, natures of conflict, and sources of conflict. After all, the integration of alternative energy sources into the new energy equilibrium can fuel global instability resulting from the shifting geographies of supply.[79] Defense sectors need to prepare for these risks and dynamics as they seek to securitize the drivers and elements of the alternative energy megatrend and expand the use of renewables.

As part of the process, the militaries may be tasked to protect the evolving international renewables-based power grids and facilities. They may also need to change their posture toward newly emerging suppliers of renewable energy, just as they needed to do for fossil fuel exporters in the past. These new factors could alter states' defense stances by relieving the need for involvement in volatile regions, such as fossil fuel-producing countries. These considerations would affect tactical deployment, and should also be examined spatially, to extract the highest level of utility from reducing the need for fossil fuels, particularly in outlying bases.

Modern, highly mechanized, and computerized militaries are currently some of the largest institutional energy consumers in the world. The U.S. Department of Defense energy consumption, for example, represents approximately 80% of total federal energy consumption.[80] This demand burdens defense budgets, restricts logistical flexibility (especially in frontline operations), and endangers lives when lengthy supply lines must be protected. Meanwhile, in-theatre reliance on energy is exposed to risks associated with transporting fuels to and within areas of operation; the impact of fuel dependence on operational effectiveness; the cost of energy itself; and energy-related regulations and policies with which the defense establishment must comply; as well as broader energy-related national policies.

Energy, therefore, is a factor of power projection, military dominance, and geopolitical control. Indeed, "it may be said that in its widest sense on its material side, history is the story of man's increasing ability to control energy."[81] The megatrend reinforces the notion that power projection is a survival imperative, with the political considerations of sovereigns placing them, as characterized by Thomas Hobbes, in continual jealousies and the posture of gladiators.[82] Within this framework, alternative energy represents a natural area of interest for defense planners, even though its practical use in military operations and practices remains relatively minor and is subject to further technological advances.

The defense sector has a clear stake in protecting a nation's energy security. The adaptability of policy approaches toward meeting this role is a central issue facing national defense establishments and international military alliances. Energy, after all, is the blood that sustains the armed forces and their operations. The projected defense integration of alternative energy resources and technologies can enhance the energy security of the defense community.[83]

The defense sector's securitization mandate is expanding to include environmental security considerations as well. Environmental threats can disrupt military capabilities and erode the efficiency of facilities and bases as they affect combat environments as well as base and operational logistics. Evolving environmental risks affect military commitments and capabilities, requiring a flexible strategic planning that takes into consideration unanticipated factors stemming from environmental challenges. The role of alternative energy development is critical in alleviating or preventing the environmental issues. The integration of alternative energy developments by leading militaries, coupled with their deployment in non-military domains globally, could restrain environmental degradation and prevent conflicts over energy resources.

The seeming inevitability of the alternative energy megatrend raises the question of desirability and the extent of its integration into defense practices. An important consideration in that regard is the potential impact of the alternative energy integration on operations, logistics, and effectiveness vs. efficiency trade-offs that prevail in current military doctrines. While the alternative energy developments will provide militaries with new solutions, they will also expose them to constraints and vulnerabilities. The latter include technological vulnerabilities, cyber threats, and risks of physical disruption.[84] Meanwhile, the systematic protection, security supervision, and development of policy regulations concerning the use of alternative energy in the military and civilian domains will present their own set of unique challenges. The defense sectors will need to account for these concerns and factors as part of their securitization agendas.

2. Alternative energy: an element of the growing spectrum of technologies spurring defense transformation.

Rapid technological advances over the last few years, the enormous complexity and plethora of security challenges, and growing securitization imperatives have predetermined a transformation of the defense sector at the beginning of the 21st century. Warfare is one area where change can occur swiftly, with transformative events clustering together to wrench the established paradigm of practices and notions into a new channel or framework. Although such sweeping changes do not occur frequently, they are spread across time. When a significant concurrence of such changes takes place, it results in a transformation referred to as a "revolution in military affairs."[85]

(1) The impact of technological advances on defense transformation.

Under the influence of diverse societal approaches and inherent knowledge, the ability to translate new technology into military advantage has fluctuated throughout history. For instance, despite being the inventors of gunpowder, the Chinese were not able, unlike the Europeans, to achieve the military dominance provided by subsequent firearms inventions. The gunpowder, the industrial, the nuclear, and the information revolutions are all examples of the spatio-temporal convergence of revolutionary events that have reshaped the face of war and military practices. The rationalization of such revolutions is not a form of technological determinism; the reality is often to the contrary, with human ingenuity spurring the development of truly revolutionary technologies. Nuclear submarines, for instance, provide an excellent example of a byproduct of a political imperative to pacify the destructive legacy of nuclear weapons.

New technologies provide major battlefield advantages, enabling a transition to a new level of military organization, strategy, tactics, thinking, and preparedness. Technological developments and material changes, however, are typically not the core elements of a defense transformation, which should not be mistaken for a sudden achievement of dominance through integration of less costly and more effective technology. As General H.R. McMaster indicated, this notion was "firmly rooted in a widely accepted yet fundamentally flawed conception of future war: the belief that surveillance, communications and information technologies would deliver 'dominant battlespace knowledge' and permit U.S. forces to achieve 'full spectrum dominance' against any opponent mainly through the employment of precision-strike capabilities."[86] What creates revolutions in military affairs is how humans perceive and use technological advances.

Several global shifts in military practices have changed warfare policies and approaches throughout history. A convergence of broader trends and technological advances defining and re-defining the application of military force has accompanied these shifts as they have transitioned from one epoch of international relations to another. For instance, the industrial and now the information revolution have redefined the roles and capabilities of modern militaries, which have increasingly shifted their reliance on industrial mass production to the utilization of complex, computerized systems deemed critical for military operations. Meanwhile, defense establishments have institutionalized related technological changes and reshaped military doctrines, which have supplanted the previously established methods and goals of warfare.

The process of defense transformation and the Law of Armed Conflict (LOAC)[87] entails a reinterpretation by the militaries of the conduct of war, which includes aligning military approaches with the latest technological advancements. Integration of technological advances into military strategic planning is a challenging task requiring precise and timely assessment of technology's future impact as it "will inevitably be conducted in conditions that planners describe as 'deep' or 'high' uncertainty, and in these conditions, foresight will repeatedly fail."[88]

Meanwhile, in most cases, technological advances, even those derived exclusively for military purposes, are not viewed as strategic "game changers," but rather as tactical improvements. Two 20th century weapons systems provide useful examples of belatedly impacted military strategic planning. As late as 1940, the naval planners still considered the aircraft carrier a second-tier maritime platform. Although developed in the interwar period, "British, American, and Japanese navies failed to realize fully the contribution that airpower could make to the conduct of war at sea."[89] By 1942, its strategic importance became obvious. Similarly, most interwar military planners downplayed the role of the submarine. Not even the near strangulation of British commerce during WWI by German U-boats could convince them to integrate submarines into strategic plans or to develop adequate anti-submarine warfare measures.

Part of the rationale for dismissing the U-boat as a secondary military capability during the interwar period has applicability today. Instead of modifying the law of war at sea to adapt to the new capabilities of the U-boat, the 1936 Second London Naval Treaty that bound U-boats to the same rules as surface ships proved insufficient to deter the new threat. Submarines are an inherently stealthy weapon, and no amount of legal wrangling could alter that reality. Consequently, anti-submarine warfare did not adequately evolve, instead coming to rely on faulty assumptions. Similarly, the warfare rules that apply to emerging technologies are remarkably opaque.

This is true, for example, of cyber operations increasingly targeting critical infrastructure.

A global technological revolution, which feeds on the propagation of various technologies, amplifies the significance of technological innovations for militaries seeking to enhance their power projection capabilities and ensure their strategic edge over other great powers in the coming decades. Technology magnifies the desire to project power and transforms this desire into a material force, especially when disruptive technologies are concerned, of which history provides demonstrative examples. The use of recurved composite bows, for instance, enabled the Mongols to dominate the Central Asian steppes; the nascence of artillery established the dominance of the West; and the invention of nuclear weapons arguably altered the logic of and approach to war. By the same token, disruptive or destructive alternative energy technologies can introduce new parameters of space and time for the military, reshaping the conduct of wars as well as reformatting relationships and redefining power projection capabilities in a multi-centric world.

(2) Alternative energy: a potential game-changer in Great Power Competition.

Technology per se does not offer simple solutions or guarantee the execution of the set objectives. In the area of defense, as in any field, technological knowledge and capabilities do not always equal wisdom. As militaries integrate new technologies, including alternative energy technologies, they invariably confront the need to re-examine their organization, strategy, and tactics. The capacity to transform is especially relevant when it comes to the introduction of disruptive technologies propelling revolution in military affairs.

Disruptive technologies have challenged the tasks of force presentation[90] and organization as well as force composition and fielding of modern militaries.[91] The use of unmanned systems illustrates the challenge.[92] Not only have such systems allowed for new levels of power to be delivered on the battlefield, but they have also expanded the tactical grasp and staying power of forces.[93] Although these advantages are not available to the same extent to all militaries, the technological basis for their development exists and evolves rapidly, undercutting the technological edge of the United States as innovative producer and user of such systems.[94]

This challenge to the overall technological dominance has prompted technology leaders to invest in new applications to preserve existing or acquire fundamentally new tactical or strategic advantages. One of these developments is the growing focus on directed energy weapons, which provide militaries with unanticipated capabilities and, potentially, new forms of air power.[95] Additive manufacturing is another potential game-changing technology, as it does not require an industrial base and threatens to upend the evolving economic and military balances. It gives an increasing number of state and non-state actors the ability to produce advanced weaponry.[96] New technologies are clearly expanding the defensive-offensive capabilities of actors by widening the range of and options for command and control of armed forces. New networking capabilities, for example, allow for quick processing of battlefield intelligence, taking decision-making speed to a new level and allowing commanders to give orders to both soldiers and unmanned platforms.[97] They also improve target acquisition and reaction times, already requiring new tactics and strategies to maximize the benefits of these new technologies.

Similarly, the alternative energy megatrend could help develop new military capabilities and reorganize military practices as part of the defense transformation. While offering immediate military benefits, such as a more efficient use of energy sources, enhanced operational effectiveness, and reduced mission risks and costs, alternative energy developments can also serve as a springboard for unimagined technological breakthroughs for military and civilian applications. This could ultimately lead to the creation of new military platforms and systems, and the networked fighter of the future. Advancing the technologies that underpin the trend can generate new capacities in operations and nurture new aspects of military readiness.

The military has an established history of adapting to technological innovations and is expected to succeed in the effort if it has a right mix of policies and incentives for the task. As Sir Winston Churchill noted when recalling the decision to move the British Navy from coal to oil, "the camel once swallowed, the gnats went down easily enough."[98]

But the integration of alternative energy developments is only one side of the coin when it comes to defense transformation, which must consider the capacity of such technologies to reshape the international system and concomitant responses to deal with related geopolitical consequences. After all, these technologies are bound to transform the why, who, and how of warfare, becoming an essential element of the broadening securitization mandate of the defense sectors. As disruptive technologies, they can cause or address problems depending on circumstances. The speed of technological innovation makes it hard to keep abreast of new military capabilities, easier to be misled on the actual balance of power, and to fall victim to strategic miscalculation. Thus, they could change the ability of actors to impose military dominance, at the same time rebalancing military power relationships. With broader security considerations gaining prominence as part of the securitization, alternative energy developments offer new opportunities and choices in defense policy development and encourage the formation of broader "security communities," just as they generate new challenges.

3. The transformation of defense strategies: the megatrend highlights new capabilities, missions, and areas of strategic engagement and cooperation.

Anticipating shifts in the international balance of power and maximizing related advantages is at the heart of statecraft. So is the understanding of ways to harness the anticipated military power by relying on technological advances without overemphasizing their role. Taking advantage of technology is not simply an issue of getting there first, but of institutionalizing the changes and retaining related advantages. Although early innovators hold the advantage, history has demonstrated that military innovation has sped up continuously, enabling weaker adversaries to use new technologies in conflicts with stronger opponents. For example, despite holding a technological advantage, U.S. forces in Afghanistan have faced challenges from insurgents pursuing asymmetrical warfare. This has prompted the development of new technological solutions and the next step in projecting the "warrior of the future"[99] in different or new war settings. The introduction of new technologies as part of the defense transformation is imposing new imperatives on defense planners and commanders to ensure defense readiness amid increased uncertainty, since "when war starts, the only consequence that is inevitable is the unintended."[100]

The strategic challenges imposed on decision-makers necessitate the use of new resources. As pointed out by Admiral Michael Mullen, "burgeoning technological and operational changes are dramatically altering the way we fight, requiring new platforms and capabilities."[101] These new capabilities and limitations will impact individual combatants, presaging the introduction of the "warriors of the future." Importantly, they will change the values that actors associate with military engagement, transforming the cost-benefit analysis of future wars. With alterations in strategic value judgments, the perceived balance of military power will itself change, prompting actors to undertake steps to reverse notional inadequacy, spurring others to advance their defense sectors.

As is the case of other technological advances, alternative energy technologies and their defense integration present a set of solutions and constraints. Just as oil is used on a wide scale today, renewable energy could become the norm of the future, providing for fundamentally new ways of energy use and power projection, and enabling a reduction in dependence on specific energy supplies and producers. Western defense establishments and institutions face a growing pressure to adapt their structures and operations to the sources of energy supplies, endowing often unstable producers with leverage and power—the gains an expanded renewables use could take away while reducing the importers' exposure to supply risks. As former U.S. Secretary of Defense Robert M. Gates pointed out, "The real lesson here [is that] it only requires a relatively small amount of oil to be taken out of the system to have huge economic and security implications."[102]

In expanding the use of renewables, the defense sectors and militaries will need to consider the effects of the alternative energy integration on effectiveness vs. efficiency calculations. It is considered that "measuring defense efficiency and effectiveness is about measuring the fighting power a given country generates per unit of expenditure."[103] Even though it is easier to measure the financial expenditure on energy, the output it produces for the military differs among actors, dictated by political considerations and types of military units. Therefore, according to the "competing interests" and other military doctrines, one view of the trade-off between effectiveness today and efficiency in the future posits that effectiveness trumps efficiency today.

For instance, the Weinberger and Powell doctrines[104] that dominated military thought prior to September 11 assert that the effectiveness in military operations comes at the cost of efficiency. They advocate a military of a decisive weight and force to overwhelm the enemy. These doctrines allow for a conclusion that energy efficiency is subordinate to effectiveness when conducting military operations. However, it can be argued that a greater efficiency of energy use can augment tactical power (as forces are not reliant on energy logistics lines), acting as a force multiplier.[105] The trade-off between effectiveness and efficiency could also be considered as a foundation for the creation of new weapons systems. While new weapons systems could improve operational effectiveness, they could also increase the demands on the military, especially if they fall into the wrong hands or introduce new factors into the calculations of allies and adversaries.

Ultimately, the integration of alternative energy-related advantages within the defense sector will be contingent on passing the effectiveness vs. efficiency test. Effectiveness and efficiency trade-offs form an integral part of modern military doctrines and would be reflected within the scope of new engagements and defense imperatives for addressing the emerging tensions and conflicts.[106] Such integration of alternative energy developments would need to address a wide range of options, referent objects, and threats as part of the broader securitization agenda.

By revealing the shape of the evolving defense transformation, the alternative energy megatrend suggests the need for new levels of military preparedness to address new areas of instability. Military force postures will need to be adequate to the new security threats of resource depletion, energy security, transnational crime, economic instabilities, pandemics, and "failed states." Defense organizations like NATO will need to integrate new technologies. An assessment will be required of the efficacy of existing frameworks in handling conflicts over alternative energy sources or regional unrest induced by a decline in traditional energy relations between major consumers and producers.

New safeguards will likely be necessary to handle the environmental externalities stemming from strategic resource depletion or the production of alternative energy in susceptible regions. Finally, domestic and international norms must be developed to guide the integration of alternative energy technologies. These norms will be imperative for the emergence of a favorable, non-confrontational platform for cooperation among major militaries worldwide.

4. The defense benefits promised by alternative energy: not just adapting to the new strategic environment, but rather new forms of power projection and cooperation.

From wind and coal to oil and electricity, energy use in military operations has been a dominant strategic and tactical consideration since ancient times. The invention of the steam and internal combustion engines made warfare significantly more energy intensive, allowing for rapid movement and maneuvering capabilities by ever-larger motorized military formations. The armed forces started relying on more sophisticated and resource-hungry platforms and equipment, particularly following the introduction of oil, the dependence on which has grown exponentially over the last century.

In naval operations, select countries deployed nuclear-powered submarines and larger surface combatants, such as cruisers and aircraft carriers, which relied on fossil fuels and nuclear power. Just as the overall factor of energy and changes stemming from its integration into the military operations had far-reaching, often unanticipated, consequences for the military and warfare, alternative energy integration into defense industries and military operations could pave the way for new ways to use energy and project power.

Defense sectors seek to incorporate the benefits and advantages offered by the alternative energy megatrend across several defense transformation targets in pursuit of specific objectives. From a tactical perspective, alternative energy resources can enhance new military capabilities and address logistical and operational challenges. They can also enhance military power projection capabilities while modifying the operational effectiveness and efficiency of the full spectrum of military operations as they concern military bases, expeditionary forces, and forward facilities. Strategically, the defense establishments, industries, and militaries already utilize, integrate, and institutionalize the use of renewables as part of the securitization and defense transformation.

In a panel discussion on preparing military leadership for the future, Gen. James Cartwright, USMC (Ret.) made the salient remark to "innovate in an incremental way." While this remark was made with reference to military tactics and equipment, the remark is perhaps most applicable to the megatrend and its development. Innovation that changes the reference architecture often requires too much time and energy and faces stubborn institutional resistance and cultural acceptance. Rather than "reinventing the wheel," tactics, techniques and procedures must be thoroughly researched, repurposed, and improved so that innovation can be "integrated into the institution."[107]

More broadly, the growing use of alternative energy in defense practices provides a basis for more rapid technological advancement. If incentivized properly, the defense integration of renewables could advance a society's technological base. For instance, the integration by the U.S. military of energy technologies paved the way for the commercialization of nuclear power, with the first U.S. nuclear plant becoming operational three years after the 1954 commissioning of the USS *Nautilus* submarine. The military's investment into renewables-related R&D could lead to new plateaus of innovation, spurring technological progress and economic growth.

(1) Optimizing the military's energy supply, use, and logistics: near-term tactical benefits and long-term defense energy security.

Despite their current lack of practical viability, alternative energy technologies could become a contributing factor to a new level of energy resilience, supply flexibility, and logistics flexibility, as well as operational effectiveness. Specifically, the alternative energy technologies have the potential to transform the military's energy use by changing the trade-off between efficiency, effectiveness, and power projection aspects. Defense policies and doctrines would need to balance these trade-offs and take into account both the asymmetric nature of today's conflicts and operations and the possibility of more traditional force-on-force scenarios. The defense sector views alternative energy as a means to increase efficiency without greatly reducing effectiveness. For instance, the military aims to reduce the levels of operational energy requirements in order to improve operational effectiveness. However, obsessively searching for efficiency may be harmful if it jeopardizes the effectiveness of a mission by putting a disproportionate emphasis on the need to conserve resources.

Major militaries have been and largely remain geared for high-intensity warfare, a state of affairs reflected in their defense logistics, infrastructure, postures, and energy needs. Following the end of the Cold War, increased focus on stability and disaster relief operations has forced additional requirements on defense establishments.

The military is heavily dependent on infrastructure, both in terms of forward-operating facilities[108] and the forces' home basing. This reinforces the imperative to reduce operational energy consumption and energy needs of the fixed building stock and other infrastructure. Installations account for a quarter of the DoD's energy use. The DoD maintains more than 300,000 buildings on more than 500 installations with 2.2 billion square feet of space and spends nearly US$4 billion a year to power them.[109] These fixed installations are ideal test beds for next-generation energy technologies, as they are not faced with the challenges of frontline operations. Although missing ambitious legislative goals of reducing energy intensity by 30% by 2015 (relative to a 2003 baseline), the DoD still met two-thirds of its target (19.9%) and, as of 2016, was more than halfway in achieving a 25% renewable generation mandate by 2025.[110]

Integrating alternative energy technologies and applications in defense bases and infrastructure can bring numerous benefits while simultaneously diversifying base energy supplies and removing dependencies on restricted energy supply sources and types of energy. Alternative energy systems can improve efficiency as well as augment and, perhaps, replace fossil fuel-based generator systems. Not surprisingly, numerous defense establishments are working toward minimizing or eliminating the fossil fuel supply vulnerabilities. Faced with austerity measures, they are pursuing efficiency improvement initiatives, aiming to reconcile the imperatives of operational effectiveness with fiscal and environmental concerns.

The strategic need to project and sustain force quickly and decisively necessitates firm defense energy resilience, which is just as important as proper training and equipment. The reliance of forward bases and facilities on extensive energy use to support expeditionary military operations and related risks makes uninterrupted energy supplies to and within theaters of operations a major concern and priority. In the case of NATO, for example, land forces pre-positioned in European forward bases require an extensive system of hardened fuel dumps and supply routes. Furthermore, Eastern-flank NATO countries, especially the Baltic states, still find themselves completely dependent on potential adversaries for energy resources. Alternative energy developments hold the potential to enhance supply diversification and provide flexible logistics capabilities the forces need in order to meet the complex challenges of future operational environments.

Together with water, energy is one of the largest logistical requirements for armed forces relying on efficient and secure transport for expeditionary missions. Solutions to reduce operational energy needs may include operationally viable energy alternatives.[111] The megatrend's projected impact on defense operations is proportional to the intensity of the imperative to reduce the military's demand for fossil fuels in forward operational theaters. Recent military interventions, such as in Iraq, Afghanistan, and Africa, reveal that military forces are increasingly required to conduct high-tempo (and resource-intensive) operations in hostile environments with little indigenous infrastructure. Addressing these obstacles requires the maintenance of large infrastructure and supporting facilities, the cost of which, in financial outlays, tied-up combat and logistic resources, and human lives, is increasing. Energy price volatility, too, carries its own risks. For instance, a US$1 increase in the price of petroleum-based fuel would cost the U.S. military billions of dollars in additional fuel costs.[112]

Energy considerations often contribute to the strategic positioning of forces and limit the spatial scope of military operations. The reliance on fossil fuels has determined the command and organizational structure of defense establishments. If the fossil fuel tether is severed, operational capabilities will be enhanced, and forces will be capable of delivering overwhelming power within a much wider radius. In this context, powering defense mobility with renewables allows actors that have a lead in such technologies to bring their advantages to where they are most effective in distant theaters.

Alternative energy developments can also provide new levels of operational flexibility by facilitating the tailoring of mission logistics to diverse mission requirements that may involve multiple large-scale operations in disparate war theatres. High fuel demand not only restricts the range of operations, but also makes all deployed forces more vulnerable.[113] Hydrocarbons themselves act as a combustible and exhibit their own kinetic vulnerabilities. The protection of convoys, meanwhile, requires the use of armored vehicles, unmanned platforms (for reconnaissance and strike), attack helicopters, and fixed-wing fighters and bombers, a significant commitment of troops and resources that must be diverted from other operations. Reducing the burden of convoy protection frees soldiers for combat operations, strengthening the military's operational and tactical capacity and allowing for "greater flexibility to shift and deploy" between operational theaters.[114]

Though the use of alternative energy sources and technologies would by no means obviate the need for logistics lines (as the military still needs food, water, ammunition, and other supplies), it could decrease the exposure of logistics convoys on the roads, thereby reducing the danger to personnel engaged in these operations. By saving lives, renewable energy applications also provide new opportunities to save dollars. For example, tangible savings of fuel demonstrated in the field tests of the Ground Renewable Expeditionary Energy Network System (GREENS), which the U.S. Marines had undertaken in 2009–10, prompted the Marine Corps Systems Command to ensure a rapid development and accelerated procurement of the system's final design.[115]

The emphasis on expeditionary operations entails greater complexity of supply, particularly the security of supply routes on land and sea. Militaries need to protect sea-based energy production and supply lines stretching across international waters. For example, about 65% of the oil and natural gas that Western Europe consumes each year travels through the Mediterranean, including via pipelines from Libya and Morocco. To ensure these and other energy supplies are secure, NATO, the EU, and U.S.-led coalitions conduct counter-piracy operations to suppress the threat to oil tankers and other maritime traffic passing along the Gulf of Aden between Yemen and Somalia. Ships assigned to NATO's "Operation Active Endeavour" mission have been patrolling the Mediterranean since October 2001, inspecting vessels and escorting cargo ships where necessary. There is no reason why future security-of-supply imperatives could not shift operations elsewhere, say to the Strait of Hormuz or NATO's "high north" region near Norway.

This is relevant given the effects of global warming on the opening of the Arctic sea lanes.

The adoption of alternative energy solutions would not remove the need for protection of sea-based power facilities or supply routes, as some alternative energy infrastructure which may be based on maritime platforms and rely on sea lanes to reach alternative energy users will also need protection. For instance, tidal and wave power generation and capacity raise a number of maritime security issues and the issue of safety of energy transmission. Projects like Desertec, which involves transmitting Saharan sun-powered energy across the water between North Africa and Europe, illustrate related prospects and challenges.

To achieve cost-effective, versatile, and individualized capabilities, the armed forces will need to consider factors other than logistics support and security of supply. An expected increase in expeditionary missions suggests a need to adapt to different climates, terrain, and force composition requirements. The increasing preponderance of asymmetric warfare in modern conflicts has strained military logistics and mobility. To address related challenges, the U.S. military is pursuing innovative efforts to augment energy supplies by using renewable energy.[116] Defense logistics modernization and transformation should be flexible to accommodate new approaches and even break with tradition in order to deliver tactically overwhelming force, on which future military engagements will continue to rely. Overall, a convergent approach toward alternative energy applications, greater efficiency, and fuel savings could achieve longer endurance levels and the ability to refuel less often and stay engaged in combat longer. However, they also can prove to be less agile against countermeasures. Because stealth and deception capabilities[117] can offset many of these liabilities, it is important to view alternative energy applications as part of a larger set of capabilities delivering tactically overwhelming force.

(2) Powering the warfighter: force multiplier in front-line operations and the progenitor of new warfighting capabilities.

The core imperative of the defense transformation is to ensure and enhance the ability to deliver unmatched and overwhelming power. Finding advantages before others and applying them to achieve superiority accentuates the link between technological development and weaponization. As former U.S. Secretary of Defense Chuck Hagel pointed out, "Throughout history, militaries have had to adapt to new threats, new weapons, new dynamics, [and] new geostrategic realities. Those that did not, could not, or would not adapt, were defeated, and disappeared."[118] It is not surprising that new weapons applications emerge (including those associated with alternative energy technologies) during this process of adaptation, promising benefits for defense sectors as part of the defense transformation.

Though it is unlikely that renewable energy systems could replace fossil fuel-powered generator systems in the short to medium term, they definitely have the potential to serve as force multipliers in the future, providing for improved deployability, stealth, enhanced survivability, and greater maneuverability. They could also increase efficiencies, allowing for better management of energy and warfare systems. It may also be noted that the deployment of technological solutions by the defense sector is not always an issue of cost or viability but, rather, of human nature's influence on the decision-making process of the military. Perhaps technology would be even more widespread in certain areas, such as unmanned craft, reconnaissance, and energy, if it were not for the desire to maintain human control.[119]

Legacy aircraft systems have impressive logistics trails. Manned, fossil-fueled tactical aircraft inherently require a significant deployment of manned, fossil-fueled vehicles just to keep them airborne.[120] The size and weight of military platforms dedicated to keeping humans protected is substantial. In this respect, the evolution of unmanned systems greatly complements the shift to alternative energies.

To help meet the demands and address the challenges of the multi-centric world, especially the increasingly frequent and far-flung non-traditional conflicts, defense establishments could lean on alternative energy developments to create overmatch capabilities[121] on all formation levels. Militaries have historically been early developers of new technologies, and will likely perceive the next iteration of alternative energy developments in the same way they have viewed cyber security—as, in the words of former U.S. President Ronald Reagan, "a vital element of the operational effectiveness of the national security activities of the government and of military combat-readiness."[122] That technological advancements have tended to originate from or are quickly assimilated by military applications only reinforces this expectation.

Besides boosting energy efficiency and fuel conservation, alternative energy advances can enhance flexibility in logistics chains. For instance, they could allow aviation platforms to travel greater distances and remain on station longer. With the increased independence and "staying power" provided via non-fossil fuel technologies (e.g., nuclear-powered naval vessels), they could help develop the unmanned air, ground, and sea systems, potentially unleashing a revolution in military capabilities. Current unmanned platforms and automated intelligence-gathering devices suffer from restricted mission times due to energy sources of limited duration and power. New equipment is being developed to address the issues, like the experimental Energetically Autonomous Tactical Robot[123] or intelligent power manager systems like Protonex's SPM-612 (Squad Power Manager), which weighs less than a pound and employs energy from many sources, including solar, vehicle, fuel cells, and scavenged energy.[124]

The "super-soldiers of the future" will require a range of new capabilities in communication, networking, stamina, firepower, and range. Alternative energy technologies can enhance the warfighting capabilities of combatants in major ways, improve command and control speed and precision, allow commanders to conduct operations with unprecedented speed and cohesion, and potentially offer new ways of delivering power to targeted areas of the battlefield. Ultimately, such technologies could also lead to the emergence of nanotechnology-based military applications, self-contained and ultra-secure operations centers, and biological and chemical tools for biomass conversion, microwave weaponry, and fusion propulsion.

Some of these developments may materialize in a few years, others in a generation or more. Enhancing warfighting capabilities by integrating alternative energy developments is challenging, in part because of a historic trend toward fewer, albeit more complex, weapons systems. The average lifecycle for new acquisitions is longer. The weapons platforms in design today are thus likely to be part of much more complex web of energy interdependencies. They are also required to perform a wider range of missions and functions.[125]

Overcoming associated challenges is critical to a nation's ability to sustain and enhance its strategic edge. Technology provides new ways of achieving dominance by combining the anarchic competitiveness of international politics with the inherent inventiveness of the human species. It makes it easier to control localities, resources, people, and states, providing new avenues for geopolitical competition and new metrics for assessing capabilities of geopolitical agents. Together with power projection capabilities supported by technologies, these considerations make alternative energy a likely factor in the development of enhanced warfighting capabilities.

The promise of new technologies in general, and new ways of powering the warfighter in particular, point to the likely transition of military operations to a new frontier—space. Creating space capabilities, such as kinetic space weapons or microwave emission platforms, would not only introduce a new "high ground" for the 21st century battlefield, but would also reshape the contested geopolitical terrain. This could make possible space-to-space or space-to-ground military capabilities, requiring new military strategies.[126] These considerations must ultimately give way to cost-effective solutions. Considering a "congested, contested, and competitive" space environment,[127] where adversaries can neutralize satellites at little cost, U.S. Strategic Command advocates the development of "more resilient, more distributed capabilities."[128]

However, beyond nuclear power, the potential to "weaponize" alternative energy technologies, especially in the space domain, is still in the realm of science fiction. Renewable technologies are yet to beam microwave "rays" from orbit, even though similar experiments with solar power have shown potential. Although the renewables' capacity for new weapons developments is restricted, it is accelerating and might soon lead to the development of transformational warfighting capabilities.

(3) The anticipated unintended side effects: improving society's technological base through defense sector-induced technological advancements.

The defense establishment has always been a hotbed of new technological developments expanding a society's technological base. There is no reason that the defense use of alternative energy will prove an exception.

Ever since the need to quickly project military power over vast distances helped drive the Roman Empire two millennia ago to develop an extensive road infrastructure, security has been a major driver of new technology and infrastructure development initiatives. Military institutions have regularly proved able to take on projects that are too large, risky, or unprofitable for private industry alone.[129] Thus, over the last century, the U.S. DoD and affiliated defense organizations have accomplished a number of projects, achieving monumental breakthroughs, such as the Internet.[130]

The U.S. military has played a critical role in spurring an overall technological development, as it is the main player capable of bridging the so-called "Valley of Death"—the gap between the early stage of a technology development cycle and its commercialization as an application.[131] This value in research and the "bringing to market" factor cannot be understated.

Aided by the availability of an extensive infrastructure of laboratories and facilities, the defense establishment has an enormous capacity to convert technological innovation into a spectrum of practical benefits. Military technological advances have the capacity to provide momentum to a wide range of civil developments, with securitization producing unanticipated side benefits.

The imperatives of achieving technological breakthroughs to address challenges of the defense, military, and civilian sectors are as strong as ever. It is often during periods of conflict or major geopolitical stress and uncertainty that major breakthroughs are achieved. Just as the blockades of the War of 1812 increased coal prices, which expanded the use of anthracite for smelting, so may the current and anticipated energy needs spur a wide-scale use of renewables.[132] The societal and military legacy of technological research and development in handling large-scale projects in the United States provides a platform for revolutionary alternative energy developments and broader technological advances. A collaboration among the technologically endowed NATO countries could provide an additional boost to the expansion of the broader technological base.

The military is a tested and well-placed actor to explore ways of using new technologies to promote its objectives. The defense establishment will most likely play a significant role in the actual propagation of the alternative energy megatrend, including within the non-military domain, due to the significance of energy security for the military and its capacity to absorb innovation. This can be construed from the current operational planning, efforts to enhance national security (including the energy domain), and historical examples.[133]

The defense and military transformation, which appears inevitable given the mounting challenges blurring civilian and military lines, will place greater importance on ensuring appropriate facility to integrate civilian and military developments in order to facilitate the adaptation of defense technological developments into broader advances for society. Advantages could arise from partnerships between defense establishments and private contractors. Private sector engagement would make the technologies developed sustainable by commercial forces rather than government subsidization.

5. Practical uptake of renewables by defense establishments worldwide: U.S. maintaining a leading role.

Led by the United States, several countries are changing their attitudes about the military significance of alternative energy use and are incorporating related technologies and outcomes into their policies, doctrines, and operations. Whether motivated by the need to reduce fossil fuel consumption or address environmental security concerns, these attitudes are not limited to a few defense establishments but span geographical boundaries thanks to the diffusion of technologies.

This concerns U.S. allies within NATO, a decades-old alliance that requires revitalization to remain relevant in the post-Cold War environment. While renewables integration is not a priority for NATO, energy security overall is of strategic importance to the alliance. Due to the pervasiveness and widespread impact of the megatrend's drivers, the integration of alternative energy in NATO practices and approaches could play a role in the revitalization of the alliance.

Countries other than the technologically savvy NATO states are also emerging as civilian and military centers and hubs of technological developments in a number of areas, including alternative energy. China, among a few other non-NATO member countries, has notably taken important steps in integrating alternative energy technologies into its military operations.

(1) Defense-generated demand: fueling the overall alternative energy market.

The U.S. defense market for alternative energy developments has already demonstrated significant robustness, achieving levels of support and resilience greater than the overall U.S. renewables sector. For instance, between 2011 and 2015 the U.S. military nearly doubled its renewable power generation, whereas in the same time period, the entire U.S. economy added only about 2.6% of new renewable power generation.[134]

The U.S. Army Energy Initiatives Task Force established in 2011[135] has been supporting the renewable energy market development by leveraging private sector and defense resources through procurement projects at multiple installations.[136] Through competitive bidding procedures, defense establishments offer contract awards for alternative energy technologies and provision of alternative energy supplies.

The U.S. defense sector is also a pioneer in the field of advanced research projects, which include alternative energy developments. The U.S. Defense Advanced Research Projects Agency (DARPA) focuses on the most far-reaching scientific discoveries and innovations. With an annual budget of approximately US$3 billion, DARPA's mission stretches across all security sectors.[137] Because of its wide-reaching and cross-cutting mission, DARPA typically addresses challenges and technologies that have multiple end uses and are three to ten years from commercialization. Alternative energy projects undertaken by the agency[138] are fueling research on multiple energy-related fronts—algae-based jet fuel, nano-batteries, wave energy, solar and wind technology, fuel cells from microbes, and space-age technologies.

These projects are to provide breakthroughs that can then be widely applied beyond the defense community.

The private sector, including defense companies, is already taking advantage of the defense sector-driven demand for alternative energy solutions. For example, Lockheed Martin is developing an Ocean Thermal Energy Conversion technology that uses temperature differences between warm surface waters and deep cold water to generate power. Boeing is developing a highly energy-efficient solar-powered drone that can stay aloft for several months to serve as a platform for remote sensing, reconnaissance, and scientific experiments. The business case for development and use of alternative energy is expanding and might involve the development of ever-more effective weapon systems, tactical mobility platforms, and net-centric sensors.

The expanding integration of alternative energy developments by private defense companies reflects their advantageous position and capabilities to merge civilian and defense applications to enhance the overall technological base of a society. These companies possess the skills, the infrastructure, and commercialization capabilities to initiate and complete the entire cycle of a technology development.

(2) The U.S. Department of Defense: directives, policies, and initiatives.

The U.S. DoD is the largest single energy consumer in America.[139] Coupled with increasing operational demands, finding new energy solutions has become a constant priority for the department, which plays the leading role in the development and integration of alternative energy solutions. As stated by former Under Secretary for Defense Michèle Flournoy, the DoD "looked at [energy and climate change] both as a factor in the future security environment—how competition for energy, how climate change could actually affect the operating environment for the U.S. military in the future—but we also looked at it from the perspective of the Department of Defense being one of the largest, if not the largest, energy consumer in the United States. And how do we gain further efficiencies in our facilities, in our use of fuels and so forth? How do we become a market leader potentially in driving innovation and investment in more sustainable energy sources?"[140]

The DoD is expected to spend approximately US$10 billion on renewable energy by 2030 and is "positioned to become the single most important driver of the cleantech revolution in the United States."[141] This leadership role reflects the U.S.' overwhelming military strength and could drive defense-specific and broader technological superiority. This leadership role remains a guide for the NATO alliance, underpinning the U.S.' military dominance.

The DoD draws its mandate to use clean, renewable energy from the National Defense Authorization Act, which calls on the department to produce or procure 25% of its energy from renewable sources by 2025, and from the Energy Independence and Security Act, which sets key goals for facility power use and authorizes the use of innovative mechanisms for leveraging private financing of advanced technologies.[142]

The DoD developed an Operational Energy Strategy to implement the mandate and seek three main goals: "to improve future capability, reduce risk, and enhance current mission effectiveness."[143] These targets entail "achieving increased warfighter capability as the salient outcome while advocating for programs and initiatives that both reduce energy demand and enhance energy supportability."[144] The Operational Energy Strategy envisages enhancing the assurance of energy supply through diversification of energy sources and considers the integration of a range of alternative energy technologies across the full range of air, sea, and ground platforms. For instance, renewables solutions may mitigate the impact of commercial power grids' disruptions for the installations and achieve savings based on self-generation.

The DoD's mandate also extends to ensuring environmental security. Driven by national and international legislation and policy, the department is pursuing "green" initiatives that are drawing on and propelling the alternative energy megatrend. The American Recovery and Reinvestment Act provided US$12.02 billion in 2009 and 2010 to the DoD, funding 45 energy conservation-related projects in 17 states. The initiatives are focused on achieving general facility energy improvements—from installation of wind turbines, solar photovoltaic systems, and solar thermal systems in buildings and infrastructure to the testing of various forms of experimental renewables. The U.S. Army's "Net-Zero" approach to energy use offers another example, ensuring that a military installation produces as much as or more energy than it consumes.[145]

Notwithstanding the technological obstacles, the pursuit of military advantages and energy security will most likely push forward the development of alternative energy technologies. Conversely, an expanded integration of alternative energy technologies by the defense sectors and the militaries will result in a transformation of the military energy systems, capabilities, and doctrines in the years ahead.

(3) U.S. Navy, Air Force, and Army: the military's renewable energy programs in practice.

The different branches of the U.S. military have taken steps to integrate alternative energy technologies and outcomes into their planning and force development that differ more in pace and intensity than in approach. The specific energy needs and approaches of each branch differ on many points, albeit overlapping in some cases. The uneven level of effort and focus is linked to their immediate experience and direct operational effect of energy security and environmental threats on the imperatives driving the alternative energy integration. Besides, the assessment of appropriate alternative energy applications is still ongoing. The challenges of integrating alternative energy in the military will inevitably take on different forms across the operational and installation landscape. The services will individually address the new variables in the context of the operational environment.

The Navy has been a proactive integrator and user of alternative energy technologies and initiatives aimed at addressing challenges of operational security, climate change, and energy security. It is already producing or procuring at least 25% of its energy consumption from renewable sources. In FY 2016, some 28.2% of its energy consumption came from renewable energy sources, a testament to its successful initiatives to expand the use of renewables.[146]

For instance, the Navy launched the Arctic Roadmap, a comprehensive strategy to help navigate challenges in a thawing Arctic. It also announced its "Great Green Fleet" initiative to create a carrier strike group using alternative energy fuels, including nuclear power for the carrier and a blend of advanced biofuel and petroleum for the escort ships. Pointedly, the first oil-burning destroyer, the USS *Paulding*, was commissioned in 1910. A year later, the USS *Nevada* class battleship was burning oil instead of coal, marking a transition to a completely different fuel type. Today, the Navy is committed to a similarly dramatic shift away from petroleum-based fuels.[147] In addition to biofuels, the Great Green Fleet, consisting of aviation, surface combatants, and submarines, will rely on hybrid-electric propulsion technology, fuel cells, and, predominantly, nuclear power. Unveiled in 2012, the Great Green Fleet sailed in 2016.[148]

By far the largest consumer of fuel within the DoD (accounting for more than half of the department's petroleum use per year), the U.S. Air Force has focused its efforts predominantly on securing energy access to enhance operational effectiveness. Alternative jet fuel use expanding the fuel options available to the fleet is considered a part of the solution. The first flight of an aircraft with all engines powered by a biofuel blend was performed in March 2010.[149] By 2017, the U.S. Air Force had certified its entire fleet to fly on two alternative aviation fuel blends.[150] Increased use of cost-competitive drop-in alternative aviation fuel blends for non-contingency operations is considered one of the strategic means to assure supply, according to the Air Force Energy Flight Plan 2017–2036.[151]

The Air Force is also using renewable energy to power its bases in order to improve their energy resiliency and reduce costs. For example, it built a 13.2-megawatt solar array on Nellis Air Force Base in North Las Vegas, Nevada, in 2007 and another solar array in 2015, providing another 15 megawatts of electricity to the base. The array is made up of 43,200 highly efficient photovoltaic panels cleaned by specially designed robots. Another significant project is a 14.5-MW solar array built at Davis-Monthan Air Force Base in Tucson, Arizona. [152]

The Army is currently the largest installation energy user within the DoD, consuming up to 35% of total facility energy in FY2016.[153] The extensive network of Army installations makes it especially vulnerable to the risks of commercial power grids' disruptions caused by infrastructure drawbacks or natural disasters, making it a priority for the Army to ensure operational energy security. Its policy is to ensure that all U.S. facilities and bases can operate, at least partially, off the grid by 2030—a task that will require an expanded use of all types of renewable energy sources and technologies.[154] In fact, the Army's portfolio of renewable energy initiatives, guided by various operational needs, is already rather diverse.[155] The "Army Net Zero Initiative" is one of its flagship programs; it will introduce 25 Net Zero installations by 2030. The installations are intended to produce as much energy on site as they consume. Seventeen pilot projects were undertaken in 2015.[156]

(4) NATO approaches: new challenges driven by the evolving global security environment.

Although not a top priority, energy security considerations have been of strategic importance to NATO. The role of the alliance in guaranteeing the security of its members is gradually encompassing energy security as an important aspect of its policy initiatives. This stems from the evolving security landscape and the imperatives of change facing the alliance since the end of the Cold War and dissolution of the Warsaw Pact. As part of its transformation, NATO could provide added value in the areas of information and intelligence sharing, stability operations, international and regional cooperation, crisis management, critical infrastructure protection, and international energy collaboration.[157] An expanded use of renewables will be crucial for NATO's energy security, technological transformation, and operational efficiency and effectiveness. Yet, it will need to address a number of issues impeding its reliance on renewables infrastructure.

Already, Allied leaders acknowledge that disruptions to the flow of resources, especially energy, can threaten the collective security interests of the alliance members. They are supporting institutional and international efforts to assess energy infrastructure risks and ways to ensure its protection from attacks, sabotage, and manipulation. However, the complexity of energy security threats, let alone threats posed to the overall security environment, may indicate that "instead of energy security, we shall have to acknowledge and live with various degrees of insecurity."[158] Still, the alliance is reviewing ways to protect domestic energy infrastructure from terrorist attacks.[159] For example, EU countries are building a database of critical energy infrastructure nodes, particularly those which would have the most severe cross-border impact if disabled.[160]

Direct physical threats to energy supplies, systems, and markets are not the only types of threats defining NATO's operational security environment and requiring the securitization of the alliance's agenda, policies, and procedures. Threats of energy supply manipulation or cessation are, too, shaping up to become formidable threats—a state of affairs made clear by the Russian-Ukrainian energy disputes in 2006 and 2009 that held Russian gas supplies to Europe hostage.[161]

Despite the challenges, the alliance is also working to enhance energy security as part of targeted policies. NATO's Strategic Concept unveiled at the Lisbon Summit in 2010 devotes considerable attention to the issue given European dependence on imported energy, the growing significance of the link between energy and environmental security, and the rising threat of armed attacks on energy supplies by terrorists and pirates.[162] The alliance is specifically reevaluating its energy security role across a range of domains from policing and protecting the sea lanes to supporting individual member states in facing up to energy challenges. Moreover, NATO reinforces its energy policy capacity by leaning on its direct military-to-military contact with countries in select regions.

Potentially serving as a *casus belli*, energy supply disruptions increasingly prompt joint work by NATO and the EU to protect critical energy infrastructure from malfunction, sabotage, manipulation, and attacks.[163]

However, NATO and the EU have yet to articulate publicly a strategy to protect out-of-area energy infrastructure in times of peace.[164]

The alternative energy developments could help NATO reduce dependence on foreign sources of energy supplies from countries considered hostile and mitigate the risks of energy-related tensions and conflicts. Yet, while future alternative energy developments might result in numerous benefits as far as operational capabilities of NATO's military forces are concerned, the full effect on the Alliance's ability to project power and maintain defensive capabilities will remain unclear until alternative energy technologies are tested and deployed on a wider scale.

Beyond energy security, the alliance could face new challenges from deteriorating environmental conditions in areas where technological development has not been sufficient to offset environmental damage. NATO members recognize the problem, as environmental security is already driving the securitization and transformation of the alliance. The environmental security threats are expected to spur NATO to deal with environmental disasters or terrorist attacks on energy facilities. More broadly, NATO could accelerate the development of alternative energy security policies and become a hub of renewables infrastructure development. It could then pass on its policymaking functions to organizations more suited to dealing with environmental security threats,[165] especially given NATO's limited capacity to engage the private sector in addressing the challenges spanning both the civilian and military sectors.

The time could not be more opportune, as the deployment of alternative energy technologies already raises new operational challenges for the alliance and individual EU members and companies. As former NATO Secretary General Jaap de Hoop Scheffer said in 2008, climate change will alter energy exploration and transit routes, impacting global security. Scheffer made specific reference to NATO's "high north" region near Norway, arguing that "[a]s the polar icepack melts and the Northwest Passage to Asia opens up, an increasing amount of shipping will pass through one of the most remote and inhospitable parts of the world. Intervening in the event of an environmental disaster or even a terrorist attack would be very difficult indeed."[166]

The U.S., NATO, and the EU understand the implications of environmental security considerations on energy and other aspects of security, but the integration of these implications in their strategic doctrines remains limited, with the security of energy supply being the predominant concern. Clearly, NATO can do little about energy efficiency or alternative energy policy on its own (other than implement measures at its own headquarters or common-owned facilities) since decisions are made by individual member nations. "Tasking NATO is one thing; getting a consensus on it is another," the saying goes.[167] This is especially the case with the EU, which is only starting to develop a coherent European defense policy and would not be able to define the problem or the solution for the European militaries, despite the growing imperatives of making the EU's members' separate and joint defense structures more efficient and effective.

Cyber security is yet another critical attribute of NATO's securitizations agenda, especially if viewed in tandem with the alternative energy developments. The alliance is cognizant of the growing cyber security threats to the continent's cyber infrastructure and energy grids, which grow more complex as the use of renewables and energy storage devices expands. Interstate transmission lines will increasingly dominate the securitization of energy supplies, with renewables becoming a regular target. To illustrate, a hacking group known as "Dragonfly" infected a number of renewable energy companies in Europe in 2013, compromising their industrial control systems. In a separate case, a sophisticated malware attack left 225,000 customers in Ukraine in the dark in 2015, taking it months to recover from the attack.[168]

Finally, geopolitical imperatives are also driving NATO's transformation, forcing its member militaries to adapt to the post-Cold War realities of the multi-centric world featuring transactional coalitions and hybrid threats.[169] The Atlantic Alliance is tasked with guaranteeing the security of its members, but in the 21st century the threats to NATO countries are more mutable and opponents more difficult to discern.[170] As this mission gradually encompasses broader security considerations, NATO will require specific policy initiatives and a broader reevaluation of its role in the energy, economic, and environmental security of its members. To revamp NATO's role would, therefore, necessitate a revision of material approaches and strategies. This will especially concern the alternative energy megatrend, which is expected to propel geopolitical developments in ways that will make or break NATO as a successful 21st century alliance.

Enhancing NATO members' operational capabilities is a timely and necessary undertaking in view of the requirements that could be placed on the alliance in the event of an alternative energy-related conflict. Such confrontations could run along the lines of past energy conflicts, such as the OPEC crisis of 1973, albeit with their distinct characteristics.

The institutional and structural problems within NATO, however, are bound to constrain its ability to address the geopolitical challenges effectively. A lack of cohesion between NATO members' internal security considerations, politically diverging views on global environmental priorities, grievances regarding member country contributions, and the overall goals of the alliance as well as the existing military technology gap within NATO[171] are impeding the defense transformation of the Alliance. The megatrend's drivers and underlying technologies could therefore become an element of a new framework for the alliance's revitalization and transformation.

(5) China: leading with a long-term vision.

The development of renewable energy applications by the military is not limited to the United States and other NATO members. China has become a significant force in this field as well as a robust competitor. It, too, demonstrated a special awareness of the significance of energy of all sources for military applications and, unlike individual NATO allies (other than the U.S.), is actively advancing and pursuing the development and integration of alternative energy developments.

The broadening of security considerations, which is propelling the global defense transformation, is a key aspect of national security considerations in China, and, to a larger extent, in Asia in general. China's substantial economic growth over the last few decades has translated into increased national defense capabilities and stronger imperatives to protect its internal and external position as well as stability, which appear to be correlated with China's continuing economic performance. China is modifying and further transforming the world order in accordance with its understanding and aspirations.

China's defense transformation incorporates a new understanding by the political elites of the significance of defense in the country's long-term strategy. China's willingness to adapt to the transformation is also a reflection of the need to enhance the state's ability to deal with potential internal and external threats to stability for China and the parts of Eurasia that China considers critical to its development.[172]

China's heavy dependence on foreign energy supplies to power its soon-to-be world's largest economy as well as its reliance on the security of the sea lanes for trade underscores its penchant for the development and integration of renewables as part of the defense transformation. It has taken full advantage of the booming renewable energy industry at home in recent years to enact energy efficiency and renewable policies for its armed forces.[173] China is poised, if it is not already, to become the world's leading producer and user of alternative energy technologies.

China has also begun to transition to a new level of economic production focused on technology and innovation. This transition holds the potential to accelerate the development of alternative energy industries and their integration into the country's armed forces, presenting challenges and opportunities for China's allies and adversaries. Initiatives such as China's Strategic Energy Action Plan (SEAP) (2014–2020) and the 13th Five-Year Plan (FYP) for economic and social development (2016–2020) set ambitious targets for expanding renewable generation and reducing GHGs. The 14th FYP (2021-2025) is expected to expand on China's sustainable development goals and increase targets for renewable technologies.[174]

Beyond energy security objectives, China is actively pursuing renewables technologies associated with directed-energy weapons development.[175] China has a history of innovations—from paper to gunpowder—that have modern applications, and renewables may prove to be one more technological development that China makes its own, this time for power projection capabilities and energy security given the country's exposure to supply and trade risks.

Coupled with the country's amassed economic clout, China's substantial R&D investments could yet translate into various breakthroughs, including in the field of alternative energy. However, China is still far from matching the U.S.' capabilities in scientific, technological, R&D, and military applications of alternative energy technologies. Its growing military has yet to undergo a conventional modernization, let alone one featuring or resting predominantly on high-tech systems or alternative energy sources and technologies.

(6) Uneven developments in the rest of the world: sufficient momentum yet to be gained.

Although countries other than the United States have undertaken steps to integrate alternative energy use in their defense sectors, the technologies they integrate are predominantly focused on experimental and proof of concept-level deployments. And while the defense communities of several countries have acknowledged the importance of energy security, they have done little to integrate alternative energy developments into the full range of defense solutions. Still, the private sectors in these countries can serve as a powerful driver for the development and integration of alternative energy technologies by their militaries. Just as military technology requirements can be, and often are, the catalyst for commercial integration of technologies, the private sector can, too, boost the development and integration of renewables by the militaries.

Renewables integration is expected to impact military tactics and doctrines across the globe. For example, anticipated shifts in the field of transportation due to renewables integration will impact the militaries in a profound way. For instance, China, India, France, Britain, and Norway all seek to ban the production and sale of vehicles powered by fossil fuels between 2030 and 2050.[176] This means renewable technology shifts may swing from the commercial to the defense sectors.

While European Union defense establishments have yet to fully develop a unified approach to alternative energy, some countries are making specific advances in select areas. The militaries of Denmark and France, for example, lead the way in integrating alternative energy applications to enhance energy efficiency and combat the effects of global warming. To that end, they are employing both country-specific defense initiatives and a wider agenda.[177] Denmark focuses on energy optimization of buildings, use of clean energy in operations, and energy conversion, as well as transformation of practices and approaches toward more "climate-appropriate and energy-appropriate behavior."[178] France has undertaken R&D initiatives for renewable energy applications, such as flexible camouflaged solar cells, as well as the "Advansea concept ship" (ADVanced All-electric Networked ship for SEA dominance).[179] Other initiatives include the joint efforts of the French naval defense conglomerate DNCS and the Irish company OpenHydro to develop tidal power generation technological capabilities.

The UK Ministry of Defence pursues alternative energy developments as a source of new capabilities and as a way to adapt to the impact of climate change. Its 2009 Defence Technology Plan[180] and the Strategic Defence and Security Review[181] are targeting new energy security approaches, having spurred innovative developments to reduce the military's energy costs. The ministry has also undertaken extensive projects concerning directed energy weapons, energy storage, and energy systems being pursued on a public-private partnership basis.[182]

Aside from these few cases, the integration of renewables by the defense sectors of European nations has been rather limited. This demonstrates the difficulty of achieving common policies across the relatively unrelated segments of society. If any "guidance" or models to emulate come out of the EU or NATO, they will likely be only loosely related to military imperatives.[183]

A limited interoperability and lack of common policies have hindered the integration of alternative energy developments within European militaries, despite some individual successes.

There is absolutely no uniformity across NATO or EU militaries for energy efficiency and alternative energy policy. Nor is there any agreement about the strategic implications of alternative energy, the ongoing international struggle for resources, or possible conflicts stemming from climate change, except in the broadest, vaguest, and thus "un-actionable" terms. Meanwhile, austerity measures by European nations are squeezing out potential defense sector investments in alternative energy technologies while reducing defense spending across the board.

In the rest of the world, militaries seeking to maintain their edge have demonstrated only a general focus on renewables integration, a process which is transpiring at uneven pace and reflecting divergent strategic objectives and interests of each concerned nation.

A leader in overall technological development—especially in the field of military technology—Israel employs solar-based battery chargers for use in operational environments and has developed new approaches to providing energy to military bases. The Israeli Air Force launched its biggest alternative energy project, the solar power station in the Ramon Air Force base, in early 2017 to be followed with two new solar power stations in 2018.[184] In addition, it is testing new technologies for powering drones and other UAV from the solar energy. The interaction between the Israeli defense and civil sector is highly intensive in the area of renewables, as energy security and independence are closely tied to the general security of the state.

Rich in shale oil, natural gas, uranium, hydro-resources, and grain-based fuel production capacity, Canada is among the world's largest energy producers. Like its NATO allies, the U.S. and the UK, Canada has independently moved toward making its armed forces less reliant on fossil fuels. Unlike other major NATO members, however, Canada's Department of National Defense and the Canadian Armed Forces only recently developed a comprehensive "Defense Energy and Environment Strategy,"[185] which considers alternative energy-powered installations and options such as using blends of synthetic fuels for the military fleet. Regardless, the country is ideally placed to exploit its massive hydro-resources and is already testing renewable and energy-efficiency techniques in the wind, solar, and biofuel sectors for their wider application in the military. With heavy cross-border energy flows, Canada also keeps a close watch on how its neighbor to the south, the

United States, is approaching the development and integration of alternative energy sources and technologies.

6. The uneasy question of renewables' viability: do they meet defense requirements?

The extent of renewables integration in military operations, procedures, and strategies hinges on their ability to boost military effectiveness, efficiency, and warfighting capacity while transitioning armed forces to an environmentally sustainable energy use. The process of integrating renewables is, however, subject to the premise that power projection capabilities should not be sacrificed for efficiency improvements. According to this premise, military adoption of renewable energy technologies is contingent on addressing outstanding vulnerabilities that could impair the military's ability to perform its core functions.

(1) Core impediments: operational, security, and infrastructure.

Just as with fossil fuels, the defense sectors and the militaries will face significant operational, security, and infrastructure challenges in integrating renewable sources and technologies, as this requires a major reorganization of resources, systems, practices, and regulations. Meanwhile, geopolitics will add its own complexity. Access to and a steady supply of critical materials for the manufacturing of alternative energy technologies will prove crucial, as renewables assume a growing share of the military's energy and warfighting infrastructure in the coming years.

The major technical operational impediment to renewable energy integration is energy storage.[186] A key component of a combatant's operational requirements, energy storage has been the subject of intensive focus by the military. Military vehicle operations conducted independent of an internal combustion power source as part of increasingly asymmetrical missions illustrate the challenge.

Another critical operational issue is equipment interference, which is most pertinent for wind turbines as they have a unique electromagnetic "signature" varying based on environmental conditions.[187] Wind turbines in proximity to military training, testing, and development facilities can adversely impact operations below 2000 feet altitude.[188]

For instance, wind turbines located close to the Comprehensive Test Ban Treaty monitoring sites can adversely impact their functions by increasing ambient seismic noise levels.[189] Measures to mitigate this problem are available, but they have their drawbacks, explaining the opposition of the British and German militaries to the installation of wind towers close to the military infrastructure. Due to the incomplete testing of electronic emission and the magnetic effects of alternative energy technologies, it is not yet clear whether, or to what extent, equipment interference issues will impede renewables defense integration.

Infrastructure vulnerabilities as well as equipment performance and compatibility issues present their own set of challenges. Expanding the use of renewables suggests an increased need to protect the renewables infrastructure from attacks, accidents, and natural disasters. Defense establishments are, therefore, likely to focus on the vulnerability of the new infrastructure.[190]

Sub-stations and transformers are particularly vulnerable to attacks because they are usually unmanned, in remote locations, and have few physical barriers. The larger sites would likely employ force protection measures. However, the consequences of their compromise would be comparatively greater. Still, the global impact of terrorist attacks on energy transmission infrastructure has thus far been relatively limited because of the security measures that were incorporated when such infrastructure was built. But it is yet to be established what level of redundancy, security, and safety elements must be added to the renewable energy infrastructure to mitigate its soft-target status. Protection against cyberattacks on computerized energy networks, for instance, will be crucial given the frequency and evolution of cyber operations targeting energy infrastructure, and so will the disaster relief and crisis management operations in the aftermath of severe climatic events or natural disasters.

The issue of access to and the steady supply of critical and rare earth materials needed for the manufacturing of alternative energies will add its own complication. Countries with lithium, indium, cobalt, and tellurium resources are emerging as critical suppliers of renewable resources and may abuse their position by manipulating production and export of these commodities or threatening to end them. The role of militaries to ensure access to energy resources will, thus, not evaporate with the anticipated reduction in reliance on traditional energy sources and supplies.

It is possible, and highly desired, that efforts to address the above impediments and vulnerabilities lead to practical solutions that sustain the effectiveness and efficiency of military operations. New applications of renewable technologies may be developed that are tied to securitization efforts—both core defense considerations and broader security, such as energy or environmental. There is indeed a marked focus on sources and technologies that improve energy and broader security. Such technologies include greener alternative fuels and new aerospace designs that consider fuel efficiency as a key performance parameter.

(2) Institutional inertia: the disconnect between operations and strategy and institutional impediments.

In any transformative process, the inertia of past practices is likely to reduce benefits and could hinder the development of a new trend or implementation of a new mission. This is true of the defense transformation, as institutional impediments could have a negative impact on the integration and anticipated expansion of alternative energy technologies and practices. While there are positive signs of changes in perception in the wider defense community, a paradigmatic thought shift has yet to occur whereby "the people who run the...military have to be futurists, whether they want to be or not."[191]

Resistance to the deployment of alternative energy solutions stems from the divergence between tactical and strategic imperatives, which has resulted from the broadening of the defense mandate. New tools and approaches have yet to permeate the operational considerations of the defense establishments. The disparity between priorities and capabilities of the military to deploy renewables on a wide scale indicates that the learning curve necessary for such integration may be insurmountable at current levels of technological progress and preparedness.[192] It would necessitate a multidimensional and flexible approach based on new educational systems, training constructs, and a continual absorption of new technologies.

Integration would require a balance between logistical support, manpower, and supplies, as well as a consideration of a host of other issues critical for defense missions: enhancing operational ability; reducing unnecessary force protection vulnerabilities while protecting logistics lines; reducing significant logistical weight from handling and hauling fuel; decreasing vulnerability to energy supply disruptions; and maintaining the strategic importance of energy security within the relevant area of operation.

The expanding securitization agenda, meanwhile, will pose a set of additional obstacles as they are related to new practices of stewardship, civilian integration, and environmental protection, among other security considerations. For example, the legal, technological, social, and environmental contexts created by the introduction of alternative energy technologies will complicate significantly the conflict resolution, posing major challenges for the defense establishment.[193] The resulting plethora of regulations and norms, as well as potentially new treaties on the global or regional scale, may not accelerate but stifle the development of renewables applications or impede their unrestrained development and integration.

(3) The technological integration impediments.

The modern militaries increasingly rely on various types of technology to maintain operational energy security, to ensure warfighting capabilities, and to conduct missions in challenging environments. Units and soldiers are becoming hi-tech hubs of command, control, and operations, capable of conducting autonomous and coordinated missions. This trend represents a new level of operational intensity, which increases the complexity of combat operations even if it provides seemingly viable solutions for diverse missions. However, such complexity may undermine the warfighting effectiveness if methodologies and practices are not duly adapted to harness the advantages offered by technologies and mitigate their vulnerabilities.

Adapting new technologies has immediate and long-term effects on operational effectiveness and efficiency, especially for alliances since allies exhibit different levels of technological development and capabilities. There is a trade-off between new capabilities and the advantages of commonality, and adapting common technologies to different use would have to ensure flexibility in approaches and design options. Defense applications of renewables, for instance, can benefit from openness toward utilizing specialized equipment, as well as hybridization and the introduction of modular technologies that can improve operational flexibility.[194]

Thus, technological interoperability and compatibility have been persistent concerns for NATO, which comprises a diverse set of nations possessing different defense capabilities and exhibiting varying levels of technological development.[195] When multinational forces are operating together, effectiveness and efficiency can swiftly deteriorate when one unit's equipment cannot work in conjunction with another's, or when incompatibility results in impaired mission success or even blue-on-blue casualties. NATO is therefore pursuing an extensive integration and standardization of equipment and systems across the militaries of its member states.

The process of alternative energy defense integration will thus entail difficult long-term and immediate trade-offs,[196] likely causing operational and strategic frictions, especially in alliance and coalition operations where resource interoperability has been a long-standing issue. As a result, the militaries will have to rely on the use of both legacy fossil fuel and alternative energy systems for quite a long time despite the anticipated defense integration of renewables.

(4) The cost of alternative energy defense integration: foreseeable short-term burdens and potential long-term advantages.

A major drawback to the integration of alternative energy solutions in defense strategies is the prohibitively high cost of achieving the impact that fossil fuels can deliver with lesser short-term costs. At the same time, militaries can be and are effective promoters of alternative energy applications because they have more political room for generating financial resources to spearhead the alternative energy development and integration. The intrinsic economic impediments to renewable technologies' mass deployment are discussed more extensively in Chapter 4 of Part 3. But suffice it to say that defense establishments are unable to justify increasing energy costs in the medium term without the promise of significant efficiency improvements, especially because they face additional costs in human lives, training, and strategic placement.

A lack of incentives supporting the defense integration of alternative energy compounds the cost burden of militaries. This is despite some apparent advantages of the alternative energy technologies and their integration by the defense sectors. Select NATO member states, for instance, lack sufficient incentives (including programs leveraging savings from fuel use) to advance renewables integration. Uneven pace of defense investment growth within the alliance[197] also makes spending on new technologies a challenging proposition.

Finally, defense establishments and respective governments cannot but consider the opportunity costs for the military and the society of not pursuing or advancing the integration of renewables. These costs can be in the form of deficient defense capabilities, loss of human lives, and limited expansion of the overall technological base. Calculating such costs is difficult given the unknown and unmeasured impacts of renewables integration on military and non-military domains. However, austerity measures and considerations in select countries, including the United States, will put the opportunity costs into focus of both national agendas and defense planning.

III. Environmental security revisited—the alternative energy megatrend redefining the securitization of the global habitat.

What is the environmental security significance of the alternative energy megatrend? Prompted by growing societal pressure to address threats to the global habitat, environmental security has achieved a new level of significance within national security agendas. A range of environmental security policies and regulations has emerged worldwide, which in turn is propelling the development of alternative energy. At the same time, national and regional policy and regulatory measures appear to be converging toward global governance frameworks.

Driven by both technological developments and societal expectations, the megatrend promises a range of environmental security benefits—alleviating threatening levels of carbon dioxide emissions, reducing damaging energy by-products, and offering new approaches to alleviate health and environmental side effects of economic activity. The following discussion also sheds light on how societal notions and beliefs propel the megatrend beyond the technological reality.

The alternative energy megatrend contributes to the emergence of "environmental geopolitics" as an increasingly important aspect of international relations. The "greening" of geopolitics means taking the logic of a state-centric world system onto a worldwide and society-oriented level.

1. The modern redefinition of environmental security: the emergence of actionable environmental policies promised by alternative energy.

Tracing the megatrend's future trajectory shows that the modern environmental security vision is a hybrid one—a view of nature through the perspective of modern technologies. The pursuit of conscientious use of resources, of a humanity at one with nature, and cohabitation rather than exploitation do not reflect a demand for an actual return to how things were in the past. Rather, it is a modern vision of how nature and humanity should interact in a way that does not impinge on standards of living, levels of consumption, and prosperity.

The pursuit of continuous betterment of human existence is thus intertwined with an acceptance that society's adverse effect on its environment must be addressed sooner rather than later.[198] This has resulted in a growing determination by states, non-state actors, and civil society to incorporate the mitigation of risks to the welfare of humanity into environmental security approaches, which is reinforced by an intensifying public support that expects "green" efforts to yield benefits beyond a reduction in carbon emissions.

The risks of degradation of the habitat are becoming closely interlinked with other vital interests for state and non-state actors, and are encroaching on relations between them, creating rivalries, tensions, and even conflict. Environmental threats thus pose a challenge to policymakers "as an externality to the international system, rather than an internal variable which can be addressed in terms of familiar political structures and their supporting social values."[199]

In the early 21st century, alternative energy developments have emerged as a tangible solution that enables state and non-state actors to address the most pressing environmental challenges, including climate change, ecosystem degradation. and scarcity of essential resources. As a new piece in the policy toolkit, alternative energy developments are providing new venues for influencing geopolitical, environmental, and other global security considerations. They have achieved widespread acceptance, shaping the definition and, importantly, the practice of environmental security itself.

(1) Environmental security: broadening the concept of securitizing the global habitat and concomitant political considerations.

From efforts to alter the natural habitat to the search for a better living space, environmental security has shaped human history since ancient times.[200] Environmental disasters, such as drought and famine, which often forced great migrations in the past, continue to take a heavy toll on societies worldwide. The devastating effects of the El Niño weather pattern, Hurricane Katrina in the United States, the earthquakes in Haiti, Chile, and Japan, and the typhoon in the Philippines are phenomena—in some cases amplified by climate change—that even developed countries have trouble coping with, let alone preventing.

As environmental threats strike irrespective of national boundaries, they are a subject of global societal concern, making environmental security a highly politicized issue not only within but also across nations.[201] However, policies designed to address threats to the environment have historically been limited in scope and results. They have predominantly been focused on preventing and rectifying the effects of environmental disasters as well as addressing environmental pollution, waste, and endangered species. Differing interests amongst state actors' goals in addressing environmental security issues have generated various cross-border approaches that have not yielded concrete advances. The deficit of viable policy actions to a certain extent is due to states obstinately distinguishing environmental security from explicit threats to national interests. Environmental threats have often proven too diffuse, their causes too difficult to determine, and their effects too hard to measure in order to be considered objects of securitization, which entails identifying, defining, and developing appropriate new policy responses to address them.

154

Although environmental security's place in policy agendas is yet to be firmly established, its importance and relevance for national security have been growing over the last decades as the impacts of environmental threats have become more tangible. It has already demonstrated a growing scope and an ability to influence broader swathes of policymaking by serving as a policy tool rather than just as a policy concept. The concept of the "global commons," which originally emerged in a military context, has been an important factor behind the advance of environmental security as a policy component in the contemporary agendas of state and non-state actors.[202] The concept gained prominence in the 1960s and is based on the idea that sovereign control over shared goods such as water, air, and other natural resources was unsustainable, prompting new perspectives on environmental security, such as the popular limits-to-growth thesis. The thesis argues that economic growth and industrialization in developing countries must be checked in order to avoid exceeding Earth's life-sustaining capacity. In response, international action on population control began in the latter half of the 20th century. As early as 1973, John K. Galbraith warned that damage to the environment was "a clear and present danger," noting "the explosion of concern over the environment" and calling for legislation to set parameters for "the permissible damage of consumption and production to the environment."[203] Ironically, the "clear and present" designation provides states the opportunity to securitize environmental issues and act unilaterally in order to address the perceived direct impact of environmental threats.

The emerging environmental security considerations in the second half of the 20th century continued to focus on environmental degradation as a cause for societal misery that could potentially provoke conflict between actors, despite the lack of a specific "instigator" or "enemy." Thus, the concept of environmental security required a broadening of the strategic considerations of importance to the state, such as socio-political autonomy, physical survival of the state and population, and a targeted level of economic wellbeing.

The concept and policy of environmental security does have a certain presence in national security considerations in instances where threats to the human habitat and the resources it provides may lead to violent conflict or disputes between and within states. Examples of clashes between nations over resources such as water go as far back as the campaigns of Alexander the Great in Persia between 355 and 323 BC[204] or even, as recent findings suggest, the Neolithic massacres in Talheim (Germany) and Asparn and Schletz (Austria) caused by significant increases in populations followed by adverse climatic conditions and resource stress.[205] More recent conflicts driven at least partially by the struggle for resources are numerous, including those in Angola, Congo, Indonesia, Liberia, Sierra Leone, Somalia, Senegal, and Sudan.[206] While such conflicts are more likely to be domestic rather than international, intra-state violence can weaken governments and regional security, which in turn increases the potential for inter-state clashes. It is noted that the war in Syria—and the refugee crisis associated with it—among other causes "can be linked to a prolonged period of drought in the country that drove the rural poor into the cities only to find their future limited by authoritarian rule and inaction."[207] Because a combination of complex factors not directly related to environmental security is usually the cause of such conflicts, including ethnic, economic, and class factors, the cause-effect relationship between environmental security and violent conflict is not clear cut and therefore undermines policymaking by states to prevent related risks.

Despite its rising significance, the concept of environmental security almost always remains separate from the traditional national security debate.[208] That said, threats to the environment are increasingly being identified as a systemic global risk, which has until now defied the traditional security frameworks of causality and liability. This has prompted observations that "energy security" trumps "environmental security" as far as government policies are concerned.[209] It is at this juncture that alternative energy enters the environmental security debate as a viable tool of securitizing the habitat, given its benefits in addressing the evolving environmental security challenges.

(2) Alternative energy redefining the policy toolkit: providing practical means for mitigating environmental threats.

The alternative energy megatrend is providing a mechanism for the redefinition of environmental security, offering actors a practical means of addressing environmental security threats. It is increasingly integrated into broader security policies to address issues outside the scope of environmental security. Due to the advent of modern alternative energy technologies, environmental damage, such as climate change, becomes subject to viable and proactive policy mechanisms.

The transformational effect of the alternative energy megatrend on environmental security is gaining shape through gradual acceptance and continued technological advances in the field. This acceptance is bridging the securitization gap between threats that are still difficult to identify and policy responses that would effectively address them. As a multi-dimensional phenomenon, the alternative energy megatrend could provide solutions to deal with multi-dimensional challenges that are often hard to fathom. From a national security perspective, alternative energy developments could play a significant role in alleviating a number of formidable environmental security challenges: habitat degradation; deforestation; environmental refugees; food insecurity; loss of biodiversity; water scarcity and resource depletion; the propensity for more natural disasters; and the global conflicts that could result from environmental distress. Achieving such a mitigation capacity requires formulating multilateral environmental security arrangements that alleviate environmental degradation while not damaging the economy or diminishing living standards.

Actors are increasingly incorporating alternative energy solutions into emergency measures, at times going outside established political processes. Considerations about most cost-effective and least damaging ways of mitigating climate change are at the heart of this expanding policy practice.[210] Alternative energy points to the potential for technological solutions to replace political solutions, creating a direct relationship between technology and the environment.[211] In essence, the megatrend's promise transforms environmental security from an aspiration and a statement of future intent into an actionable strategy that could target threats that previously had no viable solutions. In this manner, the progression of the alternative energy megatrend is becoming a matter of governance.

Besides offering solutions to environmental issues, renewable technologies also offer new methods of using the global habitat for humanity's needs without professedly exploiting or harming it. Man's interaction with nature has resulted in the emergence of human-defined ecologies, where technologies coexist with nature. However, natural resources are no longer seen as existing independently of human activity. Alternative energy technologies provide for minimal disruptive impact on nature due to their renewability and capacity to blend with existing environments without unduly changing them.

The integration of alternative energy developments into environmental, economic, and other broader security approaches is associated with their perceived link with human welfare, health, and prosperity. From the pursuit of a healthy lifestyle to the imperative of so-called "green living," environmental security issues are becoming part of everyday life, embedded in ideology and various belief systems shaping notions of development, welfare, and security. Disparate groups—from conservation clubs and Europe's Green parties to corporate CEOs and political leaders in the developing and developed world —have today converged to become a modern, global, environmentally conscious movement embracing the importance of sustainable and effective environmental policies. According to a recent survey, the issues of climate change and environmental damage are positioned rather high on CEO agendas: 50% of CEOs express concern over these threats to their organizations' growth prospects.[212] Further, national and international programs supporting investment in "green" infrastructure are becoming more commonplace.[213] Roof gardens in Paris or bike sharing programs in New York City and London may not come as a surprise. However, an increasing number of cities in developing countries, such as Belo Horizonte in Brazil, Bogota in Colombia, and Accra in Ghana, have instituted wide-ranging "green" city initiatives to manage growing urban populations, waste disposal, and water management.

The intensified push for governmental measures on the back of growing public support has led to the allocation of more assets and resources towards broader environmental and security concerns. However, the growing scope of state measures are still to be fully supported with constructive global coordination. Narrow political considerations continue to restrict the scope of inter-state cooperation on environmental security, despite the trans-national effects and potency of environmental security threats. A large-scale disaster could prompt more focused actions that circumvent the limitations imposed by sovereign interests, and induce private actors to make individual sacrifices to promote overall human security. There are advantages to deepening cooperation on pre-emptive environmental security measures as well, impelling actors to pursue more active coordination.

Alternative energy developments reinforce the perceptions by environmentalists that the division of the international system into distinct geographic areas of sovereignty is an impediment to addressing environmental challenges. Some environmental security advocates contend that alternative energy holds the universal solution to environmental threats. Thus, the alternative energy megatrend plays a key role in deploying a comprehensive approach toward preventing extensive environmental damage to territorial integrity, economic growth, international stability, and individual and communal welfare. The concept of environmental security is therefore poised for a redefinition and transformation into "human habitat security," and the megatrend is expected to play an increasingly important role in this process.

(3) The effect of societal values on environmental security: the megatrend's impact on the discourse.

The alternative energy megatrend is both a technological and a social phenomenon, perceived as the convergence of societal notions, ideas, and practices and reflecting the increasing ability of society to impose its will on security agendas, particularly on environmental security. The megatrend's role in environmental security reinforces the impact that social constructs have on policymaking. Societal constructs and visions have led to an imperative to pursue renewables development that is not commensurate with either the level of viability of alternative energy technologies or with the current reality of world energy reserves. The megatrend's impact to a large extent is rooted in its ability to produce symbols of the promise that renewables hold for society. These symbols are self-reinforcing as they in turn reaffirm the societal understanding of the alternative energy megatrend. The megatrend has made substantial inroads into the societal subconscious through its saturation of the public discourse. Whereas years ago the terms "green" and "environmental" may have been equated with marginal stakeholders, today "green" is part of the media's common parlance and, therefore, that of politicians.

The modern interpolation of the megatrend in societal values appears to be at odds with past convictions "that men will continue to withdraw from nature in order to create an environment that will suit them better."[214] The reshaping of societal notions creates an ideological glue that serves as a transmission mechanism through which the mutual influence of the megatrend's drivers is exerted and from which its attributes are derived. The megatrend exemplifies the divergence between "objective reality" and "socially constructed reality." It is the expectation of what renewables can achieve and the vision of a future where they are genuinely all-pervasive that determine how humanity approaches renewables. This socially constructed reality helps propel the alternative energy megatrend. Indeed, the development of alternative energy is not a reflection of technology, but a "complex web of social interactions and patterns."[215]

The renewables megatrend has entered the macro-structures of morality, where on a general level it is integrated into the institutional domains of society—economy, politics, law, and even religion. As a quasi-ideology, it affects how these institutional domains evolve—for example by transposing environmental concerns onto economic considerations, or social responsibilities onto energy demand. The quasi-ideological bridging of disparate views and ideas, which is emerging in line with the alternative energy megatrend, leads to a level of widespread conformity through the unified understanding of intrinsic societal norms and values.[216]

Irrespective of the variety of ideological backdrops of alternative energy developments, they generate discourses that have several consistent and unifying themes—those of shared benefits that make renewables, in a sense, a "political conception itself as the focus of an overlapping consensus."[217] Realization of the megatrend results from discourse that both sustains the coherence of social order and directs its developments. Through this process of discourse, the imagery of alternative energy has interpolated itself into the ideas that underpin environmental security, politics, economics, international relations, and conflict. By shaping social orders and related developments, the vision of alternative energy developments is forming the framework for its evolution, and will contribute to the coalescence of a new reality for renewables.

2. Environmental policies: an emerging cross-border renewable energy regulatory framework.

The inclusion of alternative energy within environmental security strategies and state policies targets not just the development of solutions to environmental threats, but also broader economic, energy, and technological goals. As these policies evolve, diverse patterns emerge that sometimes work at cross-purposes, but whose common aims are reducing the impact of environmental security threats. These shared policy objectives have resulted in mechanisms such as energy price setting, renewable portfolio standards, fixed feed-in tariffs, investment subsidies, and quota systems.

With the integration of alternative energy developments into these policies and frameworks, the momentum behind the megatrend continues to build, leading to unprecedented levels of ambition and commitment. Securitization of the environment and securitization of alternative energy development feed upon one another, presenting a mutually reinforcing evolution of two concepts and related practices.

(1) Conventional alternative energy-related environmental policies: quotas, subsidies, fixed pricing, and emission restrictions.

Through the emerging regulatory framework, the megatrend leaves its imprint on virtually all aspects of society as, in the words of Gareth Porter, "environmental security is concerned with any threat to the wellbeing of societies and their population from an external force that can be influenced by public policies."[218] Almost every country has specific policies aimed at addressing environmental security risks.[219] A confluence of local, regional, and international environmental policies and grand strategies has therefore emerged. However, as noted in preceding pages, despite the plethora of policies, embedding environmental security into national security policies and practices, let alone global ones, remains problematic. Effective policymaking is challenged by the fact that environmental threats have an extended time horizon that often takes them outside election cycles and the span of attention of policymakers.

The alternative energy megatrend's impact on policymaking and politics stems to a large extent from the influence of public opinion, which is calling for environmental protection in general and the use of renewables in particular. The build-up of greenhouse gases in the atmosphere is considered a critical cause of the rise in global temperatures beyond natural climate drivers, such as variations in solar radiation, deviations in Earth's orbit, tectonic plate movement, and continental drift.[220] Thomas Friedman has reiterated what appears to be a global societal consensus: "There is still much we don't know about how climate change will unfold, but it is no hoax."[221] Thus, according to Prof. Shirley Tilghman, "it's extraordinarily important that we push the frontiers of knowledge."[222] As policies are influenced largely through message delivery, the media—and increasingly, social media—serves as the intermediary between society and policymakers. The impact of having the media at the intersection of societal influence on politics has paradoxically led to the disassociation of much of society from responsibility over environmental issues, placing it squarely on the shoulders of governments. Moreover, many governments acquiesce to or adopt policies recommended by NGOs, meaning that the quasi-ideological nature of alternative energy is empowering non-state actors to play key roles in policymaking.[223] In fact, the establishment of environmental regulatory frameworks is currently driven more by the efforts of non-state actors than by states.

The range of government policies, measures, and targets that affect alternative energy development to date have been designed chiefly to target the most urgent environmental threat—climate change.[224] The number of countries that introduced some kind of policy stating and supporting goals in renewable energy development had grown from 55 in 2005 to 195 in 2015, when the legally binding Paris Climate Agreement was signed.[225] Under the agreement, which aims to limit global warming to below 2 degrees Celsius, a majority of countries pledged themselves to scale up renewables and energy efficiency through their Nationally Determined Contributions.

In 2016, 117 NDCs were submitted, with 55 including concrete targets for increasing renewable energy, while 89 made reference to renewable energy more broadly.[226] The renewable policy targets are not always legally binding, and are sometimes revised. However, they may serve as a benchmark that can drive an increase in the share of renewable energy worldwide and, to a certain extent, inform the outlook for the future.

The global map of renewable energy policies reflects a wide variety of approaches and scopes. At the same time, they work in concert to contribute to a common environmental goal. Even if climate change is not the prime motivation behind measures such as alternative energy portfolio standards, renewables are considered capable of delivering significant greenhouse gas reductions.

While targets are an important tool, they alone do not guarantee their achievement. In this regard, governments have implemented a variety of policy mechanisms to further develop alternative energy. Regulated energy pricing systems,[227] investment subsidies,[228] fixed premium systems,[229] and renewable quota systems[230] are the mainstream government measures for supporting renewable energy development, with variations based on their specific targets.[231]

Though diverse, these policies assume continuous public involvement in the sector and rely predominantly on subsidies and restrictions. These policies, imposed either in a command-and-control or market-based form, can induce some amount of actual change since they compel corporations to address externalities presented by environmental degradation and climate change. There is no firm data, however, to support the view that this approach effectively encourages technological development in alternative energy or other sectors. It is therefore difficult to gauge the extent to which market participants will change their behavior in response to regulation and policies.[232]

Despite the perceived urgency, environmental policies are yet to fully incorporate the converging forces that drive the alternative energy megatrend. For example, many external costs—such as carbon pollution—are currently not factored into energy pricing, thus hindering competition, and slowing development of renewables. As the European Environment Agency's (EEA) Executive Director Hans Bruyninckx, put it, "[W]hile we have been successful in agreeing a wide range of policies to protect the environment, implementing these policies remains a challenge. We are making some progress towards the EU aim of creating a green economy, but we need to keep the pressure on up to 2020 and beyond."[233]

Integrating the megatrend into environmental security policies is subject to divergent priorities and sometimes conflicting interests. The policymaking and regulatory process regarding environmental security threats and alternative energy are generally hampered by a lack of clarity and political consensus. The very nature of environmental risks presents security policy with several major obstacles that complicate its implementation and sustainability:

- The threats from environmental risks are less distinct than those from other security concerns. They are not perceived as threats in their own right and their impact is difficult to ascertain.
- Addressing environmental security sometimes requires measures that significantly compromise economic interests.
- Policies to counter these threats often work only if globally coordinated and implemented.
- The costs of environmental regulation externalities are yet to be fully understood. Thus, environmental regulatory imbalances could produce an arbitrary selection of so-called technological winners and losers that could lead to dead-ends and other long-term problems.

A wide spectrum of environmental grand strategies, policies, and regulations is exerting pressure on the alternative energy megatrend's propagation, with diverse, sometimes contradictory, patterns emerging. Non-state actors' and international organizations' support for expanding renewables through environmental regulations endows the megatrend with enormous potential—though the current palette of legislative and regulatory measures can be a burden to renewables and hinder their progress in reducing environmental risks. For instance, regulations can be subject to politicization, particularly in times of austerity. The so-called "Solyndrification"[234] of the renewables debate in the United States is a case in point, where politics has damaged renewables policy momentum at the federal level. Also, while renewables present solutions that reduce uncertainty and enable state actors to maintain core national security principles, they can also become an impediment to specific security measures regarding other issues. For example, the expansion of biofuel mandates in 2007–2008 is calculated to have caused food price spikes that exacerbated food shortages in many countries. It is estimated that 20–40% of the price increases were the result of greater demand for cereals used to produce bioethanol.[235]

The aspirations and perceptions underlying the megatrend are creating societal and policy assumptions that could confine technological development and limit the full scope of environmental security preparedness and capabilities that the megatrend promises. At the same time, some level of regulation of alternative energy development is inevitably required, especially given untested outcomes and potentially negative effects of alternative energy on environmental security.

(2) The build-up toward an expansive environmental regulatory framework: the alternative energy megatrend propelled by the coalescing global governance architecture.

Countries' top-down considerations, such as energy independence and economic benefits, as well as NGO's and global civil society's bottom-up environmental targets, shape most state strategies propelling the alternative energy megatrend. Environmental security has assumed a prominent role in global society's consciousness in recent decades because of climate change's perceived acceleration due to human activity. Civil society's growing influence on policymaking to safeguard the environment leads to a greater emphasis on collective security considerations, i.e., the perception that environmental security policies should reflect the needs of the greater good rather than those of the individual or a single country. This collective environmental security perception is based on the belief that the range of alternative energy-related regulations (including redistributive programs) reflects common goals that crystallize, for example, in the environmental justice movement.[236] In this context, a consensus has started to form about the evolving role of geo-spatial factors in international green politics. Renewables advocates maintain that the emerging geopolitical order should be reshaped in response to the challenges posed by new environmental threats.[237] However, this view is often based on predicted future threats rather than on current circumstances and results in policies that fall short in matching the alternative energy megatrend's challenges and features.

The evolving system of international environmental regulation seeks international cooperation. This requires securing nearly universal participation and often entails bypassing the individual states' systems of checks and balances, as the EU-wide environmental policy framework has demonstrated. The banner of a single unified world and the need for collective action on environmental security challenges the traditional view of the sovereign state embodied in international law. The momentum toward a global environmental regulatory framework is reinforced when countries' environmental regulations coalesce into specific regional regimes. For example, regional organizations such as the EU and the Association of Southeast Asian Nations have developed common environmental security policies. The North American Free Trade Agreement (NAFTA), and its successor, the United States-Mexico-Canada Agreement (USMCA), also incorporate environmental security issues. For example, NAFTA (and USMCA) includes provisions requiring signatory countries to meet automobile emissions standards. These and other regional agreements and treaties, although not directly focused on the role of alternative energy in environmental security, provide openings for such integration at a later time.

The emerging global regulatory framework is based predominantly on a series of principles, protocols, guidelines, agreements, and treaties that are gradually becoming incorporated as elements of global governance regimes.[238] This framework is designed to govern international conduct through both soft law and legally binding instruments that are governed by international law. Since the United Nations Conference on Human Environment held in Stockholm in 1972, hundreds of multilateral environmental agreements have been signed and ratified. These agreements bind their parties to monitor and assess the status of the environment and report their efforts in order to address environmental threats. There are also environmental conventions, often with established juridical status, such as the EU's EUR-Lex or the Reporting Obligations Database of the European Environment Agency. The United Nations Environment Program is tasked with environmental security, and provides broad guidelines beyond observation and assessment.[239] Global directives and treaties targeting specific environmental targets, such as carbon emissions, have been exemplified by the Rio de Janeiro Earth Summit in 1992, the Kyoto Protocol of 1997 and the Paris Climate Agreement in 2015.[240]

The intensity of environmental concerns and broad public support for alternative energy technologies have given politicians more capital and provided greater leeway in adopting global strategies that were previously considered unacceptable. This makes difficult choices, such as increased taxation or reduced energy consumption, more palatable in the context of domestic politics and reinforces the momentum behind a global regulatory framework. It is the classic "lesser of two evils" choice. Such leeway carries major security implications, rendering the consequences of renewables promotion more difficult to foresee. Additionally, alternative energy resources are perceived to be nearly infinite, further changing the framework of limitations and policy choices available.

Figure 5. Public Support for Renewable Power in the United States, in Comparison with Fossil Fuels[241]

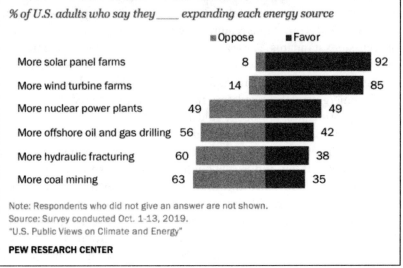

Most Americans favor expanding solar or wind power; half or fewer support expanding fossil fuels

% of U.S. adults who say they ____ expanding each energy source

▪ Oppose   ▪ Favor

	Oppose	Favor
More solar panel farms	8	92
More wind turbine farms	14	85
More nuclear power plants	49	49
More offshore oil and gas drilling	56	42
More hydraulic fracturing	60	38
More coal mining	63	35

Note: Respondents who did not give an answer are not shown.
Source: Survey conducted Oct. 1-13, 2019.
"U.S. Public Views on Climate and Energy"

PEW RESEARCH CENTER

The environmental regulatory frameworks that are emerging in different countries are gradually coalescing into a major force that propels the alternative energy megatrend. Domestic and international law is increasingly embodying a new environmental ethic that defines humankind's responsibility to protect the global environment.[242] The basis of, and momentum behind, global concern about the dangers of climate change could also provide the underpinnings for a globally enforced governance framework, through which environmental issues could have the capacity to transform global diplomacy and international relations. Such systems are already established to push forth potential solutions to environmental security threats, with alternative energy developments seen as the major tool. These mounting responsibilities will have diverse effects on international relations—one country's efforts to "free" itself from environmental threats may become another country's national security concern.

Furthermore, when considering the globalization of environmental regulation, it is important to not underestimate the extent to which the environment and alternative energy are politicized. The majority of measures that affect environmental security generally, and alternative energy development in particular, are dictated by decisions that political agents make on the basis of political convenience more often than on actual knowledge of the specific problem to be addressed. The solutions developed are not formulated with a clear goal and structural responses in mind, but rather stem from distinct agendas of agents. The result is a continuous division between "insiders" and "outsiders," who are for or against a specific industry, policy, or societal goal. This distinction in turn is globalized through the spill-over of political in-fighting and turf wars that feature alternative energy, but that rarely aim to achieve a material transformation of renewables development.

3. "Greening" geopolitics: the megatrend as a focal point for strengthening environmental security-related cooperation and competition.

The envisaged game-changing role of alternative energy resources in environmental security puts them squarely at the center of geopolitical calculations and carries broad implications for global security. The connection between geopolitics, geo-economics, and the environment implies that economic and environmental security considerations should be combined in strategy-making on a broad range of issues directly or indirectly impacting national security. Given the breadth and complexity of international relations agendas, alternative energy's projected role in environmental security could lead to both new avenues for cooperation and new points of contention.

The trajectory of the alternative energy megatrend's interpolation in environmental security discourses reflects the increasingly complex pressures exerted on policymakers in relation to environmental challenges and concerns. As "green" policies become mainstream at the national level, they reinforce the growing centrality of environmental security on a global level. This suggests that environmental security will become a more central geopolitical consideration, and its elements could provide state and non-state actors with new capabilities to exert power and influence political agendas.

(1) Cooperation and alliances for peace: factoring the alternative energy megatrend into global eco-realignments.

Since environmental risks are not limited to political boundaries, addressing them has inevitable significance for relations between geopolitical actors.[243] Alternative energy's role in environmental security is creating momentum toward broader societal support for global solutions that can enhance international cooperation while alleviating environment-related tension and international conflict. The paradigm shift that procures the critical mass for the transformation of alternative energy developments into a modern megatrend simultaneously reflects and is influenced by the transformation of "economic" man into "ecological" man.[244] By gradually elevating environmental security considerations onto a global plane, the megatrend and its projected benefits are being accepted as the "cure of choice" for the planet's environmental ills. As the leading approach for protecting the global environment from systemic disruption, the megatrend is also viewed as capable of preventing damage to territorial integrity, economic growth, and the welfare of individuals and communities. The underlying renewable energy technologies and their advances dominate public consciousness and create momentum toward specific objectives that could reduce the strain on diminishing resources and prevent conflict.

Modern geopolitics is gradually acquiring certain green overtones, incorporating the megatrend's anticipated role in addressing environmental threats. This "greening" of geopolitics is made even more pertinent by alternative energy's still unaddressed capacity to contribute to environmental risks, which can be a source of geopolitical realignments and conflicts. After all, renewables' emergence as a factor in relations among states and between state and non-state actors can be discerned in the rising tensions and preludes to potential conflicts. These can be over renewable resources themselves, the natural resources needed to develop renewables technologies, and the depletion of essential resources stemming from alternative energy development. At the same time, new areas of cooperation are spawned,[245] as the alternative energy megatrend prompts the creation of new peace alliances.

Environmental security has made national borders more porous, blurred the boundaries between foreign and domestic political issues, and pressured state actors to turn over some sovereignty to newly emerging inter- or quasi-governmental organizations. It has also drawn non-state actors, such as environmental NGOs, and international organizations, such as the United Nations and the World Bank Group, into evolving 21st century environmental geopolitical dynamics.[246] These actors seek to shape global regulatory agendas toward specific visions of environmental security through operational approaches, policy recommendations, and environmental governance regimes. Environmental geopolitics contains many perspectives, some of which are hegemonic, others marginalized by political powers. Through the prism of certain actors' perspective, environmental considerations are utilized as a tool for imposing influence of some members of the global community onto others. In any case, alternative energy development adds a whole new dimension to environmental security and geopolitics, both from the perspective of solutions that it could produce and from the standpoint of the inherent risks it can generate.

Environmental geopolitics sometimes goes beyond the high politics practiced by agents of statecraft, encompassing views of outside groups. As a result, state and non-state agents are increasingly implicated in each other's environmental practices. This interplay creates geopolitical environmental discourses that in turn influence geopolitical environmental practices. Likewise, the order may sometimes be reversed, with established practices generating their own geopolitical discourses. Environmental concerns and ecology have thus become a matter of public management with its own procedures and enforcement.

Pursuing solutions to environmental threats has led to novel and more cooperative approaches in diplomacy and international relations specifically reflecting "green" aspirations. In fact, the importance of environmental security in societal discourse has strengthened society's role in assessing the conduct of state actors. In essence, as Noel Castree asserts, "[A]lthough we do not live in a new 'environmental geopolitical order,' we arguably do live in a world where 'environmental geopolitics' is very much part of the larger interstate order that is slowly solidifying."[247] The trans-national nature of renewables development is influencing foreign policy by creating systems of collective management to regulate domestic resource use, and the externalities this usage poses on the "global commons." Meanwhile, the protection of the natural habitat has been transformed into an imperative, prompting a distinctive norm of environmental responsibility on a global scale, featuring alternative energy as a crucial factor in the struggle against environmental degradation.

State actors, with the participation of non-state actors, are emphasizing cooperation to ensure environmental security, and developing security frameworks that reshape the strategic environment and incentivize post-Westphalian forms of cooperative governance. The unprecedented scale and potency of environmental security challenges underscore the growing level of ecological interdependence that defines human interaction and raises the importance of cooperative environmental security actions. Even when environmental concerns arise in specific regions or countries—deforestation in Indonesia and the Amazon, water shortages in Asia, and food shortages in Africa—they can induce localized instability which prompts other actors to consider related impacts on global security. The drive for cooperation to bolster environmental security has led to calls for establishing prevention and dialogue mechanisms, which ensure that disputes generated by environmental stress never spiral into violent conflict within or between states.

And yet, the widespread belief that climate change, if left unaddressed, will have considerable global security implications applies a consistent level of pressure on policymakers,[248] prompted by the notion that "climate policy... equals security and peace politics."[249] Some have envisaged, for example, a "grand bargain" between energy producers and consumers that involves, according to former World Bank President Robert Zoellick, "sharing plans for expanding supplies, including options other than oil and gas; improving efficiency and lessening demand; assisting with energy for the poor; and considering how these policies relate to carbon production and climate change policies."[250] In effect, alternative energy addresses elements of both energy rebalancing and environmental security concerns, representing a practical solution in combating climate change. As former U.S. Vice President Al Gore pointed out, alternative energy can serve a dual purpose, in that "...the bold steps that are needed to solve the climate crisis are exactly the same steps that ought to be taken in order to solve the economic crisis and the energy security crisis."[251]

Cooperative mechanisms, however, do not display an exemplary track record. To date, international organizations such as the UN have yet to demonstrate an effective integration of environmental and natural resource-related considerations into their interventions and peace-building missions. The attainment of greater environmental security through the use of renewables would be the product of an extensive process of education, training, informational exchanges, capacity building, and regulatory mechanisms involving a plethora of actors. However, the megatrend's projected outcomes can promote cooperation by introducing new dimensions into the sustainability plans of policymakers worldwide.

The megatrend's environmental security role offers new options for collaborative approaches to alleviating poverty and fostering sustainable development, as it has the potential to strengthen the link between economic stability and environmental security.[252] Economic expansion by a growing number of countries has challenged the economic-environmental trade-off and its associated theories of limits to growth. Not only can new technologies, including renewables, help countries achieve economic growth at a reduced level of harm to the environment but, as former World Bank President James Wolfensohn argues, "[n]ew and clean technologies can allow the poor to achieve the benefits of development without having to face the same environmental costs the developed world has experienced."[253] The concept of sustainable development does not consider economic development as detrimental to environmental security if it can be sustained in the long run. Alternative energy therefore becomes a potential solution, and may sometimes be regarded as the "silver bullet" for solving the world's environmental ills.

Already, increased support has translated into the creation of global governance mechanisms for environmental regulation that affect the alternative energy megatrend. Popular demands to deal with environmental threats have coalesced into a widely held set of ideas and approaches that have become a fashionable quasi-ideology with global appeal. It has captured public opinion and is feeding expectations of benefits from renewables. As part of this quasi-ideology, the alternative energy megatrend is acquiring the power to convince, as evidenced in the wide range of committed supporters it has gained throughout all strata of society, including famed icons.[254]

Ultimately, alliances of peace might emerge, with alternative energy playing a pivotal role as a bonding platform amongst countries, as well as serving as a practical solution to environmental problems. Sustainable cross-border environmental security approaches would entail establishing sound governance, capable management, and sustainable use of natural resources and the environment. This would foster social, economic, and political stability. Peace alliances are often informal arrangements when they involve environmental diplomacy and institution building. There is considerable evidence of cooperative action by states in this direction.[255] These arrangements involve environmental initiatives that aim to produce both ecological and political benefits, such as the United Nations Environment Program's efforts to strengthen environmental governance at country level and to develop local capacity to meet the UN Sustainable Development Goals.[256] Alternative energy developments could become part of a coordinated international effort to alleviate potential conflicts and instability brought on by climate disasters and related socioeconomic hardships. For example, if solar-powered water pumps could reduce water shortages in regions plagued by extreme drought, they could reduce more harmful migration pressures and the resulting tribal warfare.

(2) Discord and conflicts: divergent interests and new points of contention.

The confluence of geopolitical and environmental security considerations over the course of the megatrend's progression can exacerbate the complexities of global politics, with the megatrend contributing to discord and inter-state conflicts in a number of areas and, therefore, requiring creative securitization approaches. The megatrend could spark new competition over access to renewable technologies and resources, as well as resource components needed for renewables production. Areas of conflict could emerge as a result of environmental degradation (drought, soil erosion, rising sea levels), in part caused by the active pursuit of renewables, which can contribute to scarcity of life-sustaining resources, such as water and food, generating a self-sustained dynamic of geopolitical conflicts over access to critical resources. These considerations underline the importance of viewing the megatrend as both a practical tool to address environmental security and geopolitical challenges as well as a factor of instability requiring policy measures to prevent or mitigate its negative effects.

New forms of international competition could arise over access to and availability of certain resources needed to develop alternative energy technologies. Some of these resources are located in unstable parts of the world, with actors often needing to ensure access to such resources at any cost. Bids to influence production patterns and strategies for access to renewables technologies and resources can trigger more acute competition and foster international tensions. Battery development is a prominent example as it is indispensable for solar energy deployment. Estimates show that the reserves of lithium, a vital component for batteries, may meet the growing demand.[257] However, a lion's share of reserves is concentrated in Latin America within "a lithium triangle" consisting of Chile, Bolivia, and Argentina.[258] Though these countries are currently competing for financial resources to develop their lithium reserves, political instability in the region and the Bolivian president's record of nationalizing foreign companies' assets give reason to predict barriers to international investment into new mines, hence the impending struggles over this resource.

Environmental risks and degradation could serve as points of contention between localities, provinces, and regions, leading to conflict within and between states. Disputes about despoliation of the environment have existed throughout human history, with actors causing environmental damage as a means of coercion. Modern disputes over environmental damage range from clashes between industrial centers and the countryside to the face-off between industrial economies and developing economies over each other's contribution to climate change. In vulnerable developing countries, for example, climate change is expected to exacerbate food shortages, water scarcity, and the spread of diseases, while aggravating conditions of poverty, societal tensions, and weak leadership. Global warming, as a feature of climate change, could be considered a threat multiplier for instability—it will fuel political turmoil, drive weak states toward collapse, threaten regional stability, and increase security costs.[259] Although it is difficult to judge the pace of environmental damage, its effects are now more visible due to enhanced communication capabilities. Such conditions can increase the pool of potential recruits for malevolent actors. Indeed, as noted by General (Ret.) Anthony Zinni, "It is not hard to make the connection between climate change and instability, or climate change and terrorism."[260]

With regard to environmental risks, Paul Roberts argues, "America is going to pay for climate, one way or another. It can either pay now to try to mitigate some of the effects, or it can pay later, when droughts and floods start decimating the developing world."[261] As the two largest greenhouse gas emitters, the United States and China were exploring the ways to build alliances under the aegis of addressing climate change. A Climate Change Working Group, which the two countries initiated in April 2013, was just one of the bi-lateral initiatives aimed at strengthening cooperation on technology, research, conservation, and alternative energy. These initiatives set an example of alliances that emerging economies could use as a springboard to achieve stronger geopolitical leverage by proxy. Alternately, they offer emerging economies the opportunity to take common positions on specific issues—acting not individually but rather as a block, as was first seen at the conclusion of the Copenhagen Climate Summit.[262] But, as recent events have shown, cooperation between the world's two largest economies always holds the potential to turn adversarial,[263] especially as China's economic and military capabilities continue to expand while the United States becomes apprehensive about Beijing's ambitions and its own declining power status. The seemingly cooperative gestures, in part spurred by the megatrend, could thus quickly evaporate. However, John F.W. Rogers aptly noted that "The United States can't do it alone ... It has to do it in concert with others and it has to be a leader in evolving the institutions that are going to [meet these challenges]."[264] From a security perspective, the rising importance of being seen to exert power and apply cross-border leverage unilaterally could make military actions more attractive, or at least more likely than in the conditions of the Cold War bipolarity.

The emerging concept of "environmental imperialism" and its practical manifestation can increase the likelihood of conflict as well. Developing and emerging countries view the developed North and its control over policies dealing with environmental degradation as a means of promoting its agenda and subjugating the poorer South. The South suspects that the North is using global environmental security as an instrument to promote a "green imperialism," to control worldwide natural resources, and transfer part of the environmental cost to the South. The view that the developed world and its corporations own and control alternative energy technologies has exacerbated this suspicion, leading to intense debate about the terms of alternative energy technology transfers and their respective intellectual property rights.

The essence of geopolitical conflict is often explained by the intrinsic lack of morality that is ascribed to politics. Environmental movements emphasizing sustainable development seek to correct this deficiency by pointing to the impact of environmental degradation on societies and inter-state relations, if related issues are left unaddressed. As politics are often defined as the application of power in order to dominate others, it is not considered to have or require morality or reason. This is applicable in particular to international politics, where the possibility of "civilizing" geopolitics or subjecting it to common "rules of the game" through processes such as disarmament or global governance is considered naïve at best. In effect, what is considered illegitimate in domestic politics, due to the pressure of accepted forms of state power, social norms, and communal links, is much more nebulous where geopolitics is concerned. However, the emergence of "moral" geopolitics cannot be ignored, considering the connotations of environmentalism and "green" geopolitics that emphasize ethical, sustainable, and humanistic treatment of eco-systems as a way to prevent environmental degradation. The theory and practice of geopolitics is thus undergoing further change and signaling a shift in the understanding, development, and application of the instruments of power. The potential impact of environmental degradation, for instance, has fueled societal pressures on governments to take action beyond their borders, forcing them to intervene in some form or another, even when there is no national interest at stake.

The upcoming iterations of the alternative energy megatrend can further exacerbate disputes and confrontations over the depletion of food, water, and other essential resources. Although scarcity has not resulted in dramatic escalation of organized violence yet, it has increasingly defined political struggles about control over resources and the excuse of "national interest" as rationale for the use of force. Likely price increases in renewable transportation fuels, electricity, and other forms of energy can create a platform for opposition groups to voice their grievances and shape national policy agenda, possibly having a knock-off effect in causing inter-state conflict. For example, conflicts over resources are often interlinked with pressure to kick-start domestic development and generate income, which can lead to the risk of rapid, uncontrolled exploitation of specific resources—often at sub-optimal prices and at the cost of environmental sustainability. For example, water stress is one major potential cause of future conflict, with more than 2 billion people already affected by water stress.[265] Estimates of water stress by region also point to a divide in water supplies, which may generate conflicts and significant migration waves. It is expected that by 2050 more than half of Earth's population may be living in water-stressed conditions.[266]

Figure 6. Levels of Water Stress by Region: Freshwater Withdrawal as a Proportion of Available Freshwater Sources[267]

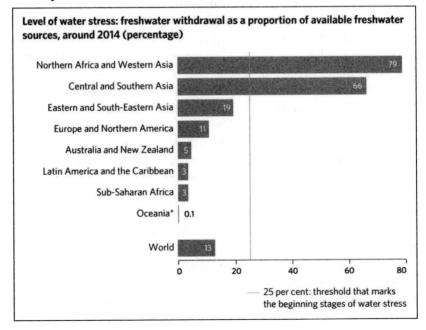

Policymakers have yet to fully consider the link between the parallel usage of resources for alternative energy and for other essentials such as water and food.[268] Examples of states going to war over water access date as far back as 4,500 BC.[269] "Greening" the world will certainly eliminate some serious risks, but it will also create new ones. Possible scarcity challenges generated by intensified production of renewables could fabricate new uncertainties that do not respect boundaries and erupt into regional or global confrontations. The sheer amount of water needed to generate certain types of alternative energy could affect the water supply of entire regions, upping the odds of resource-based conflict. The River Nile dispute between Ethiopia, Egypt, and Sudan concerning the impacts of Ethiopia's construction of a large hydropower dam is a prominent example of tensions over water access, whereby Egypt has strongly opposed the project over concerns of significant water supply reductions. Despite a succession of provisional multilateral agreements, the three parties have not been able to agree on mechanisms to contain the impact on downstream countries, and the tension is escalating with unclear outcomes.[270]

Concerns have also intensified regarding the impact of alternative energy development on food resources. The growing competition between food and energy stems in part from increasing pressure to implement alternative energy solutions, in particular, biofuels. In the United States, for example, farmers have been offered incentives to shift from growing soy to growing corn for biofuels. However, this could provide economic incentives to destroy forest land and to use arable land for biofuels feedstock production rather than for food production.

Another contentious area is the institutional infrastructure in place that is guiding the securitization of global environmental issues. That infrastructure remains subject to Westphalian influences and the dictates of state sovereignty and domestic politics, which sometimes leads to contrarian positions and tensions. The influence of national interests on "green geopolitics" is thus often counter-intuitive and appears to fly in the face of other participant states' intended objectives. This is perhaps not surprising given the lack of political predictability in a post-Cold War multi-centric world, where positions no longer align with the boundaries of the Cold War spheres of influence.

The practical implementation of international environmental security policies could prove to be another area of geopolitical contention. Alternative energy-related environmental policies have propagated beyond the state of practical applications, harkening to Saki's "people of Crete" who "unfortunately make more history than they can consume locally."[271] The environmental security aspects of alternative energy development in particular create diverging strategic interests for state and non-state actors. The current nature of renewable energy development could lead to new international tensions sparked by the enforcement of climate change commitments and regulations. The confluence of environmental regulations and security policies could have unanticipated effects because of irrational and subjective decisions and actions, reinforcing Emerson's caution to avoid getting mired in the details of history "for often the causes are quite superficial,"[272] an issue sometimes overlooked when basing policy on too subjective a view.

While doom-and-gloom environmental scenarios paint a picture of global catastrophe if environmental security risks are ignored, the likelihood of a major catastrophe can be overstated. Whether analyzing the predicted disappearance of the polar ice caps or more frequent and damaging storms, it is important not to misinterpret the likelihood of environmental degradation's correlation to violent conflict as it would be an exaggeration to suggest that violence is an inevitable outcome.

(3) The environmental viability of alternative energy applications: the overlooked issue of "green geopolitics."

The role of alternative energy developments in the "greening of geopolitics" is subject to the environmental viability of the underlying technologies. Current alternative energy technologies have yet to achieve the status of practical solutions to environmental challenges and can even inadvertently produce side effects that can have debilitating effects on the environment. Ironically, existing alternative energy technologies are not intrinsically "clean" or "safe" and their side effects include exacerbating threats they were meant to tackle in the first place. Questions about the likely side effects of alternative energy production, storage, and transmission have not been fully assessed, and the possibility of pollution and other environmental damage cannot be discounted. The side effects of renewable technologies may generate "unforeseen events that could cause a major discontinuity or fundamental change" in an environment.[273] The course of the alternative energy megatrend's evolution itself will depend on dealing with the environmental vulnerabilities of these technologies, along with the environmental security pitfalls they create.

The impact of alternative energy applications upon human health and the environment have not yet been fully explored. For example, technologies used for geothermal power and waste incineration release harmful gases—carbon dioxide and sulfates—and can also lead to land slippage and degradation. Tidal and wave technologies are still at an early stage of development, but evidence is emerging that they can damage the biosphere.

The health effects of wind generation are a controversial topic. There are health concerns about noise pollution caused by some wind farms, with side effects including headaches, dizziness, and sleep deprivation. This may lead to local protests and to site closures. For example, two wind turbines located in Falmouth, Massachusetts, are set to be dismantled after residents' complaints. Studies conducted up to date suggest that noise from wind turbines may be a real problem for local communities if the wind farm is situated closely to dwellings.[274] The strong opposition of residents to on-shore wind farms prompts developers to look for new, potentially more costly solutions. Thus, a European electricity transmission system operator announced radical plans to build a wind power hub atop an artificial island in the North Sea, in order to supply electricity to households in the Netherlands and in the UK. However, the economic feasibility of the project is debatable.[275] Overall, the alleged sources of pollution from wind power generation, such as noise, shadow flicker, visual domination, or reflected light, will require developing suitable applications to mitigate associated health risks and could change lifestyle patterns significantly.

Currently, wind power also entails an additional environmental cost because of the need to bundle wind generation with fossil fuels. Wind farms are also land-intensive; they produce only a fraction of the energy of a conventional power plant but require hundreds of times the acreage.

Despite prevailing public opinion, solar power generation might also have side effects adverse to human health and the environment. The environmental and health impacts of large-scale deployment of solar thermal and photovoltaic (PV) systems currently are not fully understood.[276] A recent review of utility-scale solar energy systems' (USSE) environmental impacts shows the complex set of effects related to biodiversity, water use and consumption, soils and dust, human health and air quality, transmission corridors, and land-use and land-cover change, which "may occur at differential rates and magnitudes throughout the lifespan (i.e., construction, operation, and decommission) of a USSE power plant, which varies between 25 and 40 years."[277] Issues associated with land use, water use, and the numerous hazardous materials used in the production of PV cells are among the most prominent. Evidently, solar power development will require environmental trade-offs based on a thorough understanding of direct and indirect environmental impacts of solar energy application.

In spite of broad support, biofuels have the potential to cause demonstrable environmental side effects. Observations to date particularly point to air emissions and land and water use challenges. Biomass and fossil fuel power plants both involve the combustion of a feedstock to generate electricity. Therefore, biomass plants raise similar concerns about air emissions as fossil fuel plants.[278] Although biomass emits less sulfur dioxide and mercury than coal, for example, it still emits pollutants (e.g., nitrogen oxides, sulfur dioxide, carbon monoxide, and particulate matter). All in all, the increased use of biomass combustion to generate electricity in an emission-constrained environment merits further assessment.[279] In addition, some biofuels use significant amounts of water. Along with hydropower, biofuel has the largest water footprint of all renewables.[280] Burning biomass releases carbon dioxide into the atmosphere. According to the European Environment Agency, some biomass projects might emit more carbon than the fossil fuels they are being subsidized to replace.[281] Land use challenges largely depend on whether energy crops are displacing food production and whether sustainable land use is practiced. If farmers replace their food crops with energy crops, largely because of subsidies encouraging this practice, the result could lead to shortages and increased prices for food staples such as corn. As noted by Jörn Scharlemann and William Laurance, regardless of how effective sugar cane is for producing ethanol, its benefits quickly diminish if carbon-rich tropical forests are being razed to make the sugar cane fields, thereby causing vast increases in greenhouse gases in the atmosphere. These comparisons become even more lopsided if the full environmental benefits of tropical forests such as biodiversity conservation, hydrological functioning, and soil protection are included.[282]

Second-generation biofuels[283] and the use of genetically modified plants as a source of alternative fuels are also being given serious consideration. Second-generation non-food crop biofuels such as switchgrass might seem like a solution to the food vs. fuel conflict inherent in ethanol production. However, the energy it takes to unlock its cellulosic ethanol is far greater than the energy it produces. Efforts to work out which crops are more environmentally friendly than others have focused only on the amount of greenhouse gases a fuel emits when it is burned rather than on the total environmental impact, such as loss of forests and farmland and effects on biodiversity. Farmers of corn, soybeans, and other biofuel sources are also increasingly planting genetically modified versions of these plants.

The actual capabilities of the technologies and the anticipated scale of their use might conceal unanticipated environmental side effects and lead to safety risks. Incongruity between renewable technologies' ability to address environmental threats and their untested environmental imprint are affecting the megatrend's progression, and giving rise to both expected and unanticipated environmental security outcomes.

In sum, the alternative energy megatrend's environmental security attributes introduce new complexities into the realm of international politics. Alternative energy development is often seen as holding practical solutions for environmental problems that are at the forefront of political agendas. Access to the underlying technologies can influence economic growth and can reshape stakeholders' geopolitical stances, forcing geopolitical repositioning. Doing so may create frictions spurred on by enforcement of climate change commitments and regulations.

4. The megatrend's role in mitigating environmental security challenges.

Compared with the securitization of other areas, the security of the habitat is a much more reflexive notion that is evolving under the influence of other developments. Environmental securitization covers a broad spectrum of referent objects that make up the global habitat—ecologies, flora, fauna, and human populations. Furthermore, it is the prerogative of a whole range of securitization actors, rather than single nation-states or regions. The growing relevance of environmental geopolitics is going to be reinforced by the manner in which environmental issues, such as climate change, pollution, and irresponsible use of natural resources, are increasingly recognized as global security threats. In view of the multiplicity of existential threats that are related to the environment, it is easy to understand why environmental security policies are difficult to formulate, let alone implement. Therefore, the success of environmental securitization actions is going to be subject to formulation of relevant priorities that will depend on what the future environmental security risks are projected to be.

(1) Emerging environmental security priorities in a universally securitized world: transforming policy goals into practical securitization mechanisms.

The modern concept of environmental security that has emerged after the end of the Cold War is not a reflection of environmentalism or green movements—it is an issue that actors see as key for their future existence.[284] The upcoming redefinition of environmental security that the megatrend demonstrates is expected to broaden the scope of national security considerations by incorporating issues such as sustainable development and protection of livelihoods. This broadening will inevitably introduce new levels of complexity in addressing future environmental threats, create new points of disagreements and confrontation, and will pose security questions that necessitate a new level of prioritization.

Although yet to become an overarching priority, alleviating environmental threats is going to become an element of addressing economic shocks, conflict resolution, and mitigating threats of violence between nations and within communities. Coping with these challenges calls for a more contextualized approach that identifies and places threats within a definitive threat-assessment framework. Quantifying the immediacy, impact, and solutions to different environmental threats is a prerequisite that future policies cannot afford to ignore. This necessitates setting up priorities in environmental securitization that can be transformed into practical actions.

How should priorities in environmental security be determined so that an optimal outcome is achieved? Rational assessment of future risks is not impossible, but there is a danger that a specific threat can be either over-dramatized or underestimated, leading to inadequate security responses. Developing a metric for the urgency behind specific threats to the environment is therefore highly dependent on the nature of future risks. Some risks are easier to identify in practice, enabling them to be addressed and rectified more urgently/efficiently. For example, the threat to the ozone layer from chlorofluorocarbon (CFC) gases had immediate consequences that made a global consensus possible, leading to the phasing out of these gases from industrial and domestic use.

Assigning priorities becomes less viable when the demonstrable impact of environmental security risks is more nebulous or is not unanimously accepted. Some threats in particular, such as climate change, remain an area of dispute within scientific communities themselves. Its impact is not easy to demonstrate, and assigning value to its mitigation becomes a process that gradually incorporates elements of political debates, moral stances, and economic strategies, which respectively renders such threats unfathomable to policymakers. Even when views converge on what constitutes the threat, differences may emerge regarding optimal responses. The porous nature of a number of environmental threats leads to a divergence of responses between the scientific approach to securitizing the environment and the so-called political approach, which is prompted by much wider pressures from society and interest groups.

Sound environmental security prioritization will inevitably require the determination of what objects' survival is to be protected. The choices are many and are determined by immediate political pressures, ethical considerations, economic imperatives, and long-term security strategies. However, they can be boiled down to choosing between the protection of human institutions—nation-states or humanity itself—and the biosphere. This choice provides a myriad of scenarios, where policies to protect human institutions can negatively affect the biosphere. It is probably sufficient to recall just the example of the large predators going extinct. On the other side are cases where environmental regulations would negatively affect the global competitiveness of the national industry. How does this translate into future environmental security priorities? In practical terms, addressing environmental risks in terms of national security would require policies that would be similar to those addressing other security issues—military, economic, or geopolitical. Environmental securitization will also require resources, financial commitments, revamped processes, and the assimilation of new knowledge.

First, determining priorities will entail assessing the cost of action and inaction, and the outcomes that are to be achieved. Environmental security differs from more traditional security considerations due to the undefined set of actors that can enact it, and the blurred distinction between securitization actors and audiences. With intensifying concerns over future environmental security threats, it is inevitable that different actors will designate different areas which are deemed worthy of being addressed with urgency. The divergence of values and perspectives amongst actors will therefore make reaching a consensus on costs and outcomes more difficult, necessitating new levels of cross-border cooperation and coordination. Securitizing the environment would have to become a declaration that equals an act—specific steps that in the case of the environment would entail inter-state cooperation on a new level. In order to reconcile such modification of national security approaches, in traditional realist terms it will be necessary that the actors engaging in such securitization have the power to undertake it. Irrespective of the global nature of environmental threats, future securitization would therefore still be territorially defined, and the success and legitimacy of securitization actions will be contingent on actors justifying the measures they propose to their constituencies. In other words, a priority that would be applicable to any environmental securitization would be to "do no harm," followed closely by the imperative to create a consensus of what harm consists of.

Second, another necessary element of prioritization will be to incorporate the likely repercussions of environmental degradation on other explicit and implicit national security considerations into the securitization framework. The cross-border and porous nature of environmental risks affects the geopolitical and geo-economic stances of numerous state and non-state actors. Environmental security is thus a hungry notion, and will increasingly encompass within itself issues that range from widely held environmental concerns, such as pollution and global warming, to levels and patterns of resource consumption and production practices, along with a gamut of issues that could impact human existence. In a universally securitized world, environmental securitization priorities will therefore need to be formulated with a view to the likely side effects that their implementation would have. Beyond the obvious risk of unanticipated consequences, caution should be taken to avoid—or at least minimize—the negative impact of financing, developing, introducing, and utilizing securitization mechanisms, particularly so when it concerns those relying on renewables, the wider economy, international trade, the sustainability of future energy balances, and the availability and accessibility of relevant technologies and practices.

Third, the guiding priorities when securitizing the environment would need to correspond with societies' conception of what environmental security means. In the 21st century, the notion of a safe and clean human habitat integrates humanity's struggle to tame nature, addressing environmental shocks and co-habitation with nature that is not exploitative. This societal view does not imply, however, a return to nature that entails a reduction of standards of living. It is worth recalling Jon Barnett's observation that environmental security entails achieving a balance of resources and capacity to absorb waste, "while ensuring that everyone enjoys a minimum standard of wellbeing which can be maintained despite periods of perturbation and change in environmental and social systems."[285] In other words, achieving environmental security does not equate to giving up technology, consumption, or comfort from the perspective of today's global society.

One cautionary note that appears evident is the risk of divergence of actors' interests, goals, and methods when securitizing the habitat. Environmental security is increasingly becoming a field where the interests of a growing number of actors are expressed and often clash. This divergence is accompanied by actors designating areas as being of vital interest for them. This process of designation, which will reflect on future securitization priorities, is also going to have a spatial reflection, as security measures inevitably take place in human space. When different actors have a different vision for the security of the same space, they will penetrate others' areas of strategic interests in a preemptive or reactive manner, as "the designation of spaces as exceptional, or not, enables particular kinds of interventions."[286] Of particular significance are the differences in vital interests that could arise between developed and developing economies. Such differences already exist, are unlikely to disappear, and some developing countries' insistence on "development first, environmental security after" reflects the sense of iniquity that underlies international environmental security discourses today. As a growing number of actors are willing and able to pursue environmental securitization, there is a concern that the values underpinning prioritization of security may result in approaches that are in opposition, and deliver outcomes that could present new security challenges.

(2) The coalescing shape of future environmental security threats.

This seemingly unalterable state-centric approach to environmental security is gradually changing, however. The environmental security role of the alternative energy megatrend induces the gradual de-spatialization of geopolitics, by placing growing pressure on policymakers to address the root causes of environmental damage by cooperative measures through a global scope.

The status of environmental geopolitics is an increasingly important aspect of international relations. The progression of the megatrend points to the introduction of new frameworks that can impact hegemonic potential and marginalization tendencies for power dominance interactions. The "greening" of geopolitics means taking the logic of a state-centric world system onto a worldwide and society-oriented level. The megatrend's integration into environmental securitization processes emphasizes the evolution of security calculations and bargaining positions of states, guided by shifting perceptions of their self-interests.

What can be safely projected is that the nature of upcoming environmental threats will be that of an integrator of other risks. As highlighted by Javier Solana, threats such as climate change "act as a threat multiplier, worsening existing tensions in countries and regions which are already fragile and conflict-prone."[287] Environmental insecurity will therefore create other security concerns that will affect interdependencies and widen divisions between state actors. If environmental security priorities remain focused solely on threats to human beings as a result of environmental changes, there is a risk of ignoring the correlation between environmental threats and conflict. Although the exposure of society to environmental shocks is moving toward the forefront of the global security agenda, it is yet to encompass the full scope of repercussions that environmental degradation can have.

IV. Global economic security—the alternative energy megatrend highlighting a growing reliance on geo-economic statecraft in the competition escalation.

What does the alternative energy megatrend reveal about the evolution of economic security? In considering this question, this chapter evaluates the evolving concept of economic security and its place in the overall national security agenda. The definition of economic security is no longer limited to the prevention of economic manipulation by other actors, and now encompasses a wide range of elements and considerations beyond immediate threats to sovereignty and the survival of the state.

This book examines some of the most important factors that underpin the modern concept of economic security through the lens of the alternative energy megatrend—from the need to manage profound changes brought about by the Fourth Industrial Revolution to secure economic growth to the ability to withstand external shocks and market volatility.

The chapter considers the growing role of economic statecraft in addressing increasingly important aspects of states' economic security, which sometimes exists outside the scope of any single sovereign nation. By examining the evolving concept of economic security through the prism of the alternative energy megatrend, the analysis brings forth considerations about the new significance of geo-economics for state actors seeking to mitigate threats to their economies.

The chapter evaluates the current state of the alternative energy market and considers how actors can maximize the positive economic connotations of the alternative energy megatrend in view of the market's capacity to provide an efficient mechanism for the allocation of resources.

1. The evolution of economic security: the alternative energy megatrend's foothold in economic security considerations.

Economic policy considerations, including growth, stability, development, and resilience to economic shocks, increasingly form a part of national security agendas and are vital priorities for geopolitical actors. The flexing of economic muscles—so-called geo-economics—is a relatively new term used to "describe the admixture of the logic of conflict with the methods of commerce—or, as Clausewitz would have written, the logic of war in the grammar of commerce."[288] Geo-economics has not replaced geopolitics; rather economic strength is a major foreign policy tool and determinant of geopolitical power.

Economic security considerations are a driving force of the alternative energy megatrend, as illustrated by the growing importance of affordable and accessible energy for stable economic growth and job creation. Charting the alternative energy megatrend reveals both opportunities and challenges for global economic security. On one hand, the megatrend could provide new possibilities for fueling economic growth. On the other, it could undermine economic security by increasing costs and encouraging misallocation of resources.

(1) The securitization of the global economy understood through the prism of alternative energy developments.

Economic security is a concept that has been examined exclusively through a narrow, national security-centric context, whereby it reflected only the economic cost of military actions and the use of adversarial economic measures between states. Traditional approaches to economic security placed it within the broader definition of security provided by Arnold Wolfers: "Security, in an objective sense, measures the absence of threats to acquired values, in a subjective sense, the absence of fear that such values will be attacked."[289] In the context of the traditional definition of economic security, an actor may attempt—through economic, political, or military means—to threaten the economic values of another actor. Establishing economic security also meant translating economic power into military power by increasing military spending.

The notion of economic security is constantly expanding to incorporate a number of factors that can improve or degrade the economic system's stability in different ways. This expansion is a departure from previous attempts to consider economic security primarily within the realm of explicitly intentional "economic actions that are implemented with malign intent and [which] have a capability to do significant harm as security threats."[290] It encompasses both the application of economic policy instruments to alleviate perceived threats to national interests, and it addresses the economic basis of national security—the resources necessary for a state to ensure its survival by relying on its economic power.

Any precise definition of economic security stumbles at the term "economic," which has different meanings for different audiences.[291] In some cases it refers to economic inputs, such as resources, labor, or capital. In others, it calls for the protection of specific relationships or exchanges within a given economy. Yet in others, it considers the threats to a range of social, military, or cultural commitments that depend on economic output, relations, and perceived international positions. Despite their emphasis on different aspects, all definitions of economic security share a common feature—they focus on the most pressing concerns that impact the economic welfare of nations. Increasingly, economic security encompasses threats that induce an "inability to obtain protection against subjectively significant potential economic losses."[292] In this context, economic securitization entails formulating relatively clear-cut concepts of who is to be secured, how, and by whom.

The concept of economic security is broadening, and so too is its geopolitical significance. Economic security is no longer limited to inter-state relations involving manipulation of the conduct of one actor by another. Along with concerns about the general economic vulnerability of states, economic security increasingly focuses on risks posed by emerging economic powers, and the effects of non-state actors' cross-border networks. The resulting realignment and reassessment of global economic growth strategies have generated new perspectives on economic growth and the significance of production factors, including energy. The absence of a stable and growing economy will gradually diminish jobs, military power, and a state's geopolitical standing.

The evolving logic of economic security compels states to pay closer attention to the use of economic instruments of foreign policy, and focus on economic competition and cooperation in geopolitical strategy-making. The adversarial use of geo-economics creates a new paradigm where economic policy tools are becoming geo-economic in character as the agents pursuing external and internal security tend to consider the tools like trade tariffs or infrastructure subsidies within the frame of competition and conflict. Enhancing the economic underpinnings of geopolitical power has led to the elevation of economic statecraft to a new level, which is already serving as a prioritized tool for policymakers in pursuit of power projection.

The new prominence of geo-economics raises a question—can economic security considerations that underpin geopolitical leverage and military power be superseded by other security considerations? This question is especially pertinent for the West as it faces the rise of new and emerging powers capable of competing economically and, by implication, politically and militarily.

Energy is an increasingly important factor of economic security; it is a geo-economic force powering national economies and enhancing military capabilities. Whether it is used as an intermediate or primary input, energy is required for any type of economic activity. Improving accessibility and reducing the cost of energy can provide new ways of generating growth, multiplying the impact of investment, and increasing productivity. Energy is a key sector that creates jobs and value by extracting, transforming, and distributing energy goods and services throughout the economy. As a capital-intensive sector, it spurs overall investment and is responsible for a large part of a country's productivity.[293] It often supports more jobs than it creates directly, and the energy sector's need for highly qualified workers also requires extensive human capital investments.[294] These needs produce continuous investment flows that generate additional volume and jobs for other sectors. Energy further plays a critical role in the economics of basic government services. Health services, communication, transportation, fire, and other emergency response services, as well as basic utilities, have energy consumption requirements that actors must meet.

Alternative energy developments have the potential to lower energy prices, free up resources for investment elsewhere, create jobs, reduce fossil fuel dependency, and contribute to stable economic growth. The indispensability of energy for fueling economic growth highlights potential economic security considerations that are advancing the alternative energy megatrend, particularly given its capacity to alleviate economic security risks and contribute to general welfare.

Alternative energy technologies offer a spectrum of relatively flexible and adaptable mechanisms to address the underlying factors of poverty, the development cost burden, and constrained productivity, while generating new sectors of economic activity and advancing a society's technological base. Along with non-renewable resources, alternative energy sources and technologies can affect a state's capital base and ease substitution among inputs. Renewables have the intrinsic capacity to provide a new level of resilience which protects against energy infrastructure failures and maintains supply in the case of external energy supply disruptions. In some circumstances, alternative energy could impact socio-economic dynamics that are currently either too costly or insurmountable with current technologies.

For example, low-cost and accessible alternative energy could ease the burden of energy debt servicing that contributes to developing countries' poverty.[295] As the megatrend evolves, less developed countries (LDCs) could become major producers of renewables, particularly of solar power and bio-fuels. This could provide them with new sources of growth and, in the long run, the means to achieve marked improvements in productivity, competitiveness, and standards of living.[296]

In this broad context, alternative energy developments have emerged as a significant factor wielding the ability to influence states' economic security considerations. Although not offering a sweeping solution to all economic security threats, alternative energy developments could help alleviate economic security risks that arise from traditional energy-related problems. The potential for negative economic repercussions from alternative energy developments should also be factored into the strategies that underpin local, regional, and global economic security considerations and commitments.

(2) A stabilizing factor: reinforcing economic resilience.

Although the megatrend's capacity to play a role in strengthening global economic security remains uncertain, alternative energy technologies promise a number of solutions. They can expand economic inputs and help stabilize the global economic system, create and sustain new sources of economic growth, and optimize economic development. They can also mitigate economic damage from cyclicality, volatility, shocks, and attempts at economic manipulation.

Enhancing economic security through alternative energy could engender a greater level of certainty, which is beneficial since the greater the uncertainty the less rational the behavior of market participants. Market behavior is also often swayed by moral judgments. Irrespective of their validity, such judgments prompt actions and idea constructs that skew the market's ability to distinguish between short and long-term events, and recent and more distant historical occurrences. The deployment of renewables introduces further stability, which could have broader economic security benefits.

First, the megatrend could reinforce an economy's resilience to economic growth cyclicality, volatility, and shocks. Energy prices are considered appropriate and stable if they do not hamper economic growth or create systemic fiscal and monetary imbalances. Abrupt shifts in energy prices affect productivity, consumption, and inflation, which ultimately reduces wealth and standards of living, and damages economic security. Stable growth that enhances economic security depends on access to energy supplies at a predictable and acceptable price level, which could be fostered by alternative energy. To a large extent, "cheap" and accessible energy is considered the "defining characteristic of modernity."[297] This vision of the economic promise of renewables was noted by President Bill Clinton, who stated, "There's a trillion-dollar untapped market for alternative energy and energy conservation technologies that are available right now."[298]

Second, the alternative energy megatrend could play a role in economic power projection and alleviating unproductive economic rivalries. As a factor contributing to economic growth, energy has traditionally been a source of international rivalry and conflict. However, economic processes and the market have, to a large extent, rendered meaningless factors deemed as casus belli in the 19th and early 20th century. Given the increasing interdependence of state economies, the emergence of multinational corporations, and the growth of international trade, it is more efficient to obtain new resources through economic rather than military means.

On their own, economic processes are unlikely to prevent violent conflict. However, they do negate the need for military force in achieving certain geopolitical goals and act as a constraint on potentially violent actors though, in some cases, economic rationales can actually serve as an underlying motivation for war. In general, though, economics has not been the single, overwhelming factor in war politics, as "[the] central problem is that although Man is Economic, he is also Political, Religious, and just possibly also Military (and perhaps Warlike) in nature."[299]

Third, alternative energy developments could also help counter predatory economic behavior and sometimes far reaching economic manipulation. Fossil fuel-producing states can manipulate energy markets, undermine economic growth, and even engineer disruptions in energy supplies to inflict significant economic damage. A salient example is Russia's manipulation of gas prices, which affects key importers like Ukraine and much of the European continent. Alternative energy technologies offer shelter from such price manipulation as they have enabled countries to replace or reduce fossil fuels in their energy mix.

Outstanding examples include Brazil's expansion of bioethanol use, Denmark's surge in wind power deployment, and France's reliance on a vast fleet of nuclear power plants. Both domestic and foreign policy strategies are required in responding to the economic security threats of energy price volatility and lack of access to resources. The megatrend is indeed driven by the concept of "energy as a resource," underscoring its utility in safeguarding against energy resource manipulation, and the gradual convergence of the language of resources and the language of economic inputs.[300]

Thus, alternative energy can serve as an instrument for mitigating the potential use of economic leverage to achieve geopolitical goals. The pursuit of economic leverage is often tied to resource depletion and its corollary—the "paradox of plenty"[301] that is evident in some energy-exporting countries. Viable alternative energy technologies could reduce the threat of resource depletion for countries facing energy resource shortages and help rebalance economies that are overly dependent on fossil fuel exports. In order to not replace one form of energy-related economic leverage with another, this rebalancing should incorporate multilateral or treaty mechanisms that mitigate the danger of conflicts arising from alternative energy expansion, or from states perceiving themselves as losing out in a potential alternative energy race.

Fourth, the megatrend could encourage the creation of new forms of economic cooperation with our allies and partners that alleviate economic instability. Alternative energy developments fuel a growing perception that renewables could help revamp the energy consumers-suppliers equation, resulting in the disappearance of old markets and the formation of new ones. This would mirror the transformational effects of information technologies and add a new impetus for geo-economic cooperation. Thus, the growth of alternative energy as part of the energy portfolio and new grid and distributed storage technologies will prompt changes to the electric utility business model and creation of the new types of energy markets.

For example, the hyper-connectivity empowered by the Fourth Industrial Revolution allows for the creation and management of local energy communities on the blockchain, providing an economic optimization for participants by lowering bills and valorizing assets. The high expectations placed on alternative energy allow states to exert economic power, reinforcing the megatrend's geo-economic significance. Perhaps counter-intuitively, the potential for increased geo-economic cooperation in the area of alternative energy reinforces the significance of states on the global economic stage. The societal ambitions related to renewables that are expressed by non-state actors depend to a large extent on cooperative state policies for their implementation.

Regardless of their actual contribution to economic stability, the perceived significance of alternative energy will play a role in the shaping of future economic and geopolitical power balances. For example, energy-importing countries might find economic security advantages in cooperating and coordinating their approaches with both traditional and renewable energy suppliers. This approach can be based on common goals and respective mechanisms, where consumers break out of the mold of energy competition by capitalizing on the advantages presented by renewable energy. Such evolution of economic cooperation would depend on the strength of political will for enforcing obligations in energy consumer alliances.

The stabilization role suggested by the projected evolution of the megatrend points to the possible emergence of a new, more stable global economic model. It is based on liberal democratic principles and a more caring and socially oriented post-financial crisis capitalism within a Western-defined paradigm. By reflecting the values of the Western world, this model is being rebuked by opponents as an imposition by "imperialists," or an insidious attempt to transform the social and national values of others. This model, however, has determined socio-political and socio-economic developments worldwide. Any alternatives to this order that have been put forward are influenced by it and are a response to, rather than a rejection of, the post-Cold War Western political economy.

Ironically, and not without caveats of political and economic nature, the countries denouncing this order have accrued the power to project their views by embracing the very principles of this order. While not espousing the tenets of liberal democracy or the principles of free market capitalism, these countries have nevertheless demonstrated that the Western model of development is the yardstick by which they measure their own performance and are defining themselves within its framework. This is an especially important consideration following the global economic crisis, as this crisis sparked vilification of free market capitalism and globalization, with free market critics arguing that economic security is weakened by the susceptibility to global shocks that is propagating across borders as a result of increased liberalization and economic integration.[302]

The perspective provided by alternative energy developments on the evolving concept of economic security is changing strategic value judgments. Including alternative energy promotion in the economic aspects of national security objectives will change the nature of national economic security strategies. Renewables' potential economic role may be manifold— it can fuel further economic growth, tackle cyclical systemic imbalances resulting from commodity price fluctuations and supply disruptions, create new industries, and help advance innovative methods. Alternative energy offers multiple applications, the capacity of which has yet to be tapped for purposes of development, let alone fully ascertained.

(3) A disruptive factor: economic losses, uncertainties, tensions, and conflicts.

If actors are able to ensure consistent and sustainable global economic growth, widespread prosperity and rising personal standards of living could gradually diminish geo-economic tensions. However, this outcome hinges on several factors, with availability and access to resources in the age of perceived scarcity preeminent among them. As one such resource, renewable energy is subject to the vagaries of the global system of interconnected elements. The alternative energy megatrend's outcomes could therefore actually contribute to disruptions in the global economic system and help generate obstacles to its effectiveness. Alternative energy has already proven that it can alter economic strategies and affect the shape of the global political economy. It also has the capacity to undermine economic security by increasing costs and encouraging misallocation of resources. Further, renewables could change the institutional framework of the energy sector and wider economy by altering relations between energy producers and consumers, even removing energy interdependencies.

This chaos theory-like complexity points to a number of ways in which renewables could play a disruptive role, creating major uncertainties to their projected integration into the global economy. Similar to the classic example of the butterfly flapping its wings in China creating a storm in Europe, introducing alternative energy applications on one continent can have unintended consequences that upend the economic balances and strategies of another, a reality already made manifest, for example, in high duties imposed on solar panel imports from China by the European Union in 2013 and by the United States in 2018.[303] The megatrend's advances can produce imbalances in energy supply practices and price structures, and generate new externalities threatening global economic growth. In the long run, the economic direction of the renewables trend could ripple into and unbalance other industries, engendering a domino effect on a regional and perhaps even global scale.

The new resource geography charted by alternative energy developments could help set the stage for economic contention, competition, and even conflicts as new power centers and peripheries emerge.[304] The megatrend's economic security connotations have the potential to introduce new shades and contours to the world's political economy map. Political economy determines a number of geographical elements of modern geo-politics. The megatrend is poised to become a crucial factor in shaping both political and economic geography, bringing its own risks to economic stability and national security.

As the alternative energy megatrend progresses, it raises questions about the scope of economic confrontations over new resources and technologies needed to exploit them. These confrontations could take the more benign form of novel approaches to economic statecraft or could lead to more severe active coercion through international interventions by a state or group of states. The couching of conflict in terms of "intervention" raises questions about the legitimacy of the rules that implicitly and explicitly govern international relations.[305] The post-Cold War era has created a new political environment that appears to prompt intervention in the domestic affairs of other state actors. For example, the concept that the international community or certain countries have the right to interfere in the affairs of states when governments commit war crimes or atrocities against their populations is increasingly accepted.[306] However, there is no consensus on the conditions that justify intervention in the internal affairs of another country on humanitarian grounds, let alone economic grounds, as even a morally justifiable war can be rendered, as Thomas Aquinas observed, "unlawful by a wicked intent."[307] The emerging argument appears to only justify the action of states if they want to act but does not create a duty of states to intervene.

Alternative energy developments could contribute to new forms of inter-state resource competition, which could evolve into outright conflict. The availability of and access to resources significantly affect the security of economic growth and stability, which is largely why conflict over resources is becoming increasingly focused, as opposed to the majority of seemingly chaotic conflicts. The "fog of war" appears to occlude resource-related goals less than it did ideological, political, religious, and ethnic rationales for military action. This coherence of resource conflict rationales is due to the growing importance of economic power to geopolitical dominance. The imperative to secure resources needed for the advancement of modern industrial societies is increasingly important to the economic security of states. The megatrend's outcomes can actually engender new ways of manipulating energy supplies, undermining actors' economic power. These outcomes can also contribute to new geo-economic frictions and economic shocks ignited by trade barriers and regulatory conflicts. The megatrend is already shaking up economic security balances of fossil fuel suppliers, along with LDC's calculations on accelerating their growth.

Alternative energy's trajectory also points to the likely emergence of tensions and points of dispute between developed and developing economies. The differentiation between the "core" and the "periphery" is increasingly based on economic power and levels of technological development, rather than geopolitical prestige and military dominance. While the megatrend could help blur the boundaries between the "core" and the "periphery," it may also redefine how the "core" imposes economic hegemony over the "periphery," in particular with regards to trade and technology, which could increase the likelihood of conflict. A number of peripheral countries are not capable of challenging the conventional theory of comparative advantage through international trade, specialization, and even broader industrialization. Furthermore, the concept of "free trade" can be considered a misnomer—trade is traditionally dictated by the rules imposed by the dominant trading parties. Until the end of the 19th century, actors relied on military force to uphold the rules of trade.[308] Today, some countries perceive the practice of free trade agreements as benefitting only Western states that alone enjoy the fruits of the "free" trade.[309] In light of the more diffuse and multi-dimensional nature of power networks in the post-Cold War world system and the relative decline of the more than 500 years of Western dominance, questions arise about the terms of trade for alternative energies. Energy rebalancing in response to alternative energy development could produce a regional and even international "trade policy arms race," with actors seeking to correct emerging economic imbalances in their favor. The alternative energy producers that make great strides would gain an advantage in the process, while states trailing the pack would be tempted to introduce regulatory measures, such as quotas, taxes, and import tariffs. These trade restrictions could, in turn, spark "green trade wars" in the context of the enforcement of climate change regulations.

In the longer term, the alternative energy megatrend may well contribute to the reshaping of geo-economic power balances. The accelerated rise of developing and emerging economies has allowed these economies to transform their economic power into geopolitical clout, enabling them to reshape traditional geopolitical relationships. The new focal points of power are now less distinguishable from the traditional centers in how they wield power. U.S. leadership, while still a major factor, is increasingly diffuse and likely to remain so in the future. The southeastern rims of Eurasia, in particular China, have amassed significant geopolitical clout, even though their continued economic success remains heavily dependent on Western markets, capital, and technology.[310] India, whose economy is one of the fastest-growing in the world, is yet another power center expected to exercise a growing geopolitical influence, not just in South Asia but in the world at large. Both China and India have invested considerable resources in advancing renewables development as a means of fostering economic growth.

Over the coming decades, the Fourth Industrial Revolution and the Grand Energy Game will radically change the way economies behave contributing to rising insecurity as disruption unfolds. Growing polarization of the labor force as low-skill jobs continue to be automated and cultural anxiety will challenge policymakers. Bioengineering, robots, and gene technology will raise questions about what it actually "means to be human."

The alternative energy megatrend could thus play a role in new attempts to challenge the current global economic order. If these challenges weaken liberal and open economic policies, a protectionist backlash could ensue. There is an expectation that technological breakthroughs, including those in the renewables sector, will result in a more equitable wealth distribution and greater job creation. However, economic security in the developing world has depended on cheap labor as a competitive advantage that allows them to accumulate capital and obtain technology. These technological breakthroughs could make AI and automation the main drivers of business competitiveness, not cheap labor. If the latter occurs, the increasing concentration of wealth and rising inequalities (both within and between countries) could bring about upheavals across the globe and further strengthen anti-globalization movements. The backsliding of free market and free trade policies could lead to conflicts and weaken ideological and political frameworks, ultimately harming the growing middle class and promoting equality of outcome over equality of opportunity.

The alternative energy megatrend's evolution highlights the possible emergence of a wide spectrum of new challenges to global economic stability. These outcomes could be disruptive, just as similar historical trends have been in the past, such as the impact of urbanization on Roman agriculture and the oversupply of gold and silver from Spain's New World mines. The megatrend, like other modern phenomena, could also have the concomitant effect of exposing new weaknesses in the structure of the global political economy, such as the general reliance on natural resources. Though the megatrend points to possible new advances, it could also cause geo-economic frictions, the decline of other industries, and wider economic shocks caused by new trade barriers, regulatory conflicts, and alternative energy supply and access manipulation.

2. Leviathan as a market-maker: economic imperatives and policy tools propelling the alternative energy megatrend.

The adoption of alternative energy as a political project for global change renders governments the main source of the related market growth, and the determinant of related developmental direction. Alternative energy developments enjoy government support insofar as they are seen as contributing to economic security and broader technological progress. In the short to medium-term, the state's role will be to sustain the acceleration of the renewables megatrend through a network of local, state, and regional policies, initiatives, and regulations.

In the medium to long-term, the goal of the policies is to develop private sector markets for renewable energy and gradually phase out the incentives as they become unnecessary. Already, alternative energy-related policies and incentives are increasingly designed to draw private sector players into developing alternative energy markets like biofuels, wind, and solar. In some cases, governments deliberately play a stronger role initially in order to support specific technologies and build up domestic industries through the period between the early stage of a technology development cycle and its commercialization as an application—a proverbial start-up "Valley of Death." The key policy tools used to influence and govern renewables include energy use pricing, storage, transmission, and distribution mechanisms. In the context of the megatrend, regulation currently acts as the stick while fiscal stimuli are the carrot.

(1) In pursuit of economic growth: costs, productivity, and new jobs.

Charting the anticipated trajectory of the alternative energy megatrend reveals new and diverse possibilities for fueling economic growth. Certain elements of the trend, in particular the technologies and their perceived ability to provide supplies of energy that are indigenous and independent of existing economic relations and commitments, are at the core of state actors' calculations targeting new sources of economic development. These strategies posit the opening of a broad spectrum of options to establish new industries and achieve new types of economic growth.

The capacity of the megatrend to help achieve sustainable economic growth will be contingent on the ability to substitute renewable energy sources for fossil fuels in a wide variety of uses, and on the potential for significant technological transformations. Integrating renewable energy technologies into global development policies and strategies is particularly significant for LDCs. Despite their likely high initial costs, renewables could in the long run produce efficiency savings that can offset developing countries' attempts to foster economic growth by using environmentally damaging and costly sources of energy.

The wider application of renewable technologies will help reduce energy costs as these technologies potentially are capable of providing energy at prices lower than those of fossil fuels. Such estimates rely to a large extent on an improved cost profile of alternative energy technologies. According to a recent U.S. study, "wind and solar PV have become increasingly cost-competitive with conventional generation technologies, on an unsubsidized basis in light of material declines in the pricing of system components (e.g., panels, inverters, racking, turbines, etc.), and dramatic improvements in efficiency, among other factors."[311]

Cost reductions are also based on the assumption that development of renewables will lead to both an increased level of localized production of energy and a more distributed energy system. By combining different renewable sources into an overall system, economies of scale could be achieved through substitution and reduction of infrastructure, which could in turn reduce overall energy costs. Such a scenario appears more viable for electricity generation than for fuels, at least at the present stage of automotive and engine technologies. Renewable power plants are expected to have zero input fuel costs and, importantly, lower environmental costs.

Alternative energy developments could significantly increase productivity. Despite starting from a small base, alternative energy technologies have been one of the fastest growing industries in the last decade. This has

Figure 7. Unsubsidized Levelized Cost of Energy—Wind & Solar PV[312]

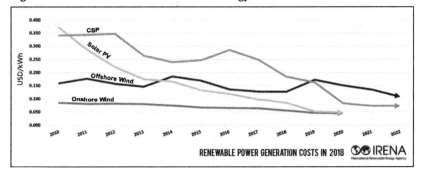

driven productivity and efficiency in related sectors and in energy end-use sectors, such as Tenon Manufacturing in New Zealand—a plant that produces pine-wood products —which increased productivity by 5% due to the wood drying more efficiently through better heat control with geothermal energy.[313] Renewable energy development, in conjunction with market opportunities and entrepreneurial advances, may also spur the creation of new industries directly or indirectly involved in the renewable energy value chain, which could lead to new economic growth paradigms. How this catalytic process takes place will determine the means by which the global economy will adapt to the resulting plethora of changes. As Alvin Toffler has pointed out, "Western society for the past three-hundred years has been caught up in a firestorm of change. This storm, far from abating, now appears to be gathering force."[314] These changes will require new operational, managerial, and consumption approaches that will shape the application of benefits from the megatrend.

Alternative energy developments have produced public expectations of new job creation. Policymakers and society increasingly regard the development of alternative energy technologies as a tool for generating economic growth and creating jobs. Indeed, renewable energy employment worldwide demonstrated an overall positive trend. It is estimated that, on average, renewable energy technologies create more jobs than fossil fuel technologies.[315]

The inferred, and increasingly accepted, link between the alternative energy megatrend and the creation of new jobs is a major political consideration. Governments worldwide have staked extensive job creation expectations on the "green economy," where renewables play a substantial role.[316] However, a slowdown after 2015 suggests that the longer-term vector of employment dynamics is not yet clear enough. The pace at which renewables are introduced, along with technologies advancements, will push employment upward. It is noted, however, that the situation differs across the renewable energy sectors; while there are consistent job increases within the solar PV and wind categories, employment in solar heating and cooling as well as in large hydropower has declined.[317] Country dynamics should also be taken into account, with a few major markets such as Brazil and Germany showing job losses in 2016.[318] Evidently, high expectations regarding renewable energy employment must be weighed against a wide set of factors, including circumstances in the traditional energy markets, investment trends, and policy changes, as well as new technology integration within the renewables sector. However, it is already clear that whatever the short-term fluctuations in jobs numbers, renewables are to fundamentally change the job market profile: jobs created are to require higher qualifications and higher pay.[319]

Regardless of their ultimate impact, alternative energy resources offer appealing options for mitigating economic instability. Both proponents and skeptics of climate change, for instance, agree that in the long run the global economy will fail to meet its growth potential without abundant and timely supplies of clean, reliable, and affordable energy. Developing alternatives to fossil fuels is considered not only prudent but also beneficial for economic growth and sustainable development. Though alternative energy deployment will likely be incapable of radically changing consumption patterns and completely removing volatility from the energy sector in its own right, it could help reshape the role of different factors of production and contribute to stable economic growth.

(2) Technological advancements: pursuing alternative energy-related transformations.

Technological developments inevitably play a role in economic growth models and strategies, as any economy can be viewed as an expression of its technologies.[320] Technological breakthroughs are widely recognized as a major source of economic growth. Alternative energy is a direct example of how technological innovation provides new opportunities to increase output while other factors of production remain the same. Joseph Schumpeter argued in his book *Capitalism, Socialism and Democracy* that new technologies could increase the productivity of a given set of resources, attributing the advances and superior economic performance of capitalism to the constant rate of technological innovation, which he called "creative destruction."[321] Robert Solow, a Nobel laureate in economics, empirically supported this proposition. He established that technological change in the first half of the 20th century accounted for 85% of output growth per worker in the United States, even though income from capital investment amounted only to about one-third of U.S. GDP. Solow's economic growth model regarding the relationship between investment and economic growth also offers guidance for the megatrend's upcoming technological developments.[322] Some have argued that technologies which enhance growth can improve productivity and generate real gains in societal and economic wealth.[323] Technological development in the field of alternative energy could thus spur the transition to a fundamentally new techno-economic basis for global society.

The alternative energy megatrend sheds light on the promise of technological "enlightenment" and could prove to be one of many sectors where specific technological advances produce broader, and continuously spreading, socio-economic effects. The megatrend and other technological trends demonstrate how technology has changed economic relations by modifying the manner in which humanity acts and influencing societies' hierarchical relations and human value judgments. The impact of technology on economic relations is reflected in the transformation of the post-industrial society of the 20th century into the technological society of the 21st century. The revolutionary changes that technological advances have brought about are reflected in the way business is conducted, goods and services are produced and sold, and people live their daily lives. For instance, the transition from family-run corporations to conglomerates owned by stockholders affected much more than corporate practices, and resulted in social reactions such as the anti-globalization and "Occupy Wall Street" movements. In the same manner, the 21st century technological revolution has transformed more than the way in which people communicate or travel. The changes are reflected in new societal customs and interactions that previously were neither possible nor relevant. In a sense, technological developments are shifting decision-making power away from politicians and into the hands of an emerging technical group within society—those that share and operate humanity's knowledge. Thus, the deployment and pursuit of alternative energy could be among the modern techno-economic phenomena that generate a popular wave of technological and academic "requalification" of the world's population with likely concomitant increases in productivity. This development would be brought about by a combination of the need for the labor force to acquire new skills and the awareness of renewables technologies' potential advantages.

Alternative energy developments intrinsically accelerate the process of innovation, both in the energy field and on a broader level. They can reinforce the promise of consistent, technologically derived economic growth. Many classical and neo-classical economists regard the accumulation of investment in physical and human capital as an important factor in long-term economic growth. These considerations also apply to renewable energy. The Harrod-Domar model, developed in the late 1940s, established a direct link between the rate of investment and GDP growth.[324] The related idea that accumulating capital in the form of investment in human capital leads to GDP growth has also gained wide currency, first in theoretical economics and later in applications related to developmental economics. For the renewables-generated economic growth to be sustainable, actors will need to ensure continued investment in human capital with a focus on technological skills.

While economic considerations are often the key determinant of the success of a given technology, it is the alternative energy technologies that are actually determining the economic framework. This is not just a matter of the economy gradually incorporating the changes in techno-logical capabilities. Economic structures are changing in order to adapt to the challenges posed by new technologies. This is already clear in the case of communication and information technologies. The alternative energy megatrend is poised to introduce similar transformative pressures. These pressures are prompted both by the wave of continuous improvements that have extensive commercial significance and by inventions that introduce brand new principles of achieving specific goals.

Economies generally create a type of ecosystem for emerging transfor-mative technologies. In the case of the megatrend, this ecosystem is already in place due to renewables' projected impact on political considerations and societal attitudes, regardless of how fast technologies are evolving and what form their final configuration may take. The economic parameters of the alternative energy sector are forming and re-forming around what can be anticipated, and even sometimes just around what is hoped for.

When these hopes and expectations will turn into a reality remains to be seen. Indeed, the renewable energy R&D investment trend, despite its ups and downs, has grown two-fold since 2004,[325] which creates opti-mistic projections. Evidently, cumulative investment has already resulted in renewable generation cost reductions, especially in solar. However, an investment breakdown by source indicates that innovation in renewable energy has not yet achieved a stage of full-scale commercialization.[326]

Albeit still in its infancy, the megatrend is already leaving an imprint on global economic security calculations. The societal pressure propelling the megatrend's evolution has persuaded policymakers that it can serve as an additional catalyst for economic growth, diversification, and developmen-tal advances. What is still in process is getting the market to take the baton.

(3) Policy toolkit: fiscal, regulatory, and financing incentives.

In line with the acceleration of the megatrend, three main types of policy instruments have emerged as mechanisms to promote renewables—reg-ulatory policies, fiscal incentives, and financing policies. The growing swathe of related policies and regulations encompasses both alternative energy-specific and broader energy rationales, often aimed at achieving a defined national or globally agreed-upon target. Most targets set objectives for renewables' shares in the electricity mix and aim for 10–30% of renewable electricity generation within the next decade or two. There are also other, less widespread targets, such as shares of total primary or final energy, shares of heat supply, installed capacities of specific technologies, and shares of biofuels in road transport fuels. For example, the EU has an agreed-upon EU-wide target to generate 20% of energy from alternative energy sources by 2020.[327] According to the EC 2017 Renewable Energy Progress Report, the EU member states are mostly on track.[328] Considering longer-term goals, the EU Parliament in January 2018 voted in favor of a new binding renewable energy target of 35% to be achieved by 2030—significantly higher than the 27% target set under the latest version of the EC Clean Energy Package 2020–2030.[329] In the United States, the Climate Action Plan from 2013 contained a goal of doubling renewable energy generation from wind, solar, and geothermal sources between 2012 and 2020.[330] However, in March 2017 President Trump signed an executive order undoing the plan, which makes the further federal-level target-setting trajectory unclear. China's Five-Year Plan (2016–2020) sets an overall goal of renewable energy capacity to reach 27% of total power generation.

The most common policies promoting the achievement of renewable energy targets are feed-in tariffs (FITs),[331] tax credits, net metering, and other forms of price controls on energy that encourage the inclusion of renewables in the energy mix. FITs generally involve a long-term contract where an eligible renewable energy electricity generator is paid at above retail price to supply renewable electricity to the grid. FITs currently remain the most common support mechanism; however, in case of large-scale project deployment, it is currently often replaced with auction-based procurement.[332]

Another widespread policy, particularly at the state/provincial level in the United States, Canada, India, and Australia, is the quota or renewable portfolio standard. Quotas typically require that retail electric utilities secure from renewables a set share of their installed capacity, electricity generated, or electricity sold, either by producing renewable energy or by purchasing renewable energy certificates from renewables generators. In addition, some governments offer direct capital investment subsidies, grants, or rebates. Investment and production tax credits and import duty reductions are also commonly used to provide financial support at the national level in many countries, as well as at the state level in the United

States, Brazil, Canada, and Australia. Another policy employed by countries is net metering, which involves renewable energy producers receiving a net award per kilowatt/hour or other measure of output. This mechanism is mostly used to support the deployment of small-scale, distributed renewable energy systems.

The targets and policies in support of renewable energy are adopted by a growing number of countries. As a recent study has shown, the adoption of all types of policy instruments has substantially grown since 2005.[333] As specific technologies and markets evolve, policies are usually adjusted. A clear example is the revision by many countries of solar photovoltaic FITs to curb the booming rate of installations, which exceeded expectations because of unprecedented price reductions in solar PV equipment costs.

International alternative energy regulations remain under the auspices of international treaties and institutions, such as the World Trade Organization (WTO). Institutions like the WTO, however, are not designed to address energy trade conflicts. Rather, WTO agreements and rules largely focus on import rather than export barriers. Most export duties remain unbound and serve as a revenue tool rather than an inducement to develop energy solutions. The existing infrastructure, dominated by incumbents and not yet configured to the specifics of alternative energy development, is undermining international regulations guiding the development of renewables. Unlike other goods, energy is grid- or pipeline-bound and is difficult to store. The multilateral framework is thus unable to deal with issues such as energy transit and creation of and access to fixed infrastructure. Within the WTO, energy is governed by the Energy Charter Treaty, which has over 50 signatories and 30 observers, 10 of which are international organizations.

The Energy Charter Treaty follows WTO guidelines and deals with investment protection, sovereignty over natural resources, environment and energy efficiency, technology transfer, access to technology, and dispute settlement. The treaty, however, does not impose rules on national energy policies, privatization, and mandatory third-party access. The Energy Charter Treaty instead aims to promote access to technology and technology transfer on a commercial and non-discriminatory basis.

3. The alternative energy market: emerging at the juncture of the private and public sectors.

An alternative energy market is gradually emerging, particularly around the more established solar and wind technologies. State-led support still dominates the development of this nascent market, though the private sector is increasingly playing a role. Capital market infrastructure is evolving around renewables facilitating interactions between market participants and capital providers. The defense industry is also poised to significantly contribute to the further development of the alternative energy market.

(1) The emerging alternative energy market: worldwide investment patterns.

Today's alternative energy market is gradually emerging as an amalgamation of public and private sector policies and operations that carry differing responsibilities for development and practical application of renewables within different industry sectors.

Modern renewable energy[334] is being used increasingly in power generation, heating and cooling, and transport. However, the share of renewable energy in total global energy consumption remains rather modest. In 2015 it represented approximately 10.2% (traditional biomass excluded). The share of renewables in major renewable energy-consuming industries is forecast to grow,[335] with the electricity sector generating most of the demand. On the supply side, the prospects are most promising for solar and wind power, which dominate spending in the sector, achieving 93% of new investment globally in 2016.[336]

The United States, Europe, and, increasingly, China have emerged as the largest markets because of their high levels of liquidity and concomitant energy imperatives.[337] Efforts are also underway to incentivize market creation in developing economies. For example, several multilateral initiatives, such as Climate Investment Funds,[338] have been launched to augment financial support in order to scale up renewable energy investments.

A range of financial instruments involved in renewables sector development includes grants and concessional finance, commercial debt and equity, loans, and risk mitigation instruments. Utility-scale solar and wind assets, accounting for the majority of renewable energy finance globally, are typically financed with a mixture of equity and non-recourse debt.[339]

Capital market is formed around renewables with a number of stock indexes tracking the sector performance, such as the S&P Global Clean Energy Index or the NASDAQ Clean Edge Green Energy Index. While the renewables market has yet to achieve sufficient cohesion and viability, interest appears to be mounting, as reflected by the growth of acquisition transaction volumes. Recent high-profile deals include Tesla's acquisition of SolarCity for an enterprise value of US$4.9 billion, which accounted for almost half the growth in corporate M&A in 2016, and Italian utility Enel buying out the 31% minority shareholders of its subsidiary Enel Green Power for US$3.5 billion. Similar transactions include the acquisition of Pacific Hydro by the State Power Investment Corporation of China for US$2.1 billion; the takeover of Spanish turbine manufacturer Acciona Windpower by its German competitor, Nordex, for US$864 million; Endesa Generacion's US$1.3 billion purchase of a 60% stake in Enel Green Power España; and the acquisition by Tata Power Renewable Energy of Welspun Renewables for US$1.4 billion.[340]

New investment in renewable energy has grown five-fold since 2004. However, the trajectory is far from even with pronounced ups and downs in the last decade. Market dynamics offer a range of explanations: a substantial fall in investment in 2016, especially in the solar (-34%) and biofuel sectors (-37%),[341] occurred following cost declines for key technologies which have influenced finance flows. Another factor was a slow-down in major markets, particularly China and Japan. However, the key factor behind these market dynamics was policy change. As noted by researchers, "[T]he peak in 2015 was partially driven by a rush to complete projects before an expected fall in policy support in key markets. Examples included cuts in feed-in tariffs in China, Germany, Japan and the UK."[342] Sharp investment declines in 2016 in South Africa, Mexico, and Morocco occurred in response to scheduled delays in their auction schedules.[343]

Market activities and investment flows are also shaped by the economic situation facing the participants' own markets. For example, oil and gas giant BP exited the solar sector after 40 years of research and development. However, this was immediately followed by a decision by India's Tata Power to buy out BP's 51% stake in their 22-year joint venture, Tata BP Solar. This decision reflected the size and growth of expectations regarding the solar market in India.[344]

Investment in alternative energy development has moved in line with government incentives, with overall economic conditions and energy needs further determining patterns of investment. Macroeconomic considerations, such as economic growth and income levels, interest rates, and broad technological advancements, largely determine the stakeholders' capacity to invest in energy alternatives. On the other hand, "green" investment is also formulated to match policy priorities and the need to address population growth, environmental considerations, and the cost of fossil fuels. A noticeable shift of capital flows to alternative energy development would have extensive implications in the future.

(2) Market-making strategies: from incentivizing public-private cooperation to integrating alternative energy into a global marketplace.

From renewable energy targets and loan guarantees to direct investment in research and development, the state plays a significant role in shaping the alternative energy megatrend. The ideological constructs and values behind the propagation of the alternative energy megatrend, as well as the innovative and insufficiently established nature of alternative energy technologies, are encouraging government dominance of the sector. Despite a recent increase in private funding, investors, risk averse as they are, largely remain unprepared to undertake investments in a sector with extensive pitfalls. The short-term return focus of the markets precludes extensive interest in business ventures that have long-term cost savings over the life cycle of a project and a pronounced positive intergenerational effect. However, over-reliance on the state puts an inordinate burden on the government, and can lead to increasingly unstable economic development that overlooks paths to growth that could prove more promising.

Certain industries are unable to allocate resources efficiently and need to rely on state support. This is the case in sectors that deal with "public goods"[345]—defense, policing, accident and emergency services, and basic infrastructure. The public good argument for state intervention in the development of new or budding technologies has been widely articulated. In essence, it is considered that externalities that the private sector cannot address or mitigate serve to hamper innovation, prompting the need for state intervention. Where technological progress affects public goods, private investors' risk aversion is an obstacle to development, necessitating state intervention in order to overcome the market's short-term bias. This support role cuts across the innovation and development stages as well as the bringing-to-market stage for any product that is classified as a public good. Furthermore, the state is the only agent with the authority to make incumbent market players internalize public good externalities that they have passed on to society, such as the dangerous carbon emissions of fossil fuels.

Often, the state acts as the ultimate rule-making and rule-enforcing body, constructing, maintaining, and protecting the market that cannot exist without it. In the post-Cold War period, the state has enjoyed its increasing ability to subject market activities to its social engineering and harmonization goals, passing some of its responsibilities to markets. For instance, while societal welfare is an indelible element of state policy, state institutions have encouraged markets to integrate welfare principles from societal constructs, prompting the concept and practice of corporate social responsibility. On the other hand, the widening of the designation of goods and services as "public" has resulted in state inefficiency, such as the efforts of the United States and other developed countries' governments to redistribute wealth through subsidizing home purchases for low-income households. This effort, among other causes, fed a housing bubble that, in the view of many analysts, caused the financial crisis.

Governments offer a wide variety of incentives for renewable energy production—essentially creating markets where none exist. Barring some sectors, such as defense,[346] governments rarely generate renewable energy directly, but their incentivizing role goes a long way toward furthering an alternative energy market. According to the International Renewable Energy Agency, the share of direct public investment varied at between 12% and 16% of the total between 2013 and 2015 (averaging US \$40 billion), before dipping to 8% in 2016 (US \$21 billion).[347] However, the actual share of public finance allocated to promote renewable energy is much larger. Thus, when various schemes of government support expenditures are taken into account, including regulatory instruments and fiscal incentives, "the share of public financing in Western Europe in 2015 increases to over 55% of total renewable energy investment, compared to almost 20% if only direct public investment is considered."[348] Such incentives' contribution to renewable energy markets development is substantial: in the Western European countries covered by IRENA's Report, for example, about 50% of the total electricity produced from renewables in 2015 was supported by renewable energy support schemes.[349]

The current status of alternative energy development is comparable to that of the Apollo Project. Political will and pressure from civil society propel the megatrend, with economic security considerations often taking a back seat to political concerns and practical needs. Scaling up renewable energy technologies to meet globally agreed climate goals implies attracting huge volumes of financial resources to the sector. To limit the rise in global mean temperature to below 2°C, the share of renewables in primary energy supply needs to grow to about 65% in 2050. It is estimated that to make it happen, a total of US \$25 trillion should be invested in renewables in the period up to 2050, which means a tripling of the current annual investments.[351] Whether the market is able to support this remains questionable, as concerns, such as price, terms of trade unpredictability, regulatory inconsistencies, and the inadequacies of alternative energy

Figure 8. Total Expenditures for Renewable Energy Support in the European Union and Norway by Support Scheme[350]

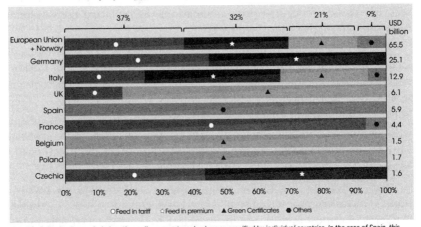

Note: The "other" category includes other policy support mechanisms as specified by individual countries. In the case of Spain, this includes investment return and operation return for existing plants.
Based on: CEER, 2017

infrastructure, all loom, reducing the private sector's flexibility and capacity to absorb renewables.

Despite efforts to jumpstart new alternative energy markets and reinforce emerging ones, there are inherent limitations to private sector financing of alternative energy research and development as a result of limited commercial applications. Due in part to the high-risk nature of renewables financing, alternative energy technologies will continue to rely strongly on state research and development (R&D) budgets (for funding defense applications, in particular). Governments support innovation in renewable technologies and related fields in order enhance local economies and businesses' global competitiveness. The Clean Energy Manufacturing Initiative is one example of a multi-directional program aimed at building "momentum around American innovation, growth, and competitiveness in clean energy manufacturing."[352] Technologically advanced countries are well positioned to see renewable energy businesses adding sustainability to their operations.[353]

However, government R&D funding often carries with it requirements that restrict the private sector's options and choices. This makes it more difficult to justify extensive R&D investments to shareholders and markets. Efforts have been undertaken to assess the risks caused by fossil fuel energy price fluctuations and uncertainty in order to better grasp the costs and returns that the alternative energy sector provides. To this end, increases in state R&D funding will only prove successful if they mitigate the energy security risks of fossil fuel price fluctuations, by replacing conventional fuels with alternative energy sources.[354]

The renewable energy market is highly volatile due to a wide range of factors, including the pace of technological advances, pressures of broader energy markets, and policy shifts. The trajectory of solar sector fluctuations in Germany is a prominent example with its turnover tripling between 2007 (€4.4 billion) and 2011 (€13.3 billion) and then falling sharply, cutting workforce almost in half when feed-in incentives were slashed and cheap Chinese modules entered the market. On the opposite end, off-shore wind power has seemingly taken off lately, largely in response to the 2014 revised German Renewable Energy Act, which stipulates incentives for produc-tion.[355] The task of promoting stability and predictability of the renewables market is of critical importance for its ability to attract investment and to deliver on its ambitious promise. Incentivizing and coordinating public-pri-vate partnerships over the course of the energy sector's transformation will therefore seemingly be the state's role for decades to come.

While the alternative energy market's development benefits from the role of the state, it can also suffer from a number of drawbacks associated with state support and intervention. In a broad sense, the state could allevi-ate the negative societal welfare impact of irrational decisions by individuals by enforcing rules and practices that are "good for them," for example by imposing penalties for littering or restricting the use of fireworks at the risk of causing fires. However, there is an inherent danger in relying on governments to be the best judges of rational behavior. Making societal welfare paramount can result in suppression of individual rights, including the right of individuals to make mistakes. Moreover, governments are made up of individuals who can also behave irrationally. In such situations, even the most benevolent intention of the state could turn out to have negative societal repercussions, as demonstrated by the U.S. prohibition laws in the early 20th century.

States also face a time lag in adapting to economic and technological advances, which is a crucial factor impacting the longevity of any busi-ness undertaking, regardless of whether it is state or private sector led. The technological transformation of Western economies has created elites who capture new market niches engendered by technological trends. This phenomenon has brought about increasing inequality, prompting states to manage technology's harmful effects on the labor market through tax policies and trade regulations. But these measures have not been able to compensate for the job-destroying side effects of new technologies. In the post-crisis global political economy, more attention is being paid to rising inequality and the loss of jobs due to technological advances. Politicians are under pressure to reverse these trends, but markets are still perceived as independent and not easily swayed by political or ideological convictions. Energy markets in particular are seen as able to withstand political influence, due to their size and the economic benefits they supply.

In practice, markets are never perfect; they are never fully "free" from interference, nor are they accompanied by perfect information. Markets are a venue for conducting the exchange of goods, services, and ideas. But they are bound by rules and regulations that restrict certain activities and curtail freedom of choice to protect the market. For example, no one is free to cheat others without the threat of punishment. In this context, the freedom of a given market is a construct that results from a consensus between society and the state over acceptable levels of regulatory constraint, either enforced or voluntary. Market regulation and the mechanisms of market operation are therefore subject to political decisions rather than rational calculations concerning efficiency and outcomes.

The evolution of market regulation is not objectively determined. It involves changing the scope of activities within a market setting, dictated by a confluence of views and attitudes of society, government organizations, and policymakers. Thus, a balance is needed that would allow for optimal government involvement in any particular market and expanded participation of the private sector,[356] in order to ease the burden of the state in fostering the development of the alternative energy market.

(3) Economic viability: will the market lose out for facilitating the megatrend's future economic security contribution?

Renewables market growth and broadening the participation of the private sector would increase the megatrend's economic security contribution. However, this will depend on resolving several challenges that the private sector at present is either unwilling or unable to tackle alone. These challenges include: the questionable sustainability of extensive state financial commitments that often have low rates of return; lack of investment capital and prolonged investment repayment periods; negative economic, regulatory, and public good externalities; distortions created by the dominance of vested interests; an uncertain customer base; a limited number of public-private partnerships; intrinsic vulnerabilities of alternative energy technologies; and inadequate infrastructure for alternative energy development and deployment.

Capital and development cost levels suggest continued championing by the state. From tight government budgets to diminished venture capital interest, the lack of capital is a leading constraint in developing and deploying all forms of alternative energy technologies. Extensive research and development, capital investment, and infrastructure requirements, coupled with disparities in cost between fossil fuels and renewables, necessitate continuous government support for the development of alternative energy technologies. However, the reality in the age of austerity is that governments have limited resources with which to meet their alternative energy commitments. Private investment and new sources of financing, such as pension funds, insurance funds and sovereign wealth funds, and new mechanisms for financial risk mitigation, will be increasingly important for easing the state financing burden.

Government support to new industries is regularly predicated on anticipated revenues from technological developments and resources, and may come in the form of tax revenues and operating revenues (for state-led companies). As the 19th century physicist Michael Faraday noted when describing the advantages of electricity to the Chancellor of the Exchequer, William Gladstone, "Sir, I do not know, but one day you may tax it."[357] Renewables are yet to offer a return through tax to offset the budgetary burdens that their development requires today. Financing the development of renewables and its related infrastructure represents a serious medium-term challenge, a constant balancing of short-term outlays against the long-term economic benefits of deploying alternatives. Given the need for governments to demonstrate well-founded financial decisions and trade-offs, there is an inherent danger of states overextending their reach and attempting to micro-manage alternative energy's propagation.

Although the economic viability of renewable energy will be enhanced with the projected decline in renewable power costs, cost impediments to renewables development are still substantial with the high R&D costs and expenses related to transmission problems. High upfront investment and a long pay-off period are considered a hurdle to market-driven development. Loss of revenue from transit payments for certain countries also comes into play, reflecting the trans-national nature of renewables and associated costs. Because of the need for cross-border applications, alternative energy development raises concerns about the frontiers' permeability and additional cost burden, as "the complexity and proximity of...boundaries give rise to trans-boundary externalities, spill-overs, and free rides."[358]

The actual effectiveness of state-supported policies is a debatable issue. Current policies that support renewables often appear to focus more on political rather than economic considerations. Indeed, the relatively minor role that alternative energy currently plays in overall energy balances makes government support difficult to justify in economic terms. Furthermore, policies in support of alternative energy often reflect the inherent contradictions of economic and environmental security, as policies that target energy independence do not necessarily align with the goal of reducing greenhouse gas emissions. Some analysts point to substantial coal reserves in the United States, the EU, and China, and their attraction for governments seeking economic growth and cheap energy. These energy and environmental security contradictions can undermine economic viability and, as argued by Jeffrey Sachs, "if we try to restrain emissions without a fundamentally new set of technologies, we will end up stifling economic growth, including the development prospects for billions of people."[359] Indeed, carbon capture and storage technologies could at some future date prove as significant from the political economy's point of view as alternative energy technologies.

Alternative energy policymaking remains uncertain because of unreliable data. In general, statistics are undeniably subject to manipulation, and many statistics-based policy considerations result in supporting positions and statements rather than a clear demonstration of specific outcomes. This is especially troubling as renewables development—a costly exercise given the low starting base and inadequate infrastructure—presents obvious questions about opportunity costs. As articulated by Margaret Thatcher, the opportunity cost consideration should include "a clear estimation of the cost in terms of public expenditure and economic growth foregone...."[360] Indeed, assessing the forgone economic growth of renewables development is wrought with uncertainties. This is especially so when considering the potential of the megatrend to result in the emergence of new industries that may also spur economic growth. Nevertheless, one may wonder if resources spent on renewables justify the lack of equivalent spending on other pursuits that may have better contributed to economic growth and stability. Given limited financial resources, are governments overlooking or underfunding other development priorities? And who will pay, who can pay, and who should receive funding for alternative energy development? Answering these questions could have long-term global consequences, considering disparities in the current financing of renewables in different regions. History provides no clear guide, as it is rife with examples of both wise and foolish decisions.

Continued state dominance carries the risk of ignoring Aristotle's premise that "those who care for good government take into consideration political excellence and defect."[361] Extensive state commitments could lead to harmful externalities and high opportunity costs. In turn, this could make or break industry sectors such as biofuels, which were purported to be clean and inexpensive but are turning out differently.[362] While the state's role in developing the renewables market is still needed, actors should seriously question the sustainability and effectiveness of continued championing of the megatrend by state institutions. The purpose of such a probe would not be to undermine but rather to accelerate the megatrend's propagation, by determining a framework for more efficient state participation and more expanded private sector involvement.

However, incentives for the private sector remain insufficient in their relevance and impact. The imperatives and rationale for private sector investment in risky sectors, including renewables, differ from states' strategic interests and impose a *prima facie* restriction to wider participation in the sector. Private sector players will, and have, invested in technological upgrades when it has been demonstrated to be in their economic or competitive interests. Examples include the switch to mini-mills in steel production, production of more energy-efficient consumer products, and manufacturing co-generation of power. As the full range of economic advantages of renewable energy to the private sector currently remains unclear, the level of private sector involvement in alternative energy development falls far short of providing the necessary market liquidity, influences, and efficiencies needed for private sector-led breakthroughs. Being a state-driven process, current frameworks and practices for alternative energy development displace the market's incentive.

Encouraging wider private sector investment in renewables will require stronger mechanisms for the facilitation of market access and a fair return on investment, the standardization of supply quality, and the establishment of compliance frameworks for concessions and subsidies, technical and customer standards, and monitoring and evaluation components.

The current structure of the alternative energy sector exposes the potential for a range of negative economic externalities. These externalities often arise from the divergence of political and economic considerations and include market distortions, and impacts on other sectors and other natural resources. Support for the megatrend will likely remain state-dominated in the future, with governments simultaneously addressing existing externalities and creating new ones.

The state's leading role in promoting renewable energy technologies can distort market operations and lead to a misallocation of resources, negatively affecting consumers. The case of California—a U.S. state which has taken the lead in introducing renewable energy—is a prime example whereby regulators are seemingly failing to effectively manage the transition from fossil fuel power to renewable energy. According to the target set by the state legislature, California is to source one-half of the state's electricity from renewables by 2030. In 2017, about one-fourth of the state's electricity already came from renewable sources. However, the success appeared controversial as the state, which in parallel was supporting the development of gas power generation, encountered the problem of power overproduction and ended up paying neighboring states to take excess electricity in order to avoid overloading its grids. At the same time, Californian consumers were paying 50% more for electricity than the average user in other states due to the burden of supporting new plants.[363]

The emergence of an alternative energy market may be impeded with regulatory externalities: "green tape,"[364] regulatory capture, barriers to entry, protectionism, and administrative arbitrage. At times, the contradictory initiatives of governments, corporations, investment firms, private equity interests, and venture capital funds, as well as climate change and environmental treaties, have created a burdensome regulatory infrastructure. This infrastructure can promote renewables, but can just as easily stifle their growth if mismanaged. The trend toward a stultifying governance framework could spawn regulatory externalities, resulting in green tape, protectionism, and opportunities for administrative arbitrage, whereby actors take advantage of the loopholes created by alternative energy-related regulation. These externalities often arise due to governments' lack of knowledge about new industries, as "it takes some time to figure out how to regulate new industries."[365]

Domestic and international regulations, by not fully adapting to the specifics of alternative energy, can cause green tape and create obstacles to market participation. As Friedrich Hayek stated, "[T]he effects on policy of the more ambitious constructions have not been very fortunate and I confess that I prefer true but imperfect knowledge, even if it leaves much undetermined and unpredictable, to a pretense of exact knowledge that is likely to be false."[366] For instance, as a result of problems with project siting, permitting, and transmission access—which are part of major energy projects—there is growing interest in small and distributed energy. However, small-scale developments encounter more problems in securing financing and face greater hurdles to their expansion.

For example, the European Commission expressed concerns over limited progress and administrative procedures gaining weight in the overall cost of renewables. The EC Renewable Energy Progress Report states that while there had been slight improvement regarding online applications and the application of maximum administrative time limits, the number of member states applying facilitated procedures for small-scale projects decreased.[367] Removing, or at least minimizing, administrative barriers can reduce uncertainty and regulatory risk for investors, in turn reducing the cost of capital.

The emergence of a new regulatory framework for alternative energy can result in protectionist policies for renewables. Protectionist measures often arise in the name of "security," be it food, energy, or job security. Indeed, it is not uncommon for protectionism to hide behind a curtain of health, safety, or even environmental regulations. The ban on EU imports of U.S. hormone-treated beef or genetically modified crops under the banner of food safety is a prime example. Protectionism induces confrontational approaches because it emphasizes conflict as a means of resolving international trade disputes. Critics of free trade have espoused the view that international trade could incite violence by less developed states that see themselves as losing out economically, and who may seek to correct the imbalance by force. With the advent of the alternative energy megatrend, some LDCs could even pursue aggressive protectionist strategies against other developing countries.[368]

The megatrend highlights the potential pitfalls of administrative arbitrage, in which manufacturers take advantage of a price difference between markets caused by disparate levels of stringency in environmental standards between different countries. Regulations have yet to address regional disparities and "effect leakage" between sectors with different energy intensity and regulatory requirements.[369] Regulations can influence broader economic policies, causing the transfer of production to move from a country or region with a tighter regulatory framework to those with less stringent environmental standards. Administrative arbitrage can also impact alternative energy industries that may be a part of related transfer arrangements. Other forms can arise if renewables development relies on foreign grants and loans conditioned on the purchase of donor-country generation equipment. This dependence increases costs and inhibits the development of domestic manufacturing industries. It also provides an artificial subsidy to manufacturers, distorting the true level of revenues that the specific technology production can generate.

Carbon emissions trading is another example of economic practices that depend almost entirely on arbitrage opportunities. Although carbon trading can further renewables development, the carbon trade market has little to do with actual alternative energy production, but provides specific business opportunities springing from environmental regulation. In the end, the advantages of arbitrage opportunities may hinder the ultimate goal of market development. In fact, the perceived inadequacy of cap-and-trade and carbon offsets reflects poorly on the technologies themselves and their long-term viability. Furthermore, the traditional framework of regulations that governs energy-related issues has been geared toward fossil fuels, and was formed in response to conflicting national and supra-national interests. Thus, such market-based mechanisms can even block the development of alternatives.

Although they can protect certain applications of alternative energy technology, intellectual property rights regulations present another challenge. While sometimes considered minor when compared with the overall costs and lack of efficiency that renewables have yet to address, there is an economic significance attached to the ability to protect intellectual property. It represents future income streams for companies, thus justifying investments in research and development.

Regulatory and policy balances often prove difficult to fine-tune because of the alternative energy megatrend's many interests, and renewables policy has yet to achieve a sustainable ratio between unimpeded market activity and state support. This lack of balance is reflected in the network of vested interests that influence political decisions and economic activities worldwide. The state's role in renewables development has created a state-capitalist sector of quasi-private sector actors, who are interested in alternative energy industries and enjoy access to state-provided funding to pursue renewables development. Unfortunately, this may limit the scope of techno-economic advances as inevitable distortions emerge and become institutionalized in the process of competition for state funding. As Milton Friedman noted in one of his famous remarks, "[The] invisible hand in politics that operates in the opposite to the invisible hand of the market" may seem to "promote only the public good," but is led by that invisible hand to "promote special interests that it was no part of their intention to promote."[370]

Furthermore, significant economic security threats arise from picking winners and losers, distorting market information and causing market failure. In particular, the relationship between the state and vested interests can encourage rent-seeking and avoidance of the costly, yet ultimately beneficial, process of efficiency and cost improvements. Along with the temptation of cronyism and even corruption that this can engender, this choking of renewables developments poses economic security threats.

Government intervention, support, and provision of preferential terms determines the direction of corporate activities and aims. If history is any guide, the better established and more politically powerful an industry is, the more likely subsidies are to persist. Subsidized industries provide politicians with a clear sequence—subsidy, growth, jobs, and tax revenue, making it easier to justify continued support for them. Energy and commodities-related industries have reaped the benefits of especially large government subsidies in the majority of developed economies. The value of global fossil fuel consumption subsidies, though steadily declining for a decade, are still about twice as high as the estimated government support to renewable energy.[371] However, the calculations of subsidies per unit of energy produced might show that solar and wind power are far from discriminated.[372] A comparison of energy output by different technologies to its price and overall volume demonstrates why other energy forms—fossil fuels or nuclear—would be considered more attractive targets for government support.[373] While numbers by themselves fail to provide clear-cut answers, they do indicate that governments are more prepared to provide financial support to industries where the projected outcome appears sufficiently beneficial and scalable.

In effect, the promise of government funding and aid artificially determines where success and failure of the market lies. The convergence of bureaucratic interests and political imperatives in the alternative energy industry has produced a speedy confluence of business and political groupings and collusion among them. These groups are using the alternative energy megatrend to promote narrow agendas and are introducing socio-political girding within the economic and technological mix that underpins the development of renewables, as the Solyndra case well demonstrated.

The concern is not betting on the wrong horse, as this risk is typical for technological development and high-tech ventures, but the speed with which vested interests have become enmeshed in the megatrend's technological development. The emergence and accumulation of interest groups and layers of bureaucracy that are in the race to capture state financing explain the growth of alternative energy-related state commitments. Much of the projected growth in government financing commitments now stems from factors beyond the usual political considerations driving subsidies—creating jobs and increasing tax revenue. The opportunities presented by state financing have become the goal of some industry participants, closing off alternative paths of development.

The growing interest of select groups of companies and bureaucrats, as well as the need for government to buttress the renewables industry, have furnished an opportunity for the emergence of a new interest group: the green energy lobby. The role of vested interests in the economy is not evaluated on the basis of a moral judgment—it is an issue of the most efficient and effective allocation of resources. Even the most benign intentions should be considered as vested interests. An NGO wishing to promote conservation in order to preserve specific flora and fauna species or activists pursuing the adoption of new cap-and-trade policies represent vested interests. In this regard, they behave in the same manner as oil companies that lobby governments. The issue to consider is not whether specific pressure on governments is right or wrong but, rather, its long-term effects on other sectors. The integration of industry and politics has created a virtuous (or vicious) circle of vested interests that anchor the megatrend's development and channel its progression.

The persistent role of vested interests, and resulting economic vulnerabilities and externalities, could jeopardize the megatrend's future contribution to the development of the renewables market and global economic security. Economic imbalances from alternative energy development could reinforce the tendency to chase government financing over entrepreneurial development. Infrastructure development imbalances and the price volatility of other commodities could also pose economic security risks. These problems may create market distortions, exacerbate perceptions of inequality or unfair distribution of resources, and even lead to a new profligate energy race between established energy powers.

4. Geo-economics in a universally securitized world: the promise and the warnings of the alternative energy megatrend.

The alternative energy megatrend highlights questions about the evolution of economic security complexities, particularly the changing threats and securitization actions of actors. In order to securitize the economy of a nation, region, or the world, it is important first and foremost to define the parts to be protected and the threats to be mitigated. States pursue economic security as an intrinsic element of national power that allows them to protect their territory and sovereignty. In the context of economic securitization, "economic policy [is often treated] in a manner different to the normal rules and practices of economic policymaking and implementation."[374] Governments regard economic security as a component of security practices that protects their existence, rule, and legitimacy.[375] It is a part of the social contract between states and national populations, which determines how economic activity is governed and securitized.

(1) From geopolitics to geo-economics and back: the megatrend highlighting the drifting emphasis on sources of power projection.

Economic security is increasingly important in international relations. Actors project economic power to mitigate threats to economic stability and growth. To a certain extent, geo-economics is gradually displacing the "naked" threat of military power in international relations. In many instances, geo-economic logic is part of geopolitical logic: a zero-sum situation where one actor's gain is another's loss. In other words, the logic of state economic policies and regulations in an international context is the logic of conflict.

While geopolitics continues to define interactions between state actors in the international system, geo-economics has become a major foreign policy tool and a factor in international relations. Economic strength is a determinant of geopolitical power, which provides actors with an enhanced ability to withstand economic shocks and avoid economic or financial manipulation perpetrated by other actors. In its essence, geo-economics creates a paradigm of autonomy and interdependence within which rivalries are situated and played out. The projection of geo-economic power can be both constructive and destructive, as it affects the positions from which actors participate in globalized exchanges, and in some cases, curtails that ability.

The goal of geo-economics is best described as the use of economic statecraft in interactions between geopolitical agents. Geo-economic approaches are continuously broadening to cover the spectrum of productivity, technological advancement, military financing, and the social pressures of inequality, diminishing living standards, and developmental perspectives of individuals and societal groups. This inevitably puts actors against each other or requires previous rivals to cooperate when confronted with new forms of economic competition.

As a tool of geo-economics, economic statecraft can be defined as the manner in which states enhance their economic power, including by systematically influencing and even threatening the economic security of other states.[376] It comprises a range of economic instruments, such as trade protection policies and blockades on essential goods, which have come to play a major role in policymaking and abetting economic security issues. The flexibility with which economic instruments can be used provides them with inherent advantages over the use of violent means, which tend to culminate with irreversible outcomes. From sanctions to trade wars, these instruments are associated with a much lower ultimate cost to the actor wielding them. Applying this set of tools is a challenging task.[377] Economic sanctions may fail to change the behavior of decision-makers while punishing the populace of a sanctioned country. To achieve intended impact, sanctions should be "smart," continuously improving their effectiveness and precision, by targeting responsible individuals and groups rather than whole states.[378] Although not always effective, sanctions and other economic instruments remain a viable option, sometimes the only form of non-military pressure available. With the broadening of security considerations, it is not too hard to imagine the application of economic instruments meant to provoke specific responses on issues like environmental or energy security.

The evolution of the alternative energy megatrend provides a new perspective on the growing complexity of economic relations. This complexity runs parallel to the current geopolitical disequilibrium of a multi-centric world system marked by an increasing number of power centers. Alternative energy can be a transformative factor that contributes to and highlights the irreversible changes to economic relations that are already occurring worldwide. Energy-based developments have and will continue to be a key contributing factor to the formation of state-centric geo-economic strategies of manipulation. Economic considerations revolving around resources in general, and energy in particular, are becoming increasingly politicized, standing as they are at the heart of intensifying geopolitical competition and tensions.

Although different states have different geo-economic goals according to their political system and dominant socio-cultural order, the state-centric approach is waning, especially as commonalities across economic security policy approaches emerge. However, the process of convergence in economic security strategies is itself influenced by the political imperatives driving specific actors' policies, which can lead to new security risks. Furthermore, the global political economy of the 21st century imposes specific constraints on state policies, making them increasingly dependent on global conditions, which in turn generate internal contradictions and lead to conflicting modes of the social relations of production. Generally, these modes are divided into a capitalist and redistributive mode distinguished predominantly by the rationale and motivation behind the accumulation and use of wealth. The former mode is characterized by the pursuit of profit in a market environment, while the latter focuses on the redistribution of accumulated wealth on the basis of political decisions. Within these modes, states have a key and multi-dimensional role. However, in either mode the "...state is constrained by its position and its relative power in the world order, which places limits on its will and its ability to change production relations."[379]

The risks associated with unstable economic realignments among states due to power shifts in the global arena are exacerbated by the increasing impact of non-state actors.[380] International organizations, social movements, and economic interest groups representing multinationals are capable of influencing state actors' policies and often aim to obtain specific benefits from manipulating international economic activities. Indeed, private businesses often rely on state support for specific economic endeavors and strategies, and states utilize non-state actors in implementing specific foreign policy strategies. At the same time, states' roles are often parallel or subordinate to private economic interests and multinational companies. Examples run the gamut from the East India Company to today's sovereign wealth funds. This has resulted in a plethora of forms of coexistence between states and non-state actors in the global economic space, characterized by different degrees of interaction, ranging from passive to state-led and state-dominated.

The growing de-territorialization of non-state actors—i.e., actors exercising political authority without explicit support of, and without directly pursuing specific benefits for, a given state—highlights the mutable impact of economic security on geopolitics.[381] This is particularly true for multinational companies that were previously associated with a specific nation-state and whose interests were aligned with those of their host state. In the 21st century, the prime examples of de-territorialized non-state actors in the energy sector are Royal Dutch Shell, ExxonMobil, and the Anglo-Australian conglomerate Rio Tinto, all of which are heavily engaged in extractive activities in Africa, Asia, and other regions far beyond their domestic markets. For many companies worldwide, the question "who are we?" is becoming particularly important, as companies' nominal nationhood is being rapidly superseded and governed by their transnational operations in what is an increasingly globalized economy.[382]

The complex geo-economic landscape is therefore creating a framework where conflicts over economic issues may propagate and escalate. It is structurally abnormal to find a state that does not wish to assume the geopolitical clout of a great power, so it is unlikely that actors will restrain themselves from using economic leverage to achieve political goals in the future. Applying tools of economic statecraft would generate responses from others, whether in the form of seeking to maintain the balance or jumping on the bandwagon of a successful strategy.[383] Although maximizing collective beneficial outcomes may work well for the global system, separate actors will still endeavor to expand their own capabilities and competitive advantages over others. Given that the areas where geo-economic power can be applied are continuously growing in number, the scope of such competition and the spectrum of geo-economic sources of conflict will also expand.

What the megatrend's evolution suggests is an impending process of competition between actors to determine the new hegemons that will set the rules to guide the upcoming global economic system. Hegemony in the modern global economy requires a unity between material and ideological drivers that achieves a consensus in a given society. This necessary consensus requires a situation whereby the state transcends from a ruling class or elite into a component of society that has support and basis within different social strata, to which it provides moral and cultural guidance and leadership.

The transition to a new leadership framework will be an element of a larger process that includes the evaluation and choice of new developmental models for global society. The increasing internationalization of economic relations will result in placing different spatial locations, resources, and assets in a new position of global dominance. However, a transition to a new, universally accepted developmental model for the global economy could become a process of constructive destruction with far-reaching socio-political and geo-political repercussions that could be construed, by a number of actors, as security threats in their own right.

(2) The rising importance of geo-economics: what does the alternative energy megatrend's evolution reveal about upcoming economic security considerations?

An expanded concept and practice of economic security has led single powerful actors to pursue securitization actions across borders and over extended periods of time.[384] Economic securitization increasingly incorporates areas that impact a growing number of economic actors and relationships—from individual corporations to whole industry sectors, and from trade relations to movement of capital and labor. This makes it more difficult to divorce economic activity by private individuals and enterprises from the strategic interests of the state. In effect, the resources available for actors to apply toward economic securitization are spread thinner and thinner. There is also a danger that securitizing a growing number of sectors could be transformed into protecting corporations from normal market conditions, or gaming markets to achieve specific politically motivated outcomes.

Besides states, which continue to represent the major agents of the international system, future economic security challenges will involve an increasing number of non-state actors—from industries that address threats to property, income, and infrastructure to supervisory bodies, trade dispute resolution organizations, and multilateral financial institutions. This is impacting the rules that govern economic activity, with rights being subsumed by specific securitization requirements.[385] The economic sectors protected by securitization will increase in scope and type, encompassing impacts on economic activity and infrastructure from criminal, terrorist, or pirate incursions, mobility of goods, money and labor, information and communication technologies, and economic institutions and processes.[386]

The broadening of economic securitization is blurring the difference between legitimate (or at least broadly acceptable) forms of protecting the security of the national or global economy and protectionist measures and administrative barriers. Policies will range from measures to distance fishing fleets from environmental protestors to state assistance to counter the growing threat of industrial espionage. Increasingly, securitization will expand to protect state and non-state actors from theft of intellectual property, technology, managerial and industrial processes, and general competition.

The megatrend illustrates that geo-economics is becoming the dominant power projection tool through which economic, political, and military advantages are achieved. State actors realize that the opportunities provided by techno-economic advances will not remain open for long before they are snatched by other parties. For instance, the major benefits of the Internet were largely realized by the United States during the "dot-com boom," the U.S.' massive economic boost in the 1990s and early 2000s. Similarly, the winner of the race to institutionalize alternative energy will likely reap similar rewards, with innovations and growth spreading across economic sectors.

The established international economic and trade roles of actors will transform as states and the international community increasingly hold national economies responsible for the stability of the global political economy. Specifically, trade and economic coercion will be tantamount to the use of force in changing actors' behavior. Furthermore, in order to increase the credibility of economic statecraft tools and signal the seriousness of their intent, actors will be willing to spend more to implement economic policies. Continuing the pursuit of national economic security in this way could lead actors to back up their economic policies with the realistic or believable threat of force or coercive diplomacy, which may actually increase the risk of economic clashes ending in military conflicts.

The megatrend's projected economic security connotations highlight the current state of economic disequilibrium. As the multi-centric world system has introduced new imbalances within existing strategic alliances, it has become more difficult to justify maintaining unified fronts against common enemies that may no longer exist, especially in light of the persistent and unifying threats of economic insecurity. In this disequilibrium, techno-economic phenomena and resource factors like energy provide actors with an edge. This will enable a multitude of actors to assume new roles in global economic, geopolitical, and military balances. "The result will be an exacerbated disequilibrium, where a return to a stable status quo may well require a major disruptive correction; renormalizing...a form of stabilization that can occur only through violence; the imposition of a stabilization, a new hegemony."[387]

Further, in the past, social change was construed along lines of rational consensus and objective judgment, often marginalizing subjective positions. This led to a distinction between "traditional" societies and "modern" societies. In the former, collective interests prevailed over individual goals, with values formulated by a given society determining interpersonal relations. In the latter, a set of universally accepted values were prevalent, and relationships were diffused rather than established within a particular framework of obligations and explicit rules. Hence, the straight-line comparison of GDP growth between countries no longer determines developmental paths. In the 21st century, size is no longer the major determinant of an actor's place in the global economic hierarchy.

Besides endowing actors with new or added power projection capabilities—be it in the economic or military domain—the alternative energy megatrend will help induce a transformation of institutional and social order paradigms, which will shape the balances between existing and emerging hegemons. Alternative energy could become a feature of new modernization processes through which major powers exert influence. In the existing modernization paradigm, the less developed and so-called traditional societies have a lower level of potential growth due to their system of rules and obligations, which hinder the expansion of science, technology, entrepreneurship, and risk-taking. Modern societies, on the other hand, are better able to develop by applying individual judgment that eventually benefits society as a whole. In order to "modernize," traditional or less developed societies need to build up a critical mass of industrial and financial infrastructure, strong and independent institutions, a knowledge base, a level of consumption that goes beyond basic goods, and an economic framework that focuses on investment of surplus wealth for purposes of stimulating further economic growth. This modernization process is therefore a set of structural and behavioral transformations that must occur in a specific order so as to provide the foundation for upwards movement.[388]

The megatrend's progression suggests that economic statecraft and securitization approaches will affect national security considerations, such as defense, energy, and the environment. The megatrend reveals that the interconnectedness of events and trends in the globalized economy means not only that negative repercussions will have unanticipated consequences, but that unanticipated consequences may have beneficial outcomes. In adapting to the demands of a universally securitized world where vulnerabilities are ubiquitous, states will need to prioritize and address specific economic threats rather than mitigate every single threat.[389]

The new technological advances and factors of production promised by the megatrend offer novel economic means of achieving geopolitical goals. With the growing integration of economic relations in the zero-sum logic of international relations, the advent of new sources of power will inevitably bring economic consequences. New forms of economic cooperation are therefore likely to emerge along the lines of regional economic security complexes.[390] In becoming a tool of economic statecraft, alternative energy offers greater flexibility and impact than military force. Indeed, renewables represent one of the new channels that reinforce the persistent importance of territoriality in international political and economic relations.

As a framework that facilitates the exertion of power, regional economic security complexes unify methods of implementing securitization mechanisms that protect objects recognized as threatened by the majority of actors within a region. This convergence of regionalism and securitization provides insight into the possible direction of international economic cooperation, and mechanisms required to address future economic conflicts.

The megatrend can give rise to new economic considerations that may place it at the heart of geopolitical competition and tensions. From the perspective of geo-economic rivalries, the management of resource access and utilization leads to intensifying resource competition, even though economic conflicts to date have been less disconnected and chaotic than military ones. Geo-economic conflicts differ from traditional geopolitical rivalries because they do not always put state actors against one another. Instead, they result in different visions of economic flows that actors attempt to impose across regions and worldwide. The different logic that governs such visions influences the security of economic activities across the affected regions, potentially impacting global trade and economic flows. In particular, the significance of non-state actors that undertake economic securitization, and the transfer of economic securitization powers from states to supranational organizations and the market, have challenged the persistently state-centric logic of geo-economic relations.

The ongoing challenges to the prevailing economic order are persistent, and may potentially cause a retreat from more open economic policies, including/such as a resurgence of protectionism. These challenges might also spur a drive to secure access to new resources, which represent new opportunities for actors to develop industries and fuel global economic growth.

In conclusion: How does the alternative energy megatrend affect the future of the energy, defense, environmental, and economic security domains?

The megatrend's security trajectory across security domains reveals a number of upcoming developments:

Energy security:

- The megatrend's reflects the confluence of imperatives and impediments to an upcoming energy shift. The outcomes and manifestations of the megatrend are already altering societal approaches toward energy security, offering options that can contribute to the stability and safety of the international energy system, energy resilience, diversity of supply, local energy independence, and global interdependence. Alternative energy is seen as a future solution to a range of broader energy and economic security concerns, such as the manipulation of energy supplies, commodity price fluctuations, and resource depletion.

- The capacity of alternative energy technologies to complement and match fossil fuels' role in the global energy system will ultimately determine the megatrend's impact on energy security. Addressing the outstanding questions about storage, transmission, demand-side management, intermittency, and the side effects of renewables will determine their future viability in the energy mix.

- Nuclear power is a special case that could influence the further iterations of the alternative energy megatrend. Nuclear power is a double-edged sword that can serve as an energy security solution for one country and be perceived as a national security threat to another. Moreover, nuclear power's intrinsic vulnerabilities—waste disposal and storage issues, infrastructure security and its financial and capital cost constraints—exacerbate the already strong ambivalence about its promotion. Nuclear power also provides a cautionary tale about irrational exuberance with emerging technologies. Once regarded as "too cheap to meter," nuclear power now struggles to compete economically with other forms of energy generation.

- With the anticipated reshaping of future societal attitudes toward energy security, it can be confidently projected that energy security-based tools of political deterrence and new bargaining chips for obtaining geopolitical leverage will likely become increasingly prevalent.

Defense:

- Defense policies, military doctrines, and strategic considerations are set to steadily assimilate specific aspects of the alternative energy megatrend as part of the ongoing defense transformation. The geographic spread of areas of strategic concern will likely necessitate new abilities to operate effectively in areas where forces are impeded from operating. Military planners are compelled to look at distributed, multi-node, networked, and semi-autonomous systems that provide higher levels of redundancy and reliability. Alternative energy offers improved military capabilities and can enhance military power. It can potentially free up defense resources, improve supply lines, mitigate rising defense energy costs, and alter force postures.

- The megatrend's future iterations are in tune with the defense establishment's broadening mandate to address energy, environmental, and economic security threats. As it takes on a more important role in defense affairs, the alternative energy megatrend is likely to trigger broader reconsiderations of the effectiveness vs. efficiency trade-offs that currently prevail in military doctrines, and encourage further testing of the viability of adopting alternative energy. The envisioned advances in the field of renewables are poised to furnish armed forces with new warfighting capabilities.

- A shift to new energy resources could destabilize regions previously deemed stable and could modify the strategic and security imperatives for the West. Hydrocarbon states that continue to ignore economic diversification risk strategic disruptions both externally and internally. In that regard, there may be a reshuffling of strategic focal points, with some resource-rich regions of traditionally preeminent strategic importance losing their position on the defense agenda, only to be replaced with other areas of strategic engagement.

- Like oil and gas, alternative energy infrastructure could become a vulnerable target requiring physical hardening, new regulations, and defenses against unforeseen attacks. Ultimately, advancing alternative energy's defense integration seems most contingent on achieving a fundamental change of mentality and the provision of further incentives.

- The defense establishment's adoption of alternative energy technologies underscores the military's enduring role in technological development. The defense integration of alternative energy will spur technological progress and innovation, leading to economic growth derived from the emergence of new industries. Alternative energy's defense applications are thus poised to play an essential role in enhancing society's technological and industrial base.

Environmental security:

- Environmental security risks have the potential to introduce imbalances in the global societal order. Although the significance of environmental security considerations is not viscerally integrated in policymaking, and especially in the bargaining positions that underpin modern international relations, there is a growing realization

229

that, in the past, environmental challenges have been associated with the fall of civilizations.[391] Environmental risks will be reflected in upcoming national security agendas.

- As renewables are ascribed a transformative capacity for addressing present and future environmental security concerns, including climate change, the megatrend will become an increasingly significant part of security and policy discourses. Renewable technologies, however, will need to be sufficiently viable and their outstanding environmental hazards, risks, and side effects addressed, which will require thought-out securitization approaches.

- The megatrend's upcoming iterations could generate new resource conflicts. Conflicts could arise due to competition over scarce essentials (e.g., water and food), regulatory contradictions, and changes in production patterns and technology transfers. Pursuit of control over resources could, by incorporating the development of renewables, broaden the canvass upon which resource conflicts could arise.[392]

- The mounting importance of addressing environmental threats could put further pressure on states to strengthen the regulatory frameworks that support the current course of the megatrend. This consideration is also spurring convergence of a growing number of local, regional, and international policies directly or indirectly related to alternative energy. The pursuit of new options for empowerment by non-state actors could also focus on the megatrend, resulting in guidelines and initiatives that would channel the megatrend's progression even if renewable development is not their main objective. Along its current developmental path, alternative energy-related and broader environmental regulation will likely continue to embrace redistributive programs driven by the public policy agenda of the environmental justice movement.

- Irrespective of the form they take, the environmental security changes highlighted by the megatrend could introduce new palpable complexities in international relations. Free riding and passing responsibility to others could damage traditional alliances, aggravate existing international strains, and result in geopolitical imbalances.

- The considerations underpinning the evolving notion of environmental security will continue to influence societal attitudes, inducing the search for globalized approaches to security. State and non-state actors will continue to pursue solutions to environmental problems that are at the top of political agendas. This search for solutions will occur with the understanding that specific environmental threats can no longer be treated as strictly localized or specific. As actors seek to maximize their interests, both cooperation and confrontation will emerge over the direction, pace, and extent of environmental securitization and related governing frameworks.

Economic security:

- While the scale of the megatrend's economic impact is uncertain, its role in upcoming economic security considerations is bound to grow. Alternative energy developments are already reshaping global economic security discourses and calculations by alleviating energy-related dependencies, catalyzing growth and job market restructuring, and providing a springboard for technological progress. Deploying alternative energy technologies could reduce susceptibility to energy supply disruptions and price shocks, contribute to alleviation of poverty, and mitigate broader economic volatility and global cyclicality. Furthermore, renewables can equip actors with new tools for relieving the threat of economic manipulation. The megatrend also suggests the possible emergence of new industries, which could provide new opportunities for countries with one-dimensional economic development to diversify and change their growth paths.

- The megatrend's impact on the future economic security landscape will depend on the economic viability of renewables and the breadth of externalities and distortions. To have a tangible effect on economic security, the alternative energy megatrend will need to achieve grid parity with fossil fuels. Making renewables economically viable will require reevaluation of the marginal cost and marginal price of energy. Such reevaluation would need to include all the positives and negatives—from the added utility of energy on demand to the added cost of carbon emissions.

- Broader private sector participation will be needed to facilitate positive and expanded outcomes from the development of renewables markets. Government intervention in support of the megatrend may grow uncontrollably, and this growing role could lead to imbalances and cross-sector side effects that could hinder the responsiveness and mitigating effects of markets. The resulting "green tape" might lead to an artificial selection of winners and losers, as well as to the emergence of overwhelmingly dominant players and vested interests. Policies will be necessary to remove or minimize barriers, such as counterfeiting and patent theft, which hinder innovation and cause negative externalities.

• State actors are increasingly relying on geo-economics as a tool of projecting geopolitical power, and alternative energy developments could provide new avenues for deploying such tools. The use of economic statecraft mechanisms and coercive economic measures is subsuming 20th century geo-economic approaches, such as modernization,[393] and is increasingly rivaling military means as the instrument of choice in international relations.

PART 4

The Metamorphoses: The Alternative Energy Megatrend's Inevitable Demise and Future Security Trajectory

"...Timaeus...you have given us a wonderful acceptable
prelude; now go on to develop your main theme...."

Plato[1]

Judging by its development thus far, the first act of the alternative energy play appears to be over. The main themes are set and the characters have been introduced. Several acts, however, remain to be performed, and just like Mozart's *The Magic Flute*, the plot may turn on misperceptions and unforeseen metamorphoses. As seen in similar socio-political and techno-economic trends in the past, the megatrend will likely unfold with surprising twists and turns.

What does the future actually hold for the alternative energy megatrend and how is this future reflected in global societal visions and security considerations worldwide? What can be done to achieve positive and security-conscious outcomes from the megatrend's evolution within the fluid security context of the 21st century world?

In considering these questions, the following chapters build on the discussions in previous parts of the book. A review of approaches and policy tools implemented by states across the globe indicates elements that may emerge from current developments. This adds one more dimension to the guiding principles and approaches to building a global framework for understanding the further progression of the megatrend. Finally, the chapter discusses how the insights provided by the megatrend can be utilized to test the emerging notion of security prioritization in a universally securitized world.

I. Charting the megatrend's future course.

Tennessee Williams's observation that "[t]he future is called 'perhaps,' which is the only possible thing to call the future,"[2] is certainly applicable to the alternative energy megatrend. The future of the megatrend is by no means set in stone. It is poised between a potential downfall and the capacity to achieve non-linear leaps and advances that would ensure its durability. A number of obstacles could slow down or even end the megatrend, while its drivers and attributes could also endow it with the power to withstand doubts about its potential. As with other trends, the alternative energy megatrend may change course or perhaps dissipate entirely. To make assumptions on its future course, one needs to consider the factors that may lead to its demise or to its ascent.

The alternative energy megatrend's longevity depends on addressing and overcoming several very real challenges: viability, environmental security risks, and integration into defense operations, among others. The evolving demand and supply of energy overall will be an even more important factor. This is particularly relevant when assessing the future use of fossil fuels, especially non-traditional fossil fuels. The future of the megatrend is inseparable from its security repercussions, which will depend on how renewables evolve as a resource.

Beyond enhancing existing capabilities and creating new options for addressing issues as diverse as energy independence, economic growth, and GHG emissions reduction mechanisms, renewables could become a factor in a future social order that will generate its own institutional framework. This framework could be similar in spread and significance to that generated by the use of fossil fuels, from the implicit understanding of the significance of energy in daily life and its importance for economic activity, to the imperatives that energy considerations have already introduced into foreign policies.

The future of the alternative energy megatrend will ultimately depend on how society and policymakers approach the megatrend. The manner in which the megatrend's underlying factors are assimilated in societal notions and ideas, and how their effect—material, ethical, societal, and cultural—will shape its future course. In the case of the megatrend, perception may indeed be reality. Actors will formulate policies and security considerations based on assessments of future scenarios. These policies will impact alternative energy developments, which will, in turn, inform policies. The perception of the megatrend's "assured longevity" will actually be its primary catalyst. Thus, the act of portending the future of the megatrend is a "self-fulfilling" prophecy.

1. The demise?

A wide spectrum of opposing views, doubts, and arguments challenge the megatrend. As history indicates, trends of this type are the result of a convergence of different yet often coordinated endeavors aimed at generating, imposing, and applying specific social, political, economic, scientific, and technical knowledge. These endeavors are as likely to fail as to succeed. What may lead to a failure?

Skepticism about alternative energy development's future has taken many forms. From the skeptics' perspective, the downfall of the megatrend is considered more a question of "when" not "if," as the momentum behind and impact of the megatrend's drivers are themselves subject to doubts. These doubts and criticisms are not simply the expression of a dissatisfied minority. They often represent rational and well-founded questions about the megatrend's fundamental elements and the side effects of its progress that point to its failure. The following points summarize the essence of the arguments predicting the megatrend's doom:

- The megatrend's role in energy security calculations is questionable. Despite continuous promotion, public subsidies, and hype, renewables make a modest contribution to the energy mix and fail to match the capabilities offered by fossil fuels. Continuous new discoveries of fossil fuels[3] as well as technological improvements enabling access to and profitable recovery of previously untapped resources[4] counter the seemingly strong imperative to pursue alternative energy developments as a response to "peak oil" and diminishing fossil fuel reserves.

- The notion that renewables are good for the environment is not without its flaws as we cannot yet fully foresee the effects of these technologies. Many of these technologies have not been sufficiently tested, and their pursuit could lead to environmental deterioration such as deforestation, land erosion, water scarcity, and noise and heat pollution, all of which also cause health hazards. Both the production and disposal of a range of renewable energy technologies entail the use of highly toxic materials, dangerous processes, and hazardous by-products. Renewables' low energy density requires greater use of land, exacerbating scarcity of essential economic resources like arable land and water. This, in turn, contributes to increased food costs and new demands on scarce metals, such as tellurium, cadmium, and lithium.

- Cost is seen as another major reason against pursuing alternative energy.[5] The most prominent technologies bolstering the megatrend are currently not cost-effective enough to bolster economic security. Intermittency, variability, and storage issues cannot be fully resolved with current technology. At the same time, experimental technologies, such as hydrogen energy, power-from-orbit, or magnetic tethers, are more in the realm of theoretical development than practical application. The deployment of renewables also requires substantial compatibility adjustments to current infrastructure as well as extensive new infrastructure, which is costly and often unfeasible.

- The defense sector integration of alternative energy technologies is problematic. There are persistent hurdles to the use of alternative energy technologies in the majority of defense operational environments. Current technologies continue to lag far behind fossil fuels in their ability to deliver the energy density that military operations require. The process of integrating renewables into defense practices would be protracted and costly. The new resources necessary for producing alternative energy technologies may open up unforeseen areas of vulnerability, increasing the demands on already burdened armed forces.

- The pursuit of alternative energy developments is seen as a crusade that is advocated by renewable energy or environmental lobbies. Ideological movements come and go, and the green ideas and methods behind the alternative energy megatrend may disappear in the same manner as ideas of anarchism declined in Europe and the United States after WWI. There is also a danger that delayed fulfillment of the expectations some societal groups have placed on alternative energy could result in a counter-reaction and decline in public support, jeopardizing the megatrend's development.

- The policies supporting alternative energy development can lead to the misallocation of funds and resources and can bring about distortions and negative externalities. Providing subsidies to support renewables is not only damaging to existing industries; it also absorbs valuable resources. The government's role in the technological development of renewables spawns a political process and conflicts over the funding for different kinds of technologies. Furthermore, policies and regulations governing renewables could potentially lead to new trade wars with a green slant, causing losses to some industries from decreased sales of their commodity, or, worse, bankruptcy and failure.

These arguments may be regarded as sufficient reasons for skepticism regarding its future, though their validity is often questioned. The point of contention is that the envisioned worldwide spread of these technologies is at best an illusion, at worst, a con. The convergence of skeptical views, however biased they may appear, also highlights the real pitfalls that can hamper or even block the megatrend's self-professed inevitability. At the end of the day, opposition to alternative energy developments condenses around one focal point: whatever solution the megatrend may offer, there are better ones that can be found, which points to the eventual demise of the megatrend as it is eclipsed by better solutions, should they prove cleaner and cheaper.

A factor that may have strong influence on the waxing or waning of the alternative energy megatrend is the development of innovative methods of harvesting energy from non-traditional, or unconventional, fossil fuel sources like shale oil and gas, tar sands, and others.[6] These sources of energy have already generated extensive inroads in the notional make-up of the energy mix, with related production capacity transforming former net energy importers into putative energy exporters, thereby changing the outlook of markets and government energy strategies. Other types of economically recoverable hydrocarbons loom on the horizon, in quantities that make current conventional reserves pale in comparison, for example, seabed methane hydrates, remote gas, or deep-sea oil. These developments suggest an inevitable correlation between alternative energy developments and the fluctuation of fossil fuels' demand and supply. Enthusiasts of these types of fossil fuels argue that peak oil remains in the distant future. Overcoming the oil shocks of the 1970s with aggressive incentives to locate and extract new sources of hydrocarbons slowed the previously resurgent development of renewables. In the same manner, the unconventional oil "revolution" that is currently underway may again change the paradigm for alternative energy developments, delaying and perhaps putting an end to the alternative energy megatrend, at least in its current form. As the ENI Chairman Giuseppe Recchi put it, "[U]nless in the next ten years we see a breakthrough in technology we cannot imagine now, today we'll bet on gas."[7]

Indeed, the future of the alternative energy megatrend is uncertain. However, the future is seen through the history, and, according to Shakespeare, "...what's past is prologue...."[8] This megatrend has already established itself as a footnote in the history of civilization. The question is: will it become a full chapter?

2. The ascent?

Projections about the alternative energy megatrend are ultimately restricted to current knowledge and driven by historical preconceptions and idea constructs. This book nonetheless posits that the megatrend's future seems assured for the time being. Globalization, the fragmentation of a multi-centric world system, and the ongoing global technological revolution have jointly catalyzed alternative energy developments into a powerful global megatrend in the 21st century. Modern alternative energy-related ideas, aesthetics, and values also support an assured future for alternative energy.

The future history of the megatrend will be closely aligned with the unfolding Fourth Industrial Revolution—a transformational change induced by "a fusion of technologies that is blurring the lines between the physical, digital and biological spheres."[9] The Fourth Industrial Revolution is bringing about a new level of interconnectedness, intelligence, and innovation, connecting people, objects, and spaces based on advanced information and communication technologies such as artificial intelligence, big data, blockchain technology, new generation mobile communications, 3D printing, and the "Internet of Things."

As discussed, the new capabilities associated with the new wave of technological breakthroughs, infrastructure, and institutional innovation are both drivers and preconditions of the alternative energy megatrend. The Fourth Industrial Revolution provides a foundation for the evolution of the alternative energy trend and turns it from a futuristic concept to a viable option able to compete with the traditional fossil-based energy mix. The promise of alternative energy to ensure a supply of cheap, clean, and practically limitless energy, seemingly far-fetched, does not look so fantastic against the background of the broad array of new technologies providing practical solutions for harvesting and distributing energy from renewable sources.

- Digital technologies can address significant technical issues hampering renewables' expansion, like the variability of energy output from intermittent renewables such as wind and solar or the decentralized model of providing energy from renewable sources (unlike nuclear power, coal, and natural gas, wind and solar energy is generated by relatively small generating stations, spread across a large area). Digitization offers solutions for the complexity of systems including a multitude of decentralized, renewable power generation units. "Smart grids" may provide the flexibility needed to reliably integrate renewable energies such as wind and solar.[10]

- Technological breakthroughs addressing energy storage, which is vital for alternative energy, occur with increasing speed. Intelligent monitoring and connectivity of devices provide for increased efficiency, machinery lifespan and sustainability, reduced downtime, and reduced energy use and total cost of ownership. Intelligent network technologies also provide platforms for integrating a wide range of stakeholders along the entire value chain and offer quick demand response and customized services. Data-driven smart technologies, solar roofs, batteries, and electric vehicles are also converting energy consumers to prosumers, offering a way for individuals to create and sell energy services, drastically changing business models.

- Innovation in the design and manufacturing of renewable energy generation components, like applying additive manufacturing model, drives down costs of production as well as operational and maintenance costs, which is critical for alternative energy wider acceptance. For example, wind turbine blade mold manufacturing will be transformed with 3D printing.[11]

These solutions may be considered early-stage developments. However, the high pace of research and development is also a significant feature of the Fourth Industrial Revolution. It may prove realistic to expect the evolution of more powerful solutions utilizing current renewable technologies as well as the emergence of breakthrough power sources such as fusion energy, which could provide emissions-free baseload power in virtually unlimited amounts.

The alternative energy trend trajectory will probably trace a zigzag path toward its own sustainability. The Fourth Industrial Revolution will not only push renewables forward but also strengthen competing solutions. A broader look at energy sector development reveals the ambiguous effects of new technologies on the pace and scale of renewables adoption. Meanwhile, traditional power sectors are also enjoying the benefits and advantages of these technologies. Customized manufacturing lowers the cost of traditional power plants. New energy technologies drive down both operational costs as well as emissions. Automated oil and gas platforms are already producing, from remote areas, parts made via 3D printing, which provides for efficient maintenance. Data-driven technologies also improve the efficiency and flexibility of energy use. For the time being, the Fourth Industrial Revolution will help fossil fuels stay in the game. The global energy mix of the foreseeable future will likely be rather complex and include various sources. It will also be fluid, with its components struggling for dominance until a new type of energy, adequate to meet the Fourth Industrial Revolution's energy needs, emerges.

The power, persistence, and direction of the drivers that make up the megatrend assure its future: energy independence and rebalancing; environmental and climate change considerations; the need for stable economic growth; envisioned technological developments; defense calculations; the pursuit of new forms of empowerment; and increasingly sympathetic public attitudes and ideologies that support alternative energy developments. A converging framework of local, state, and international alternative energy-related policies and regulations serves to unify these drivers into a major force promoting the megatrend and assuring its longevity.

On top of this set of "real world" drivers, the megatrend is driven by societal values and idea constructs. The importance that alternative energy has achieved in societal values, expectations, practices, and ideologies also supports the momentum shaping the alternative energy megatrend's propagation.

- Renewables continue to be strongly associated with certain human values, such as the desire for human interaction with nature that is not purely exploitative, the creation of a new green habitat for humanity, and the pursuit of new forms of empowerment. As these values are increasingly integrated into modern societal idea constructs, alternative energy comes to represent the practical means of achieving a new habitat for humanity and a new coexistence with nature, with the megatrend representing a new energy for a new world. The need for independent and uninterrupted access to affordable energy that does not exhaust natural resources and is both capable of being produced locally and deployed in any region of the world spurs the deployment of alternative energy technologies, sometimes irrespective of the hurdles or costs. In the process, modes of societal pressure emerge that associate the megatrend with new forms of empowerment available to state and non-state actors.

- Alternative energy developments' future appears assured due to their successful integration into a number of 21st century ideological frameworks.[12] The megatrend is continuously absorbing elements of different ideological paradigms that are bound together coherently over time and are a part of distinct ideologies that have achieved consensus among societal groups. The imperatives that assure the future of the alternative energy trend go beyond the material, in the sense that "along with making things, technology stands for something about what we are, or wish to be, and about the manner in which we live together."[13]

- The integration of the megatrend's own imagery in modern societal aesthetics at the intersection of technology and art is gaining momentum, suggesting the megatrend's assured future. This imagery suggests that alternative energy embodies an inherent goodness and freedom, combined with a new kind of power that does not exploit or force but, rather, co-exists, mutually supports, and more broadly stands for the abstractions of progress and modernity. Renewable technologies are increasingly incorporated in art forms like sculpture, painting, music, storytelling, and cinema. When artists use tidal energy to produce new sounds or embed solar photovoltaics into artwork, renewables become something altogether different and culturally significant.[14]

The almost cinematic projection of the megatrend onto societal views of the future makes the new hybrid aesthetic linked to humanity's own future especially palpable. It is increasingly achieving a harmony that provokes human reactions that are inseparable from the usability of renewables. These practical aesthetic elements of renewables can be found in art installations that generate energy as well as so-called aesthetic power plants giving rise to notions of "green architecture." The cognitive process of technological advancements that establishes the image that the megatrend imprints on societal consciousness reflects French postmodernist Jean Baudrillard's "basic reality."[16] It demonstrates the megatrend's capacity to blend

Figure 9: Solar Fountain at the Cooper Hewitt Design Museum[15]

into both urban backgrounds and natural landscapes and appeal to humans' physiological reactions to the stimulus of beauty.[17] It also incorporates the artistic and aesthetic elements of the precious, modern, and innovative—a captivating fusion of a René Magritte-like hybridization of humanity and nature, resulting in energy forms that are associated with a bright future. The megatrend's imagery has become an integral part of everyday life, forming "a social relation among people, mediated by images."[18]

The goals associated with the future of the alternative energy megatrend have already generated a range of customs, practical approaches, and methods that are increasingly incorporated in societal interactions. New technologies and forms of communication, infrastructure, and societal organization reinforce the momentum behind the deployment of alternative energy technologies. The growing support for broader technological developments is an expression of human rationality, curiosity, and spirit of adventure, reflecting notions of technological optimism, the trust in innovation, and the inherent benefits of technological progress.[19] In this manner, the values associated with renewables are incorporated into the social construction of the future, with the alternative energy megatrend's rising prominence embodying the impact of society's visions and needs on governance and decision-making.[20]

The societal perception of renewables' "assured longevity" that is essential to the megatrend's actual development is informed by subconscious notions of renewables and their association with goodness and moral correctness. The alternative energy megatrend's imprint on society's subconscious is an indicator of the nature of the transformations that are already taking place and, more importantly, of upcoming developments in the 21st century. As an idea construct, the megatrend represents an understanding of how human interaction with nature may evolve. Widely held environmental concerns have led to the emergence of popular movements, with a new focus on wellbeing, prosperity, and peaceful human coexistence with nature, and have already established a certain grassroots presence in education, family life, and popular culture.[21]

3. The dynamics.

At its current pace and trajectory, the megatrend is likely to follow a linear course of development along the path of basic research, applied research and development, and technological production and diffusion.[22] Current alternative energy technologies are predominantly secondary—and thus not radical—linear innovations.[23] This model of development hinges on essential preconditions for the persistence of the alternative energy megatrend, which in turn are based on small, incremental changes to policies, products, services, and processes. Within this model, technological diffusion with lower capital commitments, fewer restrictive practices, and fewer vested interests often precedes new and broader innovations.[24] This diffusion, in turn, attracts the private sector into the newly opened market space, intensifying technological competition.

Perhaps more importantly, the megatrend's future is reinforced by its capacity to bring about non-linear transformations of technologies, economic practices, and the structure of society.[25] The critical mass of changes and modifications in knowledge, practices, and approaches associated with renewables could trigger a non-linear leap toward a new cycle of technological capabilities and socio-political and techno-economic impacts. This leap could result in new notions of economic activity that could bring about higher-order outputs from the same inputs. The future iterations of the megatrend, whether real or aspirational, are prompting alterations in human conduct. The megatrend mimics the progression of broader technological developments, which interpolate both incremental and linear advances, as well as transformative leaps.

The progression of the alternative energy megatrend is already resulting in as many unanticipated as envisaged consequences. Breakthrough solutions in the future will arise, more often than not, from the unintended consequences of the alternative energy megatrend's next evolutionary stages, with results that are unknowable, as "any sufficiently advanced technology is indistinguishable from magic."[26] Such occurrences will result in new priorities and unanticipated values attached to outcomes.[27] However, we can only surmise to what extent Moore's law on information[28] will apply to the alternative energy megatrend in the short-term, and to what extent this law might predict the occurrence of repeated non-linear leaps generated by the pursuit of renewables.

Alternative energy technologies can be aptly classified as disruptive technologies.[29] Disruptive technologies characteristically affect markets by making products and companies obsolete, destroying old industries, challenging regulation, and generating new business and regulatory models. With this in mind, it is important to not only extract the maximum benefit from alternative energy's capacity for creativity, but to continue to closely monitor its security impact in light of the Law of Unintended Consequences—while remembering that "unforeseen consequences should not be identified with consequences which are necessarily undesirable,"[30] or may present, in economic-speak, positive externalities.

In the final analysis, the quest for alternative energy could prove more important than the actual result of the search. The true achievements may be by-products rather than targeted outcomes and bring a swath of changes in the behavior of actors. In the same manner that the development of radar resulted in the common microwave oven, or the laying of secure communication lines between Europe and America served as a precursor to the

World Wide Web, the alternative energy megatrend may produce unexpected capabilities and benefits in its upcoming iterations, in which "small differences in the initial conditions produce very great ones in the final phenomena."[31] Likewise, some questioned the large expenditures for the Apollo Project, while others continue to highlight, even today, the positive returns on human capital (more interest in science and technology occupations, advanced technologies, and improved systems engineering).[32] Although the future remains unpredictable, the alternative energy megatrend clearly constitutes a movement and an agent of global change and will transform itself as much as it transforms all that surrounds it, producing a range of security implications that, as discussed in previous chapters, encompass geopolitics, energy, defense, environmental, and economic security domains.

II. The progression of the alternative energy megatrend— making headway in a multi-centric world in the new age of Great Power Competition.

The age of "Great Power Competition," i.e., the emergence or comeback of peer competitors, has returned. Indeed, a world without Great Power Competition is just a historical footnote.

The rise of China, from a historical perspective, is the most important change in the balance of power in the early 21st century. Competition in the multi-centric world will be defined by the growth and relative weight of China and its strategical and tactical alliances. "Any U.S. administration is going to need a sustained strategy for dealing with China to set up a set of norms and rules of the road without dividing the world and plunging us into a war nobody wants; it will be the work of years before we get this right."[33]

In a multi-centric world, the Great Power Competition involves more than just the emergence of China as a great power. Asia overall has become an important center of the balance of power. Thus, a prerequisite of being a great power is a strategic presence in Asia; a presence along the lines of the Cold War Great Power Competition in Europe. Others such as India, the European Union, and Brazil are playing new parts in the new Great Power Competition.

Russia is a special case. Although it is arguably a declining power; it still, in some respects, has the capacity to behave like a Great power and could be seen as staging a limited comeback. It is a nuclear power, a permanent member of the UN Security Council, has vast territory, an abundance of resources, and is proactively exploring new technological capabilities.

Ongoing and upcoming rivalries will not necessarily replicate previous manifestations of Great Power Competition like the Cold War. The new competitors will not necessarily have the capacity, inclination, or plans to follow the United States' or the UK's path to preeminence.

1. The Americas: broadening energy security considerations and new avenues of power projection.

Alternative energy strategies in the Americas are driven by considerations ranging from energy security to maximizing certain geographic renewables advantages. The United States is vulnerable to oil supply disruptions, regional anti-Americanism, terrorist plots, and hostility by regimes possessing vast energy reserves. It is not surprising that renewables development in the United States is driven largely by the confluence of energy security concerns and civic and environmental agendas. While the U.S. federal government does not boast anything that resembles a comprehensive renewable energy policy, developing a strategic long-term approach to energy, including renewables, has become firmly embedded in energy security policies in the United States.[34]

Canada and Brazil are two other countries in the Americas where alternative energy features prominently on policy agendas. Canada currently ranks among the world's leading producers of renewable electricity, primarily from hydropower generation. Brazil is also considered to be among the world's largest renewable energy markets. It seeks to take advantage of its vast hydropower resources and play a significant role in the biofuels industry.

(1) The United States: energy security, environmental, and economic imperatives.

The history of alternative energy development policies in the United States is rather recent. These policies stem from the need for a diversified energy supply and economic growth, with both strands underpinned by environmental security considerations. Although the United States is increasingly incorporating the alternative energy megatrend's potential in its strategies, its practical uptake is constrained by a lack of funding, political will, and dependency on other countries' fossil fuels, as well as the availability of new domestic fossil fuel deposits, such as shale oil and gas.[35]

In spite of these constraints, the United States has been the source of breakthrough alternative energy technologies, and has set the tone for a number of world technology waves.[36] However, biofuels are the only renewable energy sector where the United States is the absolute world market leader. Steps intended to reverse this situation, undertaken by President Barack Obama, were followed by President Trump's attempts to dismantle the clean power legacy of his predecessor. Climate and alternative energy policies may remain a matter of intense political debate in the United States, impeding consistent energy policies on a federal level. Fluctuating approaches to federal regulation of renewable energy development create uncertainty for power producers and hamper initiatives in research and in business. "We definitely need to prepare, to adjust, to adapt to climate change to mitigate the impact of the industry on climate.... We're dealing with finite resources. There's not going to be more cobalt on this planet. There is not going to be new soil on this planet. There is not going to be new oxygen on this planet."[37]

Despite inconsistencies at the federal level, many U.S. states pursue alternative energy-related policies and have introduced regulations and mechanisms according to their specific interests and local political considerations. Thirty states have Renewable Portfolio Standard policies, which set a minimum percentage of energy a state must receive from renewable sources, and six more have non-binding policy goals. These policies have served as a key driver behind the renewable energy advancement in U.S.: since 2000 more than 62% of the growth in U.S. non-hydro renewables has been undertaken to satisfy RPS requirements.[38] State-level and regional cap-and-trade policies directly support the megatrend's propagation and are geared to address the wider range of carbon producers and emitters as well as the relatively high level of fossil fuel use in U.S. industry and transportation.

Policies targeting renewable energy supplies for low-income populations have been experimented with at the sub-national level. As of 2016, programs to expand access to renewable energy for low-income communities existed in California, Massachusetts, and the District of Columbia, and 12 states had community net metering programs to help low-income residents access solar PV by allowing the benefits of solar PV to be extended to renters, and not just to property owners.[39] State-level initiatives included New York's US$3.6 million in funding to support solar PV deployment in low-income communities and Illinois's Future Energy Jobs Bill, which also promotes solar PV deployment for low-income communities.[40]

Another supporting factor for renewable energy in the United States is that U.S. investment in renewable energy "tends to be more diverse than that of most other countries and regions, with strong showings by public markets, venture capital and private equity, and small-scale projects, as well as by utility-scale asset finance,"[41] and these markets are rather dynamic.

Thus, in 2016, there was strong growth in small distributed capacity investment, with US $13.1 billion of rooftop and other small PV projects going ahead, up 33% from 2015.[42]

Enacting renewable energy policies at the federal level is complicated by difficulties in the legislative process and the pressures of the electoral cycle. U.S. policymaking is further subject to the needs of its extensive fossil-based economy, and its oil and gas sector. There has been increasing pressure from oil companies and consumers in general to open up more federal land for drilling, make states' licensing of oil and gas drilling more efficient, and build or upgrade aging energy transmission routes and pipelines.[43] Although public opinion is influenced by environmental concerns, the prospect of the United States becoming energy independent in the near future is adding momentum to efforts to scale up production of natural gas, shale gas, oil, and shale oil. Since the crisis in Ukraine, some U.S. politicians are even calling for expedited U.S. liquefied natural gas exports as a means of influencing international politics by diminishing European dependence on Russian gas.[44]

The U.S. debate on energy and economic security has been primarily driven by the belief that the economy should not be vulnerable to debilitating shocks caused by geopolitical events. This is partly why the U.S. government, while arguably more averse to subsidies than European governments, has provided support to the private sector for energy technology development for nearly one hundred years. Energy tax incentives, for example, fluctuated in the 1980s, stagnated in the 1990s, and soared after 2005. The Obama administration's 2009 U.S. stimulus and tax incentives bill was seen as particularly generous to renewable energy, smart grids, transmission, advanced vehicles, and energy efficiency.[45] As the cost-competitiveness of renewable energy, especially solar and wind, grows, political pressure to give way to market forces will become stronger and the volume of support will inevitably fluctuate.

The development of renewables is focused on promoting energy independence and resilience. The U.S.'s overriding energy policy concern remains ensuring the stability of the energy-producing regions on which the U.S. economy depends, with the focus shifting according to the balance of domestic production and imports. The U.S. is prepared to deploy significant military resources overseas whenever energy supplies are threatened. The U.S. remains exposed to energy market volatility and disruptions, despite increased domestic fossil fuel production, necessitating a commitment to protecting global fossil fuel supplies.

National security considerations related to protecting vital U.S. interests are closely correlated with new energy developments. The U.S. energy infrastructure at present is a tempting target for malevolent actors. Several terrorist plots to damage or destroy U.S. infrastructure have been foiled in the past years, including a 2002 attempt to bring down the Brooklyn Bridge and a 2005 plan to blow up a Wyoming natural gas refinery, the Transcontinental Pipeline, a natural gas pipeline from the Gulf Coast to New York and New Jersey, and a Standard Oil refinery in New Jersey.[46] A number of hacker attempts to attack power grids in the United States were reported in 2017 and 2018.[47] Any disruption to the grid would have strategic and economic consequences. While modernization efforts reduce vulnerability and enhance efficiency, financing such upgrades remains problematic given the polarization between Republicans and Democrats and the need to cut the budget deficit to stabilize and reduce the federal debt.

Beyond energy and economic security, U.S. alternative energy advances can serve wider geopolitical goals. U.S. "soft power" is largely comprised of its use of technological leadership, of which alternative energy is a part. In the energy-related aspects of its foreign policy, the U.S. has to take into account the changing economic picture of its main suppliers and neighbors. Latin American oil exporters continue to rely on energy revenues, and U.S. dependency on imports strengthens those countries' leverage. To prevent any potential damage to its energy security, the U.S. pays attention to the stability and development of its Latin American energy suppliers (fossil or otherwise).

Most primary energy production, conservation, and energy efficiency activities have received subsidies for many years. There are differing views on what constitutes an appropriate scale of support and the support mechanisms themselves and whether these subsidies should be extended. However, the fate of U.S. policy options affecting the alternative energy megatrend will ultimately depend on the technologies' economic viability. The economic costs related to the attainment of geopolitical gains from alternative energy development have yet to be fully calculated. The U.S. government thus faces complicated policy choices. These considerations prompt the further securitization of the national energy system.

(2) Canada: maximizing potential.

The alternative energy megatrend has already elicited significant attention by successive Canadian governments, resulting in a diverse alternative energy portfolio. Canada generates a large share of its electricity (66% in 2015) from renewable sources. Hydropower currently accounts for 62% of the country's power mix.[48] Several large hydroelectric projects are currently under construction.[49] In addition to being a world leader in hydropower generation, Canada is also a major producer of wind power and has undertaken projects in generation from biomass, solar, geothermal, and tidal sources. Canadian alternative energy policies have catalyzed renewables development by requiring renewable power shares (RPS) of 5–20%, meaning that electricity companies are required to produce the aforementioned percentage of electricity from renewable sources. Overall, these priorities reflect the broader Canadian security and foreign policy aim of using soft power to address threats to human security.[50]

However, Canada is not immune to changes in political priorities and the scale of support measures has been revised in recent years. In mid-2016, for example, the Ontario government suspended the second phase of its renewable procurement program, cutting CAD 3.8 billion in planned renewable energy contracts. In addition, in an effort to lower electricity bills for consumers, 758 renewable energy contracts were cancelled in 2018.[51]

Canada's alternative energy policies do not exhibit an overt intent to establish a specific international position in the renewables sector, but have a rather marked domestic slant driven by the significance and potential of non-traditional fossil fuel reserves the country possesses. The Canadian government has set ambitious goals to compete with U.S. clean energy producers but it remains unclear how these goals can be achieved. For example, the Canadian government's 2007 ecoENERGY for Renewable Power Program offered a guaranteed production incentive for new projects over a 10-year period. However, no new contribution agreements were signed after March 31, 2011.[52] Another contentious barrier to policy support for renewables is the oil shale and gas industries in Canada, especially in Alberta province, where the majority of these new resources are found. Successful international challenges of subsidies and trade restrictions have struck another blow to province-specific policies aimed at creating local renewable energy industries.[53]

(3) Latin America and the Caribbean: Brazil aiming to maintain its frontrunner status.

Brazil seeks to maximize the advantages it can extract from the alternative energy megatrend. As the biggest economy in Latin America and an emerging power with resources and financial strength on a global scale, it is the clear leader in alternative energy development in the region. Nearly 76% of its electricity comes from renewable sources, primarily from hydropower.[54]

It has focused predominantly on sectors where it perceives it has competitive advantages, in particular biofuels and hydro. Currently Brazil is the world's second-largest biofuel producer and ranks fourth among the bioenergy capacity leaders.[55] The National Policy on Climate Change establishes the expansion of renewable and clean energy usage as a part of the national strategy for the country's medium to long-term development. The alternative energy megatrend has also provided Brazil with a tool for exercising one of its foreign policy priorities: building South-South relationships based on a framework of southern solidarity and specific strategic interests.[56]

Alternative energy sources make up a relatively large proportion of energy use in Latin America because of its geographical endowments, in particular biomass and water resources. But this could change as more countries (e.g., Argentina, Chile, and Brazil) discover reserves of shale oil and gas underground or underneath their territorial waters. However, as energy diversification is regarded in the region as a means to foster energy security, and as policy instruments have driven crucial cost reductions, the development of renewables will likely be a sustainable trend.

With targeted financial support for certain alternative energy technologies, Latin America could become a global leader in the field. In 2015, Mexico and Chile joined Brazil for the first time in the list of the top 10 largest renewable energy markets globally.[57]

Energy security concerns, in the context of rapidly falling costs of non-hydropower renewables, are driving broader renewable energy development in Latin America. Despite the enormous hydro potential and the traditional political support for this source, the region is vulnerable to hydrological cycles and extreme weather events like El Niño. Developing large-scale projects is further complicated due to social and environmental issues, as in Chile and Panama.[58]

Non-hydropower renewables installed capacity tripled between 2006 and 2015 in Latin America.[59] Support for renewable energy is found across the region, as indicated by over 300 pro-renewable policies. The most widespread policies include fiscal incentives, regulatory instruments, and financial mechanisms.[60] Latin America's renewables sector is also supported by national public financing institutions which accounted for over one-third of new clean energy project financing in Latin America in 2015.

2. Europe: a millennial strategy.

Overall, Europe is considered an established world leader in alternative energy developments even though within the EU the mix of fossil fuel and alternative energy differs substantially from country to country, and the member states have different alternative energy policy priorities.[61] The commitment to renewables ranges from the EU's strong embrace of alternative energy technologies to Russia's distinct lack of interest due to its considerable fossil fuel reserves, nuclear power capacity, and its willingness to use its current energy leverage as a foreign policy tool. There is, however, an emerging common agenda among European countries that underscores how alternative energy could prove to be a significant tool of power projection. Most EU countries' high energy dependence on external sources, the growing significance of environmental considerations, and the megatrend's potential to spur economic growth provide considerable momentum to alternative energy development. This momentum is reinforced by the fact that the European public has largely welcomed alternative energy as a component of popular concepts of sustainable development and a "circular economy."

(1) The European Union: the durability of the consensus on energy security challenges.

The EU is one of the global alternative energy leaders. Its investment in alternative energy is in response to political pressure to address energy security, climate change, and other environmental security challenges. The rationale for such a focus was articulated by German Chancellor Angela Merkel's statement: "Europe must also lead the way in renewable energies, energy efficiency, and the protection of our climate."[62] EU policy consensus, however, faces a number of obstacles, including a lack of funding, inconsistent regulations, and the absence of a functioning and effective alternative energy market.[63]

The EU is the world's leader in installed solar PV and wind capacity, as well as in average renewable electricity capacity installed per person.[64] With the annual average compound growth rate of 7.4% in RES-E (electricity from renewable energy sources) capacity per unit GDP over the period 2005–2016, the EU is visibly transforming the energy resource base of its economy.[65]

EU alternative energy policies aim to mitigate the EU's specific energy security risks and vulnerabilities, particularly given the region's heavy dependence on external supplies. The EU's dependence on foreign energy is currently about 54% and is projected to rise as North Sea oil and gas reserves are depleted. The EU has a number of fossil fuel suppliers, such as Russia, Norway, and countries in North Africa, the Middle East, Central Asia, and the Persian Gulf. But EU policymakers recognize the dangers of excessive dependence on these suppliers. Many of them are located in unstable regions prone to internal strife which can result in supply disruptions. Over one-third of the natural gas consumed in the EU is supplied by Russia, whose disputes with transit countries threaten to disrupt supplies.

With this in mind, raising the share of renewables in the EU energy mix has become a strategic priority. The EU Renewable Energy Directive establishes an overall policy for the production and promotion of energy from renewable sources in the EU. It requires the EU to meet at least 20% of its total energy needs with renewables by 2020.[66] In 2018, renewable energy represented 18.9% of energy consumed in the EU.[67]

The EU's renewable energy market has had its ups and downs. Market growth slowed in 2015 due to the economic crisis, a downturn in the building sector and low oil prices. Despite the slowdown for some renewable heat technologies, geothermal-based district heat has expanded, especially where resources are optimal and where building construction has continued. The market for heat pumps has continued to grow, especially in France, Finland, and Poland. New EU rules came into force, amending existing legislation to limit to 7% the share of biofuels in transport from crops grown on agricultural land. Biofuel production remained largely stable.[68]

Pursuing the development of renewable energy is, therefore, part of the EU's answer to its growing dependence on foreign energy. Former French President Nicolas Sarkozy stated that "we are going to make as significant a change of direction on renewable energy as General de Gaulle did for nuclear energy in the 1960s."[69] This does not mean that the EU is turning its back on fossil fuels, merely that it is willing to pursue alternative energy development on a far greater scale.

The national renewable energy action plans of all EU countries identify the steps they intend to take to meet their renewables targets. These plans include sectorial targets for electricity, heating and cooling, and transport, planned policy measures, the mix of renewables technologies they expect to employ, and planned use of cooperation mechanisms.

Energy policymaking in EU countries remains primarily the responsibility of member states despite efforts to introduce blanket frameworks, such as the European External Energy Policy and the 2020 emission targets. Member states' strategic interests, which encompass environmental and economic aspirations as well as energy security, guide EU policies and generate momentum for the alternative energy megatrend's progression. These efforts are "an economic and geopolitical signal"[70] that could lead to the creation of a unified energy market in Europe. Such a market would be premised upon cooperation not only in traditional energy markets but increasingly in the alternative energy development sector.

EU members have achieved different levels of competence and specialization in different types of renewables. The commercial exchanges of these capabilities within the EU create a mutually complementary framework of interests and needs. This may also affect the EU's energy diplomacy since it will strengthen its bargaining position with its main energy suppliers—Russian and the North African gas producers—as well as strengthen ties with new energy suppliers.

Alternative energy development in the EU is also seen as the means to achieving higher economic growth. Regulatory mechanisms offer a source of financing to further develop these technologies and enhance their economic feasibility. Although the EU as a whole is not making large investments in alternative energy (aside from countries with a strong innovation and technological base like Germany), cap-and-trade demand pricing presents a source of revenue for technological development.

EU alternative energy developments are further underpinned by specific environmental security considerations. The EU's overall energy and environmental security strategy adds momentum to the alternative energy megatrend. In 2007 the goals set by EU leaders (enacted in legislation in 2009) can be summed up as "20-20-20" targets: reducing greenhouse gas emissions by 20% (from 1990 levels); increasing the share of renewable energy in the energy consumption mix to 20%; and improving energy efficiency by 20%, all by 2020.[71] By 2017, the EU was mostly on track to meet these targets.[72]

The EU's support for renewables involves a mix of regulatory and subsidy mechanisms, the most notable of which are feed-in tariffs. Other support mechanisms are the Strategic Energy Technology Plan (SET Plan),[73] and demand-side cap-and-trade measures that govern carbon emissions pricing on large-scale power producers and other industrial sectors. The carbon cap-and-trade system has a tight focus on EU emissions targets and large carbon emitters. Outside of power generation, the EU members' policies rely on comparatively high fuel taxes, rather than cap-and-trade.[74]

However, questions remain about the future of EU policies and the extent to which they incentivize lower emissions and promote alternative energy. For example, the European Commission's proposal to reform the Emissions Trading System (ETS) required years of debate prior to its adoption by the European Parliament.[75] The ETS, whose functioning has been seriously called into question, is one of the main EU-wide environmental mechanisms. Other countries (e.g., Australia and South Korea), California, and some Chinese provinces have adopted schemes similar to the EU's ETS.

But these and other actors monitor the ETS's evolution more to avoid its shortcomings than to emulate it.

A major consideration for the EU is that the factors propelling the alternative energy megatrend can ultimately influence alliances and have long-term geopolitical implications. Renewables development could help the EU avoid certain strategic and geopolitical approaches that could prove harmful to the continent in the long run. It could also bolster the foreign policy interests of the EU's major member states.[76] It remains uncertain, though, how alternative energy development in the EU will affect relations with its major fossil fuel suppliers, and who will ultimately gain from such developments.

The EU's pursuit of global leadership in renewables has also increased tensions, even with its allies. Several disputes have already erupted, most notably the clash between the EU and the U.S. over biofuel exports, which resulted in the EU introducing an anti-subsidy duty in 2009. The evolving energy security strategies of different member states are challenging the EU's overall environmental security commitments. As the EU deepens its reliance on alternative energy development and reduces its share of gas imports from Russia, the Middle East, and North Africa, it is expected to confront resistance from these regions that may take the form of retaliatory actions along economic lines.

(2) Russia and other non-EU countries: moving beyond testing the waters from the shore.

As one of the most significant energy-producing countries in Europe and globally, Russia will be directly impacted by the evolution of the alternative energy megatrend. Russia has yet to focus on alternative energy development and until recently perceived the pursuit of alternative energy as detracting from state energy policies and national interests. However, it has never actually opposed the development of alternative energy technologies and is a leader in hydropower capacity and biomass.

By the end of 2015, total installed renewable power generation capacity represented about 20% of Russia's total power generation capacity.[77] Hydropower accounts for all of this capacity, followed by bioenergy.[78] There is some evidence that Russia is taking steps to expand its solar PV, onshore wind, and geothermal capacity. One of the largest solar power plants in the country, in Dagestan, began operating in 2013. Off-grid systems are being built with increasing frequency in Siberia and the Far East, where population density is very low. In 2014, a new PV station was launched in the

Altai region. At the end of that year, two further solar PV stations began production. Geothermal capacity, located in eastern Russia, also came into operation in 2015.[79]

However, the lowering of renewable energy targets suggests that Russia will not pursue an accelerated deployment of renewables in its energy mix in the near future. In January 2009, the Russian government announced plans to increase the share of renewable energy generation from less than 1% to 4.5% by 2020 (hydropower excluded). In 2013 the target was considered unrealistic and a lower target of 2.5% was introduced for 2020.[80]

Current government support for renewable energy market growth will hardly bring about a substantial breakthrough. In 2013, Russia adopted Decree No. 449 on the Mechanism for the Promotion of Renewable Energy on the Wholesale Electricity and Capacity Market to stimulate economic activity in the renewables sector. The scheme is considered overly complex, providing little certainty to investors. The cornerstone of the scheme is the "Agreement for the Supply of Capacity," which allows renewable energy investors to benefit from regulated capacity prices. The Russian capacity market, however, rewards power plants for their ability to produce electricity on demand, an ability often lacking in renewable energy generation facilities due to the supply variability. The decree also obliged renewable energy project investors to use equipment in each installation which is at least partly produced or assembled in Russia, even if cheaper and more efficient foreign alternatives are available.[81]

Whether or not Russia eventually decides to pursue alternative energy development, the megatrend will factor into its long-term strategic and national interests. Because of its strong dependence on fossil fuel exports, Russia is vulnerable to any changes in energy imports by European, and increasingly, Asian customers as well. For example, in response to the seizure of Crimea, Europe and the U.S. devised strategies to reduce their dependence on Russian energy. This prompted Russia to seek new long-term contracts with Eastern partners, notably China.[82] This raises the question of how Russia would react to a global drop in demand for oil and gas. As Russia is a relatively high-cost producer, a collapse in oil and gas prices could spell another sharp and long-term downturn for the Russian economy similar to the one it experienced from 1986 to 1999.

Russia continues to demonstrate a willingness to utilize its energy leverage in foreign policy interactions with Europe.[83] For Russia, energy represents a geo-economic and geopolitical advantage beyond its intrinsic value as a commodity.[84] Russia and other major energy suppliers cannot be expected to readily relinquish this competitive advantage. At present, Russia can exercise a significant degree of influence on Europe given the latter's dependency on its energy supplies. Russia therefore does not need explicit military strategies to complement its energy policies.

This status quo may change, however, should other sources of supply become available, crowding out Russian oil and gas, or if alternative energy achieves a greater level of penetration within the energy mix. Russia would face stark choices and different calculations regarding the viability of a militarization of its energy policy. Modern Russian history indicates that the reaction is likely to be within modes of traditional, spatialized geopolitics, with national interests serving as the determining factor of any policy. The outstanding question is whether the scales will tip toward compromise or confrontation.

A scenario in which Russia acts aggressively to protect energy rents cannot be ruled out. Russia's energy policy pursues two main goals. First, it wants to build assets and resources within the state-owned energy entities, such as Gazprom, Rosneft, and Transneft, and key players in the electricity sector, like Inter RAO, RusHydro, and Rossetti, with national interests superseding investors' interests. The second is maximizing its competitive advantages in energy in order to attain specific internal and external political goals that include influencing the world energy system and ultimately the policies of the West, particularly those of Europe.

Beyond Russia, other non-EU European states are implementing renewable energy policies at different speeds. For example, in 2016, 62.9% of Switzerland's domestic electricity production came from hydropower.[85] Another example is Norway, which is both a progressive, advanced, and environmentally conscious country and a major producer of fossil fuel. According to Norway's Petroleum and Energy Ministry, 98% of electricity production comes from renewable energy sources.[86] Other non-EU European countries, such as Serbia, are developing their energy policies in line with EU directives. According to the National Action Plan for Renewable Energy Sources adopted by the Republic of Serbia, the share of renewable energy in gross final consumption of energy should be 27% by 2020.[87]

3. China: pursuing regional hegemony via a broader strategy of national development and security with renewables-related geopolitical leadership.

China is the world's largest energy consumer and second-largest economy. To support its economic growth, it must seek out new sources of energy, especially those that are independent from politically volatile regions or vulnerable to interference by other great powers. A key component of this strategy is the development and deployment of alternative sources of energy.

China has shown the most consistent pursuit of renewables of any alternative energy player. This is part of an overall strategy aimed at a China-centric Asia. China sees renewables development as part of an effort to secure additional energy supplies. Securing access to advanced and affordable energy technologies and promoting cleaner and renewable energy sources is the main strategic incentive for renewables development. However, the pursuit of renewables has other elements that resonate with the country's growing economic clout and its growing geopolitical power.

China is the strongest alternative energy player in the world. By the end of 2016, it ranked first, ahead of the United States, Brazil, Canada, and Germany, in total renewable power capacity and in the rate of capacity growth.[88] Its intensive pursuit of alternative energy development is driven by several factors: economic growth, energy security, its own vast pollution problems, and leadership positioning in Asia. Utilizing its extensive financial and human resources, China is following an aggressive strategy that no other country has been able to successfully match.[89] China is the global leader in annual investment in renewable energy.

Figure 10: Renewable Energy Capacity Investment by Country[90]

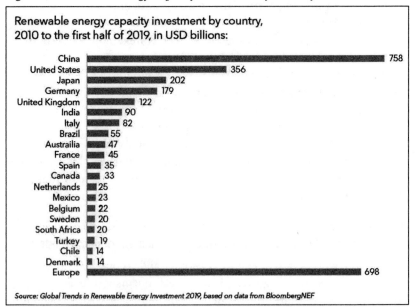

Renewable energy capacity investment by country, 2010 to the first half of 2019, in USD billions:

China	758
United States	356
Japan	202
Germany	179
United Kingdom	122
India	90
Italy	82
Brazil	55
Austrailia	47
France	45
Spain	35
Canada	33
Netherlands	25
Mexico	23
Belgium	22
Sweden	20
South Africa	20
Turkey	19
Chile	14
Denmark	14
Europe	698

Source: Global Trends in Renewable Energy Investment 2019, based on data from BloombergNEF

The country is also a leader in manufacturing solar and wind equipment and its associated components. In BNEF's annual ranking of onshore and offshore turbine manufacturers for 2016, out of the top 10 companies, four and five correspondingly were from China.[91]

China has demonstrated its willingness to use technological advances to add to its power projection capabilities. Its proactive alternative energy policies should not be attributed to some form of "Westernization" or viewed as a vestige of "modernization," but rather represent a deeper understanding of the interrelation between technological development and geopolitical power—a realization that China has already demonstrated and intends to fully utilize. Technology is not an imposition of the West's will on China but a tool that is available to whoever grasps it.

Energy security is intimately linked with economic growth and continuously influences China's strategic and geopolitical calculations. This is reflected in the Chinese stance toward alternative energy. Beyond its need for energy to maintain its current rate of economic growth, energy independence is part of China's vision for the future development of Asia. China's energy diplomacy has been deployed on several continents, and the advent of renewables is unlikely to change energy's prominent position in China's national security considerations.

China's geopolitical strategy remains bound by the geography of buffer zones and spheres of national interest.[92] In this context, the Chinese government's national security position strongly influences alternative energy development. Its leadership's view has been consistent: "China has to look at supply security and the name of the game in energy security is diversification."[93] However, Chinese energy policy is not a coordinated and seamless whole.

Although there is a central guiding hand, the practical result is more of a common direction than an imposition of a central will on a wide range of players involved in the Chinese energy market.[94] Despite its renewable energy leadership, Chinese energy consumption is still dominated by oil and coal, and a scenario in which renewables generate most of China's energy needs lies in the distant future.

China is increasingly becoming an anchor and gravitational center for a new sphere of influence demarcated by its geo-economic and geopolitical reach.[95] The spread of China's influence, particularly in Asia and Africa, is causing a realignment of economic, cultural, and political power across the globe. China's strategic leadership aims have been demonstrated in its stance toward the development of alternative energy and its overall global framework for climate change policy. In 2015, after a period of restrained policy towards global climate regulation, China's top leader, President Xi Jinping, for the first time attended the United Nations Climate Change Conference, claiming China's leading role in the design of global mechanisms governing environmental and energy issues.[96] Advancements in renewables and a growing role in international efforts to tackle climate change would further bolster China's geopolitical position and provide it with additional leverage in its relations with the West.

China is already forced to play a leading role in global energy markets as a major energy importer, pursuing joint energy strategies with other actors like Russia. China's ambitions on a global scale remain unclear. At the very least China is expected to continue its policy of securing its near-abroad and coastline.[97] Its ambitions may remain those of a regional power but that would be due to lack of intent rather than capability as its increasing influence in Eurasia gives it preeminence and endows it with the capacity to challenge even the United States.

China continues to face growing energy demands and local environmental imperatives, with alternative energy providing one solution to meeting those needs. The megatrend's potential could furnish China with an array of opportunities to meet a wide range of energy and economic security needs. Its implications provide a new putative source of geopolitical and economic strength, producing power realignments beyond the context of Asia's multidimensional regional and global rivalries. In this regard, China has staked a leadership claim in alternative energy development, often at the risk of running afoul of international regulations in the drive for market-leading energy diversification and economic growth.[98]

4. Asia-Pacific: pursuing alternative energy developments to match the regional hegemon.

For the other major economies of Asia (India, Japan, and Australia) alternative energy represents a source of energy security and offers economic and geopolitical advantages. The region is a massive consumer of energy without established energy resources. With the megatrend presenting the potential for immediate benefits to their economies, alternative energy is an area in which these countries are seeking to match China. The pursuit of energy security is also part of the growing willingness of Asian economies to utilize resources as a means of propelling economic growth and projecting geopolitical power.

(1) *India: energy, economic, and environmental security considerations amid the pursuit of regional and global positioning.*

Like China, India views alternative energy as a factor in the creation of geopolitical and economic strength, prompting significant support for renewables. India's intensifying energy security focus supports the development of alternative energy, particularly solar and wind power, with ambitions sometimes disproportionate to the benefits of current renewable energy technologies.

The Indian government is applying a broad strategy that increasingly incorporates support for renewables to ensure an ample supply of energy for its growing economy. In 2016, India ranked sixth globally in new alternative energy investment. It is also one of the top five wind power producers in the world. This growth in alternative energy investment was supported by several initiatives, including the government's Jawaharlal Nehru Solar Mission, which aims to deploy 20,000 MW of grid-connected solar power by 2022,[99] and the launch of a system for trading Renewable Energy Certificates.[100] India's forward-looking targets and anticipated investment requirements are set forth in consecutive "New and Renewable Energy" five-year plans. Indian states are actively expanding renewable power deployment through the adoption of new net metering policies and the use of tendering.[101]

As additional incentives, the Indian government applies two climate-focused instruments to develop renewable energy technologies: the National Action Plan on Climate Change (NAPCC) and the Clean Development Mechanism (CDM) of the Kyoto Protocol. Many of the measures India is adopting to foster renewables are also aligned with its broader national interests, such as enhancing energy security, reducing costs, and avoiding the use of valuable foreign exchange reserves. India's energy aspirations are thus achieving momentum, and in effect, boosting the alternative energy megatrend.

Energy and renewables are becoming a significant part of India's overall geopolitical stance in Asia. It conducts consumer coordination activities with other major energy importers. At the same time, India has undertaken measures to enhance its energy security, especially in view of its longstanding concerns over tensions with Pakistan. These measures have centered on building strategic oil reserves and acquiring energy facilities abroad.

India is thus following a strategy similar to that of China, which could spark tension between the two powers if they find themselves competing over the purchase of a specific resource or asset. Although India's focus on renewable sources is relatively weak in comparison to China's, a rivalry between these two large energy importers over alternative energy should not be discounted, even though greater benefits may be accrued through cooperation.[102]

India is becoming more forceful in expressing its position on renewable energy and environmental and climate change as part of a more assertive foreign policy stance. In particular, at the Durban Climate Change Conference in 2011, India sought to gain as many concessions from Europe and the United States as possible, with the spotlight on legally binding climate change parameters. India also proactively supported the Paris Climate Accord in 2015. The need to meet increasing energy demand because of population growth, along with India's plentiful alternative energy resources, could lead to significant progress in renewable energy development. If successful, alternative energy promotion will strengthen India's position vis-à-vis its current energy suppliers and its neighbors. In this context, India increasingly relies on multilateralism to support its global repositioning and ambitions. It carefully balances its role as a spokesperson for emerging and developing countries with its membership in international fora and new groupings of major powers, such as the G20, the Major Economies Forum, and the Asia-Pacific Partnership.

(2) Japan: searching for a sustainable energy model in the aftermath of Fukushima.

Japan's alternative energy policies are primarily driven by energy security imperatives and its desire to limit dependence on fossil fuel imports. For many years, this strategy involved reliance on nuclear power to mitigate its dependence on foreign energy sources. This strategy was dramatically affected by the March 2011 earthquake, tsunami, and subsequent disaster at the Fukushima Dai-ichi nuclear power plant. The Fukushima accident and its aftermath have had profound repercussions on Japan's public psyche and energy security policy. The earthquake and tsunami caused a series of equipment failures, nuclear meltdowns, and the release of radioactive materials. After the meltdown of the Chernobyl reactor in 1986, it was the second most serious nuclear accident in history and only the second accident (along with Chernobyl) to measure a seven on the International Nuclear Event Scale.[103]

Prior to the Fukushima disaster, Japan's primary focus was on nuclear energy expansion with more modest targets for renewables, such as geothermal and solar energy.[104] The disaster has led Japan to consider radically transforming its energy sector policies, with renewable technologies now seen as an alternative to both fossil fuels and nuclear power. In the summer of 2011, the Japanese Ministry of Energy, Trade, and Industry (METI) put forth a proposal for a 30-year-long plan to develop energy efficiency and renewable technologies, which complemented the earlier introduction of higher feed-in tariffs.

In response to the accident, almost 80% of the public expressed support for the phase-out of nuclear power, and renewable energy is now widely viewed as a critical energy source for Japan's future. Fukushima and Nagano have set targets of 100% for renewables, and Tokyo and Osaka have become more interested in restructuring their electricity markets. In 2016, Japan was among the top five countries by renewable power capacity with solar power as the leading component of renewable energy mix.[105]

Japan's established tradition of technological leadership and leveraging innovation for economic growth will likely drive its renewables sector. It appears to be one of the few countries willing to push the boundaries of established alternative energy technologies, with some investment into solar energy from space. As a resource-poor yet technologically endowed country, Japan is conducting extensive research and development in renewable energy and pursuing several development directions, including more experimental technologies such as wind lenses, ocean current power generation, and wave power. Technological breakthroughs in these fields could bolster Japan's geopolitical position, barring recent complications with nuclear power.[106]

Japan's increasingly intensive pursuit of national and energy security expressed through a more assertively nation-centric strategy has generated tension with other Asian powers. There has been a ratcheting-up of friction between China and Japan regarding the sovereignty of the Diaoyu/ Senkaku islands, with strong energy security connotations. Gas was discovered under the sea close to the five islets in the late 1960s. From China's perspective, Japan triggered a conflict by nationalizing the islands in 2012. Both Japan and China continue to navigate around the islands, creating the potential for standoffs and even a clash. Although these tensions do not have energy as their sole cause, they are indicative of the relative instability of regional relations and the extent to which foreign policy may be affected by future energy competition.[107] Furthermore, the potential decline in Japan's prominence when compared to emerging China and India could reshape geopolitical and security dynamics in Asia. Japan's commitment to reducing GHG emissions under the Kyoto Protocol, however, establishes it as a key leader in the Asia region, which is important for Japan from a geopolitical perspective.

(3) Australia: addressing energy security considerations with respect to reliance on natural resources for economic and national security.

Australia stands apart from its Asian neighbors due to its coal reserves and natural gas. However, it too is implementing alternative energy policies as it strives to meet its environmental and energy security objectives.

Australia is assessing several renewable options, including wind, solar, wave energy, and biofuel. It has been able to achieve a number of policy targets through the Small Renewable Energy Scheme (SRES), which uses uncapped fixed-price certificates that are bought and sold in a national certificate market. Other measures include the expanded Renewable Energy Target Program and the Clean Energy Future Plan.[108] In addition, in 2012 the Australian Renewable Energy Agency (ARENA) was established to support technological innovations in renewable energy, funding projects from research to pre-commercial deployment. Its investment priorities include delivering secure and reliable electricity, accelerating solar PV innovation, and improving energy productivity and renewable energy export.[109]

In 2009, the Labor government introduced a cap-and-trade system, the "Carbon Pollution Reduction Scheme" (CPRS). The scheme, however, was a source of bitter political controversy, leading to its eventual failure. A successor to the CPRS, the Carbon Pricing Mechanism (CPM), was passed into law as part of the 2012 Clean Energy Future Package (CEF). However, implementation remains controversial. Many of the challenges facing the CPM and other parts of the CEF package are due to the fact that a single policy measure is being applied to different technologies, each with different costs and outputs. Further, Australia's abundance of coal gives it a large cost advantage over other energy sources and accounts for roughly 75% of the continent's energy supply. Moreover, substantial shale gas deposits may exist in the Cooper Basin, in the state of South Australia. Still, Australia has extensive renewable resources that, if brought online, could fortify the country's energy security and geopolitical standing.

5. The Greater Middle East and Africa: experimentation restricted by the dominance of fossil fuels in the Middle East and the "Grand Energy Game" replayed in Africa.

Alternative energy development in the Middle East and Africa is more limited than anywhere else in the world. Some nations, such as Israel and South

Africa, are regional anomalies and have set out distinct targets to accommo-date economic and energy security concerns. However, for the majority of countries in these regions, local developments have prohibited the creation of a coherent and comprehensive alternative energy sector. Instead, most renewable energy developments have been novel showpiece experiments.

Nonetheless, a small number of states, particularly in the Middle East, are aligning their strategies with the projected direction of the alternative energy megatrend. They regard the megatrend as a path toward achieving the position of minority shareholders in the upcoming energy equilibrium. The culmination of these efforts positions the Middle East to enhance its geopolitical standing for both regional and external actors. It could also make Africa a new heartland over which great powers compete in a reprise of elements in the "Grand Energy Game."

While relatively little renewable power capacity has been deployed in most countries, interest in CSP and solar PV is growing rapidly. Iraq, Jordan, and the UAE all held tenders for renewable power in 2015. Jordan brought its first utility-scale wind farm online, Israel led the region for solar PV capacity additions, and major steps were taken towards domestic manufacturing of solar technologies in several countries, including Saudi Arabia.[110] Solar thermal markets also expanded in the Middle East. In 2015, Oman announced plans to host the world's largest solar thermal facility, which will produce steam for the oil industry. Mandatory green building certifications in the United Arab Emirates (UAE), for example, have helped spur solar cooling markets in the region.[111] However, there is a wide range of obstacles including ineffective legislation, the presence of traditional cen-tralized framework, and underdeveloped infrastructure.

The majority of African countries regard alternative energy as a means of creating new avenues for channeling aid and facilitating transfers of technology and financing from developed countries and international insti-tutions. This consideration reflects the stark reality of continued, almost exclusive reliance of African countries on the production and use of tra-ditional energy sources. However, the potential exists for Africa's natural resources and the financial capabilities of the Middle East to be harnessed to develop alternative energy and create new avenues for power projection.

(1) The Greater Middle East: ambitious projects constrained by inconsistent commitment.

Due to the overarching significance of fossil fuels for the geopolitical stances and economic policies of Middle Eastern countries, alternative energy development in the oil-rich Middle East is not a government priority. Despite the incredible output capacity for solar energy resources in all Middle Eastern countries, the majority of the countries in the region tend to view development of alternative energy technologies as predominantly ideology-based and a challenge to their nation's continued prosperity.[112]

However, some Middle Eastern states may consider a more active pursuit of renewables development as a means to boost job creation, especially given that growing revenues from traditional energy exports can be used to support new employment programs and the sustainable development of alternative energy industries. Jobs are a particular issue for the majority of countries in the Middle East and Northern Africa that have large youth populations. Although renewable energy technologies may not generate many non-skilled job openings, the development of relevant research and industrial infrastructure may fit neatly with ongoing policy measures seeking to generate jobs, irrespective of the actual economic benefits these jobs engender.

For some countries in the region, alternative energy development is often based on the prestige it brings. The UAE in particular has demonstrated a commitment to reducing dependence on oil and gas revenues.[113] In addition, the UAE has shown a commitment to sustainability and is using fossil fuel revenues to construct "one of the most sustainable communities on the planet, Masdar City," a development that integrates solar energy and cutting-edge technologies to provide an optimal living environment harmonious with nature.[114] Another ambitious mega-project, also designed to demonstrate the scale and potential of local achievement, is building the world's largest solar energy park by 2030. As part of this plan, a large solar power plant was constructed in 2017.[115]

The dominance of fossil fuel resources has a substantial influence on the stability of the Middle East. If oil revenues were to dry up from a dramatic drop in oil prices as a result of mass deployment of alternative energy sources before regional economies were diversified enough to withstand the shock, economic destabilization would ensue. Increasing instability could lead to the fall of ruling families and dictators and create political vacuums. Furthermore, stagnating or falling incomes and high or increasing unemployment may fuel radical Islamist groups, many of which are anti-Western.

Future alternative energy developments may change regional power balances by providing an opening for non-Western emerging powers seeking a role in Middle Eastern politics. Countries like China and India could gain political leverage by supporting Middle Eastern renewables, an area that does not impinge on the Middle East's traditional ties with the United States and the developed West.[116]

(2) Israel: rapid technological advancements driven by security considerations.

Israel's alternative energy policies are predominantly driven by the pursuit of technological development and national security considerations. Israel is often spoken about as an "energy island": the country has an isolated power supply as its grid is not connected with those of its neighbors for political reasons. Until recently, Israel was a fuel-poor economy that relied extensively on fossil fuel imports, particularly gas from Egypt. The discovery of the Tamar and Leviathan gas fields in 2009 radically changed the situation. Gas supplies from these deposits may meet a substantial share of Israel's energy needs for decades ahead, and the possibility of exporting gas to Egypt is under discussion.

Israel started to systematically develop solar energy as early as the late 1970s. Following the 1973 oil crisis, a regulation required rooftop solar thermal water heating systems to be installed on all residential buildings.[117] The next wave of interest in renewable energy came in 2009 when the Israeli government established a target to reach 5% electricity generation from renewable sources by 2014 and 10% by 2020. An expanded scientific and development effort to introduce alternative energy into its economy with the goal of increasing its energy security was undertaken. However, the target was not achieved, and the share of electricity generation from renewable sources in Israel in 2016 was just 3%. However, in April 2016 the Israeli government adopted a resolution increasing the target share up to 10% by 2020 and 17% by 2030. New solar facilities are currently under construction and are scheduled to start operations by 2020, among them Ashalim, the world's tallest solar tower.[118]

Israel's expansion of alternative energy development will be driven by its proven competitive advantages, like traditionally strong research and development capabilities as well as new-found deposits. Combined with increased use of domestic natural gas, Israel can utilize alternative energy as a balancing factor in its relations with its energy-rich neighbors. These considerations are already leading to advances in alternative energy technologies in the country, particularly in solar and wind power, which provide ready-made channels for the megatrend's increased adoption.

Israel is a leader in renewable energy research and development.[119] Relying on its advanced technology incubators, as well as on extensive fiscal stimulus for new developments, Israel has moved closer to solutions for storage and other infrastructure challenges that the alternative energy megatrend faces in general. With a sustained history of technological advancements, Israel might be better positioned than many other countries to have a vibrant alternatives sector. As noted by Prime Minister Netanyahu, "We have the brains, but we also have the will."[120]

(3) Africa: testing alternative energy pilot projects in the background of new power plays for resources.

In Africa, the megatrend is impacted by the reality that the continent is a battleground characterized by international competition over natural resources. Fossil fuels, biofuels, and waste are the most important sources of energy in Africa, with new developments in alternative energy lagging. Fossil fuel resources will continue to determine the future of alternative energy in Africa, particularly in Sub-Saharan Africa where Nigeria and Angola have abundant reserves of oil and gas.[121] Furthermore, the revenues generated by oil and gas exports are notoriously poorly managed and are characterized by corruption and lack of transparency. Weakness in governance in many parts of Africa makes development of new technologies difficult and competition over resources more volatile.

Support for fossil fuel exports is generated by the ongoing process of energy infrastructure integration between North Africa and Europe. New pipelines are being built that will enable Algeria and other countries in the Maghreb to export additional oil and natural gas to Europe. In view of the importance of fossil fuel revenues, Northern African countries may be loath to invest significantly in renewables. Their model for exporting fossil fuels to Europe is already in place and additional infrastructure will enhance it. However, some countries may be able to channel their growing revenues from exports of traditional energy resources toward the development of alternative energy resources and technologies.

In addition, for the majority of African countries, the megatrend could secure greater amounts of economic aid, transfers of technology, and financing. Africa has an opportunity to exploit a range of renewable energy sources, in particular its abundant solar resources. East Africa possesses almost all of the geothermal resources on the continent and Central Africa has a large share of hydro resources. The East and North have the greatest potential for the development of wind energy.[122] However, at present, alternative energy development on the continent is patchy, with only a few initiatives that have not yet surpassed the test stage.[123]

In addition to the extensive role of fossil fuels in the region, alternative energy on the continent also suffers from a lack of financing, an inability to integrate renewables in deficient power generation infrastructure, and the failure of national governments to design the framework and necessary preconditions to support renewables development. Multinational companies and sovereign wealth funds could help address these challenges and play a leading role in promoting alternative energy in Africa. Alternative energy developments could be used by African countries as a path toward further aid and technological support, and boost development. Some initiatives by multilateral organizations are already in place (such as the Build-Operate-Own/Build-Operate-Transfer projects) to introduce private sector participation and market-oriented behavior in the alternative energy sector. The private and public sectors could also invest in off-grid or distributed generation applications of renewable energy technologies. These systems, which are independent of unstable electric grids in Africa, could provide rural locations and even cities with increased energy security and reliability during periods of intermittency.

Unfortunately, the political instability of the region suggests that concerted action by governments to support the development of renewables remains far off. If major energy consumers shift away from fossil fuels, Africa will be especially vulnerable to civil wars, ethnic rivalries, and corrupt institutions. There are also broader security considerations for Europe and the U.S., as the availability of oil revenues has sparked civil and military clashes in Angola and between Sudan and South Sudan. Resolution of the underlying causes that spark civil wars and ongoing ethnic tensions across the region does not seem imminent in most cases.[124] The continent is also a source of regional security threats, such as Al Qaeda in the Islamic Maghreb (AQIM) and Boko Haram, which have a capacity to affect the rest of the world.

Rivalry over economic and political spheres of influence in Africa could be prominent in the development of the alternative energy sector. A new global race for markets between the East and the West, particularly China and the United States, could turn Africa into a backdrop for geopolitical flexing, with alternative energy the means through which power is displayed.[125] Africa is proving to be a focal point where various actors' geopolitical and geo-economic strategies and rivalries clash. China, for example, has become the leading foreign investor in Africa. While several Western countries are trying to offset China's preeminent position, it currently has the upper hand in its dealings with African countries. Chinese investments in Africa come with no strings attached when it comes to enforcing labor, environmental, and corporate governance standards, cracking down on corruption, and promoting democracy and human rights.[126]

(4) South Africa: finding its place at the BRICS table.

South Africa is one of the few countries on the continent that actively embarked on alternative energy development early in the 2000s, which was then limited to non-grid services to targeted rural communities.[127] The policies supporting renewable energy in the country tie in with its efforts to achieve a new international position as a member of the BRICS club, with energy playing a significant role in pursuing such a position. Targeted policy measures are slowly facilitating the introduction of renewable energy technologies. The Renewable Energy Feed-In Tariff (REFIT) was introduced in 2009 and was replaced in 2011 with South Africa's Renewable Independent Power Producer program (SARIPP), aimed at involving business into renewable energy projects. The program has demonstrated significant resilience and is still considered a flagship public-private partnership model for South Africa.[128] In January 2016 the income tax was amended to further incentivize renewable energy initiatives in the private sector.[129] The ambitious national objective of 30% clean energy in the country's energy mix was set.[130] However, current measures will not suffice as the thorough transformation of the country's energy market still has a long way to go. Considering the country's switch in focus from renewables to nuclear power and repetitive refusals of the national utility to sign Power Purchase Agreements with solar and wind power producers, one could expect quite a bumpy road ahead.[131] The South African renewable energy market will gradually expand and gather speed only if strong support measures are maintained and refined.

The growing range of alternative energy-related policies and strategies in different regions and countries throughout the world indicates diverse actors' geopolitical stances and strategies. The broad scope of policies and regulations that affect alternative energy developments charts the paths actors may use to enhance geopolitical power and achieve domestic energy security.

Whether driven by the desire for energy independence, the imperative of diversification, or the quest for environmentally sustainable development, the diverse regional and country-specific policy and strategy patterns in the Americas, Europe, Asia, and Africa display important elements of the future global framework guiding the megatrends progression. However, using the often-quoted words of William Gibson, the future is already here—it's just not very evenly distributed.

III. Rebalancing U.S. policies for the new age of Great Power Competition—prioritization imperatives in the universally securitized world.

The previous chapters explored various factors that policymakers should consider when forging ahead in a responsible manner. This chapter addresses the critical need for the United States to rebalance its policies and prioritize security objectives in light of the new Great Power Competition.

The alternative energy megatrend's security trajectory is charted across the distinct features of the multi-centric world; a world on the cusp of the new Great Power Competition. As always, the Great Energy Game is an intrinsic part of this competition.

Modern society has arrived at a new crossroad under the emerging Great Power Competition, where the path towards good stewardship of nature finally intersects with the quest for abundance of resources. From this crossroad, a new course must be charted.

The wide range of technological and economic advances that have brought society to this juncture and captured the popular imagination is exceedingly complex. These advances predictably challenge the machinery of policymaking and policy execution across all major economies and international institutions.

First and foremost, the United States retains the most important comparative advantage—the still Western-framed world. At the core of this comparative advantage are democratic institutions based on the tradition of human liberty. While this comparative advantage is not owned by the West, it appears that the West is, for now, best equipped to take advantage of these institutions and promote their practices.[132]

This comparative advantage is premised upon maintaining military superiority compared to adversaries; supporting free societies; promoting rule of law and rules-based order; ensuring relevant alliances wherever the United States is seen as a preferable security partner and a relatively attractive power across the board. Developments at home are of equal importance, e.g., sustaining prosperity, innovation and liberties amid the inevitable political, ideological, and technological shifts and upheavals; and developing a much more resilient culture.[133]

As far as the alternative energy megatrend is concerned, regional and country-specific policy and strategy patterns that propel the megatrend vary widely, reflecting diverse drivers and actors' strategic ambitions and capabilities. However, they form a universe where the megatrend appears as its common thread, leading to the emergence of global commonalities in policies and approaches. The connotations of this convergence are multi-fold, holding implications for energy security, economic growth, and geopolitical leadership, as well as modifying the geopolitical codes that govern actors' behavior.

Both state and non-state actors, as complex interacting agents with often clashing strategies, are increasingly pursuing new and influential positions in global politics. New actors affect the dynamics of power competition by challenging the dominant norms to espouse their own interests and values. New considerations arise when these interests converge with the megatrend's anticipated progression. The determinants of geopolitical importance fluctuate persistently, with no single factor dominating. Rather, stances are determined by a greater heterogeneity of interests, considerations, and historical memories. In order to adequately adapt to these complexities, it is necessary to create a framework that reflects a coherent understanding of this continuously broadening and deepening security context.

1. Factoring the new and upcoming security complexities of the alternative energy megatrend's progression: the securitization policies.

The alternative energy megatrend's security trajectory reveals the need to emphasize the benefits and minimize the drawbacks that can arise from its development. To achieve this goal it makes sense to look for specific policy focal points that can generate foreseeable and tangible benefits, and, more importantly, do no harm.

Redefining policies, therefore, should establish the parameters of what should be undertaken, with particular attention to mitigating any negative side effects and unintended consequences. The megatrend could turn into a strategic security distraction and even a diversion if policies to securitize it are not integrated into a broader security framework.

Alternative energy-related securitization policies need to deal with the megatrend's potential effects on energy security in particular. The global security architecture is designed for the protection of oil and gas fields, extraction facilities, transport routes, energy transmission infrastructure, and energy trade balances.

Securitization should take into account the impact of related policies on human activities and environments within different societies. Attention should also be paid to how policies are disseminated as this determines the extent of their acceptance. The emerging security responses would also need to be accompanied by changes to the multiple structures, organizations, treaties, and frameworks that make up the global energy institutional and security infrastructure.[134]

The relevant policies should therefore have a clear-cut framework that allows for the determination and assimilation of the causes of any damaging impacts and the mitigation of threats that emerge from it. This underscores the need to reconsider global energy governance and institutional frameworks as part of securitization efforts seeking to mitigate negative effects.

In the short to medium term, policymaking would inevitably subject the megatrend to the interests and needs of the state, trumping other considerations. In this regard, policy mechanisms, without impinging on the democratic process, should be as divorced from political influence as possible. They should also be focused on specific security factors and referent objects,[135] which would necessitate addressing both the megatrend's broadening geographical footprint and devising domestic, regional, and international policy mechanisms that can adapt to unanticipated challenges.

These types of policies and institutions are by no means unique to the U.S. experience. In fact, beginning in the early 20th century, political entities recognized the importance of establishing independent regulatory agencies in order to provide for strategic, non-partisan stability in the achievement of policy outcomes. The Federal Energy Regulatory Commission (FERC) and the Environmental Protection Agency (EPA) remain prominent energy-sector institutions that were designed to promote independence from political intrusion. However, agency independence is only as valid as the political will to abstain from interference and coercion.

Securitization policies should integrate the cross-border nature and global spread of the megatrend. Global security would benefit from policy approaches that institutionalize the megatrend's geopolitical impact and broader security repercussions on an international level. Multilateral policies are needed to tackle the security threats that affect relations between states, and between state and non-state actors. The international relations "transactions" that mitigate the inherent anarchy of the world system would require coordination. Domestic policies for renewables development would gradually converge with and become subject to a range of international undertakings.

An additional international platform may be needed to ensure dialogue and transparency with other energy players, such as China, Russia, and India.[136] At the same time, the institutional framework for securitization should remain relatively independent from the influences of single actors.

In essence, institutions should ensure that securitization policies address relevant threats efficiently, effectively, and impartially.

The eventual global securitization framework would need to take into account the nation-centric focus on protecting vital national interests related to alternative energy developments. This process would unavoidably interact and conflict with multilateral policies. National interests will inevitably affect securitization mechanisms, irrespective of the nature of international treaties and arrangements. Policymaking should seek to allay inter-state strains and frictions that arise over access to and control over resources. Countries are unlikely to turn over national sovereignty to some supranational power or organization, whether a global civil society or global governance structures.

The megatrend's securitization would depend on balancing various actors' diverging policy imperatives and approaches.[137] The alternative energy megatrend's geopolitical, energy, defense, environmental, and economic effects will influence the risk-reward calculations of national and international policymakers.

For example, for organizations like NATO, the process of integrating alternative energy in defense practices in a secure manner may require cooperation with the alliance's partner countries in those energy security areas that pursue associated alternative energy developments. From a strategic perspective, the energy rebalancing effect of alternative energy sources could be effectively utilized to supplement national and collective defense undertakings by promoting regional stability either unilaterally or via alliance or coalition operations.

Policies need to focus on ensuring the security of new energy infrastructure. This would encompass the secure integration of infrastructure into the existing production, distribution, and consumption facilities, while maximizing the use of existing infrastructure and final consumption goods, such as electricity or fuel for vehicles. Duplication of critical equipment, provision of fuel diversity, development of other sources of energy, and reliance on fewer vulnerable infrastructure chains, among other securitization measures and processes, can also serve to enhance the resilience of the energy security system.

The less substitutable a new energy source is for existing infrastructure, the rockier the transition, and the more likely it will be to pose threats to economic security. Dealing with infrastructure threats calls for a more flexible but threat-focused regulatory framework, extensive development of and capital investment in cyber infrastructure innovation, and strengthening protection against industrial espionage and cyberattacks.

The tentative efforts by various players to establish a niche regional presence within the alternative energy sector mark the initial steps toward the establishment of a vibrant global competitive alternative energy mega-market. The potential scale of such a market is great, which could reinforce its sustainability. Developing a worldwide market would go a long way in reinforcing the megatrend's economic security contribution and resolving the most pressing concerns about the megatrend's viability, capacity, and adaptability. Such a mega-market implies a new type of approach that is not concerned with the process, but instead with monitoring and controlling the inputs and outputs.

Facilitating the creation of a global alternative energy market could expand the options for ideas, applications, and, ultimately, breakthroughs. The achievement of beneficial outcomes, technological advances, and practices from the megatrend will depend on an uninterrupted and intensifying process of innovation. In the contemporary world, innovation is increasingly becoming a social process, resulting from an accumulation of knowledge and practices under the influence of different elements of society.[138] Advances are regularly produced by interactions that resemble those of the market and can lead to mass-developed user innovations.[139]

Historically, user-generated innovation processes have been vehicles for practical ideas, and, in the words of Jean-Jacques Rousseau, the world is "indebted to the mechanical arts for a great number of useful inventions which have added to the pleasures and conveniences of life."[140] This long-standing principle applies in the modern context—Jack Ma has stated that "innovation is always outside of [big companies]."[141] The spread of user-generated innovation is strongly supported with the advent of open-source invention and knowledge.

However, the right technological and organizational conditions, as well as novel economic approaches, practices, and valorizations, will be necessary for innovation to flourish. Focusing policies on new incentives to innovate and promoting relevant infrastructure and institutional framework could help facilitate these conditions and advance innovation. Creating a rules-based framework that enables the widespread dissemination of user-originating information is important for securitizing innovation and removing or minimizing barriers to the development of alternative energy technologies.

Who can manage a socio-political, techno-economic, and ideological global megatrend? It is in fact naive to consider controlling the alternative energy phenomenon, as such worldwide trends rise and fall at the seeming whim of diverse factors that are usually visible only in hindsight. In dealing with the alternative energy megatrend, it might be most realistic to try to grab the bull by the horns and hope to not fall off, rather than tame it, with the core questions revolving less around controlling the idiosyncrasies of the megatrend and more on riding out its course intelligently. Most importantly, an adroit and vigorous pursuit of market-based, socio-political, and techno-economic innovation should be accompanied by prompt consideration of the megatrend's security implications.

Paraphrasing Jean-Paul Sartre's observation that late afternoon is always too late or too early for anything one wants to do, today we find ourselves "at 3 p.m." with respect to the next stage of alternative energy development. Society, however, should not relinquish the prerogative to at least manage, if not anticipate, the projected and unforeseen developments and outcomes that the alternative energy megatrend will bring.

As the megatrend's progression has demonstrated, security concerns can spur concerted action, but can also be "much less useful in proposing desirable futures."[142] Meaningful prioritization of security necessitates a broad and comprehensive view going beyond projections of the future determined by conflicting local visions, and ideas of individuals, societal groups, and nation-states governed by differently perceived conditions. Assigning global priorities will require maximum flexibility and a level of transparency and predictability that will balance out or at least minimize the potential for uncertainty. An awareness of the upcoming security complexities that the analysis of the alternative energy megatrend reveals would help formulate these priorities in a way that enables more adequate future securitization policies.

2. Proactively shaping the emerging security context of the Great Power Competition: the tentative emergence of new principles underpinning the global security architecture.

During the post-Cold War paradigm shift, the security context is determined by the gradual disappearance of long-standing confrontations that had global war as their worst-case outcome and international relations the main arena where the threat of war was being securitized. Since the willingness to undertake aggressive war has largely been curtailed, a perception is emerging that external, human-generated threats are diminishing, reshaping the practicalities of warfare. This transformation is bringing about a new understanding of the role of international politics as a securitization mechanism in violent conflict. It is shifting attention beyond balances of military power to economic capabilities and access to natural resources.[143]

However, it is possible to draw certain parallels with historical transitions between civilizational eras that have already occurred. Past examples provide a better understanding of what advantages actors seek to derive during such transitional periods. Those that were quick to take up the advantages offered by the new conditions, technologies, and changes in security practices were the ones to take leading roles in the next era. Compare, for example, the conservative approach to naval developments of Ming China to the European powers. The modern phenomena and trends that accompany such a transition act as both its early harbingers and the engines of change that bring about the new system.

Tracing the alternative energy megatrend's future security trajectory provides a view of a new multi-faceted and multi-dimensional geopolitics in a microcosm. As the 21st century multi-centric world system takes shape, the megatrend sheds a new light on the interplay between a shrinking geography of globally felt impacts, international relations, international law, and security. The megatrend shows how the modern globalization processes have reduced the distance between geopolitical causes and effects, introduced new dimensions through which geopolitical influence is seen to propagate, and emphasized the shortened available reaction time for actors to formulate responses to threats. At the same time, local events increasingly take on a regional and even global significance, becoming more immediately tangible for a greater number of actors, groups, or individuals, irrespective of their geographical location.

Overall, the upcoming evolution of the megatrend's driving forces suggests that the world system will increasingly display anarchical characteristics. The balancing influence of past geopolitical hierarchies will be less pronounced, whereby attempts at multilateral arrangements and the emergence of more and new geopolitical institutions will not prevent individual state actors from successfully exerting influence on others. Throughout the latter half of the 20th century, the inflexible rules of the bipolar world system restricted the ability of states to maneuver within the narrow confines of the zero-sum balance of power. During the Cold War, minute shifts of posture could lead to conflict and war. Today, with no single global rule-writer and rule-enforcer, anarchy is likely to become an increasingly significant factor among the forces shaping the geopolitical equilibrium. While reflecting and conforming to a realist framework, the process of securitization should also take into consideration the constructivist perspective—the inevitable impact of a continuously broadening field of actors that can instigate securitization actions aimed at enhancing institutional capacity to deal with the security threats and challenges of the new era.

As elements of anarchy rise to the fore of international relations, a number of states will continue to use the concept of "power balance" when formulating their foreign policies. However, the viability of maintaining such a balance will be challenged. In a global system seeking to find equilibrium, buffeted by the growing ambitions of an increasing number of actors, the balancing role of power will be diminished due to the reduced ability of hegemons to impose an overwhelming influence on the world system.

Although a balance is feasible considering the historical precedents, attaining a stable equilibrium will require statesmen and policymakers to discard other considerations in favor of achieving the balance. Further, states will need to adapt to the securitization roles of non-state actors—from media calls to the images of species facing extinction broadcast by green movements. Still, it is important not to make a simplified conclusion that conflict is inevitable due to human nature, and that it is a civilizational inevitability. The complex requirements imposed on securitization will particularly challenge such simplifications in this transitional period.

Nonetheless, the Great Power Competition in the transition toward a new world system will engender a securitization system that is likely to remain based on values that coincide with Western ideas, even if no longer predicated on Western dominance and hegemony. Western-originating social, political, economic, and cultural influences and pressures, as well as the respective value judgments about referent securitization objects, will continue to uphold the process of securitization. Liberal democracy, a cornerstone of Western values, will continue to face challenges from autocratic regimes and states. Ultimately, the institutional integrity of Western democracies will signal whether these assumptions hold against internal and external threats.[144] The Western imprint endows the process of securitization with its own directional momentum and stability, and is bound to underpin the emerging global security architecture. The priorities and goals that modern international politics would continue to pursue would be integrated into the rules and institutions of this security architecture, and will seek to alleviate the polarization and divergence of interests that arise due to the pressures of fragmentation tendencies.

This transition's upheavals could strengthen the rationale for using securitization as an additional form of power projection by actors seeking to ensure their survival and competitiveness. Securitization has been and will continue to be jealously guarded by individual states, as they consider it one of the cornerstones of national sovereignty. They will continue to endeavor to keep securitization out of the communal set of concerns that states are willing to entrust to international institutions or global cooperative arrangements. However, the immediate reality is that strategic interests of actors will not always coincide, and the resulting clashes will require their own mitigation alongside measures to address the specific security threats requiring policy intervention in the first place. Furthermore, securitization in a universally securitized world will inevitably have cross-border elements that rely on geopolitical dialogue and interactions. Given the close link between technological development and weaponization, the process of securitization will necessarily involve interaction among actors with a view to establishing appropriate proliferation regimes.

The alternative energy megatrend demonstrates how actors will seek new capabilities amid ongoing and projected transformations that accompany power transitions on the global stage. It also shows how these changes will affect strategic perceptions and national interests. Expectations of global changes will be inseparable from the growing perception by actors that they are capable of not only influencing their own development but also overcoming external influences and impediments.

Despite the indisputable dominance of the United States in a range of key areas, other actors are increasingly convinced that they too can influence global processes and pursue strategies that entail changes to the existing world system. This is evident in recent Chinese naval assertiveness in the South China Sea, Russian incursions on Ukraine, and Brazil's increasing audacity in assuming leadership over Internet governance, particularly the Internet Corporation for Assigned Names and Numbers (ICANN), a historically U.S.-led body.

The same is applicable to energy exporters that seek security and geopolitical advantages. Energy-resource-rich Russia is a prime example, driven as it is by a range of geopolitical goals in its interaction with energy importers in both the West and the East. Ensuring a more judicious application of this advantage would likely entail consistent engagement by consumers in the East, the EU, and the West as a whole, which would make exporters like Russia, for example, a stakeholder in global energy balances and security. As Strobe Talbott points out, however, "The search for common solutions to common problems—including the global economic crisis and climate change—will require a rule-based, consensual international system to which Russia will have to adapt if it is to be a full beneficiary of what that system has to offer."[145]

Combining systemic changes with previously successful but now inadequate security approaches creates security meta-narratives that alter perceptions of the security context. When actors build strategies on the basis of meta-narratives that are skewed by divergence between specific understanding and system conditions, their security strategies may integrate misconceptions that are likely to create preconditions for conflict. This may lead to growing security anxieties and the emergence of new risks. Specifically, the link between security and the ability to control geography through military and diplomatic means will become more fragile. As a response to this insecurity caused by the disappearing safety net of the previous world system, actors will increasingly focus on controlling resources, markets, and institutions while undermining the ability of adversaries to do so.

The scope of security roles is likely to expand to effectively meet the evolving challenges. Although people's lives are no longer inextricably linked to the fate of their respective states, the most significant cross-border interactions will remain between states and involve military, diplomatic, and economic exchanges. Already, the ability to wield power through securitization is becoming available to an increasing number of actors, from the UN's initiatives to address environmental degradation to the new capabilities of states like Germany to determine the economic security policies of the entire EU.

These new power capabilities will not be limited to the traditional geopolitical cores. Future geopolitical peripheries will also have new abilities to influence the conduct of the previous cores. Such influence will become much more pronounced, potentially rendering the broad distinction between the "cores" and the "peripheries" largely meaningless.

As addressing security threats is no longer the exclusive purview of nation-states, a "top-down" provision of security can no longer be the sole securitization approach. Although the world system may gradually be transforming into something that evinces the same characteristics as pre-Westphalian Europe, returning to the Westphalian order is unlikely to provide a blanket solution to global security problems. In fact, the evolving global security regime would inevitably have to consider ways of limiting the use of large-scale violence; the exportation of "externalities" and application of "beggar thy neighbor" policies, or one state's attempt to remedy their economic maladies at the expense of another state's economy; and the distortion of global economic exchanges through the use of "bureaucratic language," protectionism, and administrative hurdles, as well as potential abuses of states against their own citizens. This may bring about disruptions more akin to late-1920s trade wars amongst developed nations.

In order to keep pace with the challenges of the universally securitized world, geopolitical knowledge needs to integrate the other forms of knowledge that underpin security priorities—military, economic, energy, environmental, technological, and socio-political. This is not to say that nuclear conflict and/or proliferation is no longer a top priority for many countries. Indeed, North Korean and Iranian ambitions to join the group of nuclear-armed nations is an abiding security concern for many countries.[146] However, the new reality is that the threat is shared amongst a wider group of states, as is increasingly the trend in other security realms as well.

The mutual influence between the megatrend's drivers and various national security concerns points to the increasing difficulty of relying solely on national security justifications as a precondition for optimal outcomes. Specifically, once it becomes problematic to distinguish whose security is protected and what is being securitized, geopolitical relations predicated on a dual use of diplomatic relations and military threats to command a given space can no longer ensure the influence and security outcomes sought by actors.

Rather, the need for different national militaries to sustain international markets will be more pressing, as a globalized political economy is going to require increased policing by actors to mitigate growing rivalries over new resources, new markets, new industries, and new technologies. Sharpened competition and conflicts would likely be expressed in various regional and global economic crises and intensification of regional conflicts.

The merging of the "core" and the "periphery" has actually reinforced the power of the global market, making it even more difficult for isolationist or self-development models to thrive. In fact, national development is increasingly subject to regional goals seeking to harness the greater resources of regional blocs. If energy-related international politics is any guide, expectations that humanity's choices will be rational and wise are not particularly well grounded. In the universally securitized world, it is easy to transpose this lack of rationality or its even more popular cousin, short-termism, onto other aspects of security. This raises the question of defining whose security is being pursued: today's populace or the next generation's? Even though security continues to be primarily the purview of states in the globalized 21st century, this does not result in overwhelming dominance.

In sum, in the post-Cold War world of the developing new Grand power Competition, geo-economics is likely to gain a more prominent role in policymaking and securitization, even if geopolitics and military means to deal with evolving security challenges will play an expanded role as well. The impact of global trade on security has underpinned securitization policies of states throughout the 20th century, and is likely to play a similarly, if not more, significant role in future securitization.

The alternative energy megatrend also points to transformational change in strategic perspective worldwide. The megatrend's roots in history and its future directions provide a context that suggests the outlines of the upcoming societal and political order. Societies have a lifespan; they emerge, grow, flourish, and then die, but, as argued by Toynbee, "the continuity of history...is not a continuity such as is exemplified in the life of a single individual. It is rather a continuity made up of the lives of successive generations."[147] The transition from one era to another is often heralded by technological advances as well as socio-political and military changes that transform whole societies. The megatrend and the geo-political anarchy of the post-Cold War era are harbingers of such a societal transformation.

3. Policy prioritization: avoiding the pitfalls in formulating desirable securitization goals in the age of Great Power Competition.

In the multi-centric world, dealing with and prevailing in the Great Power Competition not only requires withdrawing from the "forever wars," but also avoiding the inertia and temptation to do everything, everywhere, all the time. This requires dynamic prioritization of potential threats.

Selecting pertinent security approaches in a universally securitized world requires careful calibration and clear metrics that integrate both localized and global knowledge.[148] Determining where primary securitization focus should lie is complicated by the need to integrate the broader ramifications of insecurity to specific objects, as "the multiplicity and interconnectedness of potential threats—and the actors behind them"[149] need to be addressed before appropriate ranking of threats can be made.

Past localized and self-referenced experiences, ideological views, or political views that introduce specific beliefs about likely future outcomes limit the perspectives of actors because they are predicated on particular and local knowledge that often distorts perceptions and misdirects from stated goals or desirable outcomes. For example, France's reliance on Belgium's line of defense against Nazi Germany, the course of action practiced in previous years, turned out to be misled, and failed to prevent German troops from overrunning Belgium.[150]

Although the principle that the past can provide a useful perspective on the future is sound, in practice it can expose policymakers to dangers and diminish the ability to react to the unexpected. The social learning and decision-making that underpin securitization would therefore be susceptible to not just the interference of power and interest, but also the often-misguided influence of past knowledge.

The different idea constructs that guide the value judgment of individual actors create the basis for prioritization and identification of security threats and enemies. In the process, political imperatives that reflect self-referential points of view, as well as the vagaries of the election cycle, constrain prioritization. As the megatrend demonstrates, a single factor, such as environmental degradation, can fit into different narratives and scenarios—military, economic, energy, and socio-political—making the process of securitization particularly prone to politicization.

In the universally securitized world, different actors, groups, and societies perceive the same security threats and the same mitigation mechanisms differently, prompting the pursuit of different policy measures with varying targeted and actual outcomes. Political imperatives also lead to the fallacy of composition, characterized by the inability of actors to achieve the same material changes simultaneously. In terms of security, this implies that securitization actions by one actor may prompt others to undertake their own steps based on the perceived need to protect vital interests or in response to pressing political considerations.

Security prioritization would therefore need to provide the necessary terms of reference—valuation of security threats and desirability of securitization outcomes—that are broadly acceptable to a majority of actors and go beyond the notions of fixed space, community, and identity that governed the conduct of previous hegemons. Addressing problems of global security would benefit from developing concrete scenarios, grounded in specific sectors with comprehensible material parameters and incorporating pressing concerns that are easy for society to understand. The perspective provided by the alternative energy megatrend will facilitate the formulation of what represents desirable and undesirable outcomes of security strategies and policies. Most importantly, future scenarios will allow for specific, commonly understandable, and acceptable values to be attached to different risks and securitization outcomes, which is imperative when assigning priorities.

As the different threats to state survival and dominance—economic, energy, environmental, and military—are often intertwined and mutually influencing, securitization approaches need to maintain a balance that combines various security narratives that are not self-referential and exclusively focused on a single security aspect. For example, the hope that alternative energy technologies could provide an answer to national energy security dilemmas can exist in complete separation from the promise that renewables could provide a tool to create new areas of growth and be a new source of employment for other (or even the same) actors.

This kind of meta-securitization approach would necessitate treating risks and mitigation mechanisms with a certain level of abstraction, often intentionally divorced from local context. Still, practical approaches to prioritization require some common points of reference, with sufficiently pragmatic relevance in order to be applicable. One option to achieve this is minimizing insecurities by developing benchmarks for threats and their impacts that reflect both local and global considerations. This would entail formulating and assigning a commonly acceptable order of urgency and long-term impacts of specific threats on specific securitization objects that are considered of vital interest and require protection.

For security prioritization to be viable, it needs to achieve a balance between the requirements of both urgency and necessity that under-pin actors' value judgments. Urgent issues require immediate reaction to prevent a pending undesirable outcome. Often, the general public places a set of demands on the state to address a specific crisis, resolve a given situation, or simply pursue a new goal. Such demands tend to be case-specific, often during crises, rather than regular occurrences, stemming from natural events, actions by other actors, or by new knowledge becoming public and generating a reaction within societal groups. On the other hand, necessary issues are more goal-oriented and represent benchmarks or elements that need to be achieved in order to arrive at a desired outcome. In many instances, necessary issues have a longer time frame than urgent issues, in particular when a response to a crisis is required. Securitization actors are continuously balancing the urgency and necessity of specific acts, with various levels of success.[151]

Prioritization, therefore, would need to be guided by necessity, but retain sufficient flexibility to respond to urgency by maintaining substantial focus on selected security sectors. It will also need to take into account the inevitable mutual influence that these sectors have on one another. Furthermore, prioritized security policies and strategies should incorporate the likely and unanticipated side effects of specific policies on other sectors and securitization objects.[152] Security prioritization has its own dialectic between immediate interests and long-term goals that influence the securitization actors and their audiences, and shape securitization actions. Securitization actors prioritize their goals on the basis of their perceived needs, such as the protection of populations from invasion and violence, and within the scope of the usually limited resources and capabilities available to address multiple threats. When threats to specific objects are identified, they are assigned values that reflect the imminence of the threat and the scope of its impact. The less immediate and tangible the projected impact, the less priority is assigned to it. In that regard, threats that actors do not consider tangible are less likely to be successfully securitized. Once the imminence and impact of the threat is determined, it needs to be matched with resources that can be deployed to address it. Prioritization therefore needs to be both effective and efficient, so that the quantification of resources allocated to deal with selected threats is optimal.

Prioritizing security would also necessitate a new approach to safety that integrates evolving societal needs and ideas of what represents desirable outcomes. Newly emerging notions, such as that of human security, differ from the concept of safety that governments have been prepared to guarantee their populations, often requiring cross-border coordination to achieve them.

A number of methods already under consideration should be integrated into a safety framework that is sufficiently flexible and adaptable to be applicable on a global scale. Both primary and secondary prevention, i.e., the elimination of hazards and reducing the risks associated with them, should be combined into a series of safety principles that would need to merge multiple purposes with redundancy. Safety would also be subject to new managerial approaches that analyze the risks and prepare contingency plans and standing responses to uncertainties.

To address the imbalances in the perceptions of insecurity created by diverging policy-formulating scenarios, an overarching framework may be needed to channel approaches and practices in line with commonly acceptable security priorities. This framework would not need to take the form of a global government (and such a government may not be viable in practice), but it could emerge as a global governance structure that directs the focus of actors toward commonly held values.[153]

The following diagram provides a simplified illustration of how actors in such a body would collectively prioritize objects to be securitized and securitization mechanisms. Note that the classification of West vs. East (and core vs. periphery) is an over-simplification intended to illustrate general historical, cultural, and governance differences between countries in these regions.

A suitable prioritization approach may entail the selection of a limited number of security sectors that correspond to the most pertinent issues

Figure 11: An Illustration of Collective Global Securitization (Prioritization of Objects & Mechanisms)

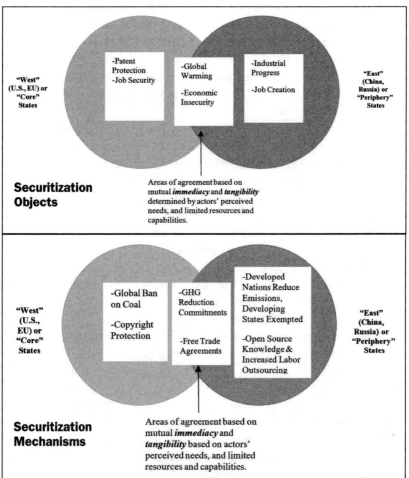

on national security agendas. A common-sense avenue may be found in selecting sectors, such as geopolitics, defense, energy, the economy, and the environment. These sectors address the urgency of security issues by factoring in both the likely sources of security threats—actors and nature—and the necessity of maximizing desirable outcomes in an interconnected world where no actor or event can be considered in isolation.

Considering the security trajectory of the alternative energy megatrend, prioritization factors in both the deepening of security and the necessary precision that would render securitization meaningful. Within such a prioritization framework it is possible to achieve quantifiable outcomes that can be subject to a sufficiently comprehensive cost-benefit analysis of security threats and their mitigation.

Such approaches could involve the creation of AI techno-behavioral systems and solutions that address the interests and needs of specific actors, and those of their neighbors and the global community. This security architecture needs to be adjusted to accommodate the next stage of development and energy security challenges that are likely to emerge. Thus, a redefined security architecture would require strengthening security mechanisms for protecting alternative energy-related vulnerabilities.

The alternative energy megatrend highlights the broadening of the notions and the agenda of specific security domains—energy, defense, environmental, and economic as well as the growth of their significance to national security. The megatrend's trajectory across these security domains also elucidates how different security aspects interact and are mutually influencing. Alternative energy-related strategies and policies are growing to encompass an evolving framework of regulations and incentives. The adoption of such local, regional, and international regulations and policies driven by sometimes divergent political considerations, as well as short- and long-term security concerns, generates new security complexities and challenges.

The alternative energy megatrend is poised to be further and better integrated in energy, defense, environmental, and economic security strategies, offering a wide range of new capabilities. As the intensity of security imperatives requires a broader scope of securitization mechanisms, the megatrend will increasingly help mitigate specific threats, serving as a vehicle for the pursuit of particular developmental strategies by offering potential indigenous and localized solutions. However, the alternative energy imprint on the future shape of these domains will be determined by the pace and scope of its expansion within the evolving energy mix and the actors' ability to overcome some of the current alternative energy vulnerabilities, so to meet the new ones.

In conclusion: What are the plausible scenarios for the megatrend's linear and nonlinear developments in the new iteration of Great Power Competition?

- A set of strong, often contradictory conditions, reinforced by the technological revolution, have catalyzed alternative energy developments into a powerful 21st century global megatrend. These conditions are expected to ensure its longevity, though its downfall cannot be ruled out given the range of doubts regarding its viability. The direction and pace of the alternative energy megatrend's evolution will be largely contingent on new technologies in the context of energy supply-demand dynamics and the extent to which it will be an element of power projection in the evolving Grand Energy Game. However, it will ultimately depend on its continued relevance vis-à-vis societal visions and aspirations.

- The power of the megatrend's drivers will vary in accordance with diverse internal and external conditions, and be affected by the availability, accessibility, and cost of other forms of energy. With so many factors affecting its future, the doubts and doomsday scenarios could be seen as viable. However, alternative energy developments appear to have charted a future trajectory that indicates their durability, with strong political underpinnings and public commitments spurring the megatrend.

- Tracing the integration of alternative energy into national strategies and policies across the globe reveals a diverse universe of ambitions and approaches with uneven distribution of capabilities. At the same time, this patchy landscape contains elements of a future global framework that could guide the megatrend's progression. The megatrend's developments also highlight the new power projection capabilities and new tools that states could deploy in their foreign policies as an additional way to ensure their survival and to strengthen their competitiveness.

- In light of the new Great Power Competition and the related transformations of the Grand Energy Game, the future iterations of the megatrend will require appropriate securitization which should take into consideration the law of unintended consequences. The appropriate security mechanisms should address the potential weaknesses and side effects that result from alternative energy developments, in particular their diverse energy, defense, environmental, and economic security impacts. Moreover, securitization will require institutions that incorporate alternative energy-related security mechanisms within the emerging global governance frameworks, thereby aligning the goals of foreign, defense, development, economic, and energy policies.

• The alternative energy megatrend offers a perspective for better understanding the power dynamics that will unfold during the upcoming transformation of the world system and the security challenges it will bring about. It highlights future security priorities and objectives that will be needed in order to meet the evolving challenges of the universally securitized world. The future security scenarios highlighted by the megatrend present the essence of the upcoming security context. These future scenarios will help determine the priorities that could bring desirable outcomes, going beyond balancing military power and capabilities. Future security complexities are embedded in the interactions of the forces that determine the geopolitical equilibrium and underpin the global security architecture.

• The megatrend's drivers provide a useful picture of the world system poised on the threshold of a new civilizational era; an era far beyond the post-Westphalian world into the new technological world. In the upcoming world system, the balancing factors that contribute to potential equilibrium will change, and the imperatives that make archetypal geopolitical divisions no longer apply to the same extent. Although still remaining within a Western-determined paradigm, the evolving multi-centric world system and security environment will be affected by actors' new objectives, which could translate into clashes based less on ideology than on perceived civilizational values. In this fluid situation, which will be further shaped by the unfolding Great Power Competition, different security priorities will emerge that entail the clear formulation of desirable goals and security metrics, integrating localized and global knowledge, as well as value judgments.

- Overall, the megatrend's security trajectory reveals a future security environment that will be characterized by a number of trends unfolding as a new iteration of the Grand Energy Game under the dark clouds of the new Great Power Competition. These unfolding trends include: a volatile energy system that is yet to adjust to the impending shift in societal perception about energy security and to the energy options that technological breakthroughs provide; an extensive process of defense transformation on a global scale that will revamp global military power balances; an increasingly intensified policy and societal focus on environmental security that will see its importance growing in national security and global governance agendas; and a continuous rise of economic security's importance that will result in geo-economic calculations taking on the characteristics, imperatives, and significance that geopolitics and military considerations held in the 19th and 20th centuries.

- The alternative energy megatrend in the age of Great Power Competition reveals the need for new visions, strategies, and policies. Security prioritization will therefore need to provide the necessary terms of reference—valuation of security threats and desirability of securitization outcomes—that are broadly acceptable to most actors, rather than the previously dominant notions of fixed space, community, and identity. With future security threats merging, meaningful securitization should focus on security domains and sectors that are actionable and correspond to the perceived vital interests of both the relevant securitization actors and the securitization audiences that would approve the legitimacy of their actions. Securitization priorities will thus be based on managing the conflicts and global cooperative arrangements in which differing actors reach agreement on objects of shared immediacy and tangibility, and the mechanisms through which to securitize them. The historical irony is that most of these cooperative arrangements will be seen and executed in the context of the Great Power Competition.

AUTHOR'S NOTE

To conclude on a lighter note, when finalizing this study, I was spending time with a group of friends on a tiny island, who were understandably curious about this endeavor. An attempt at a brief explanation led to a request that I present them with the essential theses of the book, expressed in different literary traditions—from Dashiell Hammett and Hemingway to Fyodor Dostoyevsky and Thomas Mann. In the process of doing so, I was struck by the fact that, no matter what literary style or tradition was used to describe the megatrend—whether a short detective plot, an exercise in philosophy, or a study of the human condition—the same refrain emerged throughout.

The megatrend is essentially a springboard for the transformation of something that has been commonplace in human understanding as a specific object with a specific meaning that has suddenly, without undergoing any material changes, become something completely different. When renewable energy sources are revealed as a unified phenomenon, their well-known characteristics are tangibly transformed, not simply seen in a different light, but somehow altering the material world that surrounds us.

Tracing the megatrend's development and security trajectory provides a new understanding of the world, and is both a symbol and harbinger of things to come. The whole notion of alternative energy tells the story of change, improvement, and a better world within reach.

From there the discussion moved to the search for knowledge. What could be better and more engaging?

The Epilogue to The Prologue:
Is the Alternative Energy Megatrend a
Search for a 21st Century Arcanum?

*"When I the starry courses know, and Nature's wise
instructions seek, with light of power my soul shall glow,
as when to spirits spirit speak."*

Goethe[1]

The discussion continued...

When one reaches a fateful juncture, one looks back for an experience that may offer guidance in the unchartered territory. Fortunately, history offers a welcome example of an equally sweeping quest, viz., the search for the philosopher's stone known as the Arcanum.[2] Indeed, the Arcanum was the undercurrent of bold human endeavors for centuries.

As the alternative energy megatrend carries society forward, classical policy analysis and scenarios can be less illuminating than humanity's amazing experience of that other fabled quest for liberating abundance. A reflection on the history of the Arcanum may provide an understanding of the future evolution and the efficacy of responses to the technological revolutions within the alternative energy megatrend.

In ancient Greece, the search for knowledge was considered beneficial in its own right, culminating in the teachings of philosophers who were posing the deeper questions about the means of human existence, and its meaning. Once the notion of matter was accepted, the philosophers moved on to the pre-scientific search for methods to transmute matter into what the societies deemed most valuable, be that gold, wisdom, or immortality.

Centuries later, the body of methods purporting to bring humanity closer to the attainment of these goals became known as the Arcanum, the mystical precursor to a unified theory of the universe. The natural philosophers of the 16th, 17th, and 18th centuries sought to discover the code that would allow man to reach abundance, by communicating with nature in an elemental, intimate manner, and ultimately to possess its essence. This secular quest became the carrier wave that advanced chemistry, physics, mathematics, biology, anatomy, history, literature, and psychology.

Like the current search for manifold ways to deliver energy from alternative resources, the quest for the Lapis Mysterium, the Philosopher's Stone, captivated diverse and courageous minds around the world in a global endeavor. It was driven by desperation in the face of weak human powers, old age, disease, and ignorance, and it propelled humanity towards the Ages of Exploration and Renaissance. In much the same way, the current megatrend's pursuit of new bountiful and omnipresent energy resources started with the Malthusian desperation, the fear of outliving nature's bounty, and desire for almost cost-free abundance.

And much like the ancient Arcanum, the modern alternative energy megatrend holds the capacity to break the boundaries of economic laws, open new paths to prosperity, and transcend the social strictures. It offers the promise of mastering nature's elements, achieving a status of perpetual renewal and growth, and creating a world where humanity is at one with nature, at which point the "end of history" can be postulated.

1. Some contemporary parallels: recurring patterns in the unending pursuit of advancement and empowerment.

The examination of the historical parallels to the modern alternative energy megatrend sheds light on the contemporary significance of past developments. These parallels suggest that as the alternative energy megatrend permeates more and more deeply the way society views social and economic challenges, it inevitably acquires the trappings of a quasi-ideology, or faith, in the attainability of the ultimate goal. While scientifically questionable, such ideology becomes an inspiring drive that may lead to genuine discoveries way off the beaten paths. Instead of the search for the Fountain of Youth, the adepts of alternative energy believe that they will bring energy diversification and independence, sustainable development, the alleviation of poverty, and further self-determination by state and non-state actors in ways that translate into geopolitical shifts.

The pursuit of the undiscovered has always motivated human endeavor. Examples include the search for a route around Africa and to locate the mythical Prester John, instigated by Henry the Navigator in the 15th century, as well as the quest for the East Indies by Western European kingdoms. While adventurers and explorers typically claimed lofty and sometimes mystical goals, they were actually driven by a range of diverse imperatives. At the present juncture, the lesson of the Arcanum that may be most useful is for us to accept the unpredictability of means towards the desired end, and the ultimate irrelevance of how attainable the end is. The search for the Philosopher's Stone, although unsuccessful, has animated the development of science, given purpose to unrewarded pursuits, and provided a common purpose and common language to thousands of searching and troubled minds across cultural, spatial, and temporal divides. The fact that the magical solution to man's woes has not been found in no way negates the drive for the search.

The quest for abundant alternative energy sources is similarly valid in itself. Policymakers would be well advised to look back at human history and reflect on how they can best allow the new energy frontiers to be explored and challenged rather than defined.[3] How to channel the human passions for a miracle cure to perceived problems is more important than to debate whether the problem is real, or as dire as we choose to believe. The momentum behind the alternative energy megatrend could be viewed as the societal adaptation to one more form of humanity's quest for knowledge, emancipation, and empowerment.

The Arcanum was sought as the path to the eternal, bringing perpetual youth and renewal. By vanquishing disease, endowing the practitioner with a vitality that defied purely physical dangers, and allowing humans to look beyond the daily struggle with nature, it opened avenues beyond the materialistic. Seeking to discover the Elixir of Life, a source of rejuvenating power that would conquer all diseases and even time itself, showed the path to possible transcendence into a brighter future for the next generations. Like the Arcanum, alternative energy provides a source of infinite renewal. It has established a place in human consciousness that has a quasi-ideological nature, where faith in the advent of renewable energy appears unshakeable. The very nature of alternative energy speaks of regeneration, rebirth, and youthfulness, having already assumed a stature of modernity and progress that is speedily becoming an aspiration worldwide.

Humanity striving toward advancements is often prepared to ignore the costs, or "let the mind of men be blind to fate in store, let it be permitted to the timid to hope."[4] Likewise, the achievement the Arcanum sought, whether personal enrichment, eternal life, or spiritual enlightenment, did not entail a transformation of an individual's actions, moral stance, or lifestyle. Rather, these were supposed to occur spontaneously, upon mastering the Arcanum. It was further seen as the "Anagoge"—the ascent to a new plane of development, providing the backbone for the Enlightenment period, and removing the shackles that held human horizons so close to the ground.

In a similar way, the technologies underpinning the megatrend are subject to continuous improvement, modification, and development, generating new fields and areas of research at the cutting edge of contemporary science. Most importantly, the alternative energy development process has brought into its fold leading scientists and academic institutions from across the world.

The Arcanum was identified as the route to beneficial co-existence with nature via perfection, universality, and purity. By extracting the pure essence from elements that exist everywhere, it was seen as a path of spiritual salvation via achieving the true knowledge of the whole of nature and creation.[5] The Arcanum offered the prospect to transmute not only matter, but also spirit, with "the ultimate transformations in the alchemical process...sought...in the material or in the spiritual realm."[6] As a melding of practical and ideological frameworks, the Arcanum offered the capacity to purify the soul and the being of the practitioner, leading to the ability to "penetrate these hidden mysteries of Truth."[7]

In the same manner, through a "virtuous cycle" of investment, technological improvement, and economic growth, alternative energy development is seen as having the power to reconfigure lifestyles and empower humanity to use nature without damaging nature, which brings it toward a global consciousness that is at one with our environment. The sought-after, seemingly God-like, ability to make more out of less by more enlightened use of the resources available would allow man "not only to operate according to his nature and to what is usual, but also to operate outside the laws of that nature, in order that...he would succeed in preserving himself as god of the earth."[8]

The search for the Arcanum was considered to be the path to ultimate prosperity. By providing the impetus for bolder approaches and broader visions, it promised the means to lead "from darkness into light, from this desert wilderness to a secure habitation, and from poverty and straights, to a free and ample fortune."[9] The quest for new alternative sources of energy has similarly offered a path of human development unconstrained by the hurdles of resource depletion and insurmountable capital needs, and is associated with the drive to reduce poverty and vanquish the specter of scarcity and diminishing living standards.

Alternative energy developments promise new boundless sources of energy that can be secured without skimping on humanity's energy consumption and rebalancing patterns of resource use. In other words, you may continue with your life, but these "magical" technologies will enable you to feel morally superior, because they will not damage your habitat.

Examining the historical parallels provides a glimpse of the potential future of the alternative energy megatrend and a better understanding of the megatrend's essence, connotations, and implications. Like the Arcanum, alternative energy offers a potential short-cut toward human advancement. Both derive their ambition from humanity's general aversion to sacrificing something in order to achieve something else.

With a nod to Hegelian dialectics, considering the alternative energy megatrend in the same context as the traditions surrounding the Arcanum provides the opportunity to anticipate rational reactions and expectations that the megatrend may elicit. Within the crucible of traditions, the actual object—in this case, alternative energy—is not changed intrinsically, but how it is perceived is constantly being reworked, building from the past, overcoming contradictions, and moving toward the future. Invariably, at critical junctures, dissatisfaction with specific paradigms arises. They are overturned, and new paradigms are established.[10] This can produce outlier outcomes, which in the globalized 21st century world will include global security issues, new ideologies, and moral dilemmas.

Emancipation from the fear of and a way to master nature's elements is at the root of the human drive to seek new energy. In prior ages, alchemists would stop at nothing in seeking a fountain of personal vitality. In the modern age, society has not hesitated to unleash atomic power or drill miles into Earth's crust to discover energy. However dangerous, the trend is sustainable because, inter alia, it has staked high moral grounds. Sustaining a romantic, passionate belief in alternative energy is the best investment by society in its future. Rather than scrutinizing the data that may cast doubts on the science behind climate change, it is ultimately more productive to accept it as an empowering dream, ideology, or faith and let it mobilize human endeavor as the Arcanum did for modern science. We will all be better off for it.

2. The "differentia specifica" of the modern meanings: a securitized habitat and mastery over nature within reach for everyone and everywhere.

In making the comparison between the two, highlighting the differences between the alternative energy megatrend and the Arcanum actually enables a better understanding of modern life and its complexities. The reflection of the megatrend through the perspective of the Arcanum underscores the innate capacity of the renewable energy phenomenon to be transformative and its ability to evolve beyond its own past, so that "the ways in which what happened, and what is said to have happened are and are not the same, may itself be historical."[11] It explains why the purpose, direction, and trajectory of alternative energy developments continuously change, but are never unified until the right catalyst comes along. Although the ability to predict the future always remains in doubt, as we would have to predict future knowledge in order to predict the future and we would need to know what our future knowledge is and be in possession of it at the present time,[12] there are undeniable advantages to estimating the future through the prism of the past.

The story of the Arcanum holds valuable lessons about the cul-de-sacs that humanity needs to avoid. The pursuit of the Arcanum was shrouded in mysticism that allowed the initiated to function in relative safety and obscurity. "The Arcanum itself was something wholly alien, something into which a man could not be initiated; he could only be dependent on it."[13] To avoid the risk of being sidelined and perverted, our modern pursuits must be rooted in transparency, accessibility, and understanding.

The propagation of the alternative energy worldview will wither if it becomes the credo of the elites, conducted by practitioners locked away in ivory or golden towers. Access to energy has never been the problem of the elites; by the same token, viable solutions will likely be democratic. Abundant locally generated energy can become part of everyday human existence, at least as accessible as the supermarket down the street.

Ultimately, the Arcanum stumbled over its fixation on the happiness for the one, rather than for all. It was driven by the mentality of a gold-digger who has no intent to share his nuggets or the treasure maps. Contrast that with the pursuit of alternative energy, which is presumably beneficial for everyone. The Arcanum differs from the modern alternative energy phenomenon in that it was, to a large extent, a plaything of the elites, with each feudal lord or medieval king championing his own natural philosopher. Although the alternative energy megatrend's momentum is channeled by political considerations and practicalities, it aims to benefit the whole of humankind, rather than single groups or individuals. It is not a pursuit for the personal enrichment of selected members of elites or aristocracies. The modern megatrend promises paybacks beyond a zero-sum game—the benefits for an individual using alternative energy are also benefits to society. As this ideology enters societal understanding, opposition to specific aspects of alternative energy development is perceived as opposition to the forces of good.

Regardless of the trend's current status and political controversies, its future seems increasingly assured. This assurance comes from the power of its drivers and the scope of its attributes. What the future holds for alternative energy developments lies predominantly in the realm of the unanticipated, both from the perspective of the underlying technologies and the megatrend's security implications. For alternative energy to ascend to the next beneficial plateau along its course, its security implications must be taken into account and addressed in an open, market-oriented, and secu-rity-minded manner. Deciding how to address those security implications entails further studies of the megatrend, as "nothing is worse than that assertion and decision should precede knowledge and perception."[14]

Our examination of the historical parallels and divergences between the alternative energy megatrend and the Arcanum adds another dimension to understanding the megatrend's manifestations and elements, revealing its socio-historical momentum. On that canvas, the alternative energy phe-nomenon can be perceived as an illustration of humanity's approaches to major challenges, one which facilitates the understanding of why human development, and in particular technological advances, are repeatedly eval-uated from a moral perspective as much as from a material one.

Despite the wide-ranging global security implications and the chal-lenges to the intelligent integration of the megatrend in the 21st century global security architecture, there is consistent momentum behind alter-native energy developments that is founded on societal value judgments about the megatrend's outcomes. In many respects this value does not lie in the goals and targets set out at the beginning, but rather in the process of developing and acquiring knowledge itself.

ENDNOTES

FOREWORD/INTRODUCTION

1 Part 1, Chapter 1.
2 Benjamin Franklin, as quoted by J. A. Leo Lemay and P. M. Zall, *Benjamin Franklin's Autobiography*, Part III (New York: W. W. Norton & Co., 1986), 108.
3 See Lucius Apuleius, *The Golden Ass* (Cambridge, MA: Harvard University Press, 1915).
4 Integration addresses the challenges of conducting interdisciplinary studies. See Deborah Vess and Sherry Linkon, "Navigating the Interdisciplinary Archipelago: The Scholarship of Interdisciplinary Teaching and Learning," in *Disciplinary Styles in the Scholarship of Teaching and Learning: Exploring Common Ground*, eds. M.T. Huber & S. Morreale (Washington, D.C.: American Association for Higher Education, 2002), 87–106.
5 By merging the notion of security with both the social constructions that formulate emergency measures and the existing and evolving security mechanisms, practices, and institutions, this analysis endeavors to fully integrate the diverse aspects of securitization and notions of security. The definition of security is subject to debate. For example, the protection of humans from harm is the focus of the Human Security School, which emerged after the publication of the 1994 UN Human Development Report. The report outlined what are now seen as the seven fundamental elements of human security: economic security, health security, food security, environmental security, personal security, community security, and political security. See UN Human Development Report 1994: *New Dimensions of Human Security* (United Nations, 1995), http://hdr.undp.org/en/media/ hdr_1994_en_chap2.pdf. On human security, see Edward Newman and Oliver P. Richmond, eds., *The United Nations and Human Security* (Basingstoke: Palgrave Macmillan, 2001); J. Peter Burgess and Taylor Owen, eds., "Special Section: What Is Human Security?," *Security Dialogue* 35, no. 3 (September 2004): 345–87; Mary Kaldor, *Human Security: Reflections on Globalization and Intervention* (Cambridge: Polity Press, 2007); and Rita Taureck, "Securitization Theory and Securitization Studies," *Journal of International Relations and Development* 9, no. 1 (2006): 53–61.
6 Even though the term "Great power competition" was, and is, vastly used in different theoretical and practical frameworks, the concept of a new "Great power competition" raised to prominence in 2017. The 2017 National Security Strategy, the 2018 National Defense Strategy (where this concept was considered as a "long-term strategic competition") and the 2018 National Military Strategy all have the term "great-power competition."
7 The distinction between minor and great powers was recognized with the signing of the Treaty of Chaumont in 1814.

PART 1

1 Heraclitus, *Fragments*, trans. Brooks Haxton (New York: Penguin Classics, 2003), 19.
2 As a notion, social construction of reality is based on the understanding that the emergence of ideas and the formation of knowledge among persons and groups that are

interacting in a social system gradually coalesce into a framework. Over time, this framework of concepts and mental representations becomes the structure that determines the actions of these individuals and groups. Furthermore, these concepts eventually become habituated, making these individuals and groups endeavor to fit into reciprocal roles in relation to each other. The emerging interplay and its setting gradually permeate other layers of society and influence it members to enter into and play out these constructs. When these reciprocal interactions become habitual and embedded in practice, they are said to be institutionalized. In the process of this institutionalization, meaning is embedded in society's actions that results in specific behavioral patterns and valorization that determines future developments. On social construction of reality, see Thomas Luckmann and Peter L. Berger, *The Social Construction of Reality: A Treatise in the Sociology of Knowledge* (London: Penguin, 1991); David Newman, *Sociology: Exploring the Architecture of Everyday Life* (Thousand Oaks, CA: Pine Forge Press, 1995). Regarding constructivist approaches in science, see, for example, Olav Eikeland, "From Epistemology to Gnoseology—Understanding the Knowledge Claims of Action Research," *Management Research News* 30, is. 5 (2007): 344–58.

3   Rob B. J. Walker, "Security, Sovereignty, and the Challenge of World Politics," *Alternatives* 15, no. 1 (Winter 1990): 11. For more on political geography, see Kevin R. Cox and Murray Low, "Political Geography in Question," *Political Geography* 22 (2003): 599-602.

4   In the 21st century, the notion of national security has expanded to include the security of the resources the state needs to sustain itself and exert power internationally, in particular energy. It encompasses the objective of figuratively fueling national defense and literally addressing the vulnerability posed by dependency on external energy suppliers.

5   Historically, it was thought that "a nation is secure to the extent to which it is not in danger of having to sacrifice core values, if it wishes to avoid war, and is able, if challenged, to maintain them by victory in such a war." Walter Lippmann, *U.S. Foreign Policy: Shield of the Republic* (Boston: Little, Brown and Company, 1943): 51.

6   Narrow security is underpinned by the issues of agency and intent. Issues that lack those elements are relegated to the domestic "low" politics agenda. With the recognition that threats that combine the capability and intent to result in violence are increasingly likely to emanate from without, narrow security has a distinct international flavor. See David Baldwin, "Security Studies at the End of the Cold War," *World Politics* 48 (1995): 131.

7   Hans Morgenthau, "Another "Great Debate": The National Interest of the United States," in *Classics of International Relations*, ed. J. Vasquez (Englewood Cliffs, NJ: Prentice Hall, 1982), 973.

8   On the broadening of security considerations, see Richard Wyn-Jones, *Security, Strategy and Critical Theory* (Boulder, CO: Lynne Rienner, 1999); Mohammed Ayoob, "Defining Security: A Subaltern Realist Perspective," in *Critical Security Studies: Concepts and Cases*, eds. K. Krause and M.C. Williams (London: UCL Press, 1997), 121–47.

9   Environmental security includes mitigating the depletion of resources, the environmental impact on economic activities, environmental threats to territorial integrity and livelihoods, and intra- and inter-state conflicts resulting from damage to the human habitat. On the different aspects of environmental security and the growing linkage between environmental degradation and the security of states and their populations, see Michael Renner, *Fighting for Survival: Environmental Decline, Social Conflict, and the New Age of Insecurity* (New York: W. W. Norton & Co., 1996), among others.

10 Economic security includes issues such as economic growth, stability, resilience to economic shocks and volatility, and other forms of economic welfare both domestically and globally. See, for example, Beverly Crawford, "The New Security Dilemma under International Economic Interdependence," *Millennium* 23, no. 1 (1994): 25-55; Andrew

F. Krepinevich, Jr., "National Security Strategy in an Era of Growing Challenges and Resource Constraints," Center for Strategic and Budgetary Assessments Perspective, June 2010 (originally presented at the panel on *"Domestic Constraints on U.S. Grand Strategy,"* at *"The Geopolitical Constraints of the Financial Crises" Symposium at Princeton University's Center for International Security Studies, May 13-14, 2010*). It also includes the consideration that it is "the material basis of military strength [and] has traditionally been a starting point for assessments of military potential." Emily O. Goldman and Leo J. Blanken, "The Economic Foundations of Military Power," in *Guns and Butter: The Political Economy of International Security*, ed. Peter Dombrowski (Boulder, CO: Lynne Rienner Publishers, 2005), 37.

11   ADM James G Stavridis USN (Ret.): "At the top of my list is the growing gridlock among our national leaders. ... Tied to that is an increasing strain of nationalism and authoritarianism in a variety of countries around the globe. ... Finally, I am deeply concerned about the health of the planet, including global warming, drought, rising sea levels, melting ice caps, and increasing levels of violent storms. That is a dangerous list, but I remain cautiously optimistic about facing these challenges, because some things are going right." *Lessons In Leadership: One On One With Admiral James Stavridis*, March 26, 2019, available at: https://thrive-global.com/stories/lessons-in-leadership-one-on-one-with-admiral-james-stavridis/.

12   Kissinger, Henry. "The Future Role of the IEA." October 14, 2009, Paris, France.

13   The process of intensifying regionalization has run counter to globalization. Region-alization has been characterized by the formation of new cores and peripheries, the development of new forms of power projection by them, and the increasing fluidity of defining cores and peripheries, stemming from a variety of regional normative and social forms, whether hegemonic, particularistic, or universalistic. There are different levels of regionalization: geographical, social, organized cooperation, regional civil society, or a region as an "acting subject" with a distinct identity. In addition, the rise of regional-ism has been accompanied by a gradual erosion of "nation-state projects" that has been accelerated by the removal of the Cold War anchors. See Björn Hettne, "The Double Movement: Global Market versus Regionalism," in *The New Realism: Perspectives on Mul-tilateralism and World Order*, ed. R. W. Cox (New York: United Nations University Press, 1998).

14   According to the Copenhagen School, securitization can be represented as a so-called "speech act." From the perspective of securitization theory, saying is doing. It is another way of fashioning the world. On the practical power of speech, see John Austin, *How to do Things with Words* (Oxford: Clarendon Press, 1962).

15   A regional security complex, enabling a regional security agenda, was originally defined by Barry Buzan as "a group of states whose security problems are so closely intertwined that they cannot meaningfully be understood independently of each other." For more, see Barry Buzan, *People, States and Fear: The National Security Problem in International Rela-tions* (Hemel Hempstead: Harvester Wheatsheaf, 1983).

16   To a certain extent, this broadening of the framework of interaction between states has reinforced the so-called Structuralist view of international relations—that interactions between geopolitical agents have always been and remain the various aspects of com-petition between the wealthy elites and the poor, ultimately toward achieving specific economic ends. See, for example, Edward H. Carr, *The Twenty Years' Crisis, 1919-1939*, 2ⁿᵈ ed. (London: Macmillan, 1946).

17   In the same vein, existential threats to referent objects impact other objects, bringing forth risks that need to be addressed, whether or not those risks represent extant or conceptual threats. Societal pressure on policymakers has led to calls to address risks even before an actual threat is formulated and has materialized. This applies to issues as diverse as the

"War on Terror" and climate change. See Rens Van Munster, *Logics of Security: The Copenhagen School, Risk Management and the War on Terror* (University of Southern Denmark, Political Science Publications, 2005); Holger Stritzel, "Towards a Theory of Securitization: Copenhagen and Beyond," *European Journal of International Relations* 13, no. 3 (2007): 357–83.

18   The notion of security prevalent throughout the history of human civilization was based on the premise that the referent object of security is the state, as the guarantor of security of its populace. In this manner, the individual essentially transferred responsibility of his/her own security to the hands of the state, making securitization its responsibility. The acts to be securitized were therefore predominantly in the plane of inter-state and international relations, focused on defense, and increasingly after the end of World War II, energy and nuclear proliferation. This placed explicit security considerations within the realm of "high" politics, which were the exclusive domain of states as the main actors that held the responsibility to address security threats. See Emma Rothschild, "What is Security?" *Daedalus* 124, no. 43 (1995): 53-90; T. Hobbes, *The Leviathan* (Abingdon: Oxford University Press, 1998).

19   Kenneth Waltz, *Theory of International Politics* (Reading, MA: Addison-Wesley, 1979), 168.

20   On the issue of intent and capability in securitization, see David Singer, "Threat-Perception and the Armament-Tension Dilemma," *Journal of Conflict Resolution*, 2 (1958): 90, http://www.jstor.org/discover/10.2307/172848?uid=3739656&uid=2&uid=4&uid=3739256&sid=21103253585827.

21   On "low" and "high" politics, see Robert Owen Keohane and Joseph S. Nye, Jr., *Power and Interdependence* (Harlow: Longman, 2001).

22   Jessica T. Mathews, "Redefining Security," *Foreign Affairs* 68, no. 2 (1989): 162–77, http://www.foreignaffairs.com/articles/44331/jessica-tuchman-mathews/redefining-security.

23   Apart from geographical restrictions, another important aspect of securitization that has changed as a result of globalization and the rapid advent of communications technology is time constraints, i.e., time before a threat determined by the securitization act has occurred, which is the time available to securitization actors to mitigate this threat.

24   For example, using religious, racial, or sexual discrimination as a basis for formulating the threats would be less successful with certain audiences. It is highly unlikely that securitization measures to address fundamentalist terrorism in the Middle East would be successful if they propose banning the practice of Islam.

25   The acceptability of securitization requires the creation of a number of assumptions of political relations, values, and the choice of approved securitization tools, which means that securitization is a joint enterprise between the actor and audience. See Matt McDonald, "Constructing Insecurity: Australian Security Discourse and Policy Post-2001," *International Relations* 19, no. 3 (2005): 297–320.

26   For example, the statements of Warren Buffett on economic security may result in economic securitization acts (whether or not implemented by him), or a series of reports by media networks that enjoy worldwide trust, such as CNN or the BBC, which may result in global action to securitize issues from education to wildlife preservation. See K. Booth, "Security and Emancipation," *Review of International Studies* 17 (1991): 313–26, http://didierbigo.com/students/readings/booth1991emancipationsecurity.pdf.

27   One of the oldest examples is associated with the urging of Demosthenes for Athenian action against Philip of Macedon, whose aggressive policies Demosthenes considered a threat to the life of Athenians. This contextualization of securitization is sometimes considered to represent the act of "constructing" security. In a more modern example, attempts to securitize the world's financial system were proven inadequate by the global financial and economic crisis of 2007–2008, resulting in pressure by both securitization

actors (states, multilateral organizations, industry associations, etc.) and audiences (media, political parties, non-governmental institutions, popular societal movements, etc.) to introduce new rules to address the perceived threat to the global financial and economic system.

28 Robert Kagan, "Power and Weakness," *Policy Review* 113 (June/July 2002), http://www. hoover.org/publications/policy-review/article/7107.

29 History has numerous examples of the introduction of securitization acts that have now become the norm. Securitization measures such as military conscription or the formation of professional armies were not normal practices. For example, in ancient Rome, citizens that were part of Roman armies had to pass specific property requirements, and the army was called up for specific action and then soldiers were discharged back to civilian life. It was only around the end of the 2nd century BC that conscription reforms became prevalent, often attributed to Gaius Marius. (See Sallust, *Sallust*, trans. John Carew Rolfe (London: Harvard University Press, 1960). Over the next period of more than two centuries, the Roman state experienced continuous problems in conscripting for the army, as this was deemed out of the norm. Today, a number of countries worldwide practice regular, non-emergency military conscription without visible societal resistance.

30 On the erosion of academic and practical coherence of the discipline of security due to broadening and deepening, see Stephen Walt, "The Renaissance of Security Studies," *International Studies Quarterly* 35, no. 2 (1991): 211–39, http://graduateinstitute.ch/files/live/sites/iheid/files/sites/political_science/shared/political_science/1702/1-Walt-1991-ISQ-Renaissance-security-studies.pdf.

31 There is concern that a continuous broadening of security considerations diffuses securitization to a level that renders it unrecognizable and impossible to implement. See, for example, Gregory Koblentz, "Biosecurity Reconsidered: Calibrating Biological Threats and Responses," *International Security* 34, no. 4 (2010): 96–132.

32 Policies are reasoned choices, defined sometimes as "all human actions based on deliberate comparison of alternative possible outcomes in terms of known standards or principles." See E. J. Meehan, "The Concept 'Foreign Policy,'" in *Comparative Foreign Policy: Theoretical Essays*, ed. W. F. Hanrieder (New York, David McKay, 1971), 269.

33 On the interrelations and mutual impact of security approaches, see Ulrich Beck, *Risk Society: Towards a New Modernity* (London: Sage Publications Ltd., 1992).

34 Desecuritization reflects the view that there is an inordinate focus on the role of states as the primary securitization actors, and that securitization is not taken far enough, but rather interposes issues that would impede the ability of securitization actors to act intelligently and devote the necessary focus to dealing with extant security problems. This is a view of desecuritization closer to the Habermasian view, where empowerment and emancipation of the security audience is itself the most optimal form of securitization. See, for example, J. Ann Tickner, *Gender and International Relations: Feminist Perspectives on Achieving Global Security* (New York: Columbia University Press, 1992).

35 The implicit rules that govern interaction in this world retain the anarchical characteristics of realist geopolitics. The behavioral roles of actors will continue to be dictated by self-referenced vital interests, but with the inevitable impact of external influences factored in behavioral calculations. See Philip Cerny, "Plurilateralism: Structural Differentiation and Functional Conflict in the Post-Cold War World Order," *Millennium* 22, no. 1 (1993): 27-51.

36 In the realist tradition, the conditions for such order are: "First, all societies seek to ensure that life will be in some measure secure against violence resulting in death or bodily harm. Second, all societies seek to ensure that promises, once made, will be kept, or that agreements, once undertaken, will be carried out. Third, all societies pursue the goal of

ensuring that the possession of things will remain stable to some degree, and will not be subject to challenges that are constant and without limit." See Hedley Bull, "Society and Anarchy in International Relations," in *Diplomatic Investigations*, eds. H. Butterfield and M. Wight (Cambridge, MA: Harvard University Press, 1968), 35-50.

37 See John Naisbitt, *Megatrends: Ten New Directions Transforming Our Lives* (New York: Warner Books, 1982).

38 See World Energy Council, *World Energy Resources Hydropower 2016.*

39 See, for example, "China's Yunnan Defends Dam Building as Activists Head to Court," *Reuters,* March 12, 2018, https://www.reuters.com/article/china-parliament-hydropower/ chinas-yunnan-defends-dam-building-as-activists-head-to-court-idUSL4N1QP3U1.

40 The government of Guyana estimates that building the Amaila Falls plant will cost $840 million. The China Development Bank will lend most of the money and the Inter-American Development Bank will lend $175 million. Guyana Power and Light (GPL), the state-owned electricity company, will have to pay approximately $100 million to the Amaila Falls consortium, which will increase electricity bills in at least the short-term. The developers of Amaila Falls have already had to pay $56 million for political risk insurance. However, if the project succeeds and the plant someday operates at its maximum capacity of 165 MW, it would provide more power than Guyana currently consumes. For more discussion see "Hydropower in Guyana: Shrouded in Secrecy," *The Economist,* May 4, 2013, http://www. economist.com/news/americas/21577090-small-dam-big-argument-shrouded-secrecy.

41 Hydroelectric plants whose capacity is 20 MW or less.

42 For example, Syria and Iraq are protesting against current Turkish projects to build 22 dams on the Tigris and Euphrates rivers, resulting in a reduction in the flow of these two major rivers downstream from the dams. Water available for farmers would be reduced, and the ecological balance of the rivers themselves and the land along their banks threatened.

43 The rotation of turbine blades creates an electrical current, which is harnessed on wind farms and used by national electrical grids. Alternatively, small individual turbines provide electricity to remote locations or individual homes.

44 U.S. Department of Energy, "History of U.S. Wind Energy," *Energy Efficiency and Renewable Energy*, https://www.energy.gov/eere/wind/history-us-wind-energy.

45 Ibid.

46 REN21. *Renewables 2017 Global Status Report.*

47 Ibid.

48 Ibid.

49 For example, Elon Musk has claimed that if "the only thing we had was solar energy - that was the only power source – if you just took a small section of Spain, you could power all of Europe."

50 See James Newton, *Uncommon Friends: Life with Thomas Edison, Henry Ford, Harvey Firestone, Alexis Carrel & Charles Lindbergh* (New York: Harcourt Brace Jovanovich, 1987), 31.

51 Solar PV directly converts solar energy into electricity using a PV cell made of a semiconductor material. CSP devices concentrate energy from the sun's rays to heat a receiver to high temperatures. This heat is transformed first into mechanical energy (by turbines or other engines) and then into electricity. See *International Energy Agency*, http://www.iea. org/topics/solarpvandcsp/, accessed May 13, 2014. At the end of 2012, global PV capacity passed 100 GW. See REN21, *Renewables 2013 Global Status Report* (Paris: REN21, 2013), 40.

52 World Energy Council, *World Energy Resources Report 2016*, https://www.worldenergy.org/ wp-content/uploads/2016/10/World-Energy-Resources-Full-report-2016.10.03.pdf.

53 Ibid.

54 REN21, *Renewables 2017 Global Status Report.*

55 CVP is a type of PV technology that uses lenses or curved mirrors to focus sunlight into small and highly efficient solar cells.

56 Industrial biomass comes from plants like miscanthus, switchgrass, hemp, corn, poplar, willow, sorghum, sugarcane, and a variety of tree species ranging from eucalyptus to palm oil. The particular plant matters more in processing than for the end product. Algae-based biofuels and second generation (cellulosic) ethanol should open new opportunities for development once they overcome the pilot stage. See Nancy Stauffer, "Research Spotlight: Algae System Transforms Greenhouse Emissions into Fuel," *The MIT Energy Research Council*, 2006, accessed December 5, 2013, http://web.mit.edu/erc/spotlights/alg-all.html.

57 By the end of 2012, almost 83 GW of biomass power capacity was in place. See REN21, *Renewables 2013 Global Status Report*, 27.

58 Rudolf Diesel, *The Theory and Construction of a Rational Heat Engine* (London: E & F. N. Spon, 1894), 9.

59 REN21, *Renewables 2017 Global Status Report*.

60 Challenges include the lack of an industrial chain for growing, harvesting, processing, and using biomass. Also, both bioethanol and biodiesel are less efficient in terms of energy content compared to petroleum-derived fuels.

61 Bioethanol blend in old vehicles causes corrosion on engine internal surfaces such as fuel rails, and only a small percentage of the current automotive fleet is designed to run on fuel that combines more than 10% bioethanol. In the U.S., for example, only 3% of motor vehicles are designed to accommodate fuel blends. For more details see International Energy Agency, "Technology Brief T06—June 2010" (Paris: IEA, 2010), https://www.iea.org/publications/freepublications/publication/etp2010.pdf.

62 For years, the U.S and Brazil, the world's two biggest producers of ethanol, were at odds over U.S. subsidies and tariffs. The U.S. imposed a tariff on imported ethanol of 54 cents per gallon. This tariff was applied to protect American corn farmers who could not produce ethanol as cheaply as sugarcane growers in Brazil. In January 2012, the U.S. government allowed the 30-year-old subsidy for U.S. producers to lapse and eliminated the steep tariff on imports of ethanol. This breakthrough prompted the U.S. and Brazil to cooperate in promoting the production and consumption of ethanol, to lobby for new markets in Africa and Latin America, and for a uniform global standard. See Brian Winter, "Insight: U.S. and Brazil—At Last, Friends on Ethanol," *Reuters*, September 14, 2012, accessed December 3, 2013, http://www.reuters.com/article/2012/09/14/us-brazil-us-ethanol-idUSBRE88D19520120914.

63 Geothermal energy harnesses the heat produced when hot rocks heat water underground. The steam released from drilling powers electric generators. Geothermal power does not suffer from intermittency, enabling it to serve as a base-load power source when the technological impediments to its application are resolved. However, the right combination of permeable rock formations and trapped hydrothermal energy is relatively rare in nature. See Ronald Dipippo, "Ideal Thermal Efficiency for Geothermic Binary Plants," *Geothermics* 36, no. 3 (June 2007), and *The Future of Geothermal Energy—Impact of Enhanced Geothermal Systems (EGS) on the U.S. in the Twenty-First Century* (Cambridge, MA: Massachusetts Institute of Technology, 2006), http://www1.eere.energy.gov/geothermal/pdfs/future_geo_energy.pdf.

64 See the project site at www.forgeutah.com/.

65 https://www.cornwall.gov.uk/business/economic-development/geothermal/.

66 Quoted in *Nature* 344, is. 6262 (March 1990): 102.

67 "There are currently three different ways to get tidal energy: tidal streams, barrages, and tidal lagoons. For most tidal energy generators, turbines are placed in tidal streams. A tidal stream is a fast-flowing body of water created by tides. A turbine is a machine that takes

energy from a flow of fluid. That fluid can be air (wind) or liquid (water). Because water is much denser than air, tidal energy is more powerful than wind energy. Unlike wind, tides are predictable and stable. Where tidal generators are used, they produce a steady, reliable stream of electricity." See National Geographic Education, accessed March 29, 2014, http://education.nationalgeographic.com/education/encyclopedia/tidal-energy/?ar_a=1.

68 REN21, *Renewables 2017 Global Status Report.*

69 World Energy Council, *World Energy Resources 2016.* For more on wave power, see, for example, K. Gunn and C. Stock-Williams, "Quantifying the Potential Global Market for Wave Power," paper presented at the *4th International Conference on Ocean Engineering,* Dublin, October 17, 2012.

70 World Energy Council, *World Energy Resources 2016.*

71 Fuel cells combine hydrogen and oxygen to produce electricity and are often compared to batteries. However, the fuel cell will produce electricity as long as fuel (hydrogen) is supplied, never losing its charge. NASA has used liquid hydrogen since the 1970s to propel space shuttles and other rockets into orbit. Hydrogen fuel cells power the shuttle's electrical systems, producing a clean by-product (pure water), which the crew drinks. Fuel cells operate best on pure hydrogen, but natural gas, methanol, or even petrol can produce the necessary hydrogen. On fuel cells technologies application, see Sandra Curtin and Jennifer Gangi, *Fuel Cell Technologies Market Report 2016* (Washington, D.C.: U.S. Department of Energy, 2017), https://energy.gov/sites/prod/files/2017/10/f37/fcto_2016_market_report.pdf.

72 Ibid.

73 Launched in 2006, the ITER project was by 2018 halfway to completing initial operation. The testing of fusion power operation is expected around 2035. The partner countries are the EU, China, India, Japan, Korea, Russia, and the U.S. See https://www.theguardian.com/environment/2017/dec/06/iter-nuclear-fusion-project-reaches-key-halfway-milestone.

74 https://www.bloomberg.com/news/features/2017-10-20/renewable-energy-threatens-the-world-s-biggest-science-project.

75 The EU contribution is 45.6%, with the other 6 partners each contributing 9.1%. The Members contribute very little money to the project: instead, nine-tenths of contributions are delivered to the ITER Organization in the form of completed components, systems or buildings. https://www.iter.org/proj/Countries.

76 European Fusion Development Agreement, *Fusion Electricity: A Roadmap to the Realisation of Fusion Energy* (EFDA, November, 2012), 66, https://www.euro-fusion.org/fileadmin/user_upload/EUROfusion/Documents/Roadmap.pdf.

77 Obtained from https://www.bloomberg.com/news/features/2017-10-20/renewable-energy-threatens-the-world-s-biggest-science-project/, accessed December 12, 2017.

78 On magnets and electricity see https://www.eia.gov/energyexplained/index.cfm?page=electricity_magnets.

79 Scientists in Japan have conducted experiments in converting solar power to laser and in sending energy in microwave form to Earth. The Japan Aerospace Exploration Agency (JAXA) aims to put into geostationary orbit a solar power generator that will transmit one gigawatt (GW) of energy to Earth, equivalent to the output of a large nuclear power plant, by 2030. The energy would be sent to the surface in microwave or laser form, where it would be converted into electricity for commercial power grids or stored in the form of hydrogen. This option holds the greatest promise for the ultimate goal of securing a non-polluting, unlimited source of energy. See "Practical Application of Space-Based Solar Power Generation," interview with Yasuyuki Fukumoro, *Japan Aerospace Exploration Agency,* April 2010, http://www.jaxa.jp/article/interview/vol53/index_e.html.

80 See Byung Yang Lee et al, "Virus-Based Piezoelectric Energy Generation," *Nature Nanotechnology* 7 (May 2012): 351–356.

81 See Freeman Dyson, *Disturbing the Universe* (New York: Harper & Row), 212. Dyson distinguishes civilization types on the basis of energy production and use. Type I masters all forms of terrestrial energy, extrapolating that a Type I civilization would be reached in 100–200 years. Type II would have harnessed stellar energy, and Type III would have exhausted that and tapped new types of energy sources.

82 "What countries have to do is that they have to satisfy three Es: they have to satisfy economic growth, they have to satisfy environmental sustainability and that is done through energy use." Hon. Condoleezza Rice, *Common Ground Panel at Notre Dame*, March 20, 2019, South Bend, Indiana.

83 For more on the driving forces that determine future change, see Joel Garreau, *Radical Evolution* (New York: Doubleday, 2005); James Canton, *The Extreme Future* (New York: Dutton, 2006).

84 Addressing the security implications of the composite parts allows the securitization of the megatrend as a whole through a process that transcends and represents a higher state of securitization than the securitization of each separate driver. This meta-securitization is securitization both on a higher abstract level, and also a unification of the securitization of disparate elements of the whole. On meta-securitization and meta-processes see Willard Van Orman Quine, "Logic Based on Inclusion and Abstraction," *The Journal of Symbolic Logic* 2, no. 4 (December 1937): 145–52, http://philpapers.org/rec/QUILBO accessed January 9, 2014, as well as Ludwig von Bertalanffy, *General System Theory: Essays on its Foundation and Development* (New York: George Braziller, 1968), and on meta-analysis as a quantitative effect estimate, see Gene V. Glass, "Primary, Secondary, and Meta-Analysis of Research," *Educational Research* 5 (1976): 3–8, http://www.jstor.org.

85 According to the Eurobarometer polls, nearly two-thirds of respondents agree that reducing fossil fuel imports from outside the EU can increase the security of EU energy supplies, and that reducing fossil fuel imports from outside the EU can benefit the EU economically. See Special Eurobarometer 45, *Climate Change* Report (EC, September 2017), https://ec.europa.eu/clima/sites/clima/files/support/docs/report_2017_en.pdf.

86 About 83% of conservative Republicans favor more solar panel farms; so, too, do virtually all liberal Democrats (97%). Similarly, there is widespread agreement across party and ideological groups in favor of expanding wind energy (75% and 93% correspondingly). See Cary Funk and Brian Kennedy, *The Politics of Climate* (Pew Research Center, October 2016), http://assets.pewresearch.org/wp-content/uploads/sites/14/2016/10/14080900/PS_2016.10.04_Politics-of-Climate_FINAL.pdf.

87 "Rethinking Renewable Mandates" by Gail Tverber, Our Finite World, July 31, 2019, accessed June 17, 2020, https://ourfiniteworld.com/2019/07/31/rethinking-renewable-mandates/

88 See, for example, Robert Mabro, *Oil in the 21st Century: Issues, Challenges and Opportunities* (New York: Oxford University Press, 2006).

89 R. James Woolsey, "High Cost of Crude: The New Currency of Foreign Policy," testimony of R. James Woolsey (U.S. Senate Committee on Foreign Relations, November 16, 2005), accessed June 12, 2011, http://www.gpo.gov/fdsys/pkg/CPRT-109SPRT28001/html/CPRT-109SPRT28001.htm.

90 Because of the increased demand, competition for oil and other fossil fuels will continue to intensify and can lead to major conflicts. With the current and projected rates of consumption, some analysts estimate that we will run out of oil by 2051. See M. King Hubbert, "Nuclear Energy and the Fossil Fuels," in *Drilling and Production Practice* (American Petroleum Institute, 1956), 7–25, and David Deming, "Oil: Are We Running Out?," in *Petroleum*

Provinces of the 21st century, AAPG Memoir 74, eds. M.W. Downey, W. A. Morgan, and J. C. Threet (Tulsa: The American Association of Petroleum, 2001), 45–55.

91 See Julian Simon, *The Ultimate Resource 2* (Princeton: Princeton University Press, 1998).

92 On environmental threats and climate change, see, for example, B. Metz et al., *Climate Change 2007: Mitigation, Contribution of Working Group III to the Fourth Assessment, Report of the Intergovernmental Panel on Climate Change* (Cambridge: Cambridge University Press, 2007); Greenpeace and European Renewable Energy Council, *Future Investment: A Sustainable Investment Plan for the Power Sector to Save the Climate* (Greenpeace, 2007), accessed December 3, 2013, http://www.greenpeace.de/fileadmin/gpd/user_upload/themen/klima/greenpeace_studie_future-investment_engl.pdf; *Stern Review on the Economics of Climate Change* (London: HM Treasury, 2006).

93 On July 9, 1970, Richard Nixon transmitted Reorganization Plan No. 3 to the U.S Congress by executive order, creating the Environmental Protection Agency (EPA) as a single, independent, agency from a number of smaller arms of different federal agencies.

94 On the "Smart City" concept, see, for example, Andrés Monzón, "Smart Cities Concept and Challenges: Bases for the Assessment of Smart City Projects," in *Smart Cities, Green Technologies, and Intelligent Transport Systems*, eds. M. Helfert et al. (4th International Conference, SMARTGREENS, 2015, and 1st International Conference VEHITS 2015, Lisbon, Portugal, May 20–22, 2015, Revised Selected Papers, Springer International Publishing, Switzerland 2015), https://www.springer.com/cda/content/document/cda.../9783319277523-c2.pdf.

95 Archimedes' lever is a popular metaphor derived from a saying ascribed to the philosopher Archimedes that if he had a fulcrum and a lever long enough, he could move Earth. It is a symbol of providing a point that is "outside" that can be applied to change the "inside" conditions, i.e., to make something unreachable obtainable.

96 Peter Truscott, "European Energy Security: Facing a Future of Increasing Dependency," *Whitehall Paper* 73 (London: Royal United Services Institute for Defence and Security Studies, December 11, 2009): 54, accessed December 24, 2013, http://www.rusi.org/publications/whitehall/ref:I4B228CBFED62F/#.UtG8l55dW8c.

97 *The Next Economic Growth Engine: Scaling Fourth Industrial Revolution Technologies in Production*, World Economic Forum White Paper, in collaboration with McKinsey & Company, January 2018, http://www3.weforum.org/docs/WEF_Technology_and_Innovation_The_Next_Economic_Growth_Engine.pdf.

98 On the strategic technology trends and most essential technologies with broad industry impact and significant potential for disruption, see PwC Global, *Tech Breakthroughs Megatrend: How to Prepare for Its Impact* (PwC, Global Technology Megatrends, 2016), https://www.pwc.com/gx/en/issues/technology/tech-breakthroughs-megatrend.pdf; David W. Cearley et al., *Top 10 Strategic Technology Trends for 2018* (Gartner, October 3, 2017), https://www.gartner.com/technology/research/top-10-technology-trends.

99 Massimov, Karim. "THE NEXT MASTER OF THE WORLD: Artificial Intelligence." Amanat Publishing House LLC, 2019.

100 Flaherty T., Schwieters N., and Jennings S., *2017 Power and Utilities Industry Trends* (PwC, 2017), https://www.strategyand.pwc.com/media/file/2017-Power-and-Utilities-Industry-Trends.pdf.

101 William Petty, *A Treatise of Taxes and Contributions* (London: Obadiah Blagrave, 1679), 53.

102 See Emanuel Adler and Beverly Crawford, *Progress in Post-War International Relations* (New York: Columbia University Press, 1991).

103 On the issue of "policy-as-violence" and the link between military and geopolitical power in security, see Michael Dillon, "Governing Terror: The State of Emergency of Biopolitical Emergence," *International Political Sociology* 1, no. 1 (March, 2007): 8.

104 See Thomas Robert Malthus, *An Essay on the Principle of Population* [Oxford World's Classics reprint, 2008 (1798)]. His theory of population posited that population grows in geometric progression and food in arithmetic progression which may lead to mankind having no resources for survival.

105 On the mutual influence between societal orders and technological development, see Wiebe Bijker, *Of Bicycles, Bakelites, and Bulbs: Toward a Theory of Sociotechnical Change* (Cambridge: MIT Press, 1995).

106 Auguste Comte, *Positive Philosophy*, ed. and trans. Harriet Martineau (New York: Calvin Blanchard, 1858), 30.

107 The impact of the technological revolution on society and socio-political phenomena is determined by its persistence in the face of shifting societal attitudes. See A.M. Hommels, *Unbinding Cities: Obduracy in Urban Societechnical Change* (Cambridge: MIT Press, 2005).

108 Stephen Hadley. Podcast. *Tom Donilon and Stephen Hadley talk with Michael Morell on "Intelligence Matters"*. CBS News, January 29, 2020.

109 The defense importance of overall technological, and alternative energy developments in particular, is continuously changing due to the rise of China and other important non-Western military powers, as well as other actors. On the role of technology in national security, see Michael G. Vickers and Robert C. Martinage, *The Revolution in War* (Washington, D.C.: Center for Strategic and Budgetary Assessments, 2004); R.V. Ericson and A. Doyle, *Uncertain Business: Risk, Insurance, and the Limits of Knowledge* (Toronto: University of Toronto Press, 2004).

110 Colin Flint, *Introduction to Geopolitics* (New York: Routledge, 2006), 39.

111 Socio-material factors are the elements of societal practices, which are defined as "embodied, materially mediated arrays of human activity centrally organized around shared practical understanding." See Karin Knorr-Cetina, Theodore R. Schatzki, and Eike von Savigny, *The Practice Turn in Contemporary Theory* (London: Routledge, 2001), 2.

112 Manichaeism is an old religion taught by Mani, an apostle in Mesopotamia in the 240s. Manichaeism is based on a strict breakdown of everything into good or evil. Seeing things as always having two opposed sides is what we now call dualism.

113 Jennifer Taylor, "Ethics of Renewable Energy" (paper submitted to *World Wind Energy Conference*, York, York University, 2008), 5, accessed May 22, 2012, http://www.ontario-sea.org/Storage/27/1872_Community_Power-_Bringin_Ethics_Back_into_Energy_Politics.pdf.

114 Robert S. Litwak, *Détente and the Nixon Doctrine: American Foreign Policy and the Pursuit of Stability, 1969–1976* (Cambridge: Cambridge University Press, 1984), 5.

115 Paul Quirk, "Energy Report: Ethical Analysis of Renewable Energy and Conservation," October 17, 2012, accessed December 21, 2013, http://www.scribd.com/doc/39500159/Ethical-Analysis-of-Renewable-Energy-and-Conservation.

116 Václav Havel and Paul Wilson, "The Power of the Powerless," in *Open Letters: Selected Writings 1965–1990*, ed. Paul Wilson (New York: Vintage Books, 1992), 15.

117 Hans Jonas, *The Imperative of Responsibility: In Search of an Ethics for the Technological Age* (Chicago: University of Chicago Press, 1984), 6.

118 Such regulatory mechanisms generally include taxes and charges, tradable permits, voluntary agreements, subsidies and incentives, production quotas, price restrictions and guidelines, research and development, and information dissemination. Policies include feed-in tariffs that provide renewable energy generators with a premium above the price of electricity generated from conventional fuels, and quota systems requiring retail electric utilities to secure a set percentage of their energy mixes from renewable resources. Other regulations have been considered, such as net metering, power cost equalization, and fuel stabilization.

119 See, for example, Bill McKibben, *Enough: Staying Human in an Engineered Age* (New York: Henry Holt and Company, LLC, 2004).

120 Henry Kissinger and George Shultz, "Finding Common Ground," *New York Times*, September 30, 2008, http://www.nytimes.com/2008/09/30/opinion/30iht-edkissinger.1.16585986.html?pagewanted=all&_r=0.

121 See José E. Alvarez, *International Organizations as Law-Makers* (Oxford: Oxford University Press, 2005).

122 See United Nations General Assembly, "Transforming Our World: The 2030 Agenda for Sustainable Development," resolution adopted by the General Assembly on 25 September 2015, A/RES/70/1 (October 21, 2015), http://www.un.org/ga/search/view_doc.asp?symbol=A/RES/70/1&Lang=E. The resolution adopted by heads of state and government at a special UN summit contains 17 Sustainable Development Goals (SDGs) and 169 targets in areas such as climate change, economic inequality, innovation, sustainable consumption, peace, and justice, as well as "access to affordable, reliable, sustainable and modern energy for all." Targets are defined as aspirational and global, with each government setting its own national targets guided by the global level of ambition but taking into account national circumstances. In order to ensure progress and long-term accountability, the 2030 agenda includes a follow-up and review mechanism which will allow all partners to assess the impact of their actions. At the global level, this is overseen by the High-Level Political Forum on Sustainable Development.

123 The existing international legal framework is based on obligations and commitments between countries on price floors, quota measures, and subsidies on energy. See Robert Howse, *World Trade Law and Renewable Energy: The Case of Non-Tariff Barriers* (United Nations, New York and Geneva, 2009), accessed December 12, 2013, http://unctad.org/en/docs/ditcted20085_en.pdf.

124 Richard Haass, Statement of President of the Council on Foreign Relations Richard N. Haass, Committee on Armed Services, U.S. House of Representatives, Washington, D.C., March 11, 2009.

125 Local and regional regulatory measures to safeguard environmental security consistently incorporate a broader international component, influenced by new commitments and international undertakings developed by such international platforms as the Paris Climate Accord of 2015.

126 As a notion, social construction of reality is based on the understanding that the emergence of ideas and the formation of knowledge among persons and groups that are interacting in a social system gradually coalesce into a framework. Over time, this framework of concepts and mental representations becomes the structure that determines the actions of these individuals and groups. Furthermore, these concepts eventually become habituated, making these individuals and groups endeavor to fit into reciprocal roles in relation to each other. The emerging interplay and its setting gradually permeate other layers of society and influence its members to enter into and play out these constructs. When these reciprocal interactions become habitual and embedded in practice, they are said to be institutionalized. In the process of this institutionalization, meaning is embedded in society's actions that results in specific behavioral patterns and valorization that determines future developments. On social construction of reality, see Thomas Luckmann and Peter L. Berger, *The Social Construction of Reality: A Treatise in the Sociology of Knowledge* (London: Penguin, 1991); David Newman, *Sociology: Exploring the Architecture of Everyday Life* (Thousand Oaks, CA: Pine Forge Press, 1995). Regarding constructivist approaches in science, see, for example, Olav Eikeland, "From Epistemology to Gnoseology—Understanding the Knowledge Claims of Action Research," *Management Research News* 30, is. 5 (2007): 344–58.

127 Nicholas Onuf, *Making Sense, Making Worlds: Constructivism in Social Theory and International Relations* (Abingdon: Routledge, 2012), 6.

128 Aristotle, "Metaphysics VII, 1032a26-32," in *The Complete Works of Aristotle*, vol. 2, ed. J. Barnes (Princeton: Princeton University Press, 1984), 1630.

129 The idea constructs for renewables development can be associated with what are traditionally considered total ideologies that color how actors see the world around them. For detailed discourses on ideology see Karl Mannheim, Ideology and Utopia: An Introduction to the Sociology of Knowledge (New York: Harcourt Brace Jovanovich, 1985); Anthony Downs, An Economic Theory of Democracy (New York, HarperCollins, 1957); Philip E. Converse, "The Nature of Belief Systems in Mass Publics," in *Ideology and Discontent*, ed. David E. Apter (New York: The Free Press, 1964), 206–61.

130 Societal constructions about the past are not so much a reflection of the notion that the past determines the future, but rather reflect the understanding of how humanity advances through a process of learning, which is, in itself, "the process by which we become able to use past and current events to predict what the future holds." See Yael Niv and Geoffrey Schoenbaum, "Dialogues on Prediction Errors," *Trends in Cognitive Sciences* 12, no. 7 (2008): 265.

131 See Dennis G. Shepherd, *Historical Development of the Windmill* (Ithaca: Cornell University, 1990).

132 See Polybius, *Historiae*, vol. 1, trans. G. Whittaker and W. B. Whittaker (Salzburg: Lehner, 1823).

133 See Pliny the Younger (A.D. 61/62–c. A.D. 112/113), *Letters*, trans. William Melmoth (New York: P.F. Collier & Son, 1909–14).

134 On the technological and scientific advances during the Enlightenment and the Industrial Revolution, see Giuliano Pancaldi, *Volta: Science and Culture in the Age of Enlightenment* (Princeton: Princeton University Press, 2005); Joel Mokyr, "Useful Knowledge as an Evolving System: The View from Economic History," in *The Economy as an Evolving Complex System, III: Current Perspectives and Future Directions*, eds. Lawrence E. Blume and Steven N. Durlauf (New York: Oxford University Press, 2006), 307–37; Douglass C. North and Robert P. Thomas, *The Rise of the Western World* (Cambridge: Cambridge University Press, 1973).

135 On the ascent of the Western world to its modern position of dominance in North-South relations, see Diamond, Jared M., *Guns, Germs, and Steel: The Fates of Human Societies* (New York: W. W. Norton & Co., 1999).

136 Such a re-conceptualization of socio-political developments and notions is explored by diverse theories of social change. See N.J. Smelser, *Theory of Collective Behavior* (New York: Free Press, 1963); also see A. Touraine, *The Voice and the Eye: An Analysis of Social Movements* (New York: Cambridge University Press, 1981).

137 See Eric Jay Dolin, *Leviathan: The History of Whaling in America* (New York: W. W. Norton & Co., 2008).

138 See Bill Kovarik, "Henry Ford, Charles Kettering and the Fuel of the Future," *Automotive History Review* 32 (Spring 1998): 7–27.

139 "Fuel Cell Origins: 1840–1890" (Smithsonian Institution, January 21, 2013), accessed May 12, 2013, http://americanhistory.si.edu/fuelcells/origins/origins.htm.

140 Geothermal Technologies Office, *A History of Geothermal Energy in the United States* (U.S. Department of Energy, 2006), accessed January 23, 2013, https://www1.eere.energy.gov/geothermal/history.html#1851.

141 John H. Lienhard, *Solar Power in 1884* (University of Houston), accessed January 1, 2014, http://www.uh.edu/engines/epi2871.htm.

142 See Michael Brian Schiffer, *Taking Charge: The Electric Automobile in America* (Washington, D.C.: Smithsonian Books, 2003); Ernest Henry Wakefield, *History of the Electric Automobile: Hybrid Electric Vehicles* (Warrendale, PA: Society of Automotive Engineers Inc., 1998).

143 W.R. Nitschke and C.M. Wilson, *Rudolf Diesel, Pioneer of the Age of Power* (Norman, OK: University of Oklahoma Press, 1965), 139.

144 This tax had increased the cost of ethanol, reducing its competitiveness as a fuel. See Joseph DiPardo, *Outlook for Biomass Ethanol Production and Demand* (Energy Information Administration, Washington, D.C., 2000), accessed December 15, 2013, http://www. agmrc.org/media/cms/biomass_E6EE9065FD69D.pdf.

145 John Lund, *100 Years of Geothermal Power Production*, Geo-Heat Center Bulletin (Geo-Heat Center, September 2004), accessed December 17, 2013, http://geoheat.oit.edu/bulletin/ bull25-3/art2.pdf.

146 See Sheila Bailey and Ryne Raffaelle, *Space Solar Cells and Arrays* (New Jersey: John Wiley & Sons, 2003).

147 In 1979, the Carter administration installed 32 solar panels to heat water at the White House. The Reagan administration removed those panels in 1986. See David Biello, "Where Did the Carter White House's Solar Panels Go?," *Scientific American,* August 6, 2010, accessed December 5, 2013, http://www.scientificamerican.com/article.cfm?id=carter -white-house-solar-panel-array.

148 Henry Kissinger, "Speech to The Pilgrims Society of Great Britain"; see Bernard Gwertzman, "Kissinger Urges Pooled Efforts in Energy Crisis," *New York Times,* December 13, 1973, http://select.nytimes.com/gst/abstract.html?res=F50815FF385D127A93C1A81789D 95F478785F9.

149 Jacques Ellul, *The Technological Society* (New York: Vintage Books, 1967), 247.

150 Technology development becomes a social responsibility issue for governments and citizens alike, with an obligation to "see that science is applied to the right social and political ends." See Imre Lakatos, "The Social Responsibility of Science," in *Mathematics, Science and Epistemology: Vol. 2, Philosophical* Papers, ed. John Worrall and Gregory Currie (Cambridge: Cambridge University Press, 1978), 258.

151 On the interaction of society with its environment and Actor-Network Theory, see Bruno Latour, *Reassembling the Social—An Introduction to Actor-Network Theory* (London: Oxford University Press, 2005).

152 The notion of "paradigm shift" as introduced by Thomas Kuhn in 1962 denotes a shift from an accepted theory in natural sciences to another, which completely replaces the first one. See Thomas S. Kuhn, *The Structure of Scientific Revolutions,* 3rd ed. (Chicago: University of Chicago Press, 1996). While subject to extensive critique, including its application to social sciences, it is a useful theoretical summarization that serves as a tool and explanatory model for highlighting the major elements of the post-Cold War dynamic, illuminating the major ones among them and providing a better understanding of the alternative energy developments as a modern trend.

153 Edward Wenk Jr., *Tradeoffs: Imperatives of Choice in a High-Tech World* (Baltimore: The Johns Hopkins University Press, 1986), 11.

154 Ludwig von Mises, *The Ultimate Foundation of Economic Science: An Essay on Method* (Liberty Fund Inc., 2006), 127.

155 This demographic shift incorporates a range of elements: extensive population growth in rapidly developing and emerging economies, intensified migration within developed economies, and a new generation faced with bleaker economic prospects. It is characterized by the predominance of fertility "plateaus" across most of the world, with global fertility rates reaching a peak, bar some exceptions. These plateaus, coupled with lower

levels of mortality and increased life expectancy, are one of the factors fueling the growing demand for energy. See, for example, U.S. Department of State, U.S. Agency for International Development, "Security, Democracy, Prosperity," August 2003, Strategic Plan FY2004–2009; UN Population Division, *Population Challenges and Development Goals* (New York, United Nations, 2005).

156 Globalization itself has enhanced the visions associated with the alternative energy megatrend, as globalization has its own ideological content, pros, and cons, and is dominated by the interests of the financial and economic players central to world markets and institutions. This ideology reflects how specific social groupings impose their political priorities and economic interests on government policies, societal views, and practices, and on global market activities. It remains unclear whether these idea constructs will follow a Western-centric liberal democratic model, as Confucian and Islamic societies have inherent cultural differences that prompt different approaches. Overall, liberal globalization ideology has been met with resistance—on the political level, through the process of fragmentation, and on societal and individual levels, through the rising focus on inequality and consequent polarization of economic interests.

157 See Harold James, *The Creation and Destruction of Value: The Globalization Cycle* (Cambridge: Harvard University Press, 2009); Bryan Mabee, *The Globalization of Security: State Power, Security Provision and Legitimacy* (Chippenham and Eastbourne: Palgrave Macmillan, 2009); and Norrin M. Ripsman and T.V. Paul, *Globalization and the National Security State* (Oxford: Oxford University Press, 2010).

158 It should be noted that globalization's effects defy easy characterization and cannot be easily broken down into simple formulas and opposing constructs (the simple dichotomies of nationalist/globalist, modernist/pastoralist, or liberal/fundamentalist). See Eleonore Kofman and Gillian Youngs, *Globalisation: Theory and Practice* (London: Pinter, 1996).

159 Roger A. Arnold, *Microeconomics* (Mason: Cengage Learning, 2008), 476.

160 Martin W. Lewis and Karen E. Wigen, *The Myth of Continents: A Critique of Metageography* (Berkeley: University of California Press, 1997), ix; see also J.V. Beaverstock, R.G. Smith and P.J. Taylor, "World-City Network: A New Metageography?," *Annals of the Association of American Geographers* 90, no. 2 (2000): 123–34.

161 According to former U.S. Under Secretary of State Paula Dobriansky, globalization has "resulted in a much more interconnected world with unprecedented freedom of movement." Paula Dobriansky, "Threats to Security in the Western Hemisphere," remarks at the Inter-American Defense College, Washington, D.C., October 20, 2003, https://2001-2009.state.gov/g/rls/rm/2003/25564.htm.

162 See Richard S. Silberglitt, *The Global Technology Revolution 2020, Executive Summary: Bio/ Nano/Materials/Information Trends, Drivers, Barriers, and Social Implications* (Santa Monica: Rand Corporation, 2006); Scott Barrett, "The Coming Global Climate-Technology Revolution," *Journal of Economic Perspectives* 23, no. 2 (2009): 53–75.

163 On the philosophical approaches to technology see Herbert Marcuse, *One-Dimensional Man* (Boston: Beacon Press, 1964).

164 Geopolitical transitions occur when actors intersect across multiple dimensions of international relations and influence global socioeconomic phenomena. These trends, including the alternative energy phenomenon, are together increasing readiness and willingness by actors to break with established consensus. There are noticeable anti-systemic responses by state and non-state actors, as well as global society—protests, social movements, crime, and terrorist attacks. These result in disruptive pressures that impact global security and skew ongoing conventional processes. On geopolitical transitions through

history, see, for example, Benno Teschke, *The Myth of 1648: Class, Geopolitics, and the Making of Modern International Relations* (London & New York: Verso, 2003).

165 The most noticeable has been the rise of Asian powers, in particular China and India, with the 1998 Asian financial crisis providing a watershed for a more forceful expression of their power projection capabilities.

166 The coming transformation is not strictly based on battery-storage development. Other technologies are on the cusp such as storing hydrogen gas that can be burned in fuel cells. This system uses nanomaterials to create a partially flexible sponge that can trap hydrogen atoms in its pores. The gas can later be released by heating the structure. Another example is a sulfur-based flow battery in which ions flow across a membrane between a sulfur-containing anode and a cathode.

167 Rob Smith. "Three Countries are Leading the Renewable Energy Revolution." *World Economic Forum,* February 26, 2018.

168 Barber, Lionel, "Outgoing FT editor Lionel Barber: how the world has changed," video interview with Miranda Green, *Financial Times,* January 16, 2020.

169 It is important not to overemphasize the role of societal notions and beliefs on the shaping of objective reality. It is not culture or mores on their own that influence how society constructs its own reality—rather reality is a hybrid of a number of factors that include societal influences.

170 Alvin Toffler, *Future Shock* (New York: Bantam Books, 1971), 15.

171 See Bertolt Brecht, *Life of Galileo* (New York: Grove Atlantic Inc., 1991).

172 *Ovid: Metamorphoses*, introduction by W.R. Johnson, trans. S. Lombardo (Indianapolis and Cambridge: Hackett Publishing Inc., 2010), 5.

173 Although popularly associated with Jürgen Habermas, the theory of truth or knowledge is not an epistemic conception of truth, and, in fact, it cannot be pigeonholed as technological determinism, as it incorporates the view that a proposition or object should be agreed upon because it is true, not the other way around. See Jürgen Habermas, *Truth and Justification* (Cambridge: MIT Press, 2003).

174 The idea constructs for renewables development can be associated with what are traditionally considered total ideologies that color how actors see the world around them. For detailed discourses on ideology see Karl Mannheim, *Ideology and Utopia: An Introduction to the Sociology of Knowledge* (New York: Harcourt Brace Jovanovich, 1985); Anthony Downs, *An Economic Theory of Democracy* (New York: HarperCollins, 1957); Philip E. Converse, "The Nature of Belief Systems in Mass Publics," in *Ideology and Discontent*, ed. David E. Apter (New York: The Free Press, 1964), 206–61.

PART 2

1 Solon, *Plutarch's Lives*, trans. John Langhorne and William Langhorne (Baltimore: William & Joseph Neal, 1834), 60.

2 Geopolitics as a term was first coined by Rudolf Kjellén, a Swedish political scientist, in 1899. It has been placed within diverse historical-geographic contexts of knowledge and praxis—from controlling, containing, and limiting access to "strategic geographical space" by specific actors to the Cold War interaction of great powers. It integrates racial, ethnic, and religious conflict, the pursuit of rights by societal groups, and others. Geopolitics today creates a representative and interpretive framework of worldviews that channel specific actions and policies that respond to a broadening of the situations that require geopolitical interpretation. See Gearóid Ó'Tuathail, *Critical Geopolitics: The Politics of Writing Global Space* (Minneapolis: University of Minnesota Press, 1996), 15.

3 Such phenomena include: technological advances, impact of religious or ethical views on the conduct of societal groups, demographic trends, and attitudes toward how economic

activity is conducted. Generally, the greater the confluence of different phenomena, the greater the effect on the conduct of and interaction between states. See, for example, U.S. National Intelligence Council, Global Trends 2030: Alternative Worlds NIC 2012-001 (NIC, December 2012), http://www.dni.gov/files/documents/GlobalTrends_2030.pdf.

4   Power can be defined as the authority or ability to exert influence over other actors in a given social or political setting. See Michael Smith, *International Security: Politics, Policy, Prospects* (Basingstoke: Palgrave Macmillan, 2010), 51.

5   On power and technology linkages, see Parag Khanna and Ayesha Khanna, *Hybrid Reality: Thriving in the Emerging Human-Technology Civilization* (TED Conferences, Kindle Edition, 2012), 79.

6   Non-state actors include intergovernmental organizations, supranational platforms, NGOs, multinational corporations, economic and political groupings such as the G7 and G20, and wealthy individuals and figures of international renown, as well as terrorist, organized crime, and other such groups.

7   See Stephen Krasner, "Realism, Imperialism, and Democracy," *Political Theory* 20, no. 1 (February 1992): 39.

8   A product of the so-called Dependency Theory, the notion of cores and peripheries emerged in describing actors that are mutually dependent, as in "an economic or political relationship between countries or groups of countries in which one side is not able to control its destiny because of oppressive links with the other side." Peter Taylor, *Political Geography: World-Economy, Nation-State, and Locality*, 3rd ed. (New York: John Wiley & Sons, 1993), 328.

9   Historically, the core-periphery relationship has also been determined by the international division of labor that arose after the emergence of strong states in Northwest Europe. These states were characterized by strong governments and large armies, which enabled them to control international commerce to an unprecedented extent, to extract the relevant benefits and growth, and to concentrate key factors of production: capital and labor. The periphery was characterized by weaker governments, often governing their populace via coercion rather than economic means, due to their economies' focus on the export of raw materials. The core exercised influence over the periphery from being the source of innovation and income and from the export of natural resources to changing the local elites and structures of power. "Not only are the states of the core the richest on the planet; their power also continues to permeate the countries of the periphery, spawning anger as well as hope." See Harm de Blij, *The Power of Place: Geography, Destiny, and Globalization's Rough Landscape* (Oxford University Press, 2008), 13.

10   *See generally*, David Petraeus, Paras D. Bhayani, "North America: The Next Great Emerging Market?" *Foreign Policy*, June 25, 2015.

11   The core-periphery relationship is hierarchical, linking the whole to its parts through rank-dependent interactions. See Johan Galtung, "A Structural Theory of Imperialism," *Journal of Peace Research* 8, no. 2 (1971): 81–117.

12   See Immanuel Wallerstein, *The Model World-System: Capitalist Agriculture and the Origins of the European World-Economy in the 16th Century* (New York: Academic Press, 1974).

13   See Fareed Zakaria, *The Post-American World* (New York: W. W. Norton & Co., 2009) and Dilip Haro, *After Empire: The Birth of a Multi-Polar World* (New York: Nation Books, 2010). For opposing views, see Stephen G. Brooks and William C. Wohlforth, *World Out of Balance: International Relations and the Challenge of American Primacy* (Princeton, NJ: Princeton University Press, 2008).

14   John Agnew, *Geopolitics: Re-Visioning World Politics* (London: Routledge, 2003), 3.

15   B. de Sousa Santos, "On Oppositional Postmodernism," in *Critical Development Theory*, ed. R. Munck and D. O'Hearn (London: Zed Books, 1999), 29–43.

16 The Paris Climate Agreement adopted at the United Nations climate conference in Paris in December 2015 was the first universal, legally binding global climate deal that set out a global action plan to avoid climate change by limiting global warming to well below 2°C. See United Nations Climate Change, *Paris Agreement,* http://unfccc.int/paris_agreement/items/9485.php.

17 The perception of the trend as a source of East-West cooperation has its merit, but a perception of the East as a threat and challenge to the West is just as likely an outcome. The possibilities for collective management of East-West security relationships have gone beyond the status quo of global institutions and arrangements that were present in the bipolar Cold War order. See Samuel Huntington, "The Clash of Civilizations?" *Foreign Affairs* 72, no. 3 (Summer 1993), 22–49.

18 Austin Williams, *China's Urban Revolution: Understanding Chinese Eco-Cities* (Bloomsbury Academic, 2017), quoted in Wade Shepard "No Joke: China Is Building 285 Eco-Cities, Here's Why," *Forbes.com,* September 1, 2017, https://www.forbes.com/sites/wadeshepard/#41077d9e3f6e.

19 The North-South rift is a more recent development that cuts across the historic East-West division, and has close connotations with the division between developed and developing countries. There is an undeniable geographic element in geopolitics that determines political priorities and interests, and, as a typical archetype of geopolitical interaction, the North-South divide sets out those divisions most clearly in modern history. See M.A.L. Miller, *The Third World in Global Environmental Politics* (Boulder: Lynne Rienner, 1995).

20 This was expressed in the notion of the Third World, which gradually encompassed the so-called Second World nations previously comprising the Communist bloc. On the evolution of the notions of First, Second, and Third World, see Dan Harris, Mick Moore, and Hubert Schmitz, *Country Classifications for a Changing World,* Working Paper 326 (Center for the Future State, Institute of Development Studies at the University of Sussex, Bringnon, May 2009), http://www2.ids.ac.uk/gdr/cfs/pdfs/Wp326.pdf.

21 The North could now be seen to include countries like China and Russia, as well as possibly Brazil, India, and South Africa. There are now North-South divisions even within regions, such as Europe, Asia, Africa, and America. For a detailed discussion of North-South cleavages, see Charles A. Jones, *The North-South Dialogue: A Brief History* (New York: St. Martin's Press, 1983); David A. Lake, "Power and the Third World: Toward a Realist Political Economy of North-South Relations," *International Studies Quarterly* 31, no. 2 (1987): 217–34.

22 See Daniel Faber, *Environment under Fire: Imperialism and the Ecological Crisis in Central America* (New York: Monthly Review Press, 1993); See Bruce Rich, *Mortgaging the Earth: The World Bank, Environmental Impoverishment and the Crisis of Development* (London: Earthscan, 1994).

23 Alexander Mirtchev, *Political Behavior: Its Nature, Forms and Development* (Library of Congress Catalogue # JA76.M56, 1987), 232.

24 Historically, developments similar to alternative energy have fallen predominantly within the purview of the state, at least initially, as it is the only institution capable of absorbing the costs, risks, coordination, and other associated burdens of their application. Alternative energy can be aptly compared to the development of the telecommunications sector, particularly the Internet. Through the Advanced Research Projects Agency Network (ARPANET), established in the 1960s, the U.S. government funded research into information management that eventually led to the creation of the Internet, a major transformational force that had widespread implications on society at large. The alternative energy megatrend has a similar potential. In fact, the U.S. Department of Energy runs the Advanced Research Projects Agency-Energy (ARPA-E) for new energy technologies.

Its namesake aspires to achieve the revolutionary impact of ARPANET with a mission to bring entirely new technologies to market. See "Arpa-E," https://arpa-e.energy. gov/?q=arpa-e-site-page/about.

25 "The Post-World War Two institutions [such as WTO, IMF, and World Bank] . . . are out-dated and need a refresher... in light of the changing dynamics of the world." "China plays a relatively small role in those institutions, yet is the primary driver of global growth. So these institutions have to be updated to reflect the reality of the new world and also to reflect that the United States' relative influence is more multi-polar than it was at the end of World War Two." David McCormick. Interview. *In Conversation: David McCormick.* Bloomberg Live. June 4, 2019.

26 See Colin Crouch, *The Strange Non-Death of Neo-Liberalism* (Cambridge: Polity, 2011) and William Robinson, "Beyond the Theory of Imperialism: Global Capitalism and the Trans-national State," *Societies Without Borders* 2, no. 1 (2007): 5–26.

27 UN Global Compact is a voluntary initiative based on businesses' commitments to imple-ment universal sustainability principles and to support UN goals. See more at United Nations Global Compact, https://www.unglobalcompact.org.

28 The basics of sustainable development concept were presented in 1987 in: World Commis-sion on Environment and Development, *Our Common Future,* http://www.un-documents. net/wced-ocf.htm. The current understanding of sustainable development includes a set of global Sustainable Development Goals adopted on 25 September 2015 by the UN General Assembly. See: Sustainable Development Knowledge Platform, *Transforming our World: The 2030 Agenda for Sustainable Development* (UN DESA, 2015), https://sustainable development.un.org/post2015/transformingourworld.

29 RE100—a global initiative launched in 2014 that calls for transfer to 100% renewable energy. Its membership list includes large multinational companies like BT Group, Corbion, Facebook, Google, IKEA Group, M&S, Microsoft, Novo Nordisk, Royal DSM, Royal Philips, Unilever, and Vestas. See the official RE100 site at http://re100.org/.

30 Third Generation Environmentalism (E3G), *Consumer Led Energy Transition* (RE100, The Climate Group, November 2016), www.euractiv.com/wp-content/uploads/sites/2/2016/11 /RE100_ConsumerLedEnergyTransition.pdf.

31 Bengt Johansson, "Security Aspects of Future Renewable Energy Systems," *Energy* 61 (November 1, 2013): 598–605, https://www.sciencedirect.com/science/article/pii/ S0360544213007743.

32 See Nikolas Rose, *Powers of Freedom* (London: Cambridge University Press, 1999).

33 See Robert Jackson, *The Global Covenant: Human Conduct in a World of States* (Oxford: Oxford University Press, 2000).

34 For examples regarding strain in the international order, *see* Richard J. Evans. "The Breakup: The Unmaking of the Postwar International Order." *The Nation,* December 17, 2019.

35 At the end of 2015. See World Energy Council, *Resources 2016 Summary,* https://www. worldenergy.org/wp-content/uploads/2016/10/World-Energy-Resources-Full-re-port-2016.10.03.pdf.

36 Elon Musk, for example, has stated that "[s]olar power [with] batteries will be the primary (not exclusive) means of sustainable energy production ... [and that] ... solar power will be the single largest source of electricity generation by the mid-point of the century." https:// www.utilitydive.com/news/elon-musks-master-plan-for-a-clean-energy-future/213246.

37 Ibid.

38 See C. L. Archer and M. Z. Jacobson, "Evaluation of Global Wind Power," *Journal of Geo-physical Research* 110, is. D12 (June 27, 2005), https://doi.org/10.1029/2004JD005462.

39 See World Wind Energy Association, *World Wind Resource Assessment Report*, World Wind Energy Association, Technical Paper Series (TP-01-14), 2014], www.wwindea.org/wp-content/uploads/filebase/technology/WWEA_WWRAR_Dec2014_2.pdf.

40 World Energy Council, *World Energy Resources 2016* (World Energy Council, October 2016), https://www.worldenergy.org/publications/2016/world-energy-resources-2016/.

41 See REN21, *Renewables 2017 Global Status Report*.

42 Ibid.

43 Jeremy Rifkin, *The Hydrogen Economy: The Creation of the Worldwide Energy Web and the Redistribution of Power on Earth* (Oxford: Blackwell Publishing, 2002), 294.

44 See http://www.bioenergytrade.org/ and Criekemans, David, "The Geopolitics of Renewable Energy: Different or Similar to the Geopolitics of Conventional Energy?," in *ISA Annual Convention on Global Governance: Political Authority in Transition* (Montréal, Canada, March 16–19, 2011), 32.

45 Relevant statistics are available at, https://www.statista.com/statistics/274168/biofuel-production-in-leading-countries-in-oil-equivalent/.

46 Criekemans, David, "The Geopolitics of Renewable Energy: Different or Similar to the Geopolitics of Conventional Energy?," 32.

47 World Energy Council, *World Energy Resources Hydropower 2016* (World Energy Council, 2016), https://www.worldenergy.org/wp-content/uploads/2017/03/WEResources_Hydropower_2016.pdf.

48 Ibid.

49 The map obtained from O. A. C. Hoes, L. J. J. Meijer, R. J. Van der Ent, and N. C. Van de Giesen, "Systematic High-Resolution Assessment of Global Hydropower Potential," *PLoSONE* 12, no. 2 (2017), https://doi.org/10.1371/journal.pone.0171844.g001.

50 World Energy Council, *World Energy Resources Hydropower 2016*.

51 Relevant statistics available at: https://www.statista.com/statistics/474652/global-total-hydropower-capacity-in-major-countries/.

52 See International Hydropower Association, "Hydropower Status Report 2017," https://www.hydropower.org/sites/default/files/publications-docs/2017%20Hydropower%20Status%20Report.pdf.

53 For example, the refusal of Britain and France to finance the construction of the Aswan Dam in Egypt led to the conflict over the Suez Canal and the second Arab-Israeli war, and it also tolled the death knell of European colonialism, resulting in President Eisenhower considering Egypt's President Nasser "a menace to the peace and vital interests of the West." Dwight Eisenhower to Robert Anthony Eden, September 2, 1956, in "The Presidency: The Middle Way," vol. 17, *The Papers of Dwight David Eisenhower*, ed. Louis Galambos and Daun van Ee (Baltimore: Johns Hopkins University Press, 1996), 2264.

54 On water and conflicts, see Kevin Freeman, "Water Wars? Inequalities in the Tigris-Euphrates River Basin," *Geopolitics* 6, no. 2 (2001), 127–140.

55 An example of this is the potential for conflict over water allocations in East Asia between China and the governments of neighboring nations, such as India, Bangladesh, Vietnam, Cambodia, Thailand, Laos, and Burma, which also rely heavily on water resources originating in Tibet, as well as in Central Asia, northern Africa, and other regions. The Tibetan Plateau in western China holds the headwaters of many of the world's largest rivers, including the Yellow, Yangtze, and Mekong. See Keith Schneider and C. T. Pope, "China, Tibet, and the Strategic Power of Water," *Circle of Blue: WaterNews*, May 8, 2008, http://www.circleofblue.org/waternews/2008/world/china-tibet-and-the-strategic-power-of-water/.

56 Geothermal energy is thermal energy generated and stored in the earth. Tidal energy is a form of hydropower that uses large underwater turbines to capture the kinetic motion of the ebbing and surging of ocean tides.

57 Geothermal Energy Association, *Annual U.S. & Global Geothermal Power Production Report 2016* (Geo-Energy.org, 2016), http://geo-energy.org/reports/2016/2016%20Annual%20 US%20Global%20Geothermal%20Power%20Production.pdf.

58 See Alexander Richter, "Rwanda Waiting for Results on Two Geothermal Feasibility Studies," *ThinkGeoEnergy*, May 3, 2017, http://www.thinkgeoenergy.com/rwanda-waiting -for-results-on-two-geothermal-feasibility-studies/.

59 *Technical Insights–Geothermal Energy Generation–Technology Market Penetration and Road- mapping*, Geothermal Reservoir Hot Spots, Frost & Sullivan, https://www.slideshare.net/ FrostandSullivan/technical-insights-geothermal-energy-generation-technology-mar- ket-renetration-and-roadmapping.

60 REN21, *Renewables 2017 Global Status Report*.

61 See relevant statistics at, https://www.statista.com/statistics/277268/rare-earth-reserves- by-country/ and https://www.statista.com/statistics/268011/top-countries-in-rare-earth -mine-production/.

62 These changes go beyond energy-related interactions and reflect societal pressure for global changes to mitigate the risk of global conflict.

63 Held, Amy, "Jeff Bezos Pledges $10 Billion To Fight Climate Change, Planet's 'Biggest Threat,'" NPR, February 17, 2020.

64 The prisoner's dilemma is a game modeling the situation when two rational individu- als might not cooperate, even if it appears that it is in their best interests to do so. For general discussion on the prisoner's dilemma, see A. Rapoport and A. Chammah, *Prisoner's Dilemma: A Study in Conflict and Cooperation* (Ann Arbor: University of Michigan Press, 1965).

65 Adrienne Arsht, Kathy Baughman McLeod, Graham Brookie, *Stories of Resilience: An Intro- duction*. The Atlantic Council. May 27, 2020.

66 The geopolitical reality within which agents operate is determined by the specific geopo- litical codes that they follow in their interaction and foreign policy stances. These codes determine agents' stances with regard to external factors as they pursue their interests. The geopolitical codes represent assumptions based on national interests about threats to these interests and set responses to them. See John Lewis Gaddis, *Strategies of Contain- ment: A Critical Appraisal of Post-War American National Security Policy* (Oxford: Oxford University Press, 1982).

67 Michael Redclift, "Environmental Security and Competition for the Environment," in *Environmental Change, Adaptation, and Security*, ed. S.C. Lonergan (Dordrecht: Kluwer Academic Press, 1999), 3–16.

68 Frederick Kempe, "How the US-European Alliance Can Become Even Stronger in an Era of Disruption." *The Atlantic Council*, February 15, 2019, available at https://www. atlanticcouncil.org/content-series/inflection-points/how-the-us-european-alliance-can- become-even-stronger-in-an-era-of-disruption/. *See also,* Dr. Karin von Hippel. "Time to Recalibrate" *Prospect Magazine*, March 26, 2019.

69 Malcom Chalmers and Andrey Kortunov, "Like It or Not, Russia and the UK Need Each Other – and Will Have to Talk." *The Guardian*, April 17, 2018.

70 Jonathan Eyal, "How Not to Win Friends and Influence People in Europe." *The Straits Times*, May 4, 2020. *See also*, Michael Codner. "Scale, Influence and Moral Purpose: Issues for the SDSR." *RUSI Defence Systems*, September 25, 2015.

71 For analysis of economic-related strife, see Michael Ross, "The Political Economy of the Resource Curse," *World Politics* 51, no. 2 (1999): 297–322.

72 An example is the London Suppliers' Group, which coordinates the global transfer of nuclear dual-use technology.

73 For example, the trend of diffusion of state power has been closely associated with sectarian and ethnic conflict, in particular in regions like the Middle East, where "the salience of sectarianism (and other sub-national identities, like tribalism and regionalism) rises as the power of the state declines." See F. Gregory Gause III, "Sectarianism and the Politics of the New Middle East," *Brookings.edu, Up Front Blog,* accessed June 8, 2013, http://www.brookings.edu/blogs/up-front/posts/2013/06/08-sectarianism-politics-new-middle-east-gause.

74 Energy already plays a role in new coalition-building among developing countries along regional lines and vectors of common geopolitical and economic interest, e.g., Venezuela and Iran. Alternative energy-based alliances would still be founded on energy supply and demand relations, and influenced by policies, accessible resources, states of technological development, and available financing.

75 Kroenig, Matthew. "The Return of Great Power Rivalry: Democracy versus Autocracy from the Ancient World to the U.S. and China," *Oxford University Press,* 2020.

76 The EU, while technically an intergovernmental organization, increasingly takes on the role of a "state actor" depending on the issue and forum.

77 Saudi Arabia plans to develop almost 10 gigawatts of renewable energy by 2023, starting with wind and solar plants in its vast northwestern desert. Anthony Dipaola, "OPEC's Top Producer Is Turning to Wind and Solar Power," *Bloomberg.com,* accessed 14 February 2017, https://www.bloomberg.com/news/articles/2017-02-14/saudis-warm-to-solar-as-opecs -top-producer-aims-to-help-exports.

78 On the still predominantly economic governance role of the G20, see Paul Heinbecker, "The Future of the G20 and Its Place in Global Governance," CIGI G20, Paper No. 5, *The Centre for International Governance Innovation* (CIGI, April 27, 2011), http://www.heinbecker.ca/Writing/CIGI-G20Paperno5.pdf.

79 As Stephen Hadley notes, what developing countries need more than "money" or "arms" is "technical expertise." "Technical assistance ... [is how we] ... build institutions." This lesson should be applied to the megatrend. When the developed world seeks to improve the energy capabilities of developing countries, the developed world must provide its experts and experience to achieve the desired results. Stephen J. Handley, Panel discussion. Frontiers in Development 2014. USAID, October 20, 2014, Washington D.C.

80 On collective responses to global problems, see Karen T. Litfin, "The Greening of Sovereignty: An Introduction," in *The Greening of Sovereignty in World Politics,* ed. Karen T. Litfin (Cambridge: MIT Press, 1998).

81 Hans J. Morgenthau, *Politics among Nations,* 4th ed. (New York: Knopf, 1967), 305.

82 See Yves Lacoste, *La Géographie, Ca Sert, D'Abord, à Faire la Guerre* (Paris: Petite Collection Maspero, 1976).

83 This notion has resulted in opinions that "the international system—what might be called the machinery of world politics—is...undergoing an Epochal shift." See C. Dale Walton, *Geopolitics and the Great Powers in the Twenty-First Century: Multipolarity and the Revolution in Strategic Perspective* (New York: Routledge, 2007), 38.

84 An example of voluntary schemes is the Verified Carbon Standard (VCS) for offset credits, which was developed by the International Emissions Trading Association, as well as the World Economic Forum, the World Business Council for Sustainable Development, and the Climate Group. The Gold Standard is also similar to the VCS, and other initiatives by business-civil society collaborations. See William Boyd and James Salzman, "The Curious Case of Greening in Carbon Markets," *Environmental Law* 41, no. 1 (2011): 73–94.

85 For example, the EU, the United Nations' Intergovernmental Panel on Climate Change (UN IPCC), other UN agencies and research institutions, independent consulting bodies, and formations such as the International Renewable Energy Agency (IRENA), as well as global economic and political platforms such as the G7 and G20.

86 They include organizations such as Greenpeace, World Wildlife Fund (WWF), Amnesty International, Médecins Sans Frontières (Doctors without Borders), Friends of the Earth, etc.

87 On the religious and political movement of Islamism and the Long War, see Jean Bethke Elshtain, *Just War against Terror: The Burden of American Power in a Violent World* (New York: Basic Books, 2003), 3.

88 Terrorist groups are predominantly focused on "the deliberate creation and exploitation of fear through violence or the threat of violence...designed to have far-reaching psychological effects beyond the immediate victim(s) or object of the terrorist attack.... Terrorism is designed to create power where there is none or to consolidate power where there is very little...to obtain the leverage, influence, and power they otherwise lack to effect political change on either a local or an international scale." Bruce Hoffman, *Inside Terrorism* (New York: Columbia University Press, 1998), 43–44.

89 There is often a dichotomy between the goals of global civil society with regard to developing countries and the goals of the countries themselves. It should be noted that for certain representatives of global civil society, globalization stands for imperialism and oppression of the developing world. In April 2000, anti-globalization protesters demanded that the WTO and IFIs actively pursue respect for human and workers' rights, environmental standards, etc., while at the same time calling for the organizations' abolition and denouncing globalization. At the very same time, the Group of 77, which represents less developed states, was meeting in Havana to draft their vision of how to increase their role in the WTO.

90 For instance, the U.S.' release of ICANN, the Internet-governing body, into the hands of global civil society portrays the modern power struggle between state and non-state actors. There has been significant pushback from U.S. politicians who express real and existential concern over the U.S.' perceived loss of control and influence in the international arena. See Agence France-Presse, "US Plan to Give Up ICANN Oversight Runs into Republican Opposition," *Gadgets.com,* accessed April 11, 2014, http://gadgets.ndtv.com/internet/news/us-plan-to-give-up-icann-oversight-runs-into-republican-opposition-507155.

91 See Cornelia Navari, "The Great Illusion Revisited: The International Theory of Norman Angell," *Review of International Studies* 15 (1989): 354.

92 It has long been believed that non-state and supra-state actors would have a significant role in the geopolitical equilibrium, supporting imperatives for international federalism and establishing its institutions.

PART 3

1 Hesiod (c. 8th century B.C.), *Works and Days*, 316.

2 For example, according to World Energy Council research, solar and wind energy may account for 20% to 39% of power generation, based on various scenarios. See World Energy Council, *World Energy Scenarios 2016,* https://www.worldenergy.org/wp-content/uploads/2016/10/World-Energy-Scenarios-2016_Full-Report.pdf.

3 See B. Barton et al., *Energy Security: Managing Risk in a Dynamic Legal and Regulatory Framework* (Oxford: Oxford University Press, 2004); See J. H. Kalicki and D. L. Goldwyn, *Energy Security: Toward a New Foreign Policy Strategy* (Washington, D.C.: Woodrow Wilson Center Press, 2005). According to the International Energy Agency, "Energy security is defined in terms of the physical availability of supplies to satisfy demand at a given price." See International Energy Agency, accessed November 29, 2013, http://www.iea.org/topics/energysecurity/.

4 Matthew H. Brown, Christie Rewey, and Troy Gagliano, *Energy Security* (Denver, Colorado, Washington, D.C.: National Conference of State Legislatures, April 2003), http://

www.oe.netl.doe.gov/docs/prepare/NCSLEnergy%20Security.pdf. According to the conference, "Energy security refers to a resilient energy system. This resilient system would be capable of withstanding threats through a combination of active, direct security measures—such as surveillance and guards—and passive or more indirect measures—such as redundancy, duplication of critical equipment, diversity in fuel, other sources of energy, and reliance on less vulnerable infrastructure."

5   See for example, Anthony H. Cordesman, "The Myth or Reality of U.S. Energy Independence," *Center for Strategic and International Studies* (Washington, D.C., 2013), https://csis.org/files/publication/130103_us_energy_independence_report.pdf.

6   See John McNeill, *Something New under the Sun: An Environmental History of the Twentieth-Century World* (New York: W. W. Norton & Co., 2000), 4.

7   Carlota Perez, *Technological Revolutions and Financial Capital: The Dynamics of Bubbles and Golden Ages* (Cheltenham: Edward Elgar, 2002), 20–21.

8   For example, auto manufacturing has developed viable engineering solutions—from flex-fuel and hybrids to plug-in electric and even hydrogen vehicles—that are technically feasible, even if not fully economically competitive at present. Some technological solutions have already achieved a certain level of popularity (e.g., hybrid vehicles, which, however, may be reaching their saturation point). Another sector that has been affected is energy, where the rate of building new coal-fired plants has slowed down substantially, although replacements are as much fossil-based as renewables-based.

9   Bloomberg, "Bitcoin Miners on Track to Use More Electricity Than All of Argentina," Fortune.com, January 10, 2018, http://fortune.com/2018/01/10/bitcoin-miners-electricity-argentina/.

10   Bill Gates has stated that "We're very far away from getting all these sources down to zero, which is what we have to do to solve the problem." While wind and solar "have gotten a lot cheaper... electricity [generation] is only a quarter of the problem" accounting only one-quarter of the world's greenhouse gas emissions. Monica Nickelsburg, "Bill Gates: Why renewable energy is not enough to solve climate change," *Geekwire*, November 26, 2018, https://www.geekwire.com/2018/bill-gates-renewable-energy-not-enough-solve-climate-change/.

11   Some types of alternative energy, such as wind, are limited to a very specific range of conditions [wind speed must be between 4–5 meters per second (m/s) to overcome internal friction and inertia, and under 20-25 m/s, above which gales, high winds, and hurricanes cause excessive vibrations to the structure build-up]. These narrow ranges severely restrict wind energy's ability to provide a consistent supply of energy.

12   New technologies in the utility industry are emerging. Micro-grids, for instance, use adaptive software to facilitate the transition between different fuel sources based on the available supply of each resource. As an example, when winds fall out of the optimal speed range, micro-grids can switch seamlessly to base-load generation, such as natural gas or coal, to ensure a consistent supply of energy to the end user.

13   Eric Schwartz, testimony of Eric Schwartz, U.S. Senate Committee on Energy and Natural Resources, January 8, 2009, http://www.energy.senate.gov/public/index.cfm/files/serve?-File_id=b71e8843-a99a-a76a-b5bb-54d2914e9a1b, accessed December 3, 2013.

14   A case in point is that of "stranded" wind energy in Inner Mongolia (China) where transmission connections are lagging far behind wind farm construction. See Shai Oster, "Vestas Bulks Up in China," *Wall Street Journal*, April 22, 2009, http://online.wsj.com/news/articles/SB124030560893038605 accessed December 2, 2013.

15   Solar power is affected by the fact that current PV and Concentrating Solar Power (CSP) produce direct current (DC), rather than alternating current (AC), which means that, at present, solar-generated power is not suitable for grid use. However, inverters can

convert DC into AC, meaning that large-scale PV power plants could feed into utility grids, making solar power generation more viable. A new type of PV module also has a built-in inverter which generates AC at the individual module level. Scientists are working hard on next-generation transmission technologies, some of which actually work better with DC as opposed to AC. New super-conducting transmission lines, for example, are designed to work with direct current. For more details, see for example W. Kramer et al., *Advanced Power Electronic Interfaces for Distributed Energy Systems* (National Renewable Energy Laboratory, U.S. Department of Energy, March 2008), http://www.nrel.gov/docs/fy08osti/42672.pdf.

16   O. Siddiqui, *The Green Grid: Energy Savings and Carbon Emissions Reductions Enabled by a Smart Grid* (Palo Alto, CA: Global Energy Partners, LLC and Electric Power Research Institute, 2008), http://www.smartgrid.gov/sites/default/files/doc/files/The_Green_Grid_Energy_Savings_Carbon_Emission_Reduction_En_200812.pdf. Note: According to the Electric Power Research Institute, the term "smart grid" is understood as the over-laying of a unified communications and control system on the existing power delivery infrastructure to provide the right information to the right entity at the right time to take the right action. It is a system that optimizes power supply and delivery, minimizes losses, is self-healing, and enables next-generation energy efficiency, and demand response applications. Smart grids provide tools to maximize energy efficiency, while micro-grids tackle the issue of intermittency in supply.

17   Joint letter of former Secretary of Defense William Cohen and former Senator Sam Nunn to President Barack Obama, April 23, 2009, accessed December 21, 2011, http://csis.org/press/press-release/cohen-nunn-applaud-obama-energy-initiative-call-bipartisan-support.

18   Current storage technologies include pumped hydro, compressed air energy storage, various types of batteries, flywheels, electrochemical capacitors, etc. See energy storage technologies overview: U.S. Department of Energy, *Grid Energy Storage* (2013), 66, https://energy.gov/sites/prod/files/2014/09/f18/Grid%20Energy%20Storage%20December%202013.pdf

19   See Jaquelin Cochran et al., *Flexibility in 21st Century Power Systems* [Golden, CO: National Renewable Energy Laboratory (NREL), 2014], http://www.nrel.gov/docs/fy14osti/61721.pdf.

20   See REN21, *Renewables 2017 Global Status Report*.

21   According to the U.S. Department of Homeland Security, cooperation through industry groups has resulted in substantial information sharing of effective and best practices across the sector. Many sector owners and operators have extensive experience with infrastructure protection and have more recently focused their attention on cyber security, but the issue cannot be said to have been truly resolved. See Department of Homeland Security, *U.S. National Infrastructure Protection Plan: 2007/2008 Update* (August 2008), accessed December 12, 2013, http://www.dhs.gov/xlibrary/assets/nipp_update_2007_2008.pdf.

22   Joel Gordes and Michael Mylrea, "A New Security Paradigm Is Needed to Protect Critical U.S. Energy Infrastructure from Cyberwarfare," *Foreign Policy Journal*, September 14, 2009, accessed December 8, 2013, http://www.foreignpolicyjournal.com/2009/09/14/a-new-security-paradigm-is-needed-to-protect-critical-us-energy-*infrastructure-from-cy-berwarfare/*.

23   P.G. Wodehouse, "The Delayed Exit of Claude and Eustace," in *The World of Jeeves* (London: Arrow Books, 2008), 305.

24   Imperialism has been ascribed a number of different meanings and values. Eminent conservative thinkers and policymakers of the 19th century—including Benjamin Disraeli, Cecil Rhodes, and Rudyard Kipling—endowed imperialism with the power to preserve the social order in more developed and predominantly Western countries. It did so by

establishing markets and securing trade channels, maintaining the level of employment within the "empire" and, most significantly, diverting attention from local issues that could generate internal tension toward matters occurring in foreign colonies. The 20th century realist geopolitical view held that imperialism was the outcome—as opposed to the means—of the ongoing tides that determine the balance of power. It also posited that imperialism was a process that contributed to the achievement of equilibrium as it reduced the dominant state's political and strategic vulnerability. This view gave rise to a number of contrary positions. Thus, the more radical views of imperialism associated it with the under-consumption that resulted from intensified concentration of wealth, which naturally lead the imperial powers to clashes over its redistribution. From a social-psychological perspective, exemplified by the views of Schumpeter, imperialism was a behavioral pattern adopted and institutionalized by states, whose domestic politics were dominated by expansionist elites, or a warrior class. Imperial endeavors were thus dictated by the needs of national security, gradually becoming embedded in long-term political considerations, and promoted and perpetuated by public opinion manipulation. The liberal view of imperialism was that it was a policy choice, not a "natural process" that was an inevitable consequence of the prevalent world system. See John A. Hobson, *Imperialism: A Study* (Ann Arbor: Michigan University Press, 1965), 59.

25 See David Harvey, *The New Imperialism* (Oxford: Oxford University Press, 2005).

26 Friedemann Müller, *Energy Security: Demands Imposed on German and European Foreign Policy by a Changed Configuration in the World Energy Markets* (Berlin: German Institute for International and Security Affairs, January 2007), http://www.swp-berlin.org/fileadmin/contents/products/research_papers/2007_RP02_mlr_ks.pdf; also see Flynt Leverett, "The Geopolitics of Oil and America's International Standing," testimony of Flynt Leverett, U.S. Senate Committee on Energy and Natural Resources, January 10, 2007, http://www.newamerica.net/files/070110leverett_testimony.pdf accessed December 3, 2013.

27 The Venezuelan hydrocarbons law is a case study in resource nationalism. The law reserves the rights of exploration, production, and initial transportation and storage of petroleum, and associated natural gas, for the state. Primary activities must be carried out directly by the state, by a 100% state-owned company, or by a joint-venture company with more than 50% of the shares held by the state. A decree issued in February 2007 required the four strategic associations to convert to joint ventures in which the state-owned oil company would hold a 60% share, but ConocoPhillips and ExxonMobil refused to transfer their investment stakes in three of the four associations in which they had equity. The Venezuelan government seized their investments. See Bureau of Economic and Business Affairs, *Investment Climate Statement—Venezuela* (Washington, D.C.: Bureau of Economic and Business Affairs, U.S. Department of State, March 2013).

28 Bolivia trails only Venezuela in Latin America in terms of nationalization of resources. The Constitution of Bolivia, adopted in 2009, specifies that all hydrocarbon resources are the property of the Bolivian people and that the state will assume control over their exploration, exploitation, industrialization, transport, and marketing. In 2012, the electric utilities (run by the Spanish multinational Iberdrola), the electricity-transmission company (owned by Spain's Red Eléctrica Corp.), and the Swiss commodities giant Glencore International's Colquiri zinc and tin mine were nationalized. See Shane Romig, "Bolivia Nationalizes Its Three Largest Airports," *Wall Street Journal*, February 21, 2013, http://online.wsj.com/news/articles/SB10001424127887323949404578312640857437314.

29 In Ecuador, per the 2008 Constitution, all subsurface resources belong to the state. The petroleum sector is controlled by two state-owned enterprises. An amendment to Ecuador's hydrocarbon law in 2010 allows the government to nationalize oil fields owned by foreign companies if they do not comply with Ecuadorian law. See "Ecuador President Imposes Oil

Nationalization Law," *Bloomberg Businessweek*, July 24, 2010, http://www.businessweek. com/ap/financialnews/D9H5LVA00.htm. In 2010, Brazil's Petrobras had to withdraw from Ecuador after its negotiations with the government failed. See "Ecuador: Nationalization of Oilfields Operated by Petrobras," *Global Trade Alert,* October 20, 2011, http://www. globaltradealert.org/measure/ecuador-nationalization-oil-fields-operated-petrobras.

30 In 2012, the Argentinean government and legislature approved the nationalization of Spanish energy multinational Repsol's stake in YPF, Argentina's biggest energy company. Since the nationalization of YPF, production has remained flat. See Eliana Raszewski and Pablo Gonzalez, "YPF Grab Backfires as Imports Whittle Surplus: Argentine Credit," *Bloomberg,* April 12, 2012, http://www.bloomberg.com/news/2013-04-11/ypf-grab-back-fires-as-imports-whittle-surplus-argentina-credit.html.

31 In 2013, the Mexican government launched a set of institutional reforms which were to make its energy sector, among others, more competitive by putting an end to a 75-year monopoly by state-owned Pemex. Mexico's constitution was amended to allow private investment in the petroleum sector. See more: R. Vietor and H. Sheldahl-Thomason, "Mexico's Energy Reform," *Harvard Business School*, 717–027, January 23, 2017, 32, https:// sites.hks.harvard.edu/hepg/Papers/2017/Mexican%20Energy%20Reform%20Draft%20 1.23.pdf.

32 https://oilprice.com/Energy/Crude-Oil/This-Unexpected-Move-Could-Derail-Mexicos-Oil-Boom.html.

33 Andreas Pickel, Explaining (with) Economic Nationalism, TIPEC Working Paper 02/1 (Trent International Political Economy Center, 2002), 2, http://www.trentu.ca/org/ tipec/2pickel1.pdf.

34 Robert D. Kaplan, *The Coming Anarchy: Shattering the Dreams of the Post-Cold War* (New York: Random House, Inc., 2000), 51. Also see Robert D. Kaplan, "The Coming Anarchy," *The Atlantic Monthly*, February 1, 1994, http://www.theatlantic.com/magazine/ archive/1994/02/the-coming-anarchy/304670/.

35 For a detailed discussion of scenarios of U.S. power and pre-eminence, see David Slater, *Geopolitics and the Post-Colonial: Rethinking North-South Relations* (Malden: Blackwell Publishing, 2004).

36 See David Bunnell, quoted in J. Brockman, *Digerati: Encounters with the Cyber Elite* (San Francisco: Hardwired, 1996), 36.

37 See Joseph S. Nye, *Bound to Lead: The Changing Nature of American Power* (New York: Basic Books, 1991). In international relations, power can be considered the production of knowledge and the imposition of this knowledge on others. By providing different actors with an understanding of outcomes that can be achieved, a set of routine meanings and organizational rules are imposed that shape networks of knowledge. This knowledge in turn describes the structural dimensions of the power that can be projected. The essence of power is the ability to impose specific reactions on others, explicitly or implicitly, through direct or indirect demonstration and generation of knowledge. The influencing of others through the projection of power is governed by rules that formulate the geopo-litical order of the day, and these rules determine what represents legitimate use of power. In the emerging post-Westphalian order, the distinction that establishes legitimacy of the use of power is increasingly blurred. In today's day and age, the power dynamic is channeled by mutable social conditions, and is more widely disseminated across notional societal boundaries with outcomes that engender divergent value judgments by a more widespread and diverse constituency. Informal or "soft" power is determined by the social position of the relevant actor. This position is represented by implicit arrangements and procedural and regulatory frameworks that structure the resources actors use and the manner in which they are used.

38 Susan Strange, *States and Markets: An Introduction to International Political Economy* (London: Pinter, 1988), 24–25.

39 Henry A. Kissinger, *American Foreign Policy*, 3rd ed. (New York: W. W. Norton & Co., 1977), 61.

40 Jerome D. Frank, *Sanity and Survival. Psychological Aspects of War and Peace* (New York: Random House, 1968), 139.

41 On transforming perceived weakness into a deterrent, see David Newman, "Contemporary Geopolitics of Israel-Palestine: Conflict Resolution and the Construction of Knowledge," *Eurasian Geography and Economics* 51, no. 6 (November–December, 2010).

42 For example, the Cold War approach to deterrence (Mutual Assured Destruction, or MAD) assumed strategic certainty and articulated it in a "manner that focused on violent containment and military superiority" to prevent aggression. See, for example, T. Hentsch, *Imagining the Middle East*, trans. F.A. Reed (Montreal: Black Rose, 1992); also see D. Campbell, *Politics without Principle: Sovereignty, Ethics and the Narratives of the Gulf War* (Boulder: Lynne Rienner, 1993).

43 See Mikkel Vedby Rasmussen, "Reflexive Security: NATO and International Risk Society," *Millennium* 30, no. 2 (2001): 285.

44 See C. Aradau and R. van Munster, "Governing Terrorism through Risk: Taking Precautions, (Un)Knowing the Future," *European Journal of International Relations* 13, no. 1 (2007): 101.

45 For example, "A massive energy infrastructure consisting of pipelines, tankers, ports, export and receiving terminals, refineries, and processing facilities has been built around the global energy trade. Significantly altering this infrastructure or constructing a new one would take a tremendous amount of time and investment. To some extent, this cost has served as a deterrent to energy supply disruptions that may have otherwise resulted from political or economic disputes." See Frank Verrastro and Sarah Ladislaw, "Providing Energy Security in an Interdependent World," *The Washington Quarterly* 30, no. 4 (Autumn 2007): 100.

46 Albert O. Hirschman, *National Power and the Structure of Foreign Trade* (Berkeley: University of California Press, 1945), 17.

47 Relations between South Sudan and Sudan are an example of such an outcome. Despite South Sudan's secession and independence from Sudan in 2011, both countries remained at odds over their common border. There are several regions along their border that both countries claimed, notably oil-rich Abyei. In January 2012, South Sudan stopped production and export of oil through the Sudanese pipeline (its only outlet for its oil) after a breakdown in negotiations over transit fees. South Sudan was thus using oil exports as a projection of power and a deterrent. Also, hostilities broke out in March 2012 in the border regions of South Kordofan (which belongs to Sudan) and Unity (part of South Sudan) over control of the oil-rich Heglig region. Both countries signed agreements settling some of their disputes later in 2012. The interruption in oil exports ultimately harmed both countries' economies. See International Crisis Group, "Sudan: Major Reform or More War," Africa Report N°194, November 29, 2012, https://www.crisisgroup.org/africa/horn-africa/sudan/sudan-major-reform-or-more-war.

48 Robert Ebel, *Energy Choices in the Near Abroad: The "Haves" and "Have-Nots" Face the Future* (Washington, D.C.: Center for Strategic and International Studies, 1997), 2.

49 David Victor, *The Politics of Fossil-Fuel Subsidies*, UC San Diego, CA (Geneva, Switzerland: Global Subsidies Initiative of the International Institute for Sustainable Development, October 2009), 34, *http://www.iisd.org/gsi/sites/default/files/politics_ffs.pdf.*

50 David Robertson, *The Routledge Dictionary of Politics*, 3rd ed. (London: Routledge, 2004).

51 For example, "Economic power is used coercively by threatening to deny some sort of economic advantage to another state, often but by no means necessarily for the purpose of gaining an economic benefit." See Klaus Knorr, *The Power of Nations* (New York: Basic Books, 1975), 14.

52 Mary Boies, "The Pursuit of Black Gold: Pipeline Politics on the Caspian Sea," *panel discussion hosted at the Council on Foreign Relations, New York,* November 13, 2007, accessed December 2, 2013, http://2001-2009.state.gov/p/sca/rls/rm/2007/97957.htm.

53 Jean-François Lyotard, *Postmodern Fables* (Minneapolis: University of Minnesota Press, 1997), 192.

54 General James L. Jones, *A Transition Plan for Securing America's Energy Future* (Washington, D.C.: Institute for 21st Century Energy, U.S. Chamber of Commerce, November 2008), 36, http://www.mcs.anl.gov/~anitescu/EXTRAS/READING/Transition_Plan.pdf. General Jones also served as President of the Institute for 21st Century Energy, an affiliate of the U.S. Chamber of Commerce.

55 General Jaap de Hoop Scheffer served as the Secretary General of NATO from January 5, 2004 until August 1, 2009.

56 General Jaap de Hoop Scheffer, speech by NATO Secretary General Jaap de Hoop Scheffer at Economist Energy Security dinner, October 23, 2008, http://www.nato.int/docu/speech/2008/s081023b.html accessed December 9, 2013.

57 Sherri W. Goodman and Paul J. Kern, "Bad Tidings," *The National Interest,* January–February 2008, http://nationalinterest.org/article/bad-tidings-1923.

58 Philippe Le Billon, *Geopolitics of Resource Wars: Resource Dependence, Governance and Violence* (Routledge, 2005), 7.

59 See George F. Kennan, "X Article: The Sources of Soviet Conduct," *Foreign Affairs* 26, no. 2 (July 1947): 566–82.

60 On the 19th century visions of technology's impact on warfare, see I. F. Clarke, *Voices Prophesying War 1763-1984* (London: Oxford University Press, 1966) and Herbert G. Wells, *Anticipations of the Reaction of Mechanical and Scientific Progress upon Human Life and Thought* (London: Harper & Brothers, 1901).

61 Hydropower is excluded from this analysis since it faces substantial challenges to future expansion.

62 Nuclear power relies on technology designed to extract usable energy from atomic nuclei via controlled nuclear reactions. The method in use today is through nuclear fission, although other methods might one day include nuclear fusion and radioactive decay.

63 At the end of 2016, hydropower contributed approximately 16.6% of electricity production worldwide. See *Renewables 2017 Global Status Report.*

64 Mycle Schneider et al., *World Nuclear Industry Status Report 2017* (Paris: a Mycle Schneider Consulting Project, September 2017), https://www.worldnuclearreport.org/IMG/pdf/20170912wnisr2017-en-lr.pdf.

65 Nuclear power, together with hydropower and wind-based electricity, is among the lowest GHG emitters when emissions over the entire life cycle are considered less than 15 grams CO_2-equivalent (g CO_2-eq) per kWh (kilowatt-hour), which is well below coal or gas. See Climate Change and Nuclear Power 2016, International Atomic Energy Agency, 2016, http://www-pub.iaea.org/MTCD/Publications/PDF/CCANP16web-86692468.pdf.

66 "1 kg of uranium has as much potential energy as 2,300,000 liters of gasoline." See H. Douglas Lightfoot et al., "Nuclear Fission Fuel Is Inexhaustible," paper presented at the *Climate Change Technology Conference "Engineering Challenges and Solutions in the 21st Century," Engineering Institute of Canada, Ottawa, Canada, May 10–12, 2006,* 1 –8.

67 As of July 1, 2017, there were 447 operational nuclear power reactors in 30 countries, and 60 are under construction in 15 countries, with a total of 403 nuclear reactors operating

in 31 countries. See "International Status and Prospects for Nuclear Power 2017," report by the Director General, IAEA Board of Governors General Conference, July 28, 2017. Due to differences in methodologies, the WNISR's (World Nuclear Industry Status Report) number is lower than that of the IAEA as the WNISR does not count the units that have not generated power for several years prior to the research year. See Mycle Schneider et al., *World Nuclear Industry Status Report 2017.*

68 Ibid.

69 Ibid.

70 The energy market is getting extremely competitive. With average generating costs of amortized nuclear power plants in the U.S. at US$35.5/MWh in 2015, nuclear power currently faces emerging competition also from renewables: renewable energy auctions are reported to have achieved record low prices at and below US$30/MWh in Chile, Mexico, Morocco, United Arab Emirates, and the United States. See Mycle Schneider et al., *World Nuclear Industry Status Report 2017.*

71 Despite the lack of trust and prevailing negative public opinion in many countries, there are a number of measures in place to address safety concerns. For example, the International Atomic Energy Agency (IAEA) codified a range of issues, including siting, construction, and emergency preparedness in the Convention on Nuclear Safety via the Action Plan on Nuclear Safety and Safety Standards (including revised requirements) that incorporated lessons from the Fukushima Daiichi accident. See International Atomic Energy Agency, *Nuclear Safety Review 2017* (Vienna, Austria: Department of Nuclear Safety and Security, July 2017), https://www.iaea.org/About/Policy/GC/GC61/GC61InfDocuments/English/gc61inf-5_en.pdf.

72 See Mycle Schneider et al., *World Nuclear Industry Status Report 2017.*

73 "Additional countries may decide to seek nuclear weapons as it becomes clear their neighbours and regional rivals are doing so. The 'domino theory' of the 21st century may well be nuclear." George Tenet, testimony of CIA Director George Tenet, "Current and Projected National Security Threats to the United States," hearing before the Committee on Intelligence, Senate Select Intelligence Committee, S. Hrg. 108–161, 108th Congress, 1 session (Washington, D.C., February 11, 2003), 28, http://www.gpo.gov/fdsys/pkg/CHRG-108shrg89797/html/CHRG-108shrg89797.htm accessed November 12, 2011.

74 On horizontal nuclear proliferation, see Daniel H. Joyner, *International Law and the Proliferation of Weapons of Mass Destruction*, (Oxford, New York: Oxford University Press, 2009), xiv–xv.

75 The acquisition of nuclear weapons by non-state actors is harder and more complicated than may seem at first glance. It is considered a "low probability, but high-impact" event by most recognized national security experts. See William Langewiesche, *The Atomic Bazaar: Dispatches from the Underground World Of Nuclear Trafficking* (New York: Farrar, Straus and Giroux, 2008). A recent UNIDIR study notes that "International and national efforts of the past 15–20 years to reduce vulnerabilities and lower the risk related to non-state actors acquiring and using nuclear weapons have yielded some tangible progress," though new vulnerabilities emerge, "opened up by the digital age and other new and emerging technologies." See Elena K. Sokova, "Non-State Actors and Nuclear Weapons," in *Understanding Nuclear Weapon Risks*, eds. John Borrie, Tim Caughley, and Wilfred Wan [The United Nations Institute for Disarmament Research (UNIDIR), 2017], http://www.nonproliferation.org/wp-content/uploads/2017/04/understanding-nuclear-weapon-risks-en-676.pdf#page=85.

76 The planned Russian-German natural gas pipeline project Nord Stream 2 is currently the "most controversial and difficult question of EU energy security", said Wolfgang Ischinger, Chairman of the Munich Security Conference. *See also,* Jeffrey Lightfoot. "Germany May

Not Like the American Messenger. But is Should Heed His Message." *The Atlantic Council*, June 26, 2020.

77 Scarlett, Sir. John. "Sir John Scarlett, Former Chief of the British Secret Intelligence Service MI6, on Geopolitics of Energy." Columbia University - Center on Global Energy Policy, June 13, 2016, New York, NY.

78 For example, see, David Omand, Joe Devanny, Robert Dover and Michael S. Goodman, "The UK Government Needs a New Approach to Intelligence." RUSI Journal, January 28, 2019.

79 In this volatile environment, regional leaders have sought new structures to manage security interests, threats, and opportunities, in particular energy. Marginalized economies excluded from the world market increasingly see renewed opportunities via collaboration with neighboring countries. Different actors (including non-state ones and ideological groups) are also progressively entering the existing global governance vacuum.

80 Obtained from Department of Defense Annual Energy Management and Resilience (AEMR) Report Fiscal Year 2017, July 2018, https://www.acq.osd.mil/eie/Downloads/IE/FY%202017%20AEMR.pdf.

81 James Fairgrieve, *Geography and World Power* (New York: E.P. Dutton, 1941), 4.

82 See Thomas Hobbes, *Leviathan*, book 1, ch. 13 (Paris: A & W Cooke, 1651).

83 In operational terms, energy security for the military represents a situation where fuel, power production/distribution systems, and end user devices possess "five characteristics: Surety: A condition which provides uninterrupted access to energy and fuel sources; Survivability: Energy and fuel sources are resilient and durable in the face of possible damage; Supply: An identified and available source of energy, whether it is traditional fossil fuels, or alternative energy (nuclear, biomass, hydrogen, hydropower, geo-thermal/pressure, wind, tidal and solar); Sufficiency: There is an adequate quantity of power and fuel from a variety of sources; and Sustainability: Operational effectiveness can be improved by limiting demand, reducing waste and effectively utilizing energy resources to the maximum extent possible." See Department of Defense, "Army Energy Security Implementation Strategy (AESIS)," January 13, 2009, http://www.asaie.army.mil/Public/Partnerships/doc/AESIS_13JAN09_Approved%204-03-09.pdf, accessed December 2, 2013.

84 See John V. Farr et al., *Methodology for Prioritization of Investments to Support the Army Energy Strategy for Installations* (New York, NY: Center For Nation Reconstruction and Capacity Development, July 2012), http://www.usma.edu/cnrcd/cnrcd_library/energy%20security.pdf.

85 On the impact of technological advances on military power projection, see Williamson Murray and MacGregor Knox, *The Dynamics of Military Revolution: 1300–2050* (New York: Cambridge University Press, 2001) and Williamson Murray and Allan R. Millett, eds., *Military Innovation in the Interwar Period* (Cambridge: Cambridge University Press, 1996).

86 Herbert R. McMaster, "On War: Lessons to Be Learned," *Survival* 50, no. 1 (2008): 19–30.

87 The Law of Armed Conflict (LOAC), aimed at preventing unnecessary suffering and destruction, is also known as International Humanitarian Law. It refers to the aspect of public international law regulating wartime conduct. The LOAC consists of both treaty and customary international law. The primary treaties include the Geneva Conventions and the Hague Convention.

88 Richard Danzig, *Driving in the Dark: Ten Propositions about Predictions and National Security* (Washington, D.C.: Center for a New American Security, 2011), 8, http://www.cnas.org/files/documents/publications/CNAS_Prediction_Danzig.pdf, accessed February 21, 2014.

89 Williamson Murray and Allan R. Millett, eds., *Military Innovation in the Interwar Period* (Cambridge: Cambridge University Press, 1996), 191.

90　"Force presentation" is a term used by the Pentagon to describe how it organizes its force structure. See Mark Gunzinger, *Shaping America's Future Military: Toward a New Force Planning Construct* (Washington, D.C.: Center for Strategic and Budgetary Assessments, 2013), 20.

91　The overall structure of the armed force includes all the organizations, military and civilian, that make up those armed forces. See "Department of Defense Dictionary of Military and Associated Terms," Joint Publication 1-02, *Joint Chiefs of Staff* (Washington, D.C.: Department of Defense, 2010), accessed July 2, 2014, http://www.dtic.mil/doctrine/new_ pubs/jp1_02.pdf, amended through June 2014.

92　The DoD projects that the percentage of unmanned vehicles will grow from 25% in total in 2013 to 70% of the DoD fleet by 2035, including new, optionally manned or pilot-augmented aircraft. See U.S. Department of Transportation Research, Innovative Technology Administration, John A. Volpe National Transportation Systems Center, *Unmanned Aircraft System (UAS) Service Demand 2015–2035. Literature Review & Projections of Future Usage,* DOT-VNTSC-DoD-13-01 (Cambridge: U.S. Department of Transportation Research, John A. Volpe National Transportation Systems Center, 2013), 137, https://fas.org/irp/program/ collect/service.pdf.

93　Combining unmanned drones with weapons capabilities can replace large multi-tasking equipment. See Matt Peckham, "Robot Swarms of the Future (Because Sometimes It Takes a Village)," *Time Tech*, April 1, 2013, http://techland.time.com/2013/04/01/watch-robot-swarms-of-the-future-because-sometimes-it-takes-a-village/#ixzz2hQROBUyJ.

94　The United States became the first country to use an armed drone in combat in 2001. Now there are at least 28 countries with armed drones. See "Unmanned Aerial Vehicles (UAVs)—Comparing the USA, Israel, and China," *TechEmergence.com*, last modified September 1, 2017, https://www.techemergence.com/unmanned-aerial-vehicles-uavs/. Researchers identified 38 drones made in six countries that were active in the conflict in Syria and Iraq. See "The Drone Database," *Center for the Study of the Drone at Bard College website*, last modified January 30, 2017, http://dronecenter.bard.edu/the-drone-database.

95　Directed-energy weapons which include active denial technology, lasers, radio frequency weapons, and anti-satellite and high-powered microwave are capable of fundamentally altering the nature of combat due to a range of advantages including the level of accuracy and speed, scalability, and a virtually unlimited magazine capacity. See: Andrew Feickert, *U.S. Army Weapons-Related Directed Energy (DE) Programs: Background and Potential Issues for Congress,* Congressional Research Service, February 12, 2018, https://fas.org/sgp/crs/ weapons/R45098.pdf.

96　Additive manufacturing is the creation of complex products and systems from digital models, also called 3D printing, which speeds up the transformation from prototype to deployment. Additive manufacturing enables the development of products, such as components for heavy weapons, without the need for a supporting production line, with the potential for infinite replication. See John Koten, "A Revolution in the Making," *Wall Street Journal Reports*, June 10, 2013, http://online.wsj.com/article/SB1000142412788732406330 4578522812684722382.html; Berenice Baker, "Made to Measure: The Next Generation of Military 3D Printing," *army-technology.com*, last modified January 23, 2018, https://www. army-technology.com/features/made-measure-next-generation-military-3d-printing.

97　One example is the Autonomous Learning Agents for Decentralised Data and Information Networks (ALADDIN) project, a joint endeavor between the British defense supplier BAE Systems and the universities of Bristol, Oxford, and Southampton as well as Imperial College, London. See N.R. Jennings et al., "The Aladdin Project: Intelligent Agents for Disaster Management," IARP/EURON Workshop on Robotics for Risky Interventions and Environmental Surveillance, 2008.

98 Winston S. Churchill, *The World Crisis*, vol. 1 (New York: Scribner's, 1923), 136.

99 The "warrior of the future" concept reflects efforts by various militaries to project the nature of future armed conflict and adapt to it. See, for example, U.S. Department of Defense, *Army Strategic Planning Guidance* (Washington, D.C.: Department of Defense, 2013).

100 Julian Lindley-French and Yves Boyer, eds., *The Oxford Handbook of War* (Oxford: Oxford University Press, 2012), 2.

101 Admiral Michael Mullen, "Sea Enterprise: Resourcing Tomorrow's Fleet," *Proceedings Magazine*, 130/1/1,211 (January 2004), http://www.usni.org/magazines/proceedings/2004-01/sea-enterprise-resourcing-tomorrows-fleet.

102 Robert Gates in "Oil Shockwave: Simulation Report and Summary of Findings," National Commission on Energy Policy and Securing America's Energy Future, 2005, http://bipartisanpolicy.org/sites/default/files/oil_shockwave_report_440cc39a643cd.pdf.

103 John Dowdy and Scott Gebicke, "Benchmarking Defense Efficiency and Effectiveness," *RUSI Defence Systems 2010*, December 20, 2010, accessed November 2, 2012, http://www.rusi.org/downloads/assets/RDS_Oct2010_Dowdy.pdf.

104 On the Weinberger-Powell Doctrine and its shifting influence on policymaking, see Ivo H. Daalder and Michael E. O'Hanlon, "Unlearning the Lessons of Kosovo," *Foreign Policy*, 116, Autumn, 1999, 128–140; Caspar Weinberger, *Fighting for Peace: Seven Critical Years in the Pentagon* (New York: Warner Books, 1990); Colin Powell and Joseph E. Persico, *My American Journey* (New York: Ballantine Books, 1995).

105 It is particularly significant for theatres like Iraq and Afghanistan, where operational inefficiency was an obstacle to effectiveness. In these countries it was necessary to "put inefficient systems...as a result, we end[ed] up with long lines of fuel trucks driving in. And we [had] to protect those fuel trucks with soldiers and with other vehicles." Vice Admiral Richard H. Truly, USN (Ret.), former NASA Administrator, Shuttle Astronaut and the first Commander of the Naval Space Command on the DoD's Efficiency Needs. See "Powering America's Defense: Energy and the Risks to National Security," *CNA Corporation*, May 2009, http://www.cna.org/sites/default/files/Powering%20Americas%20Defense.pdf accessed July 2, 2011.

106 On military logistics effectiveness and efficiency, see Steve R. Waddell, *United States Army Logistics: The Normandy Campaign, 1944* (Westport, CT: Greenwood Press, 1994). See also William G. Pagonis and Jeffrey L. Cruikshank, *Moving Mountains: Lessons in Leadership and Logistics from the Gulf War* (Boston, MA: Harvard Business School Press, 1994).

107 Gen. James Cartright, USMC (Ret.), Preparing Military Leadership for the Future, Center for Strategic & International Studies, Panel Discussion. Washington, D.C., November 13, 2017.

108 Forward-operating facilities, according to the office of the U.S. Secretary of Defense, are for "[r]otational use by operational forces" and "[m]ay be a Joint FOS or FOB. Small permanent party. Can be scaled to fit various force structures and can support sustained operations. May contain prepositioned equipment. Example would be Camp Bondsteel, Kosovo." See United States Army, *Base Camp Facilities Standards For Contingency Operations* (U.S. Army European Operations Red Book, 2004), 2, accessed June 11, 2014, http://www.eur.army.mil/pdf/Red_Book.pdf.

109 See The Pew Charitable Trust-commissioned report: Jeffrey Marqusee, Craig Schultz and Dorothy Robyn, *Power Begins at Home: Assured Energy for U.S. Military Bases* (Noblis, 2017), http://www.pewtrusts.org/~/media/assets/2017/01/ce_power_begins_at_home_assured_energy_for_us_military_bases.pdf.

110 Sierra Hicks, *Fact Sheet: Powering the Department of Defense* (American Security Project, September 18, 2017), accessed January 7, 2018, https://www.americansecurityproject.org/fact-sheet-powering-the-department-of-defense/.

111 See U.S. Department of Defense, *Army Strategic Planning Guidance.*

112 U.S. Department of Defense, *2016 Operational Energy Strategy* (Washington D.C, Department of Defense, 2015), http://www.acq.osd.mil/eie/Downloads/OE/2016%20DoD%20Operational%20Energy%20Strategy%20WEBc.pdf.

113 In 2007, at the height of the war in Afghanistan, one in every eight fuel convoys was attacked by the enemy, with one in every 24 resulting in an American casualty. See CNA Military Advisory Board, *Advanced Energy and U.S. National Security* (Washington, D.C.: CNA, 2017), https://www.cna.org/CNA_files/PDF/IRM-2017-U-015512.pdf. At the height of the conflict in Iraq, 2.4 million gallons of fuel moved through contested territory daily, requiring protection by armored combat vehicles and attack helicopters. See the CNA Corporation, *National Security and the Threat of Climate Change* (CNA, 2007), 38, https://www.cna.org/cna_files/pdf/national%20security%20and%20the%20threat%20of%20climate%20change.pdf. Furthermore, in Afghanistan, U.S. Marine Corps Commander General James Conway said that "a gallon of fuel the government buys for $1.05 can cost $400 once it's poured into a gas tank in Afghanistan," not counting the cost in lives. See Andrew Scutro, "Surge to Strain Supply Lines," *Defense News*, December 7, 2009, 20.

114 Secretary of Defense Leon E. Panetta, "Major Budget Decisions," statement given at the Pentagon, Washington, D.C., January 26, 2012, accessed March 2, 2014, http://www.defense.gov/speeches/speech.aspx?speechid=1647.

115 GREENS (Ground Renewable Expeditionary Energy Network System) is a portable hybrid photovoltaic/battery power system developed for the Marine Corps. Office of Naval Research, Ground Renewable Expeditionary Energy System Project. See Eric Shields and Alex Askari, *Design Development and Testing of the Ground Renewable Expeditionary ENergy System* (NAVSEA Warfare Centers, Carderock Division, May 2011), https://pdfs.semantic-scholar.org/presentation/738c/30be881f44abca97fbf9e4b9174ab65b696c.pdf; Office of Naval Research, "Ground Renewable Expeditionary Energy Network System," accessed February 28, 2018, https://www.onr.navy.mil/en/About-ONR/History/tales-of-discovery/ground-renewable-expeditionary-energy-network-system.

116 The DoD has set standards exceeding federal obligations requiring its installations to derive 25% of their electricity from renewable sources by 2025. If implemented on a wide-scale basis, such efforts could create new elements of operational efficiency and enhance the military's energy independence, significantly improving the U.S. and NATO's combat capabilities.

117 For examples, *see*, Meyer, Pamela. "Lie Spotting: Proven Techniques to Detect Deception." *St. Martin's Griffin*, 2011.

118 Chuck Hagel with Peter Kaminsky, *America: Our Next Chapter* (New York: HarperCollins, 2008), 163.

119 On taking away the human element in combat, see John Markoff, "Driver Not Included in This Performance Test," *New York Times*, June 15, 2007, http://www.nytimes.com/2007/06/15/technology/15robot.html?_r=0.

120 Sydney J. Freedberg Jr., "Airstrikes up in Iraq & Syria, Afghanistan Eats ISR: CENTCOM," *Breaking Defense* (blog), accessed April 17, 2018, https://breakingdefense.com/2016/07/airstrikes-up-in-iraq-syria-afghanistan-eats-isr-centcom-data/.

121 See Board on Army Science and Technology, Division on Engineering & Physical Sciences, *Making the Soldier Decisive on Future Battlefields* (the National Academy of Sciences, 2013), accessed June 12, 2014, http://sites.nationalacademies.org/DEPS/cs/groups/depssite/documents/webpage/deps_083666.pdf.

122 See President Ronald Reagan, "National Policy on Telecommunications and Automated Information Systems Security," National Security Decision Directive NSDD 145,

September 17, 1984, accessed December 2, 2013, http://www.reagan.utexas.edu/archives/reference/NSDDs.html#.UuQ1qCJFCpo.

123 The Energetically Autonomous Tactical Robot was a project for the development of an autonomous robotic platform able to perform long-range, long-endurance missions without the need for re-fueling, as it could extract energy from biomass. See "Energetically Autonomous Tactical Robot," Robotic Technology Inc., accessed October 10, 2013, http://www.robotictechnologyinc.com/images/upload/file/Overview%20Of%20EATR%20Project%20Brief%206%20April%2009.pdf.

124 See Protonex Technology Corporation, accessed October 10, 2013, http://www.protonex.com/products/spm-612. Scavenged energy is extracting small amounts of energy from ambient environments through various sources of energy. See Frank Furman, "Energy Scavenging: Expeditionary Logistics/Water Power," in *Warfighting in a Highly-Contested Electromagnetic Environment*, Innovation, Office of Naval Research, vol. 2, Fall 2012, 14–16, accessed July 11, 2014, http://www.onr.navy.mil/en/Media-Center/~/media/Files/031/DoI-News-Oct12-Vol9.ashx.

125 "Defense Spending in a Time of Austerity," *The Economist*, August 26, 2010.

126 The U.S. Air Force has already initiated strategic assessment of space operations. See Air Force Doctrine Document (AFDD) 2-2.1, "Counterspace Operations," August 2004, as well as Scott M. Fox, "Deterring and Dissuading in Space: A Systems Approach," U.S. Army War College, March 2008, accessed August 12, 2013, http://www.dtic.mil/cgi-bin/GetTRDoc?AD=ADA480178.

127 Space Foundation, "Schulte: Space Is Congested, Contested, Competitive," *Space Foundation.org*, last modified June 1, 2011, https://www.spacefoundation.org/news/schulte-space-congested-contested-competitive.

128 Sandra Erwin, "STRATCOM Chief Hyten: 'I Will Not Support Buying Big Satellites That Make Juicy Targets,'" *Spacenews.com*, last modified November 19, 2017, https://spacenews.com/stratcom-chief-hyten-i-will-not-support-buying-big-satellites-that-make-juicy-targets/.

129 For example, the Manhattan Project opened the possibility for nuclear energy, the U.S. inter-state highway system was constructed to simplify military mobilization, the Atlas Missile Project paved the way for commercial space, and ARPANET (Advanced Research Projects Agency Network), which was not exclusively defense-related, provided the foundation for the Internet. Such projects might encourage innovative research and development and the mass deployment of alternative energy beyond defense-specific applications. This is less true today than previously. See Peter J. Denning, "The ARPANET after Twenty Years," *American Scientist* 77 (Nov-Dec 1989): 530–535. Very often, civilian innovation utilizes the military as a testbed and initial customer, and non-defense organizations thus leverage competitive advantages in deploying new civilian applications.

130 See Vernon Ruttan, *Is War Necessary for Economic Growth? Military Procurement and Technology Development* (New York: Oxford University Press, 2006).

131 "Valley of Death" refers to the period between the moment a startup enterprise receives initial capital and the time when a sustained stream of revenues starts to come from the market. There is high probability that a startup enterprise will not survive this period as the costs of bringing the product to market may be higher than anticipated while the chances to attract additional financial support at this stage are minimal.

132 On the conflict between the U.S. and Great Britain and its North American colonies, see Martin Melosi, *Coping with Abundance* (New York: Knopf, 1985).

133 These include: the dramatic transformation of warfare, often referred to as a revolution in military affairs, which were brought about by the replacement of bronze with iron around 1,200 BC, the introduction of gunpowder in land and naval engagements in the 14th and 15th centuries, the inventions of dynamite in the 19th century, and the use of aircraft in

warfare and nuclear-powered weapons and ships in the 20th century. Such a transformation could be repeated in the 21st century with the military application of alternative energy.

134 Military use data from "U.S. Military Marches Forward on Green Energy, despite Trump," *Reuters*, March 1, 2017, https://www.reuters.com/article/us-usa-military-green-energy-insight/u-s-military-marches-forward-on-green-energy-despite-trump-idUSKBN1683BL. Compared with author derived data from Energy Information Administration (EIA) website, https://www.eia.gov/totalenergy/data/browser/?tbl=T10.02C#/?f=A&start=2011 &end=2015&charted=8.

135 The U.S. Army Energy Initiatives Task Force was established in 2011. In 2014 the army established the permanent Office of Energy Initiatives. See "Army Establishes Permanent Office of Energy Initiatives," *U.S. Army*, last modified October 1, 2014, https://www.army.mil/article/134994/army_establishes_permanent_office_of_energy_initiatives.

136 In 2012 a $7 billion renewable energy procurement program was launched to enable the army to procure 25% of its energy from renewable sources by the year 2025 in accordance with the congressionally directed goal.

137 See Marcy E. Gallo, *Defense Advanced Research Projects Agency: Overview and Issues for Congress*, Congressional Research Service (CRS, February 2, 2018), https://fas.org/sgp/crs/natsec/R45088.pdf.

138 For example, the Very High Efficiency Solar Cell program, aimed at developing photovoltaic modules with efficiencies over 50%, and the BioFuels program to develop an affordable surrogate for military jet fuel (JP8) derived from oil-rich crops, such as rapeseed and other plants, including algae, fungi, and bacteria. See DARPA Strategic Plan, Department of Defense, (May 2009), 45, accessed March 12, 2012, http://www.carlisle.army.mil/DIME/documents/StratPlan091.pdf.

139 Department of Defense Annual Energy Management and Resilience (AEMR) Report Fiscal Year 2016.

140 "Pentagon Official on QDR Priorities," NPR Transcript, February 3, 2010.

141 Pike Research, *Renewable Energy for Military Applications*, Navigant Research, 2012, accessed May 15, 2014, http://www.navigantresearch.com/research/renewable-energy-for-military-applications.

142 The National Defense Authorization Act (Public Law 109-364) was passed by Congress in 2006; the Energy Independence and Security Act (Public Law 110-140) was enacted by Congress in 2007.

143 Department of Defense, "2016 Operational Energy Strategy," Washington, D.C, 2015, accessed February 28, 2018, http://www.acq.osd.mil/eie/Downloads/OE/2016%20DoD%20Operational%20Energy%20Strategy%20WEBc.pdf.

144 Ibid.

145 On the Net Zero Initiative, see Pacific Northwest National Laboratory for OASA, *Army Net Zero Initiative 2015 Progress Report* [U.S. Army, Assistant Secretary of the Army (Installations, Energy, and Environment), 2016], https://www.army.mil/e2/c/downloads/455375.pdf.

146 Department of Defense, Annual Energy Management and Resilience (AEMR) Report Fiscal Year 2016.

147 For example, on April 22, 2010, the U.S. Navy showcased an F/A-18E/F Super Hornet multirole fighter jet powered by a biofuel blend. Liz Wright, "Navy Tests Biofuel-Powered 'Green Hornet,'" Navy Office of Information, *Navy.mil*, last modified April 22, 2010, http://www.navy.mil/submit/display.asp?story_id=52768.

148 Remarks by the Honorable Ray Mabus, Secretary of the Navy, "Deployment of the Great Green Fleet," Naval Air Station North Island, San Diego, California, Wednesday, January

20, 2016, www.navy.mil/navydata/people/secnav/Mabus/Speech/Great%20Green%20 Fleet%2.

149 Ian Graham, "Air Force Scientists Test, Develop Bio Jet Fuels," *the Official Website of the U.S. Air Force*, last modified March 3, 2010, https://web.archive.org/web/20100409084432/ http://www.af.mil/news/story.asp?id=123197415.

150 To create these alternative fuels, a synthetic fuel produced using the Fischer-Tropsch process and a biofuel produced by hydro processing esters and fatty acids are blended with traditional JP-8 or Jet A fuels. See: the U.S. Air Force Energy Flight Plan 2017–2036, January 6, 2017, http://www.airforcemag.com/DocumentFile/Documents/2017/AFEnergyFlightPlan2017.pdf.

151 Ibid.

152 See Sierra Hicks, *Fact Sheet: Powering the Department of Defense*; Pew Charitable Trusts, "Power Surge: How the Department of Defense Leverages Private Resources to Enhance Energy Security and Save Money on U.S. Military Bases," *pewtrusts.org*, www. pewtrusts.org/~/media/legacy/uploadedfiles/peg/publications/report/pewdodreport2013 ks10020314pdf.

153 Department of Defense, Annual Energy Management and Resilience (AEMR) Report Fiscal Year 2016.

154 See Pew Charitable Trusts, *From Barracks to the Battlefield: Clean Energy Innovation and America's Armed Forces*, the Pew Project on National Security, Energy, and Climate (Pew Charitable Trusts, 2011), http://www.pewtrusts.org/en/research-and-analysis/reports/2011/09/21/ from-barracks-to-the-battlefield-clean-energy-innovation-and-americas-armed-forces.

155 See Army Office of Energy Initiatives and Renewable and Alternative Energy Resilience Projects, available at: http://www.asaie.army.mil/Public/ES/oei/projects.html, January 17, 2018.

156 Assistant Secretary of the Army, *Net Zero Progress Report*, U.S. Army (October 2016), http:// www.asaie.army.mil/Public/ES/doc/2015%20Net%20Zero%20Progress%20Report.pdf.

157 "Bucharest Summit Declaration," *NATO*, April 2008, last modified May 8, 2014, http:// www.nato.int/cps/en/natolive/official_texts_8443.htm.

158 Statement of James Schlesinger before the Committee on Foreign Relations, U.S. Senate, Washington, D.C., November 16, 2005, accessed December 2, 2013, http://www.gpo.gov/ fdsys/pkg/CPRT-109SPRT28001/html/CPRT-109SPRT28001.htm.

159 A good example of the change in thinking required is the NATO Pipeline System, set up during the early years of the Cold War as a hardened network of 10 separate storage facilities and distribution systems spread across Europe. Renewable energy solutions and the shift in geo-military risks that came with the end of the Cold War obviously require a new approach to military energy infrastructure design, its functioning, and protection.

160 This, however, does not include military energy infrastructure or alternative energy.

161 Ariel Cohen, "Weak Energy Prices Show Russia's Achilles Heel." Forbes, June 2, 2020. *See also*, Stephen J. Hadley, "It's Time to Stand Up to Russia's Aggression in Ukraine." *Foreign Policy*, January 18, 2019.

162 See NATO, *Active Engagement, Modern Defense: Strategic Concept for the Defense and Security of the Members of the North Atlantic Treaty Organisation* (Lisbon: NATO, 2010), accessed February 11, 2012, http://www.nato.int/lisbon2010/strategic-concept-2010-eng. pdf.

163 EU/NATO cooperation is currently blocked by the political imbroglio involving Turkey and Greece and their dispute over the legal status of Cyprus. Such a quagmire prevents any formal exchanges of documents or structured military cooperation between NATO and the EU. The impasse is further complicated by prestige-driven considerations and disputed areas of responsibility and authority.

164 NATO has noted North Africa's abundant solar and wind resources. Sahara trade winds "represent the largest and most productive wind potential available on earth." The EU has proposed the construction of enormous solar farms in the Sahara that would transmit power via undersea cables to Europe. See "Sahara Trade Winds to Hydrogen: Applied Research for Sustainable Energy Systems," *NATO*, last modified May 11, 2008, http://www.nato.int/issues/science-environmental-security/projects/8/.

165 See Pierre Goldschmidt et al., *The Next Generation of Security Threats—Reprogramming NATO?* (Brussels: NATO, 2009).

166 Jaap de Hoop Scheffer, NATO Secretary General, speech at the Economist Energy Security Dinner, October 23, 2008, accessed December 2, 2011, http://www.nato.int/docu/speech/2008/s081023b.html.

167 Ian Brzezinski, "NATO and Energy Security: A Readout from Chicago," Atlantic Council of the United States, June 5, 2012, transcript available on http://www.acus.org/event/nato-and-energy-security-readout-chicago/transcript, accessed on October 9, 2012.

168 "Cyberattacks Are the New Challenge for Renewable Energy," *POLITICO*, last modified July 18, 2017, https://www.politico.eu/article/opinion-cyberattacks-are-the-new-challenge-for-renewable-energy/.

169 Russia has a "continued desire to disrupt NATO relationships." However, "NATO is much more than an organization. NATO stands for something far more powerful. NATO stands for an ideal and that ideal is freedom." AMB. Georgette Mosbacher, U.S. Ambassador to Poland, March 15, 2019.

170 *See,* George Robertson. "NATO at 70: The Durable Alliance." *European Leadership Network,* January 31, 2019.

171 See: Daniel Fiott, "A Revolution Too Far? U.S. Defense Innovation, Europe and NATO's Military-Technological Gap," *Journal of Strategic Studies* 40, no. 3 (2016): 417–437, DOI: 10.1080/01402390.2016.1176565.

172 China's strategic concern is focused on its periphery (neighboring countries, sea lanes, and sub-regions). The scope of China's periphery is mutable and changes according to numerous factors that shape the vision of China's leadership. See U.S. Department of Defense, *Military and Security Developments Involving the People's Republic of China 2014*, Annual Report to Congress (Washington, D.C.: U.S. Department of Defense, 2014), accessed June 25, 2014, http://www.defense.gov/pubs/2014_DoD_China_Report.pdf.

173 The PLA (People's Liberation Army) started to consistently reduce energy consumption a decade ago. In 2006, it reduced consumption by 55,000 tons of oil, 170 million kilowatt-hours, and 1.16 million tons of coal and other resources due to mandatory energy efficiency campaigns. This generated savings of 1.4 billion Yuan (or roughly US$180 million). According to Liao Xilong, the PLA's logistics director, the Chinese armed forces "should be leading the drive to build a resource efficient society." See "Chinese Army Goes Green in 2006," *People's Daily*, February 6, 2007, http://english.mep.gov.cn/News_service/media_news/200712/t20071217_114547.htm.

174 See "300GW of solar, 150GW of wind suggested for China's 14th 5 Year Plan," *Smart Energy International*, May 27, 2020, https://www.smart-energy.com/industry-sectors/policy-regulation/300gw-of-solar-150gw-of-wind-suggested-for-chinas-14th-5-year-plan.

175 For example, the U.S. has made claims that in 2006 China used lasers to blind its satellites. See "Marching Forward," *Jane's Defense Weekly* 44, no. 17 (April 25, 2007): 24–30.

176 Alanna Petroff, "These Countries Want to Ban Gas and Diesel Cars," *CNNMoney*, last modified September 11, 2017, http://money.cnn.com/2017/09/11/autos/countries-banning-diesel-gas-cars/index.html.

177 The UK Ministry of Defence (MoD) has effectively achieved its 12.5% reduction target through energy saving measures via a combination of solar, biomass, and ground heating

systems and "green" energy efficient vehicles. Included in this is the purchase of some 1300 "green" vehicles, including those with hybrid petrol/electric motors, to slash CO_2 emissions. The "SMART Metering Programme," a new energy management information system, and lightweight solar cells, for use by British troops based in the Helmand Province, add to the UK's progress. These initiatives promote the idea of green military energy use and reduce soldier loads by taking over from the heavyweight batteries presently in use. The ministry is also experimenting, with the help of private partners, with bringing renewable energy to its bases and facilities, while addressing any security vulnerabilities.

178 See Danish Ministry of Defence, *Climate and Energy Strategy of the Ministry of Defence 2012–2015* (Forsvarministeriet, 2012), accessed May 2, 2014, http://www.fmn.dk/eng/news/Documents/Climate-and-energi-strategi.pdf.

179 See Christophe-Alexandre Paillard, "Security and Energy Efficiency, a Smart Energy for a Smart Defense: Examples Taken from France," in *Energy Security: Operational Highlights*, no. 5 (NATO Energy Security Centre of Excellence, 2014), 13–14.

180 See "Defense Technology Plan," *UK MOD*, accessed May 10, 2012, http://www.science.mod.uk/Strategy/dtplan/Default.aspx.

181 UK Ministry of Defence, "Securing Britain in an Age of Uncertainty: The Strategic Defense and Security Review," presented to Parliament by the Prime Minister by Command of Her Majesty, October 2010, https://assets.publishing.service.gov.uk/government/uploads/system/uploads/attachment_data/file/62482/strategic-defence-security-review.pdf.

182 See UK Ministry of Defence, *Defense Technology Strategy for the Demands of the 21st Century* (London: MOD, 2012), http://ideas.mod.uk/modwww/content/dts_complete.pdf.

183 For example, the EU's European Defence Agency (EDA) is exploring with its member states (all of the EU countries except Denmark) how to develop new long-life mobile battery packs and other energy sources for use at the individual soldier level. This, however, is subordinate to the wider objective of force-protection technologies. Crucially, energy efficiency, alternative energy production, the logistics and protection of green fuel sources in areas of operation, and the wider strategic impact of climate change are not being addressed by any dedicated EDA policy.

184 "The IAF Goes Green," *Israeli Air Force website*, last modified January 2, 2018, http://www.iaf.org.il/4470-49963-EN/IAF.aspx.

185 National Defense, Government of Canada, "Defense Energy and Environment Strategy," October 4, 2017, https://www.canada.ca/content/dam/dnd-mdn/documents/reports/2017/20171004-dees-en.pdf.

186 Unlike commercial vehicle designs, military vehicles require more than load-leveling and steady energy output; energy storage must also accommodate "silent watch" and "silent mobility" applications.

187 Wind turbines can affect air defense operations by reducing the ability of sensor systems to detect and identify approaching aircraft, overflying or leaving the designated territory and then producing what is sometimes referred to as a Recognized Air Picture (RAP). This would result in "masking"'—the main anticipated effect on air defense radars, which work at high radio frequencies and therefore depend on a clear "line of sight" to the target for successful detection, tracking, and targeting. It follows that any geographical feature or structure that lies between the radar and the target will cause a shadowing or masking effect; indeed this phenomenon is readily exploited by military aircraft wishing to avoid detection. It is possible that, depending on their size, wind turbines may cause shadowing effects, varying with size, the type of transmitting radar, and the aspect of the turbine relative to it. Furthermore, several turbines in close proximity to each other, painting on radar, can present particular difficulties for long-range air surveillance radars, in a manner similar to tall buildings causing diffraction of radar waves. Decreasing the separation

distance between the turbines increases the diffraction effect. See DTI, Civil Aviation Authority, British Wind Energy Association, *Wind Energy and Aviation Interests—Interim Guidelines* (Crown copyright 2002), accessed November 2, 2011, http://webarchive.nation-alarchives.gov.uk/+/http://www.berr.gov.uk/files/file17828.pdf.

188 Since wind turbines are geographically stationary and near the surface of the Earth, they "clutter" air defense radars. Modern utility-class wind turbines, due to their large size, possess a significant RCS at all common radar bands. The RCS for one particular turbine ranged from that of a "business class" airplane to a value greater than that of a long-haul, wide-body aircraft. In addition, the rotating blades of such wind turbines create Doppler shifts equivalent to the velocities of aircraft. The amount of clutter produced will increase in direct proportion to the number of turbines within the line of sight of the air defense radar, degrading ability to perform air defense missions. A rotating wind turbine is likely to appear on a radar display intermittently (studies suggest a working figure to be one paint every six sweeps). Multiple turbines, in proximity to each other, will present several returns during every radar sweep, causing a "twinkling" effect. As these will appear at slightly different points in space, the radar system may interpret them as being one or more moving objects and a surveillance radar will then initiate a "track" on the returns. This can confuse the system and may eventually overload it with too many tracks. See Office of the Director of Defense Research and Engineering, *The Effect of Windmill Farms on Military Readiness*, Report to the Congressional Defense Committees (U.S. Department of Defense, 2006), 52, http://users.ece.utexas.edu/~ling/US1%20dod_windfarms.pdf.

189 Magnetic radiation is a likely complication for both electricity generation and storage, but could also be converted into a direct form of energy. In military applications and otherwise, magnetic fields have some highly damaging repercussions. First, they can be extremely hazardous to health. Electromagnetic fields and pulses can also inflict damage, intentional or unintentional, on military infrastructure of one or several countries combined. It is conceivable that magnetic fields generated by alternative energy technologies could duplicate the effect of a non-nuclear electromagnetic pulse (NNEMP). See DTI, Civil Aviation Authority, British Wind Energy Association, *Wind Energy and Aviation Interests—Interim Guidelines,* 39–40.

190 For example, there were 330 terrorist attacks against oil and gas facilities worldwide in the period between 1990 and 2005. See Memorial Institute for the Prevention of Terrorism, the Terrorism Knowledge Base, accessed January 22, 2014, https://www.mipt.org/Home.aspx.

191 Stephen Peter Rosen, "The Future of War and the American Military," *Harvard Magazine*, May–June 2002, accessed March 2, 2012, http://harvardmagazine.com/2002/05/the-future-of-war-and-th.html.

192 A relatively easily understood demonstration of why this assertion may hold true is the "P for Plenty" attitude of logisticians in planning military operations. The "P for Plenty" attitude describes logisticians' approach to providing supplies to units conducting operations. Military planners make sure to err on the side of oversupply to ensure that combat or other supported units receive all the resources they need in operational situations, as there is little cost to oversupply but significant costs to undersupply. In turn, while conducting missions, commanders are expected to fulfil objectives and ensure troop safety, not conserve resources. If the "P for Plenty" attitude in planning military operations was sacrificed in pursuit of increasing fuel efficiency, then military effectiveness could be diminished in the pursuit of energy efficiency.

193 The role of technological innovation in warfare in particular has generated an intensive debate since the Cold War, culminating in the strategic post-Cold War context of asymmetric vulnerabilities, multiple actors, and their varied capabilities. See C. Hables

Gray, *Postmodern War: The New Politics of Conflict* (New York: Guildford Press, 1997); F. H. Hinsely and A. Stripp, *Codebreakers: The Inside Story of Bletchley Park* (Oxford: Oxford University Press, 2001).

194 Hybrid equipment refers to combining capabilities of items that are normally separated (such as installing weaponry on infantry fighting vehicles), while modular equipment refers to the ability of changing equipment functionality through the exchange or addition of modules (such as installing grenade launching components on a rifle). See Thomas Held, Bruce Newsome, and Matthew W. Lewis, *Commonality in Military Equipment: A Framework to Improve Acquisition Decisions* (RAND Corporation, 2008), accessed November 2, 2013, http://www.rand.org/content/dam/rand/pubs/monographs/2008/RAND_MG719.pdf.

195 Interoperability and compatibility are of particular concern for joint operations. These terms refer to the ability of different national forces to conduct joint operations, in particular from the point of view of sharing doctrine, infrastructure, bases, and equipment. See NATO, *Interoperability for Joint Operations* (Brussels: NATO Diplomacy Division, July 2006), http://www.nato.int/nato_static/assets/pdf/pdf_publications/20120116_interoperability-en.pdf.

196 As U.S. Air Force General Ronald E. Keys notes, "It's a lot tougher with tactical systems. They are expensive, are with the force for 30 or more years, and you can only do so much with the turbines and diesels you have. Even if you had the technology in hand today, it will take decades to replace the legacy force. The key is that you have to plan for it and pay for it upfront." General Ronald E. Keys, USAF (), former commander, Air Combat Command, quoted in "Powering America's Defense: Energy and the Risks to National Security," *the CNA Corporation*, May 2009, accessed July 2, 2011, http://www.cna.org/sites/default/files/Powering%20Americas%20Defense.pdf.

197 NATO expects that the goal of spending 2% of gross domestic product on defense by 2024 agreed at NATO's 2014 summit will be reached by 15 of the 29 NATO member states. See Jim Garamone, "Secretary General: More Countries on Track to Meet NATO Spending Goals," *DoD News, Defense Media Activity*, last modified February 13, 2018, https://www.defense.gov/News/Article/Article/1439951/secretary-general-more-countries-on-track-to-meet-nato-spending-goals/.

198 On the efforts of humanity to improve nature, see Peter Ward, *The Medea Hypothesis: Is Life on Earth Ultimately Self-Destructive?* (Princeton, NJ: Princeton University Press, 2009); Larry Hickman, "Green Pragmatism: Reals without Realism, Ideals without Idealism," *Research in Philosophy and Technology* 18 (1999): 39–56.

199 Hugh Dyer, "Environmental Security: The New Agenda," in C. Jones and C. Kennedy-Pipe, eds., *International Security in a Global Age—Securing the Twenty-First Century* (London: Frank Cass, 2000), 139.

200 See for example Jared Diamond, *Collapse: How Societies Choose to Fail or Succeed*, revised ed. (New York: Penguin, 2011). The issue of environmental security is addressed in a number of studies, including M. Finger, "The Military, the Nation State and the Environment," *The Ecologist* 21, no. 5 (1991); O. Greene, "Environmental Issues," in *The Globalization of World Politics: An Introduction to International Relations*, ed. J. Baylis and S. Smith, 3rd ed. (New York: Oxford University Press, 2005).

201 The significance of environmental challenges initially took hold in government-sponsored approaches for integrating the risks of environmental degradation in the global South for security of states in the global North. Environmental security has since evolved beyond such center-periphery and North-South considerations. The imperative to securitize the environment is thus increasingly incorporated in multilateral discussions, where environmental damage and concomitant policies are imposing burdens both on

the developed North and the developing South. To an extent, environmental risks have been the domain of inter-state finger-pointing and blame-shifting, giving rise to discontent among developing countries from the global South about the indiscriminate actions of the industrialized North that have led to such straits. Actions by states to securitize the environment to date have been more reflexive than rule-driven, dictated mainly by societal pressure and political imperatives, rather than national security interests. For example, in the case of problems perceived to be truly global (ozone depletion and climate change being the foremost examples), the actions of a single actor without coordination with others was deemed unlikely to alleviate the security threat in question, and the instruments deployed have usually been limited. Although a global solution on ozone depletion was found, this solution had a regulatory basis and did not require an extensive transformation of global practices and did not affect livelihoods too dramatically.

202 See Garrett Hardin, "The Tragedy of the Commons," *Science* 162 (1968): 1243–1248.

203 John K. Galbraith, *Economics and the Public Purpose* (New York: Signet, 1973), 277.

204 See Peter Gleick, "Water, War and Peace in the Middle East," *Environment* 36, no. 3 (April, 1994): 6–42.

205 See C. Meyer et al., "The Massacre Mass Grave of Schöneck-Kilianstädten Reveals New Insights into Collective Violence in Early Neolithic Central Europe," *Proceedings of the National Academy of Sciences* 112, no. 36 (2015): 11217–11222.

206 See Thomas Homer-Dixon, "Environmental Scarcities and Violent Conflict: Evidence from Cases," *International Security* 19, no. 1 (1994): 5–40; also see Thomas Homer-Dixon and Valerie Percival, *Environmental Scarcity and Violent Conflict: Briefing Book* (Washington, D.C.: American Association for the Advancement of Science, 1996); Michael T. Klare, *Resource Wars: The New Landscape of Global Conflict* (NY: Henry Holt and Company, 2001).

207 Gustavo Sosa-Nunez, Ed Atkins, eds., *Environment, Climate Change and International Relations* (Bristol: E-International Relations Publishing, 2016), 2, http://www.e-ir.info/wp-content/uploads/2016/05/Environment-Climate-Change-and-International-Relations-E-IR.pdf.

208 The considerations for not including such broad issues as environmental concerns in the framework of global security have been expressed on the following basis: "(1) It is analytically misleading to think of environmental degradation as a national security threat because the traditional focus of national security—interstate violence—has little in common with either environmental problems or solutions; (2) The effort to harness the emotive power of nationalism to help mobilize environmental awareness and action may prove counter-productive by undermining globalist political stability; and (3) Environmental degradation is not very likely to cause interstate wars." See Daniel Deudney, "The Case against Linking Environmental Degradation and National Security," *Millennium* 19, no. 3 (1990): 461.

209 Roland Dannreuther, *International Security: The Contemporary Agenda* (Cambridge: Polity, 2007), 66.

210 Models rely predominantly on the phasing out of fossil-based energy through the use of alternative technologies that include renewables. The assumptions that lead to the least damaging economic outcomes relied on the premise that "all key technologies are available." See IPCC, *Summary for Policymakers*, Climate Change 2014: Mitigation of Climate Change, IPCC Working Group III Contribution to AR5 (Berlin: UN IPCC, April 2014), https://www.ipcc.ch/pdf/assessment-report/ar5/wg3/ipcc_wg3_ar5_summary-for-policymakers.pdf.

211 Technology and the environment, which have been juxtaposed throughout human history, have been the essential elements in the argument of human existence within or despite nature. For some, technology is a symbol of human advancement and triumph

over nature's challenges, while for others it is the mechanism through which humanity is dominating and exploiting nature. This divide between man and nature has been
refracted through a number of visions with distinct religious overtones, colored by cultural bias, and informed by moral values. For an elaborate discussion of morality and
technology, see K. H. Whiteside, *Divided Natures: French Contributions to Political Ecology*
(Cambridge, MA: MIT Press, 2002); B. G. Norton, *Sustainability: A Philosophy of Adaptive
Ecosystem Management* (Chicago: University of Chicago Press, 2005).

212 PwC, *20 Years inside the Mind of the CEO... What's Next?* (PwC, 2017), https://www.pwc.
com/gx/en/ceo-survey/2017/pwc-ceo-20th-survey-report-2017.pdf.

213 In 2016, the OECD established a Centre on Green Finance and Investment to catalyze
green investment and financing flows. World Economic Forum programs with developing countries include New Energy Architecture, New Vision for Agriculture, Sustainable
Transportation Ecosystem, and Water Resources Group.

214 Isaac Asimov, "Visit to the World's Fair of 2014," *New York Times*, April 16, 1964, accessed
March 22, 2014, http://www.nytimes.com/books/97/03/23/lifetimes/asi-v-fair.html.

215 Jennifer Taylor, "Ethics of Renewable Energy," paper submitted to *World Wind Energy Conference, York University, May 30, 2008*, accessed January 10, 2014, http://www.ontario-sea.
org/solar/Storage/27/1872_Community_Power- Bringin_Ethics_Back_into_Energy_Poli-
tics.pdf.

216 On human societal interactions and conformity, see Alexander Mirtchev, *Conformity and
the Political Society* (Sofia: N. M., 1991).

217 John Rawls, *Political Liberalism* (New York: Columbia University Press, 1993), 192.

218 See Gareth Porter, "Environmental Security as a National Security Issue," *Current History*
94, no. 21 (May 1995): 218–222.

219 The range of policies is rather wide, embracing general laws on environmental protection
as well as regulations on greenhouse gas emissions, water use, or biodiversity protection
in a specific area.

220 See Johan Rockström et al., "A Safe Operating Space for Humanity," *Nature* 461 (2009):
472—475.

221 Thomas Friedman, "Is It Weird Enough Yet?," *New York Times*, September 13, 2011, http://
www.nytimes.com/2011/09/14/opinion/friedman-is-it-weird-enough-yet.html?_r=0.

222 Leslie Garisto Pfaff. "Power Issue: Shirley Tilghman." New Jersey Monthly, December 9,
2008.

223 One of the most prominent examples of the intersection of quasi-ideology, NGOs and
policymaking is the influence of religion, and the religious right political movement, on
U.S. politics. Professor Mark J. Rozell, Dean, Ruth D. and John T. Hazel Chair in Public
Policy, Schar School of Policy and Government, George Mason University notes that
"With a politically potent religious conservative movement in the United States now
having a major influence in driving policy in the Donald J. Trump era, it is worth taking
a moment to consider the role that Graham played in mobilizing evangelical leaders and
activists into politics." See, "Billy Graham's bad precedent: How the preacher commingled
faith and politics, helping lead us to the present moment", New York Daily News, February
22, 2018.

224 For example, Angela Merkel has stated that "climate change is accelerating. It threatens
our well-being, our security, and our economic development. It will lead to uncontrollable
risks and dramatic damage if we do not take resolute countermeasures." https://climate-
actionaustralia.net.au/

225 D. Puig and T. Morgan, eds., *Assessing the Effectiveness of Policies to Support Renewable Energy*
(United Nations Environment Programme, 2013), http://orbit.dtu.dk/files/69996503/
Assessing_the_effectiveness.pdf; REN21, *Renewables 2016 Global Status Report*.

226 REN21, *Renewables 2017 Global Status Report.*

227 Overall, there are two types of price-based incentives to promote deployment of renewable energy. In Fixed Price Systems, the government dictates the electricity price (or premium) paid to the producer and lets the market determine the quantity. In Renewable Quota Systems (Renewable Portfolio Standards in the U.S.) the government dictates the percentage of renewable electricity in utilities' energy mixes and the market determines the price. Both systems create a protected market against a background of subsidized, depreciated conventional generators that need not account for external environmental costs. Their aim is to provide incentives for technology improvements and cost reductions, leading to cheaper renewables that can compete with conventional sources in the future.

228 Investment subsidies are capital payments made on the rated power (in kW) of the generator. Basing the amount of support on generator size rather than electricity output can lead to less efficient technology development, but such payments can be effective when combined with other incentives. Fixed feed-in tariffs involve paying operators for every kWh of electricity they provide for the grid. They have successfully encouraged wind energy in Germany, Spain, and Denmark.

229 These systems, sometimes called "environmental bonus" mechanisms, add a fixed premium to the basic wholesale electricity price. The total price per kWh is less predictable than with feed-in tariffs because it depends on constantly changing electricity prices, but a fixed premium is easier to integrate into the overall electricity market because participants react to market price signals. The U.S. and Canada, and most prominently, Spain, use this system.

230 Tendering systems involve competitive bidding for contracts to construct and operate a particular project, or a fixed quantity of renewable capacity in a country or state, while tradable green certificate programs reward renewable producers for every kWh they generate. Tendering systems have promoted wind power in Ireland, France, the UK, Denmark, and China. TGC systems exist in the UK, Sweden, Italy, and the U.S., where it is known as a Renewable Portfolio Standard.

231 See: R. Haas et al., "Promoting Electricity from Renewable Energy Sources—Lessons Learned from the EU, United States, and Japan," in *Competitive Electricity Markets*, ed. F. P. Sioshansi (Oxford: Elsevier, 2008). On the set of main policies to support renewable energy in the U.S., see "State Policies to Support Renewable Energy," *EPA*, accessed January 20, 2018, https://www.epa.gov/statelocalenergy/state-renewable-energy-resources#.

232 A policy effectiveness assessment performed by the Technical University of Denmark for UNEP showed that while there are a number of principles of effective policy that can be instrumental, no "one-size-fits-all" solution exists due to different factors holding back deployment. See D. Puig and T. Morgan, eds., *Assessing the Effectiveness of Policies to Support Renewable Energy* (United Nations Environment Programme, 2013), http://orbit. dtu.dk/files/69996503/Assessing_the_effectiveness.pdf.

233 European Environment Agency, "Towards a Green Economy in Europe: EU Environmental Policy Targets and Objectives 2010–2050," EEA Report No. 8 (Copenhagen: European Environment Agency, 2013), https://www.kowi.de/Portaldata/2/Resources/fp/Report-Towards-a-green-economy-in-Europe.pdf.

234 Solyndra was a manufacturer of thin-film solar cells based in by the American Recovery and Reinvestment Act. The company filed for bankruptcy in 2011 after receiving a $527 million loan guarantee from the U.S. government. As most of the financial support was provided by the American Recovery and Reinvestment Act, the bankruptcy set off a political firestorm in Congress, and eventually worked its way into the 2012 presidential campaign.

235 National Research Council et al., *Renewable Fuel Standard: Potential Economic and Environmental Effects of U.S. Biofuel Policy* (Washington, D.C.: the National Academies Press, 2011).

236 See B. Goldman, "What Is the Future of Environmental Justice?," *Antipode* 28, no. 2 (1996): 122–141; M.K. Heiman, "Race, Waste, and Class: New Perspectives on Environmental Justice," *Antipode* 28, no. 2 (1996): 111–121; R. Moore and L. Head, "Acknowledging the Past, Confronting the Future: Environmental Justice in the 1990s," in *Toxic Struggles: The Theory and Practice of Environmental Justice,* ed. R. Hofrichter (Philadelphia: New Society, 1993).

237 See A. Herod et al., ed., *An Unruly World?* (London: Routledge, 1998).

238 Global environmental issues and the frameworks to address them have been considered predominantly through the lens of regime theory and its focus on principles, rules, norms, and decision-making procedures. See, for example, Gareth Porter and Janet Brown, *Global Environmental Politics* (Boulder, CO: Westview Press, 1991).

239 "One of the roles of the United Nations Environment Program is to promote environmentally sound development in harmony with peace and security, and towards this end, issues of disarmament and security, in so far as they relate to the environment, should continue to receive appropriate attention," UN General Assembly Resolution 42/186, "Environmental Perspective to the Year 2000 and Beyond," paragraph 86, 96th plenary meeting of the UN General Assembly, December 11, 1987, accessed December 5, 2013, http://www.un.org/documents/ga/res/42/a42r186.htm. *See also,* John Negroponte, "The United Nations is Still Making the World Stronger." FoxNews.com, September 17, 2019, available at https://www.foxnews.com/opinion/united-nations-stronger-support-un-amb-negroponte.

240 These have established guidelines for global policies, but have not avoided reserved attitudes and stances. The Kyoto Protocol was never fully ratified, in particular by the United States, which has also a rather controversial position towards the Paris Climate Deal. In addition, they have generated disputes between the developed and developing worlds. Nevertheless, evidence indicates that corporate America effectively implemented the Kyoto Protocol on its own. *See,* Stuart Eizenstat and Ruben Kraiem, "In Green Company." *Foreign Policy,* October 21, 2009.

241 Cary Funk and Meg Hefferon, "U.S. Public Views on Climate and Energy," Pew Research Center, November 25, 2019, https://www.pewresearch.org/science/2019/11/25/u-s-public-views-on-climate-and-energy/.

242 Robert Jackson, *The Global Covenant: Human Conduct in a World of States* (Oxford: Oxford University Press, 2000), 175–178.

243 Rice, Condoleezza and Zelikow, Philip. *To Build a Better World: Choices to End the Cold War and Create a Global Commonwealth.* Gran Central Publishing, 2019.

244 For more on the "ecological society" see David W. Orr, "In the Tracks of the Dinosaur: Modernization & the Ecological Perspective," *Polity* 11, no. 4 (1979): 562–587.

245 International collaborative initiatives include the Renewable Energy and Energy Efficiency Partnership (REEEP), the Global Village Energy Partnership (GVEP), Renewable Energy Policy Network for the 21st Century (REN21), and the Global Network on Energy for Sustainable Development (GNESD).

246 The acute problem of the habitat is creating a new ordering principle of geopolitical interactions, leading to the emergence of the term "environmental geopolitics." This term encompasses the increasing relevance of environmental security for the whole pattern of inter-state relations, and the globalization of environmental considerations—broader geographical reach, greater depth, and seriousness and speed of development and dissemination. See for example Daniel C. Esty "Pivotal States and the Environment," in *The Pivotal States: A New Framework for U.S. Policy in the Developing World,* eds. Robert Chase, Emily Hill, and Paul Kennedy (New York: W. W. Norton & Co., 1999).

247 See Noel Castree, "Nature, Economy and the Cultural Politics of Theory: The 'War against the Seals' in the Bering Sea, 1870–1911," *Geoforum* 28 (1997): 1–20.

248 The Intergovernmental Panel on Climate Change, a UN community of climate scientists, predicts that a warming of more than 4.5 degrees by mid-century is possible. Theresa Sabonis-Helf, "Climate Change," in *Global Strategic Assessment, 2009: America's Security Role in a Changing World*, ed. Patrick Cronin (Washington, D.C.: National Defense University Press, 2009), 85.

249 See Hermann E. Ott, "Climate Change: An Important Foreign Policy Issue," *International Affairs* 77, no. 2 (2001): 295.

250 Robert Zoellick, "Modernizing Multilateralism and Markets," speech at the Peterson Institute for International Economics, Washington, D.C., October 6, 2008, accessed January 10, 2014, https://www.iie.com/publications/papers/paper.cfm?ResearchID=1012. This admittedly rather idealistic view does not appear to have materialized as yet, and the likelihood of achieving this "bargain" is subject to the geopolitical power that actors will perceive in the advent of renewable technologies.

251 Al Gore, "The Climate for Change," *New York Times*, November 9, 2008, http://www.nytimes.com/2008/11/09/opinion/09gore.html?pagewanted=all.

252 Alternative energy falls within the framework of the "sustainable development" thesis in response to the "limits-to-growth" concept. Sustainable development was made an identifiable policy concern and a valid strategic goal as a result of the deliberations of the World Commission on Environment and Development, established in 1987 and chaired by Norwegian Prime Minister Brundtland.

253 James D. Wolfensohn, "Securing the Twenty-First Century," address by the World Bank Group President to the Board of Governors of the World Bank Group at the Joint Annual Discussion, 2004 Annual Meetings, Washington, D.C., October 3, 2004, accessed December 25, 2013, http://www.imf.org/external/am/2004/speeches/pr03e.pdf.

254 Prince Haakon of Norway, Prince Albert of Monaco, and Princess Astrid of Belgium head a number of foundations and organizations focused on environmental and alternative energy issues. Prince Frederik of Denmark hosted the 2009 Copenhagen Climate Summit. The Prince of Wales, the most active proponent, founded the Prince's Rainforests Project in 2007 and participates in other campaigns.

255 See, for example, Ken Conca and Geoffrey D. Dabelko, eds., *Environmental Peacemaking* (Washington, D.C.: Woodrow Wilson Center Press, 2002).

256 See UNEP, "Environmental Governance Update November 2017," accessed January 19, 2018, https://wedocs.unep.org/bitstream/handle/20.500.11822/7506/-Sustainable_Development_Goals_-_UNEP_annual_report_2015-2016UNEP-AR-2015-SustainableDevelopmentGoals.pdf.pdf?sequence=3&isAllowed=y.

257 See: Jessica Shankleman et al., "We're Going to Need More Lithium," *Bloomberg Businessweek*, September 7, 2017, accessed January 19, 2018, https://www.bloomberg.com/graphics/2017-lithium-battery-future/.

258 Countries with the largest lithium reserves worldwide as of 2016, https://www.statista.com/statistics/268790/countries-with-the-largest-lithium-reserves-worldwide/, accessed January 19, 2018.

259 "Current Energy Security Challenges," S. Hrg. 111-2, hearing before the Committee on Energy and Natural Resources, January 8, 2009, http://www.gpo.gov/fdsys/pkg/CHRG-111shrg47252/pdf/CHRG-111shrg47252.pdf.

260 "US Generals Urge Climate Action," *BBC News*, last modified April 15, 2007, http://news.bbc.co.uk/2/hi/americas/6557803.stm.

261 Paul Roberts, *The End of Oil* (Boston: Houghton Mifflin Harcourt, 2004), 324.

262 Ahmad Babiker Nahar, statement by Minister of Environment and Urban Development of the Republic of the Republic of Sudan Ahmad Babiker Nahar, closing plenary session of the Summit on Climate Change, New York, September 22, 2009, accessed March 22, 2011, http://www.g77.org/statement/2009.html.

263 Barry Pavel and Ian Brzezinski. "It's Time for a NATO-China Council." *Defense One*, August 21, 2019.

264 John F.W. Rogers. "Atlantic Council's Annual Forum." Washington, D.C., December 14, 2018.

265 Water stress occurs when the ratio of fresh water withdrawn to total renewable freshwater resources is above a 25% threshold. See UN, *Sustainable Development Goals Report 2017* (New York: United Nations, 2017), accessed January 19, 2018, https://unstats.un.org/sdgs/files/report/2017/TheSustainableDevelopmentGoalsReport2017.pdf.

266 See C. Adam Schlosser et al., *The Future of Global Water Stress: An Integrated Assessment*, Report No. 254 (Cambridge, MA: MIT Joint Program on the Science and Policy of Global Change, 2014), http://globalchange.mit.edu/sites/default/files/MITJPSPGC_Rpt254.pdf.

267 UN, *Sustainable Development Goals Report 2017*.

268 See John Reilly and Sergey Paltsev, *Biomass Energy and Competition for Land*, Report No. 145 (Cambridge, MA: MIT Joint Program on the Science and Policy of Global Change, 2007), accessed November 22, 2012, http://web.mit.edu/globalchange/www/MITJPSPGC_Rpt145.pdf.

269 See Jerrold S. Cooper, *Reconstructing History from Ancient Inscriptions: The Lagash-Umma Border Conflict: 2 (Sources from the Ancient Near East)* (Malibu, CA: Undena Press, 1983).

270 Heba Saleh and John Aglionby, "Egypt and Ethiopia Clash over Huge River Nile Dam," *Financial Times*, December 17, 2017, https://www.ft.com/content/58f66390-dfda-11e7-a8a4-0a1e63a52f9c.

271 Saki, "The Jesting of Arlington Stringham," in *The Chronicles of Clovis* (Harmondsworth: Penguin, 1911), 78.

272 Ralph Waldo Emerson, *The Journals and Miscellaneous Notebooks* (Boston: Harvard University Press, 1965), 260.

273 Zalmay Khalilzad and Ian Lesser, ed., *Sources of Conflict in the 21st Century: Regional Futures and U.S. Strategy* (Santa Monica, CA: RAND, 1998), 34.

274 Anabela Botelho et al., "Effect of Wind Farm Noise on Local Residents' Decision to Adopt Mitigation Measures," *International Journal of Environmental Research and Public Health* 14, is. 7 (2017), https://www.ncbi.nlm.nih.gov/pmc/articles/PMC5551191/pdf/ijerph-14-00753.pdf. See also the results of an extensive study undertaken by the Government of Canada: Health Canada. Government of Canada, "Wind Turbine Noise and Health Study: Summary of Results," http://www.sustainabledevelopment.ca/wp-content/uploads/2015/07/Phase-VII-Health-Canada-Wind-Turbine-Study-Results-2014.pdf.

275 Adam Vaughan, "Is This the Future? Dutch Plan Vast Windfarm Island in North Sea," *Guardian*, December 29, 2017, https://www.theguardian.com/environment/2017/dec/29/is-this-the-future-dutch-plan-vast-windfarm-island-in-north-sea.

276 Some feedstock materials used in PV cells are toxic, carcinogenic, pyrophoric, or flammable. The actual hazards to health posed by these materials depend on their inherent toxicological properties and the intensity, frequency, and duration of human exposure. Widespread utilization of PV technologies requires that serious attention be given to these hazards as they relate to the sources, processing, usage, and end-of-product-life disposal. National Research Council, *Energy Futures and Urban Air Pollution: Challenges for China and the United States* (Washington, D.C.: the National Academies Press, 2007), 223–224.

277 R. R. Hernandez et al., "Environmental Impacts of Utility-Scale Solar Energy," *Renewable and Sustainable Energy Reviews* 29, January 2014, 766–779, https://www.researchgate.net/publication/257200435_Environmental_impacts_of_utility-scale_solar_energy.

278 A study of 26 biofuels on the basis of a method developed by Dr. Rainer Zah, head of Life Cycle Assessment & Modeling, EMPA, Switzerland, showed that 21 fuels reduced greenhouse gas emissions by more than 30% compared with gasoline when burned. But almost half of the biofuels, a total of 12, had greater total environmental impacts than fossil fuels. These included economically significant fuels such as U.S. corn ethanol, Brazilian sugar cane ethanol and soy diesel, and Malaysian palm oil diesel. Biofuels that fared best were those produced from waste products such as recycled cooking oil, as well as ethanol from grass or wood.

279 National Research Council, *Energy Futures and Urban Air Pollution: Challenges for China and the United States* (Washington, D.C.: the National Academies Press, 2007), 223.

280 As estimated by researchers, wind energy (0.2–12 m3 TJe-1), solar energy through PV (6–303 m3 TJe-1), and geothermal energy (7–759 m3 TJe-1) have the smallest water footprints, while biomass (50000–500000 m3 TJe-1) and hydropower (300–850000 m3 TJe-1) have the largest. The water footprints of electricity from fossil fuels and nuclear energy range between the extremes. See Mesfin M. Mekonnen, P. W. Gerbens-Leenes, and Arjen Y. Hoekstra, "The Consumptive Water Footprint of Electricity and Heat: A Global Assessment," *Environmental Science: Water Research & Technology* (the Royal Society of Chemistry, 2015), DOI: 10.1039/c5ew00026b, http://waterfootprint.org/media/downloads/Mekonnen-et-al-2015.pdf.

281 Producing 2,000 megawatts of electricity from wood in a sustainable manner requires a forest of 6,600 square kilometers. In addition, the EU's drive to scale up biomass that employs wood has resulted in an increase in its price, which affects other sectors that also use wood, such as construction. See "Bonfire of the Subsidies," *the Economist* 16, April 6, 2013, http://www.economist.com/news/leaders/21575759-europes-wood-subsidies-show-folly-focusing-green-policy-renewables-bonfireaccessed January 10, 2014.

282 See Jörn P.W. Scharlemann and William F. Laurance, "How Green Are Biofuels?," *Science* 319, no. 5859 (2008), 43–44.

283 Second generation biofuels focus on the residual non-food parts of current crops, such as stems, leaves, and husks that are left behind once the food crop has been extracted, as well as other crops that are not used for food purposes, such as switchgrass, grass, jatropha, whole crop maize, miscanthus, and cereals that bear little grain, and also industry waste such as woodchips, skins, and pulp from fruit pressing.

284 Views have been expressed that, in the context of the post-Cold War paradigm shift, environmental security has been "embraced" by the traditional security establishments that have begun to incorporate environmental issues in their planning, and policy approaches. The Clinton administration explicitly viewed environmental security in combination with diminishing conventional resources as a national security risk. It noted that resource depletion "is already a very real risk to regional stability around the world" and that "environmental degradation will ultimately block economic growth." "National Strategy of Engagement and Enlargement," the White House, February 1995, accessed January 10, 2014, http://www.au.af.mil/au/awc/awcgate/nss/nss-95.pdf.

285 Jon Barnett, "Environmental Security," in *The Routledge Handbook of New Security Studies*, ed. J. Peter Burgess (New York: Routledge, 2010), 124–125.

286 J. Dittmer et al., "Have You Heard the One about the Disappearing Ice? Recasting Arctic Geopolitics," *Political Geography* 30 (2011): 202–214.

287 Javier Solana, "The External Energy Policy of the European Union," speech at the Annual Conference of the French Institute of International Relations (IFRI), Brussels, February

1, 2008, accessed January 10, 2014, http://www.consilium.europa.eu/ueDocs/cms_Data/docs/pressdata/EN/discours/98532.pdf.

288 Edward Luttwak, "From Geopolitics to Geo-Economics: Logic of Conflict, Grammar of Commerce," *the National Interest*, no. 20, Summer 1990, 17–24.

289 Arnold Wolfers, "'National Security' as an Ambiguous Symbol," in Arnold Wolfers, *Discord and Collaboration. Essays on International Politics* (Baltimore: John Hopkins University Press, 1962), 147–165.

290 Dan Caldwell and Robert E. Williams, Jr., *Seeking Security in an Insecure World* (Lanham, MD: Rowman & Littlefield Publishers, 2006), 145.

291 For example, Samuelson, in his classic text, provides six different definitions of "economic" and says the list can be extended. See Paul A. Samuelson, *Economics*, 10th ed. (New York: McGraw-Hill, 1976), 3.

292 Lars Osberg, "The 'Disappearance' of Involuntary Unemployment," *Journal of Economic Issues* 22, no. 3 (1998): 17, http://www.jstor.org/discover/.

293 R. M. Solow, "A Contribution to the Theory of Economic Growth," *Quarterly Journal of Economics* 70, (1956): 65–94.

294 In the U.S., the energy industry was providing 6% of the overall industry employment in 2012, and is expected to invest more than $5.1 trillion in cumulative capital expenditures by 2035, adding 1.3 million new jobs by 2020 to support a total of 3 million jobs. IHS Global Insight, "America's New Energy Future: The Unconventional Oil and Gas Revolution and the U.S. Economy," October 2012, http://www.ihs.com/info/ecc/a/americas-new-energy-future.aspx accessed March 2, 2013.

295 Debt is often considered a millstone that reduces growth in the economies of the least developed countries (LDCs), blocking their development and sparking internal and sometimes inter-state conflicts.

296 Whether the opportunity provided by renewables is utilized to bring about positive change depends on how the alternative energy sources will be developed and implemented as well as on how the income from the newly acquired wealth is distributed. Renewable resources-rich countries may fall victim of the so-called "resource curse" as well as the countries with an abundance of non-renewable resources: resource sector dominance tends to lead to overdependence on resources price volatility, the underdevelopment of manufacturing and agricultural sectors, and, at the end of the day, to poor economic growth and social tension. Lack of appropriate natural resource governance, which is mostly the case with the LDCs in particular, also implies the risks of mismanagement and corruption by state actors which could impede any positive socio-economic developments. On "resource curse" see, for example, Jeffrey Sachs and Andrew Warner, *Natural Resource Abundance and Economic Growth*, Working Paper (NBER, 1995), DOI: 10.3386/w5398; Michael L. Ross, *The Oil Curse: How Petroleum Wealth Shapes the Development of Nations* (Princeton, N.J.: Princeton University Press, 2012); *From Curse to Blessing: Natural Resources and Institutional Quality*, Environment Matters 2006—World Bank Group, 2006, http://siteresources.worldbank.org/INTENVMAT/64199955-1162240805462/21125342/9FromCurse.pdf.

297 J. R. McNeill, "World Environmental History: The First 100,000 Years," *Historically Speaking: The Bulletin of the Historical Society* 8, no. 6 (July/August 2007): 8.

298 Bill Clinton, remarks at Georgetown University, November 7, 2001, http://ecumene.org/clinton.htm accessed January 5, 2014.

299 Colin Gray, "Global Security and Economic Well-Being: A Strategic Perspective," *Political Studies* 42 (1994): 30, http://onlinelibrary.wiley.com/doi/10.1111/j.1467-9248.1994.tb01672.x/abstract.

300 See Wolfgang Sachs and Tilman Santarius, eds., *Fair Future: Resource Conflicts, Security, and Global Justice* (London: Zed Books, 2007).

301 See Terry Lynn Karl, *The Paradox of Plenty: Oil Booms and Petro-States* (Berkeley: University of California Press, 1997).

302 Dani Rodrik, *Has Globalization Gone Too Far?* (Washington, D.C.: Institute for International Economics, 1997), 55–57.

303 See Dave Keating, "Trump Follows Europe's Lead with Chinese Solar Panel Tariffs," *Forbes*, January 23, 2018, https://www.forbes.com/sites/davekeating/2018/01/23/trump-follows-europes-lead-with-chinese-solar-panel-tariffs/#4a8711131a8b.

304 See Nicholas Spykman, *America's Strategy in World Politics: The United States and the Balance of Power* (New York: Harcourt, Brace, and Company, 1942), 265–341.

305 The principle of non-intervention in the affairs of another country has been the prevailing norm since the establishment of the system of sovereign nation-states at the Peace of Westphalia. It was one of the reasons why the U.S. initially did not join the hostilities in both World War I and II. Both the U.S. and USSR and their respective allies ignored the principle during the Cold War. Their interference in the affairs of other countries—especially developing ones—was justified by their respective fears that the opposing block and its ideology would dominate the world. See Nicholas J. Wheeler, *Saving Strangers: Humanitarian Intervention in International Society* (Oxford: Oxford University Press, 2000); David Fisher, *Morality and War: Can War Be Just in the Twenty-First Century?* (Oxford: Oxford University Press, 2011).

306 Liberal democracies (often after securing UN resolutions) have attacked governments or intervened in civil wars on several occasions since the end of the Cold War—Bosnia and Herzegovina in 1995, Kosovo in 1999, the first Gulf War in 1990, Somalia in 1992, Haiti in 2004, and Libya in 2011. They have done so under the premise that countries' sovereignty comes with the responsibility to protect and not repress their citizens, and that the international community has the right to interfere in a country's civil war in order to provide relief to its civilian population. The UN itself has approved military interventions led by Western countries to remove Iraqi forces from Kuwait in 1990, in Somalia in the absence of a functioning government in 1992, a force to stabilize Haiti in 2004, and in Libya in 2011 to prevent its military from massacring the civilian population in Benghazi. On the justifications for military intervention, see Michael Walzer, *Just and Unjust Wars: A Moral Argument with Historical Illustrations* (New York: Basic Books, 1977); Peter Singer, *One World: The Ethics of Globalization* (New Haven: Yale University Press, 2002); Benjamin A. Valentino, "The True Costs of Humanitarian Intervention," *Foreign Affairs* 90, no. 6 (November/December, 2011): 60–73.

307 Thomas Aquinas, "Summa Theologiae, IIaIIae40: On War," in Thomas Aquinas, *Political Writings*, ed. and trans. R. W. Dyson (Cambridge: Cambridge University Press, 2002), 241.

308 See for example Niall Ferguson, *Empire: How Britain Made the Modern World* (London: Penguin, 2008).

309 It is important to note that the global trade regulatory framework has actually operated in a balanced manner. The GATT's Uruguay Round agreements on trade in industrial goods (GATT 1994), agricultural goods, services (GATS), and intellectual property (TRIPS) monitored by the WTO forced developed countries to adopt deeper and faster cuts in tariffs and subsidies than developing countries. LDCs received special treatment. The EU has for decades given developing countries tariff-free access (or with very low tariffs) to its markets under the Generalized System of Preferences. The WTO's dispute-resolution system has often ruled in favor of developing countries and against developed ones. See for example Julio Lacarte-Muro and Petina Gappah, "Developing Countries and the WTO Legal and Dispute Settlement System: A View from the Bench," *Journal of International Economic Law* 3, no. 3 (2000): 395–401, http://jiel.oxfordjournals.org/content/3/3/395.abstract.

310 Zbigniew Brzezinski, *The Grand Chessboard: American Primacy and Its Geostrategic Imperatives*, 186.

311 Lazard, "Levelized Cost of Energy Analysis—Version 11.0," November 2017, https://www.lazard.com/media/450337/lazard-levelized-cost-of-energy-version-110.pdf.

312 International Renewable Energy Agency, "Falling Renewable Power Costs Open Door to Greater Climate Ambition", May 29, 2019, https://www.irena.org/newsroom/pressreleases/2019/May/Falling-Renewable-Power-Costs-Open-Door-to-Greater-Climate-Ambition.

313 See Cédric Philibert, *Renewable Energy for Industry. From Green Energy to Green Materials and Fuels*, OECD/IEA (IEA Publication, 2017), https://www.iea.org/publications/insights/insightpublications/Renewable_Energy_for_Industry.pdf.

314 Alvin Toffler, *Future Shock* (New York: Bantam Books, 1970), 9.

315 International Renewable Energy Agency, *Renewable Energy and Jobs Annual Review 2017* (Abu Dhabi: IRENA, 2017), www.irena.org/-/media/Files/ IRENA /Agency/Publication/2017/May/IRENA_RE_Jobs_Annual_Review_2017.pdf.

316 The European Commission estimated that reaching the goal of obtaining 20% of energy consumption from renewable sources by 2020 will create 417,000 new jobs, and an additional 410,000 will be generated if energy efficiency is increased by 20% by 2020. See the "EU Climate and Energy Package," Brussels, European Commission, accessed November 3, 2013, http://ec.europa.eu/clima/policies/package/index_en.htm.

317 International Renewable Energy Agency, *Renewable Energy and Jobs Annual Review 2017*.

318 Ibid.

319 Estimates by the Institute for Employment Research, the research institute of the German Federal Employment Agency, suggest that the share of highly skilled workers is 9% and the share of engineers is 5% higher than in conventional energy. See: Manfred Antoni, Markus Janser, and Florian Lehmer, *The Hidden Winners of Renewable Energy Promotion*, IAB-Discussion Paper 12 (Nuremberg, IAB, 2014), http://doku.iab.de/discussionpapers/2014/dp1214.pdf.

320 See W. Brian Arthur, *The Nature of Technology: What It Is and How It Evolves* (New York: Free Press, 2009), 194.

321 See Joseph Schumpeter, *Capitalism, Socialism, and Democracy* (New York: Harper & Row, 1942), 81.

322 One of the implications of which was that the rate of capital accumulation (savings rate) and capital investment had only a temporary effect on the rate of growth, eventually leading to diminishing returns as workers' wages increased relative to the cost of the new machines. See Robert Solow, "A Contribution to the Theory of Economic Growth," *Quarterly Journal of Economics* 70 (1956): 65–94, http://faculty.lebow.drexel.edu/LainczC/cal38/Growth/Solow_1956.pdf.

323 See Richard Lipsey, *Economic Transformations: General Purpose Technologies and Long-Term Economic Growth* (London and New York: Oxford University Press, 2005).

324 Despite the fact that Evsey Domar rejected his own theory in 1957, the focus on capital accumulation and investment is still the dominant paradigm, particularly in development economics, where the Harrod-Domar model has been used to design economic policy and assistance programs for developing countries.

325 Frankfurt School-UNEP Collaborating Centre/BNEF, *Global Trends in Renewable Energy Investment 2018*.

326 Diffusion of innovations trajectory was first discussed in Everett M. *Rogers, Diffusion of Innovations* (New York: Free Press of Glencoe, 1962).

327 Directive 2009/28/EC of the European Parliament and of the Council of 23 April 2009, Official Journal of the European Union, L 140/16, June 6, 2009, http://eur-lex.europa.eu/legal-content/EN/TXT/PDF/?uri=CELEX:32009L0028&from=EN.

328 See European Commission, *Renewable Energy Progress Report* (Brussels: EC, 2017), http://eur-lex.europa.eu/legal-content/EN/TXT/PDF/?uri=CELEX:52017DC0057&qid=1488449105433&from=EN.

329 https://www.pv-magazine.com/2018/01/17/eu-parliament-votes-in-favor-of-2030-binding-renewable-energy-target-of-35/.

330 U.S. Department of Energy, *Strategic Plan 2014–2018*, https://energy.gov/sites/prod/files/2014/04/f14/2014_dept_energy_strategic_plan.pdf.

331 A feed-in tariff is an incentive structure where regional or national electricity utilities are obligated to buy electricity generated from renewable sources at above-market rates set by the government. The higher price helps overcome the cost disadvantages of renewable energy sources. The rate may differ among various forms of power generation. A feed-in tariff is normally phased out once the renewable reaches a significant market penetration, such as 20%, since it is not economically sustainable to subsidize beyond that point.

332 REN21, *Renewables 2017 Global Status Report*.

333 IRENA and CPI: International Renewable Energy Agency, *Global Landscape of Renewable Energy Finance* (Abu Dhabi: IRENA, 2018), http://www.irena.org/publications/2018/Jan/Global-Landscape-of-Renewable-Energy-Finance.

334 Modern renewable energy—geothermal, solar, hydro, wind, biofuels, and biomass (excluding traditional biomass, like wood or agricultural by-products burned for cooking and heating).

335 International Energy Agency, *Renewables 2018*.

336 International Renewable Energy Agency, *Global Landscape of Renewable Energy Finance*.

337 Frankfurt School-UNEP Collaborating Centre/BNEF, *Global Trends in Renewable Energy Investment 2018*.

338 Climate Investment Funds provide financial resources to 72 developing countries to mitigate and manage the challenges of climate change and reduce their greenhouse gas emissions: https://www.climateinvestmentfunds.org/ There are also public-private initiatives launched to catalyze private sector capital into clean energy projects in developing countries and economies in transition, like the "Global Energy Efficiency and Renewable Energy Fund": http://geeref.com.

339 Limited data on financial instruments application is preventing a detailed coverage of deals breakdown by instrument. See International Renewable Energy Agency, *Global Landscape of Renewable Energy Finance*, January 2018.

340 See Frankfurt School-UNEP Collaborating Centre/BNEF. *Global Trends in Renewable Energy Investment 2019*.

341 Ibid.

342 International Renewable Energy Agency, *Global Landscape of Renewable Energy Finance*, January 2018.

343 See Frankfurt School-UNEP Collaborating Centre/BNEF, *Global Trends in Renewable Energy Investment 2018*.

344 "Tata BP Solar India Renamed as Tata Power Solar," *EnergyNext*, last modified August 31, 2012, www.energynext.in/tata-bp-solar-india-renamed-tata-power-solar.

345 A public good is a good that is both non-excludable and non-rivalrous in that individuals cannot be effectively excluded from use and where use by one individual does not reduce availability to others. See for example Hal Varian, *Microeconomic Analysis*, 3rd ed. (New York and London: W. W. Norton & Co., 1992).

346 According to the U.S. Department of Defense, the number of military renewable energy projects nearly tripled to 1,390 between 2011 and 2015. See: Reuters, March 1, 2017, https://www.reuters.com/article/us-usa-military-green-energy-insight/u-s-military-marches-forward-on-green-energy-despite-trump-idUSKBN1683BL. In addition, the U.S.

Army Energy Initiatives Task Force facilitates and streamlines renewable and alternative energy large-scale projects by leveraging private sector and defense resources to help the U.S. Army meet its renewable energy targets. The role of the defense industry in renewable energy market development was discussed in Chapter 2 (Part 3).

347 See International Renewable Energy Agency, *Global Landscape of Renewable Energy Finance*, January 2018. According to IRENA's review, consistent data on government expenditures for such policies are publicly available for only 27 Western European countries and Japan; therefore, the analysis of the situation in the area is limited.

348 Ibid.

349 Ibid.; Council of European Energy Regulators, *Status Review of Renewable Support Schemes in Europe* (Brussels: CEER, 2017).

350 International Renewable Energy Agency, *Global Landscape of Renewable Energy Finance*, January 2018.

351 "Chapter 3: Global Energy Transition Prospects and the Role of Renewables," in *Perspectives for the Energy Transition—Investment Needs for a Low-Carbon Energy System* (Abu Dhabi: IRENA, 2017).

352 https://energy.gov/eere/cemi/clean-energy-manufacturing-initiative-current-activities.

353 It was estimated that in Germany, for example, the biogas technology manufacturing industry exported 68% of its product. The solar photovoltaic sector in 2013 was doing 81% of its business abroad. Germany's wind turbine industry, located on the North Sea and Baltic coasts, sells 67% of its technology to global markets. In 2014 exports accounted for 44% of the jobs in the renewable facilities manufacturing sector. See: Paul Hockenos, "Jobs Won, Jobs Lost—How the Energiewende Is Transforming the Labour Market," *Clean Energy Wire*, last modified March 15, 2015, https://www.cleanenergywire.org/dossiers/energy-transitions-effect-jobs-and-business#Business.

354 For the U.S. economy, an analysis indicated that a putative increase of U.S. R&D investment by four times could potentially offset the risks of oil price shocks, power supply disruptions, and environmental threats. The analysis framed R&D in renewables as an "insurance" against such threats. See Robert N. Schock et al., "How Much Is Energy Research & Development Worth as Insurance?," *Annual Review of Energy and the Environment* 24 (1999): 487–512.

355 See: Paul Hockenos, "Jobs Won, Jobs Lost—How the Energiewende Is Transforming the Labour Market."

356 Private sector engagement is among key priorities of renewables state support programs, both national, like the U.S. Clean Energy Manufacturing Initiative, or multilateral, like the Mission Innovation Program launched in 2015, in Paris, France, by the governments of Australia, Brazil, Canada, Chile, China, Denmark, France, Germany, India, Indonesia, Italy, Japan, Mexico, Norway, the Republic of Korea, Saudi Arabia, Sweden, the United Kingdom of Great Britain and Northern Ireland, the United Arab Emirates, and the United States of America.

357 Michael Faraday, English physicist, responding to William Gladstone, the Chancellor of the Exchequer, when asked about the practical value of research in electricity, as quoted in Alan L. Mackay, *The Harvest of a Quiet Eye: A Selection of Scientific Quotations* (Bristol: Institute of Physics, 1977), 56.

358 See David Newman, "Borders and Bordering: Towards an Interdisciplinary Dialogue," *European Journal of Social Theory* 9, no. 2 (May 2006): 171–186.

359 Jeffrey D. Sachs, "Technological Keys to Climate Protection," *ScientificAmerican.com* (April 1, 2008), https://www.scientificamerican.com/article/keys-to-climate-protection/.

360 Margaret Thatcher, *The Downing Street Years*, (London: HarperCollins, 1993), 639.

361 Aristotle, *The Politics*, Book 3, ch. 12 (80b), trans. Benjamin Jowett (New York: Colonial Press, 1900), 5.

362 In October 2008, the UN Food and Agriculture Organization (FAO) called for a review of biofuel subsidies and policies, noting that they had contributed significantly to rising food prices and hunger in poor countries. See The State of Food and Agriculture (Rome: Food and Agriculture Organization of the United Nations, 2008), http://www.fao.org/docrep/011/i0100e/i0100e00.htm.

363 See Ivan Penn, "California Invested Heavily in Solar Power. Now There's So Much That Other States Are Sometimes Paid to Take It," Los Angeles Times, June 22, 2017, http://www.latimes.com/projects/la-fi-electricity-solar/.

364 "Green tape" refers to the sometimes unpredictable and inconclusive rules and regulations surrounding environmental issues. It can impact investment decisions and skew market-based decision-making. Government policies, often ad hoc, fail to integrate knowledge of the field, and their benefits are more anticipated than calculated.

365 Richard Rahn, "The End of Progress?," Washington Times, July 19, 2011, http://www.washingtontimes.com/news/2011/jul/18/the-end-of-progress/ accessed January 7, 2014.

366 Friedrich August von Hayek, the Sveriges Riksbank Prize in Economic Sciences in Memory of Alfred Nobel speech, 1974, accessed January 7, 2014, http://www.nobelprize.org/nobel_prizes/economic-sciences/laureates/1974/hayek-lecture.html.

367 European Commission, *Renewable Energy Progress Report*.

368 The problem is already evident on a localized scale in some U.S. states, such as Ohio, which, until mid-2014, had an in-state requirement for half of Renewable Portfolio Standards requirements to be fulfilled with in-state generation. California, another state with large renewables potential, has seen legislative pressure to restrict "imports" of clean energy by regulating a specific percentage of alternative energy to be produced in the state. In response, California's then-governor Arnold Schwarzenegger stated, "I am totally against protectionist policies because it never works. We get most of our cars from outside the state; why can't we get renewable energy?" See Arnold Schwarzenegger, Governor of California, "Press Conference in Relation to the Signing of Executive Order Requiring That the State Get 33% of Its Electricity from Renewable Sources like Solar and Wind Power by 2020," Executive Order S-21-09, State of California, September 15, 2009, accessed December 23, 2013, http://www.c2es.org/us-states-regions/news/2009/california-governor-issues-executive-order-increasing-state-rps and http://www.c2es.org/docUploads/CA%20Exec%20order%20S-21-09.PDF.

369 Effect leakage in general, and carbon leakage in relation to alternative energy development, refers to mismatches in regulation that cause market participants to move the location of production to a less-regulated country, negating any effect of emission reductions in the country with stricter emission regulations.

370 Milton Friedman, quoted in Elizabeth M. Knowles, ed., The Oxford Dictionary of Quotations, major new ed. (New York: Oxford University Press, 1999), 325.

371 According to IEA estimates, the global value of fossil fuel subsidies in 2015 was around US$ 320 billion while subsidies for renewables amounted to US$150 billion globally. See Toshiyuki Shirai, "Commentary: Putting the Right Price on Energy," International Energy Agency, last modified April 2017, 2017, https://www.iea.org/newsroom/news/2017/april/commentary-putting-the-right-price-on-energy.html.

372 See, for example, the calculations by the Institute for Energy Research in the U.S.: https://instituteforenergyresearch.org/analysis/eia-subsidy-report-solar-subsidies-increase-389-percent/.

373 The electricity generation costs for coal power stations vary between US$54 and US$120 per MWh. The comparable costs for gas-powered generation are between US$67 and

US$105 per MWh; for nuclear—US$29 to US$82 per MWh; for onshore wind—US$48 to US$163 per MWh; for offshore wind—US$101 to US$188 per MWh; and for solar—US$136 to US$215 per MWh. The extensive variance between the lower and higher cost bands is due to a variety of factors—access to raw materials, technology, linkages to infrastructure, cost levels for other factors of production, etc. See International Energy Agency, Nuclear Energy Agency, OECD, Projected Costs of Generating Electricity (Paris: OECD Publishing, 2010), http://www.iea.org/publications/freepublications/publication/projected_costs.pdf.

374 Richard Higgott, American Unilateralism, Foreign Economic Policy and the "Securitisation" of Globalisation, Working Paper 124 (Coventry: University of Warwick, Centre for the Study of Globalisation and Regionalisation, 2003), https://warwick.ac.uk/fac/soc/pais/research/researchcentres/csgr/papers/workingpapers/2003/wp12403.pdf.

375 See Richard Stubbs, "Performance Legitimacy and 'Soft Authoritarianism,'" in Democracy, Human Rights, and Civil Society in Southeast Asia, eds. Amitav Acharya, B. Michael Frolic, and Richard Stubbs (Toronto: Joint Centre for Asia Pacific Studies, York University, 2001), 37–54.

376 See Peter Hough, Understanding Global Security, 2nd ed. (London: Routledge, 2008).

377 Sanctions are a tool of statecraft that are often a "cop out ... throw[n] [] at a problem." While sanctions are most often symbolic, they are sometimes effective. For example, "economic sanctions combined with the decline in the price of oil had crippling effects on Iran." Richard Perle, Wilson Center Interview on the Effectiveness of U.S. Sanctions, April 28, 2015. To further demonstrate difficulties with sanctions, even among partnering nations, see Kristal Alley's commentary on the G20 from October 31, 2014: "The top-down approach of relying on the cooperation and full engagement of G20 leaders to achieve tangible results is further hampered by the fact that some G20 members (the U.S., EU, Japan, Australia and Canada) have imposed economic sanctions against another G20 member (Russia). Yet another G20 member, Argentina, is in default; India vetoed the Bali agreement on trade facilitation; and the U.S. Congress continues to block an earlier G20 commitment to reform the IMF governance structure. Add to this the fact that many G20 leaders simply don't like each other does not bode well for the Brisbane Summit."

378 For more on smart sanctions, see G. Lopez and D. Cortright, "Smarting under Sanctions," the World Today, 58(3), March 2002, 17–18.

379 Robert Cox, Production, Power, and World Order: Social Forces in the Making of History (New York: Columbia University Press, 1987), 399.

380 See Peter Dicken, Global Shift: Transforming the World Economy, 3rd ed. (New York: Guilford, 1998), 1–15.

381 See, for example, Rodney Bruce Hall and Thomas J. Biersteker, "The Emergence of Private Authority in the International System," in The Emergence of Private Authority in Global Governance, ed. Rodney Bruce Hall and Thomas J. Biersteker (Cambridge: Cambridge University Press, 2002), 3–22.

382 For a detailed discussion on identity and nationality, see Robert Reich, The Work of Nations (New York: Knopf, 1991).

383 In a globalized world, actors will endeavor to maximize collective outcomes. The method that has proven most successful in this is the so-called "tit-for-tat" strategy, which requires proportionate reciprocal responses to the actions of others. However, with states ultimately acting in their own self-interest, such a strategy can easily result in disproportionate actions. On "tit-for-tat" strategies, see Robert Axelrod, The Evolution of Cooperation (New York: Basic Books, 1984).

384 The Marshall Plan represented a good example of securitization by the U.S., often justified as protection of U.S. national interests via the reconstruction of Europe. Another example

is the Clinton administration's "economic diplomacy" that addressed possible security threats through geo-economic approaches. See David E. Sanger, "A Grand Trade Bargain," Foreign Affairs 80, no. 1 (2001): 67.

385 For some recent examples, consider the bailing out of financial institutions by the U.S. Federal Reserve in 2008 to prevent a threat to the financial system, bypassing established bankruptcy practices. See Matthew Karnitschnig et al., "U.S. to Take over AIG in $85 Billion Bailout; Central Banks Inject Cash as Credit Dries Up," Wall Street Journal, September 16, 2008, http://online.wsj.com/news/articles/SB122156561931242905.

386 See Organization for Economic Cooperation and Development, The Security Economy (Paris: OECD, 2004), accessed January 7, 2014, http://www.oecd.org/futures/16692437. pdf.

387 J. Pickles and J. Popke, "The Specter That Haunts: Marx and Derrida in Eastern Europe, South Africa, and Mexico," paper presented at the annual conference of the Association of American Geographers, Boston, MA, 1998, 13.

388 For analysis of the modernization paradigm, see Walt Rostow, The Stages of Economic Growth (New York: Cambridge University Press, 1960).

389 For example, promising jobs for everyone may be impossible, but it is possible to promise creating the conditions that would facilitate more people getting jobs. Overall, securitizing economic referent objects is often a matter of adjusting responses to threats not only depending on the strategic environment, but also on the specific resources, capabilities, knowledge, and respective social, political, and historical context of the threats to be addressed. See Edward Kolodziej, "Renaissance in Security Studies? Caveat Lector!," International Studies Quarterly 36, no. 4 (1992): 422.

390 Regional economic security complexes are sometimes, but not always, identifiable as regional military security complexes. In addition, any regional security complexes are not permanent, and their structure and form often adapt to changing circumstances. See Peter Katzenstein and Christopher Hemmer, "Why Is There No NATO in Asia? Collective Identity, Regionalism, and the Origins of Multilateralism," International Organization 56, no. 3 (2002): 575.

391 For example, some scientists believe that the fall of the Mayan civilization was due to environmental damage associated with deforestation and subsequent impacts of the agricultural system. See for example Nicholas P. Dunning and Timothy Beach, "Noxious or Nurturing Nature? Maya Civilization in Environmental Contexts," in Continuity and Change in Maya Archaeology, eds. Charles Golden and Greg Borgstede (New York: Routledge Press, 2003), 125–142.

392 Water and food resources are examples of renewable resources that have been at the heart of tensions and wars.

393 From the perspective of the peripheries, economic modernization has sometimes been perceived as an imposition of one developmental model or another by the current hegemons.

PART 4

1 Plato, Timaeus and Critias, trans. Desmond Lee, revised trans. T. K. Johansen (Oxford: Penguin Classics, 2008).

2 Tennessee Williams, Orpheus Descending (New York: Dramatists Play Service, 1959).

3 For example, discoveries of oil deposits in North Dakota have turned it into a major oil producer, second only to Texas among U.S. states. See "Formation Pressures," the Economist, March 16, 2013, 39, http://www.economist.com/news/united-states/21573569 -booming-north-dakota-numbers-formation-pressures.

4 Some suggest that these newly discovered fossil-based energy sources can be considered as "alternatives" to alternative energy. See Wesley Clark, "Bringing It All Back Home,"

Washington Monthly, November/December 2010, accessed November 2, 2013, http://www.washingtonmonthly.com/features/2010/1011.clark.html.

5   The cost assessments embrace the capital cost of the technologies themselves, the transmission of energy they produce, and the cost for adapting infrastructure as well as the actual marginal cost of production. On cost issues facing renewables, see, for example, Katherine Derbyshire, "Public Policy for Engineers: Solar Industry Depends on Policymakers' Goodwill," *Solid State Technology* 51, no. 8 (August 2008): 24; "3.03 Electricity Sector-Renewable Energy Initiatives," in Annual Report of the Office of the Auditor General of Ontario, 2011, http://www.auditor.on.ca/en/content/annualreports/arreports/en11/303en11.pdf; A. Rauch and M. Thöne, *Biofuels—At What Cost? Mandating Ethanol and Biodiesel Consumption in Germany* (Geneva, Switzerland: Global Subsidies Initiative of the International Institute for Sustainable Development, 2011), accessed December 2, 2012, http://www.iisd.org/gsi/biofuel-subsidies-germany.

6   Shale gas—natural gas found in shale formations—is an unconventional resource that many hope will help resolve energy security challenges, despite certain drawbacks that stymie its exploitation, deployment, and use. It has gained a foothold in the energy mix of countries, including the U.S. and Canada, which have extensive shale reserves. Shale gas is set to change the energy dependency picture, turning a number of net consumers like the U.S. into potential energy exporters, and, in effect, providing them with added power projection capabilities and geopolitical leverage. See Alexander Mirtchev, "Our Best New Foreign Policy Tool: Energy," RealClearEnergy, November 27, 2013, accessed December 11, 2013, http://www.realclearenergy.org/articles/2013/11/27/our_best_new_foreign_policy_tool_energy_107372.html. Oil shale, also known as coal shale, is not to be confused with shale, or tight, oil, which employs many of the same techniques used to extract shale gas (Oil shale is a solid, rather than a liquid. Its extraction requires mining and processing into liquid or retorting). An estimated 1.1 trillion barrels of recoverable shale oil are located in the Green River Formation in the western U.S., covering parts of Colorado, Utah, and Wyoming. Although extracting it is more costly than liquefied petroleum, it is a viable option with prices hovering around US$50 per barrel in 2017. See James T. Bartis et al., Oil Shale Development in the United States: Prospects and Policy Issues (Rand Corporation, 2005); John Kemp, "U.S. Shale Breakeven Price Revealed around US$50," Reuters, August 9, 2017, https://www.reuters.com/article/us-usa-shale-kemp/u-s-shale-breakeven-price-revealed-around-50-kemp-idUSKBN1AP25M.

Tar sands (also known as oil sands) are another fossil-based source of energy. Tar sands comprise quartz, clay, water, trace minerals, a relatively small percentage of bitumen, and oil with high sulfur content. Bitumen itself contains a range of complex organics that can be processed into oil. Although expensive to extract, there are large reserves of tar sands that could meet world demand for energy for a number of years. The estimates of tar/oil sands point to possible reserves of 3 to 4 trillion barrels of oil equivalent worldwide, with almost half concentrated in the Alberta Sands in Canada, and the second-largest deposit located in Venezuela. See Advanced Resources International, Inc., "EIA/ARI World Shale Gas and Shale Oil Resource Assessment," June 2013, accessed January 2, 2014, http://www.adv-res.com/pdf/A_EIA_ARI_2013%20World%20Shale%20Gas%20and%20Shale%20Oil%20Resource%20Assessment.pdf.

7   Giuseppe Recchi, "Eni's Recchi Says China's Priority Is Securing Energy for Growth," *Bloomberg*, June 6, 2013, http://www.bloomberg.com/news/2013-06-06/eni-s-recchi-says-china-s-priority-is-securing-energy-for-growth.html.

8   William Shakespeare, *The Tempest*, Act II, Scene 1 (London: Macmillan, 1915).

9   Klaus Schwab, "The Fourth Industrial Revolution. What It Means and How to Respond," Foreign Affairs, December 12, 2015, https://www.foreignaffairs.com/articles/2015-12-12/fourth-industrial-revolution.

10   T. Nagasawa et al., Accelerating Clean Energy through Industry 4.0: Manufacturing the Next Revolution (Vienna, Austria: United Nations Industrial Development Organization, 2017), https://www.unido.org/sites/default/files/2017-08/REPORT_Accelerating_clean_ energy_through_Industry_4.0.Final_0.pdf.

11   U.S. Department of Energy's Office of Energy Efficiency and Renewable Energy (EERE) website, accessed June 16, 2018, https://www.energy.gov/eere/wind/videos/transforming -wind-turbine-blade-mold-manufacturing-3d-printing.

12   Ideology as a notion has evolved beyond the traditional meaning of a stable and coherent belief system within the mind of an individual to encompass an organized and behavior-changing set of broader ideas. While subject to a range of definitions, overall it may be useful to consider it as "an interrelated set of moral and political attitudes that possesses cognitive, affective, and motivational components." See K. L. Tedin, "Political Ideology and the Vote," Research in Micropolitics 2 (1987): 63–94. The major ideologies of the 20th century that remain prevalent and influential in the 21st century are those of liberal democratic consumer-oriented individualism and Marxist-Leninist offshoots or nationalist ideologies. See E.A. Shils, "The Concept of Ideology," in International Encyclopaedia of the Social Sciences, ed. D. Sills (New York: Macmillan and Free Press, 1968), 66–75; P. E. Converse, "The Nature of Belief Systems in Mass Publics," in Ideology and Its Discontents, ed. D. E. Apter (New York: Free Press, 1964), 206–261; See John Gerring, "Ideology: A Definitional Analysis," Political Research Quarterly 50 (December 1997): 957–941.

13   Darin Barney, Prometheus Wired (Chicago: University of Chicago Press, 2000), 28.

14   "Incorporating colour, light and art with solar energy inspires us to think about our future in a new context." Artist Sarah Hall, www.sarahhallstudio.com.

15   Amelia Amon, "Aesthetics: Ignore at Our Peril," address delivered to the American Solar Energy Society, June 2003, Alt Technica, accessed December 5, 2013, http:// www.alt-technica.com/Aesthetics_Ignore_at_Peril.pdf.

16   Artistic representations and images have their own materiality, beyond representing or symbolizing some aspect of Baudrillard's "wider reality." In the case of renewables, this reality is one of technological aesthetics that is not just a product of societal visions, but is actually molding society's subconscious. The imagery of the megatrend projects a meaning that provides a "real world' setting for the meeting of technology and art, becoming an assemblage of signs that are part of the observer's surroundings and pointing him to the meaning of techno-aesthetics. For more discussion, see Jean Baudrillard, Simulacra & Simulation: The Precession of Simulacra, trans. Sheila Faria Glaser (Michigan: University of Michigan Press, 1994), 124.

17   Whether or not there is an objective basis for aesthetic judgment, one can observe that beauty is seen "through filters shaped by our values and beliefs." David Suzuki, "The Beauty of Windfarms," New Scientist, April 16, 2005.

18   Guy Debord, The Society of the Spectacle (Detroit: Black & Red translation, 1977), http:// www.marxists.org/reference/archive/debord/society.htm.

19   The notion of technological optimism endows technological advancements with intrinsic "goodness"—it assumes that these advancements are morally good and advantageous for the human condition. Critics of this notion equate it with techno-utopianism and scientism—an inordinate reliance on technology and science to the detriment of other human capabilities and qualities. See Max More and Natasha Vita-More, The Transhumanist Reader: Classical and Contemporary Essays on the Science, Technology, and Philosophy of the Human Future (New Jersey: John Wiley & Sons, 2013); See Walter Bodmer The Public Understanding of Science (London: Royal Society, 1985); also see Paul Slovic, "Perception of Risk," Science 236, no. 4749 (1987): 280–285.

20 The social construction of reality and actor-network theory underlines the major reason behind the complexity of the modern world system. Irrespective of the weight of the opinion of each member and group within society, the coalescence of their views into a single concept determines how geopolitical agents—states, organizations, corporations, groups, societies, and individuals—act with respect to reality. The approved actions are the result of a consensus formed on the basis of socio-political negotiations that are dictated by the established notion of what is real and what is appropriate. On actor-network as the theory that considers that societal approaches and technologies together play a constructive role in determining development, see Bruno Latour, *We Have Never Been Modern*, trans. C. Porter (Cambridge: Harvard University Press, 1993).

21 As shown in recent literature, the levels of concern regarding global warming and in some cases policy preferences for addressing the problem are affected by direct individual experiences with extreme weather events and abnormal seasonal temperature on top of the partisan affiliation, ideological beliefs, educational attainment, and other individual-level characteristics. See: Christopher P. Borick and Barry G. Rabe, "Personal Experience, Extreme Weather Events, and Perceptions of Climate Change," *Oxford Research Encyclopedia of Climate Science*, March 29, 2017, https://doi.org/10.1093/acrefore/9780190228620.013.311.

22 On the linear innovation model, see D. C. Mowery, "Economic Theory and Government Technology Policy," *Policy Sciences* 16 (1983): 27–43 and Benoît Godin, *The Linear Model of Innovation: The Historical Construction of an Analytical Framework*, Working Paper No. 30 (Canadian Science and Innovations Consortium, Project on the History and Sociology of S&T Statistics, 2005), http://www.csiic.ca/PDF/Godin_30.pdf.

23 Technologically, a radical innovation is one that creates completely new functional properties, while a secondary innovation makes major improvements in existing functionality of a technology that is already applied in practice—to an extent, the difference between the invention of the steam engine and of the miniaturization of semi-conductors. See also Frederick Betz, *Strategic Technology Management* (New York: McGraw-Hill, 1993); Melissa Schilling, *Strategic Management of Technological Innovation* (New York: McGraw-Hill, 2005), 38–39.

24 Most innovations start off slowly and their diffusion then speeds up with their increased adoptions, ultimately leveling off. Innovations have different rates of adoption by different social groups, determined by social customs, previous practices, interests, needs, and innovativeness. See E. M. Rogers, *Diffusion of Innovations* (New York: Free Press, 2003).

25 Legacy impediments to innovation and established practices did not stop Google from becoming a global force from its beginning as a small search engine only ten or so years ago.

26 Arthur C. Clarke, "Spectral Lines: Bringing You the Magic," *IEEE Spectrum* 41, no. 11 (2004): 14.

27 An escape from the confines of the current linear development model might prove similar to what Francis Bacon described as the evolutionary nature of invention: "As at the birth of living creatures, at first are ill-shapen, so are all innovations, which are the birth of time. Yet, notwithstanding, as those that first bring honor into their family are commonly more worthy than most that succeed, so the first precedent (if it be good) is seldom attained by imitations." See Francis Bacon, "On Innovation," in *The Essays* (Harmondsworth: Penguin Books, 1985).

28 Moore's law refers to the prediction by Gordon Moore (cofounder of the Intel Corporation) that as more transistors are built on the surface of silicon chips, the devices' performance doubles every year. The law was later modified to state that performance doubles every two years. Chip performance, according to the current estimates, doubles

every 18 months. See "The Law and the Profits," *Technology Quarterly—The Economist*, March 9, 2013, accessed December 2, 2013, http://www.economist.com/news/technology-quarterly/21572919-technology-forecasting-new-step-and-wait-model-claims-outperform-industry.

29 Disruptive technologies are new technologies that replace established and dominant technologies, often unexpectedly (e.g., sailing ships were displaced by steam and diesel ships; cars and trains removed most animal-drawn transportation worldwide). On disruptive technologies, see Joseph Bower and Clayton Christensen, *Disruptive Technologies: Catching the Wave* (Cambridge, MA: Harvard Business Publishing, 1995).

30 Robert K. Merton, "The Unanticipated Consequences of Purposive Social Action," *American Sociological Review* 1, no. 6, (December 1936): 894–904.

31 Henri Poincare, *Calcul des Probabilites* (Paris: Gauthier-Villars, 1912), 2.

32 Christopher Riley, "Apollo 40 Years On: How the Moon Missions Changed the World for Ever," *Guardian*, December 16, 2012, http://www.theguardian.com/science/2012/dec/16/apollo-legacy-moon-space-riley.

33 Stephen Hadley quoted in Kempe, Frederick, *Op-Ed: The U.S.-China Clash Has Entered Perilous New Territory*. CNBC, July 26, 2020.

34 President Carter, for example, expressed the energy security concerns of successive U.S. administrations and their preoccupation with the oil-rich Middle East this way: "Let our position be absolutely clear: Any attempt by any outside force to gain control of the Persian Gulf region will be regarded as an assault on the vital interests of the United States. It will be repelled by the use of any means necessary, including military force." Dubbed the Carter Doctrine, this reasoning deeply influences U.S. strategic thinking to this day. See President Jimmy Carter, State of the Union Address by President Jimmy Carter, January 23, 1980, accessed December 21, 2013, http://millercenter.org/president/speeches/detail/3404.

35 37% of U.S. primary energy consumption is currently petroleum-derived and 27% comes from natural gas. See U.S. Energy Information Administration, Annual Energy Outlook 2017 with Projections to 2050 (EIA, April 2017), https://www.eia.gov/outlooks/aeo/pdf/0383(2017).pdf.

36 On technology waves, see for example Robert D. Atkinson, *The Past and Future of America's Economy: Long Waves of Innovation That Power Cycles of Growth* (Cheltenham: Edward Elgar, 2004).

37 Gary Litman, Vice President for Global Initiatives at the U.S. Chamber of Commerce quoted in Luiza Ch. Savage, *How Russia and China are Preparing to Exploit a Warming Planet*. Politico, August 29, 2019.

38 See Galen L. Barbose, U.S. Renewables Portfolio Standards: 2017 Annual Status Report, LBNL-2001031, Berkeley Lab (Electricity Markets and Policy Group, July 2017), https://emp.lbl.gov/sites/default/files/2017-annual-rps-summary-report.pdf.

39 Todd Olinsky-Paul, "States Support Clean Energy for Low-Income Residents," Renewable Energy World, February 29, 2016, https://www.renewableenergyworld.com/ugc/articles/2016/02/states-support-clean-energy-for-lowincome-residents.html.

40 Benjamin Storrow, "Cuomo Announces Funding for Low-Income Solar," E&E News, December 8, 2016, http://www.eenews.net/climatewire/2016/12/08/stories/1060046837; Melanie Santiago-Mosier, "A Bright Spot for Low-Income Solar in Illinois Energy Legislation," Renewable Energy World, December 5, 2016, https://www.renewableenergyworld.com/ugc/articles/2016/12/02/a-bright-spot-for-lowincome-solar-in-illinois-energy-legislation.html.

41   See Frankfurt School-UNEP Collaborating Centre/BNEF, Global Trends in Renewable Energy Investment 2017 (Bloomberg NEF, 2017), https://europa.eu/capacity4dev/unep/documents/global-trends-renewable-energy-investment-2017.

42   Ibid.

43   The debate surrounding the expansion of the Keystone Pipeline System in North America highlights some of the conflicting interests. This 3,462-km pipeline already has the capacity to transport up to 590,000 barrels per day of Canadian crude oil from Alberta to refineries in Illinois and storage and distribution centers in Oklahoma. The controversial new pipeline would deliver synthetic crude oil and diluted bitumen from Alberta, and crude oil and light crude oil produced in Montana and North Dakota to refining facilities in the Texas Gulf Coast via the Nebraska hub. Construction of a pipeline to ship these products from the refining and marketing hub of Cushing, Oklahoma, to the Gulf Coast began in 2012. But the proposed 1,897-km-long Alberta-Nebraska pipeline, dubbed Keystone XL, has been held up by opposition from environmental groups, lawsuits from refineries, and the federal government's concerns about its environmental impact.

44   Damon Wilson and John Herbst. "Ukraine at the Atlantic Council: Building a Program, Protecting American Interests." *The Atlantic Council*, October 7, 2019.

45   Overall, the U.S. 2009 stimulus bill included about US$50 billion in spending and US$20 billion in tax provisions. Specific spending projects included: US$11 billion for the electrical grid, US$2 billion for advanced battery technology, and US$5 billion for home weatherization. Grants for energy programs placed US$6.3 billion in the hands of states and towns. Some US$8.8 billion went to energy research (US$800 million for clean coal, US$1.5 billion for industrial carbon capture, US$800 million for biomass, and US$400 million for geothermal energy). On the tax side, it authorized US$1.6 billion in clean energy bonds on top of the existing US$800 million. Green energy manufacturers received a 30% investment tax credit, while another 30% credit was set aside for homeowners who sought to install energy-efficient technology like wood stoves.

46   Jena Baker McNeill, James Jay Carafano, and Jessica Zuckerman, "39 Terror Plots Foiled Since 9/11: Examining Counterterrorism's Success Stories," *Heritage Foundation*, May 20, 2011, http://www.heritage.org/research/reports/2011/05/39-terror-plots-foiled-since-911-examining-counterterrorisms-success-stories.

47   Jennifer A. Dlouhy and Michael Riley, "Russian Hackers Attacking U.S. Power Grid and Aviation, FBI Warns," Bloomberg.com, March 16, 2018, https://www.bloomberg.com/news/articles/2018-03-15/russian-hackers-attacking-u-s-power-grid-aviation-fbi-warns.

48   See REN21, *Renewables 2017 Global Status Report.*

49   National Energy Board, *Canada's Adoption of Renewable Power Sources—Energy Market Analysis May 2017* (NEB, 2017), https://www.neb-one.gc.ca/nrg/sttstc/lctrct/rprt/2017cnddptnrnwblpwr/2017cnddptnrnwblpwr-eng.pdf.

50   See Lloyd Axworthy, "Human Security and Global Governance: Putting People First," Global Governance 7, no. 1 (2001): 19–23.

51   "Ontario Suspends Large Renewable Energy Procurement," *Ontario Newsroom*, September 27, 2016, https://news.ontario.ca/mndmf/en/2016/9/ontario-suspends-large-renewable-energy-procurement.html; "Ontario Government Cancels 758 Renewable Energy Contracts, Says It Will Save Millions," *CBC*, July 13, 2018, https://www.cbc.ca/news/canada/toronto/758-renewable-energy-cancelled-1.4746293.

52   See *Natural Resources Canada*, accessed January 29, 2018, http://www.nrcan.gc.ca/ecoaction/14145.

53   Feed-in tariff policies of provinces like Ontario, for example, have been challenged as illegal by Japan and the EU, with the WTO ruling in their favor that the local content requirement embedded within Ontario's feed-in tariff (FIT) program violates WTO rules.

See "Interim WTO Ruling Finds Canadian Renewable Energy Scheme Discriminatory," *Bridges Trade BioRes*, accessed October 15, 2012, https://www.ictsd.org/bridges-news/biores/news/source-interim-wto-ruling-finds-canadian-renewable-energy-scheme.

54 "Brazil—Renewable Energy," *Export.gov*, accessed October 8, 2017, https://www.export.gov/article?id=Brazil-Renewable-Energy.

55 REN21, *Renewables 2017 Global Status Report.*

56 See, Thomas "Mack" McLarty. "Chapter 16 Update: Latin America." Energy & Security Strategies for a World in Transition (2d edition), The Wilson Center Press, 2013.

57 REN21, *Renewables 2016: Global Status Report* (Paris: REN21 Secretariat, 2016), http://www.ren21.net/wp-content/uploads/2016/06/GSR_2016_Full_Report.pdf.

58 Frankfurt School-UNEP Collaborating Centre/BNEF, *Global Trends in Renewable Energy Investment 2016* (Bloomberg NEF, 2016), https://europa.eu/capacity4dev/public-environment-climate/document/global-trends-renewable-energy-investment-2016-back-overview-0.

59 International Renewable Energy Agency, Renewable Power Capacity Statistics (Abu Dhabi: IRENA, 2016), www.irena.org/DocumentDownloads/.../IRENA_RE_Capacity_Statistics_2015.pdf.

60 International Renewable Energy Agency, Renewable Energy Prospects: Mexico, REmap country report (Abu Dhabi: IRENA, 2015), http://www.irena.org/publications/2015/May/Renewable-Energy-Prospects-Mexico.

61 In 2016, in France, for example, renewable energy represented 9.9% of gross inland energy consumption while in Sweden more than half (53.9%) of energy consumed came from renewable sources. The average indicator for EU in 2016 was about 17%. See "Renewable Energy Statistics," Eurostat, January 2018, accessed February 2, 2018, http://ec.europa.eu/eurostat/statistics-explained/index.php/Renewable_energy_statistics.

62 Angela Merkel, speech by Chancellor of the Federal Republic of Germany and President of the European Council Angela Merkel, official ceremony marking the 50th anniversary of the signing of the Treaties of Rome, March 25, 2007, http://www.eu2007.de/en/News/Speeches_Interviews/March/0325BKBerliner.html, accessed December 4, 2013.

63 See generally, Robin Niblett. "Liberalism in Retreat: The Demise of a Dream." Foreign Affairs, Jan/February 2017.

64 See European Environment Agency, *Renewable Energy in Europe—2017 Update: Recent Growth and Knock-On Effects*, EEA Report No 23/2017 (Luxembourg: Publications Office of the European Union, 2017), https://www.eea.europa.eu/publications/renewable-energy-in-europe/#parent-fieldname-title. According to the EEA, in 2016, the EU had 422 GW renewable electricity capacity installed as a region and 0.83 kilowatt (kW) installed per person.

65 European Environment Agency, *Renewable Energy in Europe—2017 Update: Recent Growth and Knock-On Effects.*

66 In November 2016, the European Commission published a proposal for a revised Renewable Energy Directive to make the EU a global leader in renewable energy and ensure that the target of at least 27% renewables in the final energy consumption in the EU by 2030 is met.

67 Renewable Energy Statistics, Eurostat, January 2020, https://ec.europa.eu/eurostat/statistics-explained/index.php/Renewable_energy_statistics.

68 REN21, *Renewables 2016 Global Status Report* (Paris: REN21 Secretariat), http://www.ren21.net/wp-content/uploads/2016/05/GSR_2016_Full_Report_lowres.pdf.

69 Nicolas Sarkozy, remark by President of France Nicolas Sarkozy, quoted in Arnaud Leparmentier, "M. Sarkozy Veut Investir un Euro dans le Renouvelable pour un Euro dans le Nucléaire," *Le Monde*, June 10, 2009, http://www.lemonde.fr/politique/article/2009/06/09

/m-sarkozy-veut-investir-un-euro-dans-le-renouvelable-pour-chaque-euro-dans-le-nucleaire_1204830_823448.html.

70 Alexander Mirtchev, "The New EU External Energy Policy: An Important Move—If It Is Not Too Late," European Energy Review, December 8, 2011, http://www.europeanener-gyreview.eu/site/pagina.php?id=3409.

71 EU Energy Security and Solidarity Action Plan: Second Strategic Energy Review, European Commission, DG Energy and Transport, 2008.

72 See EEA, "Overall Progress towards the European Union's '20-20-20' Climate and Energy Targets," European Environment Agency, November 2017, accessed February 3, 2018, https://www.eea.europa.eu/themes/climate/trends-and-projections-in-europe/trends-and-projections-in-europe-2017/overall-progress-towards-the-european.

73 The 2007 SET Plan is designed to stimulate energy research in the EU. It brings together a patchwork of EU energy research policies on renewables, clean coal, smart grids, and nuclear energy in order to encourage cooperation, development, and competitiveness. Under the SET Plan, the energy research budget would be increased to €50 billion over the next ten years. This would require yearly flows from both the public and private sectors to jump from their current €3 billion to €8 billion.

74 The EU Emissions Trading System allows greenhouse gas emitters to count emission reductions outside the EU toward their compliance, as long as 50% of reductions occur within the country where the emitter is situated. See A. Denny Ellerman and Paul L. Joskow, "The European Union's Emissions Trading System in Perspective," report of the Pew Center on Global Climate Change (Washington, D.C.: May 2008), http://www.c2es.org/docUploads/EU-ETS-In-Perspective-Report.pdf. However, due to concern about the competitiveness of the EU, less stringent measures are being put in place—for example, non-EU airlines will not be required to pay for their CO_2 emissions. See Dave Keating, "EU Surrenders on Aviation in ETS," European Voice, last modified March 5, 2014, accessed May 19, 2014, http://www.europeanvoice.com/article/2014/march/eu-surrenders-on-avi-ation-in-ets/79909.aspx.

75 "Parliament Rubber-Stamps EU Carbon Market Reform," EURACTIV.com with Reuters, February 7, 2018, https://www.euractiv.com/section/emissions-trading-scheme/news/parliament-rubber-stamps-eu-carbon-market-reform/.

76 For example, Germany is leading a group of countries joining forces in the Desertec project, which aims to bring solar and wind electricity generated in the Sahara to Europe and could strengthen geopolitical ties between the EU and certain African countries. See www.desertec.org for more information.

77 Ministry of Energy of the Russian Federation, Draft of the Energy Strategy of the Russian Federation for the Period until 2035 (Moscow: Ministry of Energy of the Russian Federation, 2017), https://policy.asiapacificenergy.org/sites/default/files/Energy%20Strategy%20of%20the%20Russian%20Federation%20until%202035.pdf (in Russian).

78 International Renewable Energy Agency, REmap 2030 Renewable Energy Prospects for Russian Federation, Working Paper (Abu Dhabi: IRENA 2017), www_irena_org_remap http://www.irena.org/publications/2017/Apr/Renewable-Energy-Prospects-for-the-Russian-Federation-REmap-working-paper.

79 Ibid.

80 "Government Resolution No.512-r of 3 April 2013 on the State Programme for Energy Efficiency and Energy Sector Development, 2013–2020," the Russian Government, Government Decisions, April 3, 2013, http://government.ru/en/docs/1171/.

81 IFC Advisory Services in Europe and Central Asia, Russia's New Capacity-Based, Renewable Energy Support Scheme: An Analysis of Decree No. 449 (IFCl and Gef, 2013), https://www.ifc.org/wps/wcm/connect/f818b00042a762138b17af0dc33b630b/Energy-Suppor-Scheme-Eng.pdf?MOD=AJPERES.

82 Rakteem Katakey, "Crimea Crisis Pushes Russian Energy to China from Europe," *Bloomberg*, March 25, 2014, http://www.bloomberg.com/news/2014-03-25/russian-oil-seen-heading-east-not-west-in-crimea-spat.html.

83 See Angela Stent, "An Energy Superpower? Russia and Europe," in The Global Politics of Energy, ed. Kurt M. Campbell and Jonathon Price (Washington, D.C.: the Aspen Institute, 2008), 77–94.

84 Despite their steady development in the world, renewables have not yet reached the same size and production volumes as oil and gas to enable countries to leverage them as geopolitical power and influence. In fossil fuels-rich Russia, renewable energy sources lack the "power" component, which makes them unattractive for significant support from the state. See Svetlana Chernysheva, "The Development of Renewable Energy in Russia: Challenges and Constraints" (Master's thesis, Master of Science in Globalization, Global Politics, and Culture, Norwegian University of Science and Technology, 2014), 35.

85 See Armando Mombelli, "Renewable Energies: Switzerland Lagging behind in Europe," Swissinfo.ch, last modified May 17, 2017, https://www.swissinfo.ch/eng/politics/energy-strategy-2050_renewable-energies-switzerland-lagging-behind-in-europe/43187716.

86 "Renewable Energy Production in Norway," Government.no, last modified May 11, 2016, https://www.regjeringen.no/en/topics/energy/renewable-energy/renewable-energy-production-in-norway/id2343462/.

87 Republic of Serbia, Ministry of Mining and Energy, Energy Sector Development Strategy of the Republic of Serbia for the Period by 2025 with Projections by 2030 (Belgrade, 2016), www.mre.gov.rs/doc/efikasnost-izvori/23.06.02016%20ENERGY%20SECTOR%20DEVELOPMENT%20STRATEGY%20OF%20THE%20REPUBLIC%20OF%20SERBIA.pdf.

88 See International Energy Agency, Renewables 2017 (IEA, October 2017), https://www.iea.org/publications/renewables2017/.

89 China will spend an estimated US$1.54 trillion on clean energy projects in the next 15 years. Government investments in this sector come through a variety of channels, including state-owned investment vehicles and financial institutions, and financial and tax policies. See "An Overview of China's Energy Renewable Market," China Briefing, June 16, 2011, http://www.china-briefing.com/news/2011/06/16/an-overview-of-chinas-renewable-energy-market.html.

90 https://about.bnef.com/blog/decade-renewable-energy-investment-led-solar-tops-usd-2-5-trillion/. September 6, 2019.

91 See D. Cusick, "Chinese Wind Turbine Maker Is Now World's Largest," *Scientific American*, February 23, 2016, https://www.scientificamerican.com/article/chinese-wind-turbine-maker-is-now-world-s-largest/; "Vestas Reclaims Top Spot in Annual Ranking of Wind Turbine Makers," *Bloomberg New Energy Finance*, February 22, 2017, https://about.bnef.com/blog/vestas-reclaims-top-spot-annual-ranking-wind-turbine-makers/.

92 See Robert A. Manning, The Asian Energy Factor (New York: Palgrave, 2002).

93 Mark Qiu, CFO of CNOOC Ltd., quoted in Brian Bremner, "Asia's Oil Hunt," Business-Week, November 15, 2004, http://www.businessweek.com/stories/2004-11-14/asias-great-oil-hunt.

94 These include not only the government, but the Chinese sovereign wealth funds, the Chinese state oil companies, the People's Liberation Army, and various private or semi-private organizations. See Erica Downs, "The Chinese Energy Security Debate," China Quarterly 177 (March, 2004): 21–41; Kenneth Lieberthal and Mikkal Herberg, "China's Search for Energy Security: Implications for U.S. Policy," NBR Analysis 17, no. 1 (April, 2006): 11–16; Also, see Leland R. Miller, "In Search of China's Energy Authority," Far Eastern Economic Review 169, no. 1 (January–February, 2006): 39.

95 Robert Daly and Matthew Rojansky. "China's Global Dreams Give Its Neighbors Nightmares." Foreign Policy, March 12, 2018.

96 Xi Jinping, speech by the President of the People's Republic of China at the opening ceremony of the Paris Conference on Climate Change, Paris, November 30, 2015, https://unfccc.int/files/meetings/paris_nov_2015/application/pdf/cop21cmp11_leaders_event_china.pdf.

97 See Thomas Kane, *Chinese Grand Strategy and Maritime Power* (London and Portland: Frank Cass, 2002).

98 China's policies have made it a target of several trade complaints brought by other countries. China has retaliated with its own set of complaints to the WTO's dispute settlement body and through its own domestic trade remedy laws. The U.S. has concluded Antidumping (AD) and Countervailing Duty (CVD) investigations on imports of Chinese solar cells and modules as well as on wind towers (the large steel bases for wind turbines). Chinese solar cells and modules are also the subject of EU AD and CVD investigations. China has conducted AD and CVD investigations on polysilicon, a key element in the production of solar cells, from the U.S., the EU, and from South Korea. China has also challenged in the WTO the domestic content requirements of EU and EU member state feed-in tariff programs. China specifically named Greece and Italy as two European countries with offending FIT programs.

99 Ministry of New and Renewable Energy (India, 2013), http://www.mnre.gov.in/solar-mission/jnnsm/introduction-2/; accessed June 2, 2014.

100 See Frankfurt School-UNEP Collaborating Centre/BNEF, Global Trends in Sustainable Energy Investment 2011, UNEP-SEFI New Energy Finance Report (United Nations Environment Programme, 2011), accessed December 5, 2013, http://www.unep.org/pdf/BNEF_global_trends_in_renewable_energy_investment_2011_report.pdf.

101 Frankfurt School-UNEP Collaborating Centre/BNEF, *Global Trends in Renewable Energy Investment 2016*, 107.

102 Dermot Gately, "OPEC and the Buying Power Wedge," in Energy Vulnerability, ed. J. L. Plummer (Cambridge: Ballinger, 1982), 37–57.

103 For more details of the Fukushima nuclear plant accident, see "Fukushima Accident," World Nuclear Association, last modified June 2018, http://www.world-nuclear.org/info/Safety-and-Security/Safety-of-Plants/Fukushima-Accident/.

104 Before the Fukushima accident, Japan's 54 nuclear reactors provided some 30% of the country's electricity and the government's goal was to increase this share to 40% by 2017. See Information from JAIF and the World Nuclear Association. The government introduced the Basic Energy Plan in 2003, which called for using alternative energy sources and clean technologies, along with the development of hybrid cars, intelligent transport systems, and the use of plutonium in light-water reactors.

105 REN21, *Renewables 2017 Global Status Report*.

106 Japan's negligent management of the Fukushima power plant since the March 2011 accident has tarnished its image as a technological leader. In the most serious of a string of worrying developments, Fukushima's operator (TEPCO) admitted that at least 300 tons of highly radioactive water had leaked from a storage plant into the ground. TEPCO has also acknowledged that as much as 300 tons of radioactive water is seeping daily from the damaged reactor into the Pacific Ocean.

107 Japan has initiated its own oil exploration in the East China Sea, after China started drilling in an adjacent area. Requests by Japan for joint development have reportedly not been accepted by China. See Mark J. Valencia, "The East China Sea Dispute: Context, Claims, Issues, and Possible Solutions," Asian Perspective 31, no. 1 (2007): 127–167; Reuters, "Japan Protests over Chinese Radar in Disputed East China Sea

Drilling Rig," Guardian, August 7, 2016, https://www.theguardian.com/world/2016/aug/07/japan-protests-over-chinese-radar-in-disputed-east-china-sea-drilling-rig.

108 The expanded Renewable Energy Target (RET) began on January 1, 2010 to meet the aim of sourcing 45,000 gigawatt hours of electricity from renewables by 2020. In January 2011, the RET was split into the Small-Scale Renewable Energy Scheme (SRES) and the Large-Scale Renewable Energy Target (LRET). Under the amended scheme, the interim LRET targets will increase from 16,338 gigawatt hours in 2012 to 41,000 gigawatt hours between 2020–2030. Households and small businesses are anticipated to provide, and potentially exceed, the additional 4,000 megawatts required to meet the RET. Installation of small generation solar electricity units and solar water heaters have been encouraged through the Solar Credits Scheme and now form a large portion of generation under the SRES. The Clean Energy Future Plan aims to reduce Australia's carbon emissions to 5% below 2000 levels by 2020, and 80% below 2000 levels by 2050. This target is to be achieved through a carbon price (large emitters of carbon are financially liable for their emission) and a package of complementary measures. The carbon price was fixed for three years before transitioning to an emissions trading scheme. See Department of Resources, Energy and Tourism, Government of Australia, Energy White Paper 2012: Australia's Energy Transformation (Canberra, 2012), https://aip.com.au/sites/default/files/download-files/2017-09/Energy_%20White_Paper_2012-.pdf.

109 Australian Government, Australian Renewable Energy Agency, Innovating Energy: ARENA's Investment Plan (Canberra, 2017), https://arena.gov.au/assets/2017/05/AU21397_ARENA_IP_Document_FA_Single_Pages_LORES.pdf.

110 REN21, Renewables 2016 Global Status Report.

111 Ibid.

112 The region basks in an annual global solar radiation varying between 4 to 8 kWh/m. The region also enjoys high direct normal radiation and low average cloud cover. Producing electricity from both concentrating solar thermal power (CSP) and photovoltaic (PV) has strong potential due to the fact that the incident solar radiation throughout the region is higher than the required value for viable production. See REN21, Renewables Global Status Report, is. paper (Paris: REN21 Secretariat, 2007).

113 The Abu Dhabi Future Energy Company is financing a feasibility study on carbon capture, and has proven willing to engage in discussions on the future of solar energy and energy efficiency in buildings and industry. See Dennis Ross, "Arab and Gulf Perspectives on Energy," in The Global Politics of Energy, ed. Kurt M. Campbell and Jonathon Price (Washington, D.C.: Aspen Institute, 2008), 65–74.

114 See Suzanne Goldenberg, "Masdar's Zero-Carbon Dream Could Become World's First Green Ghost Town," Guardian, last modified February 16, 2016, https://www.theguardian.com/environment/2016/feb/16/masdars-zero-carbon-dream-could-become-worlds-first-green-ghost-town.

115 See A. DiPaola, "Dubai Starts Desert Solar Plant as Part of World's Biggest Park," Bloomberg Businessweek, March 20, 2017, https://www.bloomberg.com/news/articles/2017-03-20/dubai-starts-desert-solar-plant-as-part-of-world-s-biggest-park.

116 Michael Clarke. "After ISIS Threat, China May Have to Get off Sidelines in Middle East." Foreign Policy, March 3, 2017.

117 Noam Segal, "Israel: The 'Energy Island's' Transition to Energy Independence," Heinrich Böll Foundation North America, last modified June 20, 2016, https://us.boell.org/2016/06/20/israel-energy-islands-transition-energy-independence.

118 REN21, Renewables 2017 Global Status Report.

119 On the renewable energy research priorities in Israel, see: Ministry of National Infrastructure, Energy and Water Resources, Research and Development 2014–2016 (the Chief

Scientist Office, Ministry of National Infrastructure, Energy and Water Resources, www. energy.gov.il, January 2017), http://archive.energy.gov.il/English/PublicationsLibraryE/RD2014_2016.pdf.

120 Benjamin Netanyahu, address of Israel's Prime Minister Benjamin Netanyahu to the Presidential Conference, Jerusalem, October 20–22, 2009, https://www.kintera.org/site/apps/nlnet/content3.aspx?c=ewJXKcOUJllaG&b=7717007&ct=11145389, accessed December 3, 2013.

121 Fossil fuels represented about 54% of total primary energy supply in Africa in 2009. Oil, coal, and natural gas contributed respectively 22%, 16%, and 12% to the continent's total primary energy supply in 2009. In 2010, about 80% of the continent's electricity was generated from fossil fuels. Projections indicate that this share will remain high for the next three decades. Estimates by the African Development Bank and British Petroleum show that more than 122 billion barrels (BBLS) of proven oil reserves and almost 159 BBLS of potential oil reserves lie below the surface of the African continent. In terms of natural gas, the continent holds about 560 trillion barrels of cubic feet (TCF) of proven reserves and 319 TCF of potential reserves. See African Development Bank Group, African Development Report 2012: Towards Green Growth in Africa [Tunis-Belvédère, Tunisia: Temporary Relocation Agency (TRA), 2013], http://www.afdb.org/fileadmin/uploads/afdb/Documents/Publications/African%20Development%20Report%202012%20-%20Overview.pdf.

122 Ibid.

123 See UNEP, Global Trends in Sustainable Energy Investment 2009, UNEP-SEFI New Energy Finance Report (United Nations Environment Programme, New York, 2009), http://wedocs.unep.org/handle/20.500.11822/7799. Note: In March 2009, South Africa announced feed-in tariffs that guarantee a stable rate of return for renewable energy projects. In Kenya, investments in the first privately financed geothermal plant are underway and a wind farm is planned for construction near Lake Turkana. In Ethiopia, French wind turbine manufacturer Vergnet signed a contract to supply the Ethiopian Electric Power Corporation with turbines and the Brazilians are active in Angola setting up a sugar cane processing plant. Renewable energy in North Africa remains focused on Morocco, Tunisia, and Egypt, particularly in solar and wind.

124 The prospect of foreign investment to develop sub-Saharan Africa's fossil fuel resources could bring about the resolution of conflicts in some cases. Sudan and South Sudan temporarily halted the hostilities that disrupted the flow of oil from South Sudan's fields to Sudan's pipelines in 2012. China's interest and significant investments in Sudan's and South Sudan's oil sector and its diplomatic engagement may have played a role in ending the fighting. For the time being, Sudan and South Sudan have to cooperate, as the oil fields are predominantly in South Sudan but the pipelines and refining equipment are located in Sudan.

125 According to the OECD, 28 countries currently have discriminatory investment policies when it comes to the energy sector as energy is classified by most countries as "critical infrastructure." See Kathryn Gordon and Maeve Dion, Protection of "Critical Infrastructure" and the Role of Investment Policies Relating to National Security (OECD Secretariat, May 2008), http://www.oecd.org/daf/inv/investment-policy/40700392.pdf. See also, Roy Stapelton, M. Taylor Fravel, Michael D. Swaine, Susan Thornton and Ezra Vogel. "China is Not an Enemy." The Washington Post, July 3, 2019.

126 See Serge Michel and Michel Beuret, China Safari: On the Trail of Beijing's Expansion in Africa, trans. Raymond Valley (New York: Nation Books, 2010).

127 Department of Energy, Republic of South Africa, State of Renewable Energy in South Africa (South Africa, 2015). www.energy.gov.za/files/media/Pub/State-of-Renewable-Energy-in-South-Africa.pdf.

128 P. Papapetrou, Enabling Renewable Energy in South Africa: Assessing the Renewable Energy Independent Power Producer Procurement Programme [South Africa, WWF-SA—World Wide Fund for Nature (formerly World Wildlife Fund), September 2014], http://awsassets.wwf.org.za/downloads/enabling_re_in_sa.pdf.

129 Lee-Ann Steenkamp, Powering Up: A Look at Section 12B Allowance for Renewable Energy Machinery, *South African Institute of Tax Professionals*, last modified January 21, 2016, http://www.thesait.org.za/news/269950/Powering-up-A-look-at-section-12B-allowance-for-renewable-energy-machinery.htm.

130 Department of Energy, Republic of South Africa, *State of Renewable Energy in South Africa*, 2017.

131 REN21, *Renewables 2017 Global Status Report*.

132 For example, Dr. Matthew Kroenig advances the argument and demonstrates that in the competition with China, Russia, and others that, despite its predicaments, the U.S. is better positioned to sustain global leadership.

133 "Resilience is about mobilizing the potential we have, inspiring the human spirit in all of us and enabling communities to thrive through challenges." Adrienne Arsht, Kathy Baughman McLeod, Graham Brookie, *Stories of Resilience: An Introduction*. The Atlantic Council. May 27, 2020. Notably, the Adrienne Arsht–Rockefeller Foundation Resilience Center works to make "1 billion people resilient by 2030" whether by teaching children basic survival skills, working with architects to build structures that can withstand environmental catastrophes, or empowering farmers to develop agricultural solutions to global warming. Adrienne Arsht *quoted in*, Leena Kim. *How Philanthropist Adrienne Arsht Earned the Nickname "Badass."* Town & Country Magazine. March 2, 2020.

134 Among others these include the North Atlantic Treaty Organization (NATO), the EU, the Shanghai Cooperation Organization (SCO), the Collective Security Treaty Organization (CSTO), the Organization of Petroleum-Exporting Countries (OPEC), the United Nations, and the International Energy Agency (IEA).

135 For further discussion on the politicization of security measures, see Barbara Adam, Ulrich Beck, and Joost van Loon, *The Risk Society and Beyond: Critical Issues for Social Theory* (London: Sage Publications Ltd., 2000), 1.

136 John Podesta and Peter Ogden, "A Blueprint for Energy Security," in The Global Politics of Energy, eds. Kurt M. Campbell and Jonathon Price (Washington, D.C.: Aspen Institute, 2008).

137 There might be an opportunity for grand bargains, where, on the international level, "formal deals might be needed" to ensure that "uncooperative countries would begin to cooperate." See Frederick Kempe and Robert Hutchings, "The Global Grand Bargain," *Foreign Policy*, November 5, 2008, http://www.foreignpolicy.com/articles/2008/11/04/the_global_grand_bargain.

138 Science is often a process that involves societal interaction as a method of reflecting scientific and technological meaning, and tailoring it to the local. Science emerges from this process as a constructed result from exchanges between the use of materials and their valuation by society; it creates a cultural and social apparatus that distinguishes between what is imagined and what is real. See A. Clarke and V. Olesen, eds., *Revisioning Women, Health, and Healing: Feminist, Cultural and Technoscientific Perspectives* (New York: Routledge, 1999); D. MacKenzie and G. Spinardi, "Tacit Knowledge, Weapons Design, and the Uninvention of Nuclear Weapons," *American Journal of Sociology* 101, (1995): 44–99; Joan Fujimura, *Crafting Science* (Cambridge, MA: Harvard University Press, 1996); Harry Collins, "The Sociology of Scientific Knowledge: Studies of Contemporary Science," *Annual Review of Sociology* 9 (1983): 265–285; Monica Casper, *The Making of the Unborn Patient: A Social Anatomy of Fetal Surgery* (New Brunswick, NJ: Rutgers University Press, 1998).

139 Users generally innovate in order to utilize, rather than sell, a specific product or service. In the case of the alternative energy megatrend, most of the manufacturers are also "lead users" that set market trends and create needs that will create new users.

140 Jean-Jacques Rousseau, "Final Reply," in *Collected Writing of Jean-Jacques Rousseau*, vol. 1, eds. Roger D. Masters and Christopher Kelly (Hanover, NH and London: University Press of New England, 1992), 110.

141 https://www.techinasia.com/jack-ma-climate.

142 Simon Dalby, *Environmental Security* (Minneapolis, MN: University of Minnesota Press, 2002): 163–164.

143 "Energy security is as important as anything that we face, not just in the U.S. but globally. We see it played out on the world stage right now with Russia's aggressive behavior and tendency to use energy as [] a 21st century weapon." Gen. James L. Jones (USMC Ret.). D.C. Panel discussion. *Completing Europe: From the North-South Corridor to Energy, Transportation, and Telecommunications Union*. The Atlantic Council, April 9, 2015, Washington, D.C.

144 "China has recorded historic achievements, but its ascent to superpowerdom is not a given. Leaving aside the limited appeal of China's political and economic model, it faces the imperatives of transitioning from a low-cost labor provider to a value-added and services economy, reducing the world's largest debt-to-GDP ratio, cutting pollution and corruption, dealing with insufficiently competitive state-owned enterprises and addressing numerous other domestic challenges. ... [E]ven if China overtakes the United States in absolute GDP within a couple of decades, the United States may regain the top spot later in the century, especially if China's political model remains autocratic." David H. Petraeus and Michael E. O'Hanlon. "America is on the Way Up." *The Washington Post*, January 30, 2015.

145 Strobe Talbott, "Dangerous Leviathans," Brookings, last modified April 20, 2009, http://www.brookings.edu/research/opinions/2009/04/05-russia-talbott.

146 "North Korea 'Most Urgent' Threat to Security: Mattis," *Reuters*, June 13, 2017, https://www.reuters.com/article/us-usa-northkorea/north-korea-most-urgent-threat-to-security-mattis-idUSKBN194071.

147 Arnold Toynbee, *A Study of History* (Oxford: Oxford University Press, 1987), 11.

148 Wide acceptance and adoption of such metrics is imperative for the formulation and quantification of threats, as well as measurement and assessment of power, capabilities, and resources to address them. Quantification starts with securitization actors' determination of beneficial outcomes, with factors that endanger such outcomes designated as threats.

149 James R. Clapper, Lt. Gen., USAF (Ret.), "Unclassified Statement for the Record on the Worldwide Threat Assessment of the US Intelligence Community for the Senate Select Committee on Intelligence," January 31, 2012, 1, accessed November 11, 2012, http://www.fas.org/irp/congress/2012_hr/013112clapper.pdf.

150 See A. J. P. Taylor, *The Origins of the Second World War* (Harmondsworth: Penguin, 1964).

151 For example, the urgency of the global economic and financial crisis prompted governments to undertake bailouts of specific corporate entities, despite the long-term necessity of reducing the burden on government budgets and not creating precedents of providing a safety net to threatened businesses that were able to demonstrate that they were "too big to fail." See Gary H. Stern and Ron J. Feldman, *Too Big to Fail: The Hazards of Bank Bailouts*, with a foreword by Paul Volcker (Washington, D.C.: Brookings Institution Press, 2009).

152 For example, the United States needs to "work with China and try and get it to embrace positive, global standards. Where they do, for example, infrastructure, if they adopt global standards, build infrastructure that is fiscally, environmentally sustainable that benefits the countries in which it's built, let them have at it. We should support them. We

should cooperate with them. I think that's the kind of analysis we have to get through. Put ourselves in a position to compete, figure out those areas of priority where we have to succeed, figure out terms by which we can cooperate with China and other areas. Because we have to recognize that a lot of the problems the world faces, whether it's environmental, management technology, whether it's proliferation, whether it's financial stability, an awful lot of problems cannot be solved if the United States and China, with the rest of the world, do not cooperate together." Stephen Hadley. Podcast. *Tom Donilon and Stephen Hadley talk with Michael Morell on "Intelligence Matters."* CBS News, January 29, 2020.

153 This framework may be built based on the principles close to those described by Elinor Ostrom for local common pool resources management. See Elinor Ostrom, *Governing the Commons: The Evolution of Institutions for Collective Action* (Cambridge, UK: Cambridge University Press, 1990).

AUTHOR'S NOTE

1 A. Belward et al., ed. F. Monforti, *Renewable Energies in Africa*, JRC Scientific and Technical Reports (European Commission, Brussels, 2011), http://publications.jrc.ec.europa.eu/repository/bitstream/111111111/23076/1/reqno_jrc67752_final%20report%20.pdf.

EPILOGUE

1 Johann Wolfgang von Goethe, *Faust* (Leipzig: Brockhaus, 1881), 17.

2 The Arcanum, also known as the Grand Arcanum, represented the formula that allowed transmuting the base matter into the perfect spiritual essences: the arcana. In its most well-known form, it involved the search for the Philosopher's Stone that could change base metals into gold. Historically, though, the Arcanum incorporated a broad spectrum of fields across centuries of research and the harvesting of knowledge that provided some of the foundations for modern science. See Paracelsus, *The Hermetic and Alchemical Writings of Paracelsus*, trans. Arthur Waite (London, 1894, republished Hong Kong: Forgotten Books, 2007); Carl G. Jung, *Psychology and Alchemy: The Collected Works of C.G. Jung*, vol. 12, eds. Sir Herbert Read et al. (New York: Princeton University Press, 1953); Jean D'Espagnet, *The Hermetic Arcanum* (Whitefish, MT: Kessinger Publishing, 2003).

3 The megatrend, as a new Arcanum, can "be compared to the husbandman whereof Aesop makes the fable; that, when he died, told his sons, that he had left unto them gold buried under ground in his vineyard; and they digged over all the ground, and gold they found none; but by reason of their stirring and digging the mould about the roots of their vines, they had a great vintage the year following: so assuredly the search and stir to make gold hath brought to light a great number of good and fruitful inventions and experiments, as well for the disclosing of nature, as for the use of man's life." Francis Bacon, "Of the Advancement of Learning" in *The Works of Francis Bacon* (London: H. Bryer, 1803), 34.

4 See Lucan (Marcus Annaeus Lucanus), "Bellum Civile," in Bryn Mawr Latin Commentaries, ed. David P. Kubiak (Bryn Mawr, PA: Bryn Mawr College, 1985), ii, 14.

5 "Fire, air, water, earth, we assert, come-to-be from one another, and each of them exists potentially in each, as all things do that can be resolved into a common and ultimate substrate." Aristotle, "Meteorology," in *The Complete Works of Aristotle*, trans. E. W. Webster, ed. Jonathan Barnes, vol. 1, book 1 (Princeton, NJ: Princeton University Press, 1984), 556.

6 Carl G. Jung, *Psychology and Alchemy: The Collected Works of C.G. Jung*, vol. 12, eds. Sir Herbert Read et al. (New York: Princeton University Press, 1953): 277–279.

7 Jean D'Espagnet, *The Hermetic Arcanum* (Whitefish, MT: Kessinger Publishing, 2003), 4.

8 Giordano Bruno, *The Expulsion of the Triumphant Beast*, ed. and trans. Arthur D. Imerti (New Brunswick, NJ: University of Nebraska Press, 1964), 205.

9   Mary Anne Atwood, "The Golden Treatise of Hermes Trismegistus," in *Hermetic Philosophy and Alchemy: A Suggestive Inquiry into the Hermetic Mystery* (Abingdon, Oxford: Routledge, 2010), 113.

10 See discussion on approaches, Robert Nozick, *The Nature of Rationality* (Princeton, NJ: Princeton University Press, 1993).

11 Michel-Rolph Trouillot, *Silencing the Past: Power and the Production of History* (Boston: Beacon Press, 2012), 4.

12 See Karl R. Popper, *The Poverty of Historicism* (New York: Harper and Row, 1964), vi-viii.

13 Georg Wilhelm Friedrich Hegel, *Early Theological Writings*, trans. T.M. Knox (Chicago: University of Chicago Press, 1948), 193.

14 Cicero, *Academia* (London: McMillan, 1874), i.13.

INDEX

5

5G 42, 90

A

Adam, Barbara 366

additive manufacturing 123, 239, 330

Adler, Emanuel 308

administrative arbitrage 215-216

aesthetics 238, 241, 356

Afghanistan 124, 129, 331-332

Agnew, John 315

Agreement on Trade-Related Aspects
of Intellectual Property Rights
(TRIPS) 348

Albert, Prince of Monaco 344

Alley, Kristal xxii, 353

alliances of peace 171

alternative energy investment 14, 58,
70, 93-94, 127, 145, 162, 203-214,
247-248, 252, 254, 258, 261, 263,
269, 350, 359, 362, 365

alternative energy market 71, 136, 185,
197, 204-205, 208-211, 215, 252,
275

alternative energy mega-market 275

alternative energy vulnerabilities 29,
73, 86, 90, 92, 94, 119, 148-149,
177, 211, 287-288

Alvarez, José E. 310

American Recovery and Reinvestment
Act (ARRA) 138, 342

Amon, Amelia 356

anti-American 96, 100-101

anti-capitalist 56

anti-Western 56, 96, 100-101, 266

Apollo Project 208, 245

Apuleius xxiii, 299

Aquinas, Thomas 194, 348

Aradau, Claudia 326

Arcanum 292-298, 368

Archimedes 22, 35, 40, 308

Arctic Roadmap 139

Aristotle 31, 214, 311, 352, 368

armored vehicles 26, 130

Army Energy Security Implementation Strategy (AESIS) 329

Arnold, Roger A. 313

ARPANET (Advanced Research Projects Agency Network) 316-317, 333

Arsht, Adrienne 73, 319, 366

Arthur, W. Brian 349

artificial intelligence (AI) xviii, xxi,
xxvi, 23, 25, 42-43, 84, 90, 196,
238, 287, 308

Asimov, Isaac 341

Askari, Alex 332

Association of Southeast Asian
Nations (ASEAN) 165

Astrid, Princess of Belgium 344

asymmetrical warfare 124

Atkinson, Robert D. 358

Atmospheric Vortex Engines 18

attributes (of the alternative energy
    megatrend) xxi, xxv, 8, 10, 159,
    234, 298
audiences 3-7, 32, 44, 76, 78, 182, 187,
    285, 290, 302-303
Austin, John 301
Autonomous Learning Agents
    for Decentralised Data and
    Information Networks
    (ALADDIN) 330
Axelrod, Robert 353
Axworthy, Lloyd 359
Ayoob, Mohammed 300

B

Bacon, Francis 357, 368
Bailey, Sheila 312
Baldwin, David 300
Barber, Lionel xxii, 43, 314
Barnett, Jon 183, 346
Barney, Darin 356
Barrett, Scott 313
Bartis, James T. 355
Barton, Barry 321
Baudrillard, Jean 241, 356
Beach, Timothy P. 354
Beaverstock, Jonathan V. 313
Beck, Ulrich 303, 366
Belward, Alan 368
Berger, Peter L. 300, 310
Bertalanffy, Ludwig von 307
Betz, Frederick 357
Beuret, Michel 365
Bezos, Jeff 72, 319
Biello, David 312
Biersteker, Thomas J. 353
Bijker, Wiebe 309
bioethanol trade dispute 15
biofuels 12, 14-15, 29, 45, 67-68, 77,
    95, 98, 139, 176, 179, 189, 197, 203,
    214, 246, 251, 253, 268, 305, 334,
    346, 350, 355

biomass 10, 14, 37, 67, 133, 179, 205,
    250-251, 255, 305, 312, 329, 333,
    336, 345-346, 350, 359
bipolar 4, 40, 48, 55, 57, 105, 174, 277,
    316
Blanken, Leo J. 301
Blume, Stuart 311
Bodmer, Walter 356
Boies, Mary 327
Booth, Ken 302
bottom-up pressures 60-62, 78, 84
Bower, Joseph 358
Boyd, William 320
Boyer, Yves 331
Brecht, Bertolt 314
BRICS (Brazil, Russia, India, China,
    South Africa) 48, 75, 270
broader security 3, 5, 117, 124, 143, 149,
    156-157, 269, 272-273
Brookie, Graham 319, 366
Brooks, Stephen G. 299, 315
Brown, Janet 343
Brown, Matthew H. 321
Bruce Hall, Rodney 353
Bruno, Giordano 368
Brzezinski, Ian 336, 345
Brzezinski, Zbigniew 78, 349
Buffett, Warren 302
Bull, Hedley 304
Bunnell, David 325
Burgess, J. Peter 299, 346
Butterfield, H. 304
Buzan, Barry 301

C

Caldwell, Dan 347
Campbell, David 326, 362, 364, 366
Campbell, Kurt 362, 264, 366
Canton, James 307
Carafano, James Jay 359
Carbon Pricing Mechanism (CPM)
    264

Carr, Edward H. 301
Carter administration 39, 312
Carter, Jimmy 358
Casper, Monica 366
Castree, Noel 169, 344
Cerny, Philip 303
Chalmers, Malcom 319
Chammah, Albert 319
Charles, Prince of Wales 344
chlorofluorocarbon (CFC) gases 181
Christensen, Clayton 358
Churchill, Winston 123, 331
Cicero 369
cinematic projection 241
Clapper, James R. 367
Clark, Wesley 354-355
Clarke, Adele 366
Clarke, Arthur C. 16, 44, 357
Clarke, I. F. "Knobbie" 327
Clarke, Michael 364
Clausewitz, Carl von 186
Clean Energy Futures Package (CEF) 264
Climate Change Working Group 173
climate change 6, 11, 22, 28-29, 60, 72, 75, 77-78, 81, 90, 137, 139, 142, 146-147, 154, 156-158, 161-162, 164, 166, 170, 173, 177, 180-181, 184, 195, 200, 215, 230, 240, 247, 251-252, 260-262, 280, 296, 302, 307-308, 310, 316, 319-320, 322, 327, 332, 337, 340-341, 344-345, 350, 357, 361, 363
Climate Investment Funds 205, 350
Clinton, William 190, 346-347, 354
Codner, Michael 319
Cohen, Ariel 335
Cohen, William 323
Collective Security Treaty Organization (CSTO) 366
Collins, Harry 366
command and control 123, 133

Comprehensive Test Ban Treaty 148
Comte, Auguste 25, 309
Conca, Ken 344
Concentrating Solar Thermal Power (CSP) 13-14, 265, 304, 322, 364
convergence of drivers 19
Converse, Philip E. 311, 314, 356
convoy protection 130
Conway, James 332
Cooper, Jerrold S. 242, 264, 345
Copenhagen Climate Summit 173, 344
Copenhagen School 301-302
Cordesman, Anthony H. 322
Core 3, 5, 48-54, 60, 82, 84, 89, 120, 131, 148-149, 163, 195, 197, 271, 276, 280-281, 286, 300-301, 315
core-periphery 48, 50-53, 315
corporate social responsibility 208
Cortright, David 353
Council for Mutual Economic Assistance (COMECON) 53
Cox, Kevin R. 300
Cox, Robert 301, 353
Crawford, Beverly 300, 308
Criekemans, David 318
Crouch, Colin 317
Cruikshank, Jeffrey L. 331
Currie, Gregory 312
Curtin, Sandra 306
Cyber-attacks 95
cyber vulnerabilities 95

D

Daalder, Ivo H. 331
Dabelko, Geoffrey D. 344
Dalby, Simon 367
Daly, Robert 363
Dannreuther, Roland 340
Danzig, Richard 329
de Blij, Harm 315
de Sousa Santos, Boaventura 315
Debord, Guy 356

Defence Technology Plan (DTP) 337
Defense Advanced Research Projects
    Agency (DARPA) 136, 334
defense sector 25-26, 38, 117-120,
    123-125, 127-128, 132, 134, 136-138,
    145-148, 152, 236
defense transformation 116-117, 119-
    121, 123-124, 126-127, 131-132, 144,
    150, 228, 290
deforestation 15, 29, 157, 170, 235, 354
delayed arrival of the future 43
Deming, David 307
demise (of the alternative energy
    megatrend) 234-237
Demosthenes 302
Derbyshire, Katherine 355
Derrida, Jacques 354
desecuritization 7, 303
deterrence 102, 104-107, 228, 326
Deudney, Daniel 340
Diamond, Jared 63, 311, 339
Diaoyu/Senkaku islands 263
Dicken, Peter 353
Diesel, Rudolf 14-15, 38, 305, 312, 336,
    339, 346, 358
Dillon, Michael 308
Dion, Maeve 365
Dipaola, Anthony 320, 364
DiPardo, Joseph 312
DiPippo, Ronald 305
direct capital investment subsidies
    203
directed energy weapons 123, 146
disequilibrium xx, 9, 47, 83, 221, 225
Disraeli, Benjamin 323
Disruptive technologies 42, 122-123,
    244, 358
Dittmer, Jason 346
diversification (of energy sources) 15,
    20, 77, 91, 138, 202, 251, 260, 270
Dobriansky, Paula 313
Dolin, Eric Jay 311

Domar, Evsey 201, 349
Donilon, Tom 309, 368
doomsday scenarios 21, 288
Doppler shifts 338
Dowdy, John 331
Downs, Anthony 311, 314
Downs, Erica 362
Doyle, Aaron 309
Drivers (of the alternative energy
    megatrend) xxi, xxv, 1, 8-10, 19-20,
    23, 29-31, 44, 46-47, 55, 65, 72, 91,
    100, 102, 107, 118, 136, 144, 159,
    161, 196, 223, 234-235, 238, 240,
    271, 281, 288-289, 298, 313
Dual-use technology 115-116, 319
Dunning, Nicholas P. 354
Durlauf, Steven N. 311
Dyer, Hugh 339
Dynamic prioritization xviii, xxiv, 282
Dyson, Freeman 19, 307

E
Earth's magnetic field 10, 16, 18
East-West (rivalries, divides, cleavages)
    54-56, 66, 84, 316
Ebel, Robert 326
economic diversification 23, 229
economic growth xxi, xxvi, 19, 22-23,
    46, 78, 89, 104, 127, 144, 155, 158,
    168, 171, 180, 185-190, 192-194,
    196-202, 206, 213, 226-227, 229,
    234, 240, 246, 252, 254, 257-260,
    263, 272, 295, 300, 307-308, 333,
    346-347, 349, 354
economic leverage 191, 223
economic manipulation 185, 189-190,
    231
economic power 23, 53, 74, 99, 103-
    104, 106-108, 186-187, 190-191,
    194-195, 220, 223, 327
economic relations 51, 90, 92, 197,
    201, 221, 223, 226-227

economic rivalries 190, 227

economic security xxi, xxvi, 22, 27, 43, 69, 86, 185-197, 202, 208, 211, 218-227, 229, 231, 236, 245, 248-249, 260, 274-275, 280, 287, 289-290, 299-300, 302, 354

economic statecraft 185, 187, 194, 220, 223, 225-226, 232

economies of scale 38, 198

Edison, Thomas 13, 304

effect leakage 216, 352

effectiveness vs. efficiency 119, 125, 229

Eikeland, Olav 300, 310

Eisenhower, Dwight 318

Eizenstat, Stuart E. 343

El Niño 154, 251

electrodynamic tethers 18

electromagnetic signature 148

Ellerman, A. Denny 361

Ellul, Jacques 39, 312

Elshtain, Jean Bethke 321

Emerson, Ralph Waldo 345

Energetically Autonomous Tactical Robot (EATR) 333

Energy Charter Treaty 204

energy costs 146, 152, 198, 228

energy demand 14, 19-21, 40, 46, 66, 91-92, 112, 138, 159, 260, 262

energy density 112, 236

energy dependencies 74, 108

energy imperialism 87, 96-98

energy independence 11, 20, 27, 77-78, 88, 100, 102, 107, 138, 164, 213, 227, 234, 240, 248, 259, 270, 322, 332, 334, 364

energy infrastructure 82, 94-95, 108, 131, 141-142, 149, 188, 229, 249, 268, 274, 323, 326, 335

energy interdependence 20, 88

energy manipulation 21

energy price volatility 129, 190

energy rebalancing xxi, xxvi, 80, 170, 195, 274

energy resources 58, 63-65, 88, 96-98, 104, 107, 117, 119, 127, 129, 149, 165, 167, 200, 229, 260, 262, 266, 268, 293, 304, 306, 318, 329

energy security xvii-xviii, xxi, xxv, 3, 15-16, 20-21, 27, 43, 59-60, 66, 73, 75, 77, 86-90, 92, 95-96, 101-102, 105, 108-109, 111-112, 115, 119, 126-127, 135-136, 138-142, 145-147, 150-151, 156, 170, 210, 221, 227-228, 235, 246, 249, 251-253, 255, 258-265, 267, 269-270, 272, 274, 284, 287, 290, 308, 321-322, 324, 326-329, 335-337, 344, 355, 358, 361-362, 366-367

energy shocks 20

energy storage 17, 24, 42, 90, 93-94, 143, 146, 148, 239, 323, 337

energy supply 39-40, 45, 88, 93, 127-128, 138, 141-142, 193, 197, 208, 231, 246, 264, 320, 326, 365

energy trade conflicts 204

Enlightenment 10, 34-36, 40, 201, 294-295, 311

environmental policies 153, 158, 160-162, 176

environmental refugees 157

environmental security xviii, xx-xxi, xxv-xxvi, 22, 27, 69, 78, 117, 119, 135, 138, 141-143, 152-161, 163-172, 174, 176-177, 180-184, 213, 229-230, 234, 246, 252, 254-255, 261, 290, 299-300, 310, 319, 339, 341, 343, 346, 367

environmental threats 11, 22, 28, 61, 81, 119, 139, 153-156, 158, 160-161, 164-166, 168-169, 171, 180-182, 184-185, 230-231, 300, 308, 351

Ericson, Richard V. 309

Esty, Daniel C. 343

Ethics 28-29, 309, 326, 341, 348

European Defense Agency (EDA) 337

European Environment Agency 162, 165, 179, 342, 360-361

European Fusion Development Agreement 18, 306

Evans, Richard J. xxii, 317

expeditionary operations 130

externalities 15, 92, 126, 162-163, 169, 193, 207, 211, 213-215, 219, 231-232, 237, 244, 280

Eyal, Jonathan 319

F

Faber, Daniel 316

Fairgrieve, James 329

fall of civilizations 230

Faraday, Michael 212, 351

feed-in tariffs (FITs) xviii, 160, 203–204, 206, 254, 263, 309, 342, 365

Feldman, Ron J. 367

Ferguson, Niall 348

Finger, Matthias 339-340

Firestone, Harvey 13, 304

First World 57-58

fiscal incentives 202, 208, 251

Fisher, David 348

fixed installations 128

Flaherty, T. 308

Flint, Colin 309

Flournoy, Michele 137

food security 299

Ford, Henry 13, 38, 304, 311

forward bases 129

forward operational theaters 129

Fourth Industrial Revolution xviii, xxi, xxvi, 23, 25, 29, 42-43, 48, 63, 90-91, 185, 191, 196, 238-240, 308, 355

fragmentation 10, 108, 238, 278, 313

Frank, Jerome 326

Franklin, Benjamin 299

free market capitalism 59, 192

free trade agreements 51, 195

Freeman, Kevin 318

Friedman, Milton 217, 352

Friedman, Thomas 161, 341

Fujimura, Joan 366

Fukumoro, Yasuyuki 306

Fukushima 111, 113, 262-263, 328, 363

Funk, Cary 307, 343

future (of the alternative energy megatrend) 1, 32-33, 45, 57, 71, 92, 96, 110, 153, 229, 233-235, 237-238, 241, 243-244, 288, 296

G

G20 50, 77, 262, 315, 320, 353

G7 50, 52, 315, 320

Gaddis, John Lewis 319

Gagliano, Troy 321

Galambos, Louis 318

Galbraith, John 155, 340

Galileo 44, 314

Galtung, Johan 51, 315

Gangi, Jennifer 306

Gappah, Petina 348

Garreau, Joel 307

Gately, Dermot 363

Gates, Bill 322

Gates, Robert 125, 331

Gause lll, F. Gregory 320

Gebicke, Scott 331

General Agreement on Tariffs and Trade (GATT) 348

geo-economics xxi, xxvi, 104, 167, 185-187, 219-220, 223-224, 232, 282, 347

geographical spheres of geopolitical influence 52

geography of resources 63, 71, 79, 84, 193

geopolitical cleavages 49, 53-56, 316

geopolitical conflict 11, 172, 174

geopolitical constructs 48
geopolitical leverage 96, 98, 101-102, 107-110, 173, 187, 228, 355
geopolitics xvii-xviii, xxi, xxvi, 8-9, 47-50, 53, 55-56, 62, 72, 79, 82, 85, 104-105, 108, 148, 153, 167-169, 174, 176-177, 180, 184, 186, 194, 220, 222, 245, 257, 277, 282, 287, 290, 303, 309, 314-316, 318, 320, 324-327, 329, 343, 346-347
geothermal energy 15, 69, 199, 305, 311, 318-319, 346, 359
Gerring, John 356
Glass, Gene V. 307
Gleick, Peter 340
global alternative energy market 275
global economic order 196
global economic system 189, 193, 223
Global Energy Consumption by Fuel 21
Global Geothermal Power Potential 70
Global Gross Hydropower Potential Distribution 68
global regulatory framework 31, 89, 165
global technological revolution xx, 1, 10, 23-24, 39, 44, 84, 87, 90, 122, 238
globalization 1, 10, 39-41, 44-45, 67, 79, 166, 192, 196, 201, 238, 277, 299, 301-302, 313, 315, 321, 339, 343, 348, 362
Godin, Benoit 357
Goethe, Johann Wolfgang von 368
Golden Age redux 34
Goldman, Benjamin 343
Goldman, Emily O. 301
Goldschmidt, Pierre 336
Goldwyn, David 321
Goodman, Sherri W. 327, 329
Gordes, Joel 323

Gordon, Kathryn 357, 365
Gore, Albert 170, 344
Grand Energy Game xvii-xxi, xxiii, xxv, 19, 43, 46, 84, 100, 196, 264-265, 288, 290
Gray, C. Hables 338–339,
Gray, Colin 347
Great Game 73
Great Green Fleet 139, 334
Great Power Competition xvii, xix-xxi, xxiii-xxvi, 25, 42, 47, 83, 85, 122, 245-246, 271, 276, 278, 282, 288-290, 299
green agenda 22, 27
green economy 22, 162, 199, 342
green energy lobby 219
green trade wars 195
Greene, Owen 339
greening of geopolitics xviii, 177
GREENS (Ground Renewable Expeditionary Energy Network System) 130, 332
grid management 93
Gulf of Aden 130
Gunn, Kester 306
Gwertzman, Bernard 312

H

Haakon, Prince of Norway 344
Haass, Richard 31, 310
Habermas, Jürgen 314
habitat 11, 22, 33, 59, 89, 152-158, 169, 180, 183, 240, 296, 300, 343
Hadley, Stephen J. xxii, 309, 320, 335, 358, 368
Hagel, Chuck 131, 332
Hall, Sarah 300, 353, 356
Hardin, Garrett 340
Harris, Dan 316
Harrod-Domar model 201, 349
Harvey, David 324
Havel, Václav 309

Hayek, Friedrich 215, 352
Head, Louis 304, 310, 343-344, 346
Hegel, Georg Wilhelm Friedrich 369
Hegelian dialectics 296
hegemonic potential 184
Heiman, Michael K. 343
Heinbecker, Paul 320
Helfert, M. 308
Helium 3 (HE3) 18
Hemmer, Christopher 354
Henry the Navigator 293
Hentsch, Thierry 326
Heraclitus 299
Herberg, Mikkal 362
Herbst, John 359
Herod, Andrew 343
Hettne, Bjorn 301
Hickman, Larry 339
Higgott, Richard 353
high north 130, 142
high politics 3, 169
Hinsely, F.Harry 339
Hirschman, Albert O. 326
Hobbes, Thomas 118, 302, 329
Hobson, John A. 324
Hoes, O.A.C. 318
Hoffman, Bruce 321
Homer-Dixon, Thomas 340
Hommels, Anique M. 309
Hough, Peter 353
Howse, Robert 310
Hubbert, M. King 307
Hugill, Peter J.
Huntington, Samuel 316
Hutchings, Robert 366
hybridization 151, 242
hydropower 10-12, 33-34, 63, 68-69,
    94-95, 176, 179, 199, 246, 249-251,
    255-257, 304, 318, 327, 329, 346
hydrogen 10, 16-17, 19, 37, 236, 306,
    314, 318, 322, 329, 336

I
ideological frameworks 241, 295
imbalances in the global societal order
    229
Industrial Revolution xviii, xxi, xxvi,
    23, 25, 29, 36-37, 42-43, 48, 53, 63,
    90-91, 185, 191, 196, 238-240, 308,
    311, 355
infrastructure 5, 12, 17, 26, 30, 32, 36,
    43, 65, 76, 82, 92-95, 106-108, 113,
    122, 128-129, 131, 134, 137-138,
    140-143, 148-149, 158, 176, 187-188,
    198, 204-205, 207, 209, 212-213,
    215, 219, 224, 226, 228-229, 236,
    238, 243, 249, 265-266, 268-269,
    272-275, 322-323, 326, 335, 338-
    339, 353, 355, 364-365, 367
innovation xxi, xxvi, 42-43, 122-124,
    127, 134-137, 145, 200-202, 207,
    209, 224, 229, 232, 238-239, 243,
    254, 263-264, 271, 275-276, 310,
    315, 320, 329, 333, 335-336, 338,
    349, 351, 357-358
intellectual property rights 174, 217
intergenerational effect 207
intermittency 12-13, 16, 92-93, 228,
    236, 269, 305, 323
International Energy Agency (IEA) 88,
    304-305, 321, 350, 352-353, 362,
    366
international energy system 227
international relations 3, 41, 47-49, 54,
    58, 61-63, 75, 81, 83-84, 102, 121,
    153, 160, 166-167, 169, 184, 194,
    220, 226, 229-230, 232, 273, 276-
    278, 299-304, 308, 311, 313-315,
    325-326, 339-340, 346
inter-state resource competition 194
IRENA (International Renewable
    Energy Agency) 208, 320, 349-351,
    360-361
Ischinger, Wolfgang 328

ITER (International Thermonuclear
    Experimental Reactor) 18, 306

J

Jackson, Robert 317, 343
Jacobson, M.C. 317
James, Harold 313
Japan Aerospace Exploration Agency
    (JAXA) 70, 306
Jennings, Nicholas R. 308, 330
job creation 23, 186, 196, 199, 266
Johansson, Bengt 317
Johnson, W.R. 314
Jonas, Hans 309
Jones, Charles A. 339
Jones, James L. xix, xxii, 108, 327, 367
Joskow, Paul L. 361
Joyner, Daniel H. 328
Jung, Carl 368

K

Kagan, Robert 303
Kaldor, Mary 299
Kalicki, Jan 321
Kane, Thomas 363
Kaplan, Robert 100, 325
Karl, Terry Lynn 348
Katzenstein, Peter 354
Kempe, Frederick 319, 358, 366
Kennan, George 109, 327
Kennedy, Brian 307, 339, 343
Keohane, Robert 302
Kern, Paul J. 327
Keys, Ronald 339, 351
Khalilzad, Zalmay 345
Khanna, Parag 315
kinetic space weapons 133
Kipling, Rudyard 323
Kissinger, Henry xxii, 3, 30, 39, 105,
    301, 310, 312, 326
Kjellén, Rudolf 314
Knorr-Cetina, Karin 309

Knorr, Klaus 327
Knox, MacGregor 329, 369
Koblentz, Gregory 303
Kofman, Eleonore 313
Kolodziej, Edward 354
Kortunov, Andrey 319
Kovarik, Bill 311
Kramer, Walter 323
Krasner, Stephen 315
Krepinevich, Andrew F. 301
Kroenig, Matthew 320, 366
Kuhn, Thomas 312
Kyte, Rachel xxii

L

Lacarte-Muró, Julio 348
Lacoste, Yves 320
Ladislaw, Sarah 326
Lakatos, Imre 312
Lake, David A. 316, 365
land erosion 235
Langewiesche, William 328
Latour, Bruno 312, 357
Laurance, William F. 179, 346
Law of Unintended Consequences
    244, 289
Lawrence Berkeley National Labora-
    tory 18
Le Billon, Philippe 327
Lee, Byung Yang 307
Lesser, Ian 345
Levels of Water Stress by Region 175
Leverett, Flynt 324
Lewis, Martin W. 313, 319, 339
Lichtenstein, Roy xxvii
Lieberthal, Kenneth 362
Lienhard, John H. 311
Lightfoot, H. Douglas 327
Lightfoot, Jeffrey 328
limits-to-growth thesis 155
Lindley-French, Julian 331
Linkon, Sherry 299

Lippmann, Walter 300
Lipsey, Richard 349
Lisbon Summit 141
Litman, Gary 358
Litwak, Robert S. 309
logistics lines 125, 130, 150
London Suppliers Group 319
Lopez, George 353
loss of biodiversity 157
low politics 5
Low, Murray 300
Lucan 368
Luckmann, Thomas 300, 310
Lund, John 312
Luttwak, Edward 347
Lyotard, Jean-François 327

M

Ma, Jack 275
Mabee, Bryan 313
Mabro, Robert 307
MacKay, David 351
MacKenzie, Donald 366
magnetic radiation 338
Magritte, René 242
Malthus, Thomas Robert 25, 309
Manhattan Project 110, 333
Mannheim, Karl 311, 314
Manning, Robert A. 362
Marcuse, Herbert 313
market distortions 214, 219
Martinage, Robert C. 309
Massimov, Karim 308
Mathews, Jessica 302
McCormick, David 317
McDonald, Matt 302
McKibben, Bill 310
McLarty, Thomas F. "Mack" 360
McLeod, Kathy Baughman 319, 366
McMaster, Herbert R. 120, 329
McNeill, Jena Baker 359
McNeill, John 322, 347

Melosi, Martin 333
Merkel, Angela 252, 341, 360
Merton, Robert K. 358
meta-securitization 19-20, 284, 307
Metz, Bert 308
Meyer, Pamela 332
Michel, Serge 365
military alliances 119
military capabilities xxi, xxvi, 25-26,
  116, 119, 123, 127, 133-134, 173, 188,
  228
military force 76, 103, 126, 129, 142,
  190, 195, 226, 358
military operations 26, 119, 121, 125-
  127, 129, 133, 136, 148-149, 236,
  338
Miller, Leland R. 362
Miller, Marian A.L. 316
Mirtchev, Alexander xvii, 316, 341,
  355, 361
Mises, Ludwig von 40, 312
modernization processes 226
modular technologies 151
Mokyr, Joel 311
Moore, Mick 316
Moore, Richard 343
Moore's law 244, 357
moral imperatives 28
More, Max 356
Morell, Michael 309, 368
Morgenthau, Hans 78, 300, 320
Mosbacher, Georgette 336
Mouchot, Augustin 37
Mouchot's Solar Power
  Collector 37
Mowery, David C. 357
Mullen, Michael 124, 331
Müller, Friedemann 324
Murray, Williamson 329
Musk, Elon 304, 317
Mylrea, Michael 323

N

Nahar, Ahmed Babiker 345
Naisbitt, John 304
narrow security 3, 300
natural disasters 69, 140, 149, 157
Navari, Cornelia 321
Negroponte, John 343
net metering 203-204, 247, 261, 309
Netanyahu, Benjamin 268, 365
Net-Zero 138, 140, 334-335
new forms of economic cooperation
    191, 226
New Zealand Nuclear Free Zone,
    Disarmament, and Arms Control
    Act 1987 113
Newman, David
Newman, Edward 299
Newton, James 304
NGO (non-governmental organiza-
    tion) 72, 75-76, 80-81, 161, 164,
    168, 219, 315, 341
Niblett, Robin 360
Nile River dispute 176
Niv, Yael 311
Nixon, Richard 22, 308-309
noise pollution 178
non-nuclear electromagnetic pulse
    (NNEMP) 338
non-proliferation regime 114
non-state actors 4, 10, 32, 40-41, 49,
    52, 54-55, 60-62, 70-72, 75, 78-85,
    91, 96, 98, 102-103, 105-106, 114,
    123, 153-155, 161, 163, 167-169, 177,
    183, 187, 191, 222, 224, 227, 230-
    231, 241, 272-273, 278, 313, 315,
    321, 328
North American Free Trade Agree-
    ment (NAFTA) 165
North Atlantic Treaty Organization
    (NATO) xvii, 109, 126, 129-130,
    135-136, 138, 140-144, 146-147,
151-152, 274, 326-327, 332, 335-337,
    339, 345, 354, 366
North, Douglass C. 311
North-South divide 57-58, 316
Northwest Passage 142
Norton, Bryan G. 299-300, 311, 315,
    322, 326, 341, 343, 350
nuclear energy xviii, xxi, xxvi, 20, 39,
    95, 110-116, 253, 262, 307, 333,
    346, 353, 361
nuclear fission 327
nuclear fusion 16-17, 112, 327
nuclear power 90, 110-116, 126-127,
    134, 139, 190, 228, 239, 245, 252,
    262-263, 270, 306, 327-328
Nunn, Sam 323
Nye, Joseph 103, 302, 325

O

O'Hanlon, Michael E. 331, 367
Ó'Tuathail, Gearóid 314
Occupy Wall Street 201
Ocean Thermal Energy Conversion
    technology 137
off-grid generation 95
Ogden, Peter 366
oil crisis 21, 39, 267
Omand, David xxii, 329
Onuf, Nicholas 311
Operation Active Endeavour 130
operational challenges 127, 142
operational effectiveness 118, 123, 125,
    127-129, 132, 139, 151, 329
Operational Energy Strategy 138, 332,
    334
operational flexibility 130, 151
Orr, David 343
Osberg, Lars 347
Ott, Hermann E. 344
Ovid 44, 314
Owen, Taylor 299, 302

P

P for Plenty 338
Pagonis, William G. 331
Paltsev, Sergey 345
Pancaldi, Giuliano 311
Panetta, Leon E. 332
paradox of plenty 191, 348
Paris Climate Agreement 57, 161, 165, 316
Paul, T.V. 313
Pavel, Barry 345
Peace of Westphalia 348
People's Liberation Army (PLA) 336
Percival, Valerie 340
Perez, Carlota 322
periphery 48-55, 57, 60, 82, 84, 89, 193, 195, 280-281, 286, 301, 315, 336, 339, 354
Perle, Richard 353
Persia 12, 34, 55, 155
Persian Gardens 34
Persico, Joseph E. 331
Petraeus, Gen. David. H. 315, 367
Petty, William 308
photovoltaic (PV) 13-14, 18, 138, 140, 178, 204, 241, 332, 334, 351, 364
Pickel, Andreas 325
Pickles, John 354
Plato 354
Pliny 311
plug-in hybrid electric vehicles 93, 322
Podesta, John 366
Poincaré, Henri 358
Political geography xxiv, 14, 63, 71, 100, 300, 315, 346
Polybius 311
Pope, Cody 318
Popke, Jeff 354
Popper, Karl 369
Porter, Gareth 160, 341, 343, 357
post-Cold War paradigm shift 1, 39-40, 74, 78, 83, 116, 276, 346

post-proliferation world xxi, xxvi, 110, 114, 116
post-Westphalian 2, 9, 169, 289, 325
Powell Doctrine 125, 331
Powell, Colin 125, 331
power balances xxiv, 47, 49, 52, 56, 103, 191, 195, 266, 290
power grid 24, 118, 138, 140, 249, 306, 359
power projection xxvi, 23, 36, 49, 74, 76, 85-86, 102, 104, 118, 122, 125-128, 133, 145, 148, 187, 190, 220, 224-225, 246, 252, 259, 265, 279, 288, 301, 314, 329, 355
prioritization xviii, xxi, xxiv, xxvi, 95, 181-184, 234, 271, 276, 282-287, 290, 329
productivity 15, 90, 188-189, 197-201, 220, 264
protectionist policies 216, 352
public good 23, 56, 111, 207, 211, 217, 350
Public Support for Renewable Power in the U.S. 166

Q

Qiu, Mark 362
quasi-ideology 159, 171, 293, 341
Quine, Willard Van Orman 307
Quirk, Paul 309

R

radical innovation 357
Raffaelle, Ryne 312
Rahn, Richard 352
Rapoport, Anatol 319
Rasmussen, Mikkel Vedby 326
rational behavior 210
Rauch, Anna 355
Rawls, John 341
Reagan administration 312
Reagan, Ronald 132, 312, 332-333

Recchi, Giuseppe xxii, 238, 355
Recognized Air Picture (RAP) 337
Redclift, Michael 319
referent objects 3, 5-7, 126, 180, 273, 301, 354
regional economic security complexes 226, 354
regional security complex 301
regulated energy pricing systems 162
regulatory policies 31, 202
Reich, Robert 353
Reilly, John 345
Renewable Portfolio Standards 160, 342, 352
Renewable technologies 25, 63, 92, 101, 110, 114-115, 134, 145, 149, 152, 157, 172, 177, 180, 198, 209, 230, 239, 241, 263, 344
Reporting Obligations Database of the European Environment Agency 165
research and development (R&D) investment 127, 145-146, 202, 209-210, 212, 351
resource conflicts 69, 109, 230, 347
resource depletion 34, 89, 96, 126, 157, 191, 228, 295, 346
resource nationalism 87, 98-100, 324
resource-based economic power 104
revolution in military affairs 120, 122, 333
Rewey, Christie 321
Rice, Condoleezza 307, 343
Rich, Bruce 316
Richmond, Oliver P. 299
Rifkin, Jeremy 318
Ripsman, Norrin M. 313
Roberts, Paul 173, 344
Robertson, David 326
Robertson, George 336
Robinson, William 317
Rockström, Johan 341

Rodrik, Dani 348
Rogers, Everett M. 349, 357
Rogers, John F.W. 173, 345
Rorschach test 32
Rose, Nikolas 317, 326
Rosen, Stephen Peter 338
Ross, Dennis 364
Ross, Michael 347
Rostow, Walt 354
Rothschild, Emma 302
Rousseau, Jean-Jacques 275, 367
Roy, Stapelton 365
Rozell, Mark J. xxii, 341
Russia-Ukraine gas conflict 190, 248
Ruttan, Vernon 333

S
Sabonis-Helf, Theresa 344
Sachs, Jeffrey D. 213, 347, 351
Sachs, Wolfgang 347
Saki 176, 345
Salzman, James 320
Samuelson, Paul 347
sanctions 221, 353
Sanger, David E. 354
Santarius, Tilman 347
Sarkozy, Nicolas 253, 360
Sartre, Jean-Paul 276
scarcity 21, 84, 88, 103, 117, 154, 157, 172-173, 175-176, 193, 235-236, 295, 340
Scarlett, Sir John 329
Scharlemann, Jörn P.W. 179, 346
Schatzki, Theodore R. 309
Scheffer, Jaap de Hoop 109, 142, 327, 336
Schiffer, Michael Brian 312
Schilling, Melissa 357
Schlesinger, James 335
Schmitz, Hubert 316
Schneider, Keith 318, 327-328
Schock, Robert N. 351

Schoenbaum, Geoffrey 311

Schumpeter, Joseph 200, 324, 349

Schwartz, Eric 322

Schwarzenegger, Arnold 352

Second World 57, 316, 367

securitization xviii, xxi, xxiv, xxvi, 2-9, 19-20, 62, 72-73, 76, 79, 87, 89, 102, 105, 117, 119, 123-124, 126-127, 135, 141-143, 149-150, 152, 154, 157, 160, 172, 176, 180-184, 186-187, 219-220, 223-224, 226-227, 230-231, 249, 272-274, 276-280, 282-287, 289-290, 299, 301-303, 307, 353, 367

securitization gap 157

securitization outcomes 7, 283-284, 290

securitization theory xxiv, 3-4, 7, 299, 301

securitizing innovation 275

security complexities of the 21st century 20, 83

security context xxi, xxv-xxvi, 2, 6-8, 10, 25, 233, 272, 276, 280, 289

security dilemma 7, 284, 300

Sessions, William xxii

shadow flicker 178

Shakespeare, William 238, 355

shale gas 64, 248, 264, 355

shale oil 147, 237, 246, 248, 251, 355

Shanghai Cooperation Organization (SCO) 366

Shepherd, Dennis G. 311

Shields, Eric 332

Shils, Edward A. 356

Shultz, George 30, 310

Siddiqui, Omar 323

Silberglitt, Richard S. 313

silent mobility 337

Simon, Julian 308

Singer, David 302

Singer, Peter 348

Slater, David 325

smart grid 24, 91, 93, 95, 239, 248, 323, 361

SMART Metering Programme 337

Smelser, Neil 311

Smith, Michael 315

Smith, Richard G. 313

social construction of reality 299-300, 310, 357

socially constructed phenomenon 1, 31, 60

societal pressure 6, 20, 44, 62, 152, 174, 202, 241, 301, 319, 340

society's technological base 127, 134, 137, 188

socio-political discourse 4

soft power 74, 103, 105, 249-250

soft targets 149

Solana, Javier 184, 346

Solar-from-orbit 10, 16, 19

solar power 12-14, 37, 65, 70, 77, 93, 98, 115, 134, 147, 178, 189, 255, 261, 263, 266, 306, 311, 317, 320, 322-323, 352

Solon 314

Solow, Robert 200, 347, 349

Solyndra 218, 342

sovereign control over shared goods 155

spheres of influence 53, 176, 269

Spinardi, Graham 366

Spykman, Nicholas 348

Squad Power Manager (SPM) 133, 333

state role in alternative energy development 60

state-centric world system 153, 184

Stauffer, Nancy 305

Stavridis, James xxii, 301

Stent, Angela 362

Stern, Gary H. 367

Stock-Williams, Clym 306

Strait of Hormuz 130

Strange, Susan 103, 326
Strategic Defence and Security Review 146, 337
strategic perceptions 279
strategic value judgments 124, 192
Stripp, Alan 339
Stritzel, Holger 302
structural power 103
Stubbs, Richard 353
sustainable development 22, 30, 61, 145, 170-171, 174, 181, 200, 252, 266, 270, 293, 310, 317, 320, 326, 343-345, 355
Suzuki, David 356
Swan, Guy xxii
switchgrass 179, 305, 346

T

tactical power 125
Talbott, Strobe 279, 367
talking security 4
tar sands 64, 237, 355
Taureck, Rita 299
tax credits 203
Taylor, Alan John Percivale 367
Taylor, Jennifer 309, 341
Taylor, Peter 313, 315
technological advancement 24, 43, 59, 87, 90, 108, 110, 112, 116, 121, 127, 132, 134, 200, 206, 220, 241, 267-268, 356
technological advances 8, 14, 19, 25-26, 42-43, 46, 63, 76, 88, 91, 117, 119-121, 124-125, 134-135, 156, 201, 210-211, 226, 259, 275, 282, 298, 314, 329
technological optimism 243, 356
Tedin, Kent L. 356
Tenet, George 328
Thatcher, Margaret 213, 351
Third World 57, 59, 316
Thomas, Robert P. 311

Thöne, Michael 355
threats to economic stability 220
Three Mile Island 111, 113
Tickner, J. Ann 303
Tidal power 16-17, 69-70, 146
Tilghman, Shirley xxii, 161, 341
Toffler, Alvin 43, 199, 314, 349
Total Expenditures for Renewable Energy Support in the European Union and Norway 209
top-down (build-up/process/dynamics/pressure) 28, 48, 50, 60, 62, 84, 164, 280, 353
Touraine, Alain 311
toxicological properties 345
Toynbee, Arnold 282, 367
trade protection policies 221
trade wars 195, 221, 237, 281
trade-off between efficiency, effectiveness, and power projection 128
transformative technologies 202
transit countries 100, 253
transmission infrastructure 12, 65, 93, 149, 272
Treaty of Chaumont 299
triple bottom line 61
Truly, Richard 331
Truscott, Peter xxii, 23, 308
twinkling effect 338

U

U.S. Air Force 139-140, 333, 335, 339
U.S. Army Energy Initiatives Task Force 136, 334
U.S. Army 136, 138, 330-331, 333-335, 351
U.S. Department of Defense (DoD) 118, 128, 137–140, 330-332, 334, 336, 338–339, 350
U.S. Federal Reserve 354
U.S.-Mexico-Canada Agreement (USMCA) 51, 165

U.S. Navy 139, 334
UK Ministry of Defence (MOD) 146,
    336-337
UN Conference on Human Environ-
    ment 165
UN Global Compact 61, 317
unanticipated consequences 110, 183,
    226, 358
United Nations (UN) 30, 61, 147, 165,
    168, 170-171, 245, 260, 280, 299,
    301, 310, 313, 316–317, 320, 326,
    328, 340, 341-345, 348, 352, 356,
    360-361, 363, 365-366
United Nations Environment
    Program 165, 171, 343
United Nations Sustainable Develop-
    ment Goals 30, 171, 310, 317, 345
universal securitization xviii, xxi, xxiv,
    2, 4, 6-7, 9, 102
universally securitized world xviii, xxi,
    xxiv-xxvi, 1, 7-8, 19, 45, 49, 88, 117,
    180, 183, 219, 226, 234, 271, 279,
    281-283, 289
unmanned platforms 123, 130, 133
Unsubsidized Levelized Cost of
    Energy 198
user innovations 275

V

Valencia, Mark J. 363
Valentino, Benjamin A. 348
Valley of Death 134, 197, 333
van Loon, Joost 366
van Munster, Rens 302, 326
Varian, Hal 350
Verne, Jules 43
Verrastro, Frank 326
Vess, Deborah 299
vested interests 78, 211, 217-219, 232,
    243
Vickers, Michael 309
Victor, David 326

visual domination 178
Vita-More, Natasha 356
von Hippel, Dr. Karin xxii, 319
Von Mises, Ludwig 40, 312
von Savigny, Eike 309

W

Waddell, Steve R. 331
Wakefield, Ernest Henry 312
Walker, Rob B.J. 300
Wallerstein, Immanuel 52, 315
Walt, Stephen 303
Walton, C. Dale 320
Waltz, Kenneth 302
Walzer, Michael 348
War of 1812 135
Ward, Peter 339
warfighting capabilities 131, 133-134,
    151, 229
water scarcity 157, 173, 235
water security 3
wave energy 17, 19, 136, 264
Webster, William xxii, 368
Weinberger Doctrine 331
Weinberger, Caspar 125, 331
Wenk, Edward 312
Wheeler, Nicholas J. 348
White House solar panels 39, 312
Whiteside, Kerry H. 341
Wigen, Kären E. 313
Williams, Robert E. 347
Williams, Tennessee 354
Wilson, Damon 359
Wilson, Paul 309
wind energy 12-13, 66, 268, 304,
    306-307, 309, 318, 321-322, 338,
    341-342, 346
windmills 34
Wodehouse, P.G. 323
Wolfers, Arnold 186, 347
World Bank 11, 52, 168, 170-171, 316-
    317, 344, 347

World Economic Forum 308, 314, 320, 341
World Trade Organization (WTO) 30, 75, 204, 317, 321, 348, 359-360, 363
Wright, Liz 334

Y
Youngs, Gillian 313

Z
Zah, Rainer 346
Zinni, Anthony 173
Zuckerman, Jessica 359

ABOUT THE AUTHOR

Dr. Alexander Mirtchev is a U.S. academic and executive working in the area of global economic security, energy and geopolitics.

He is a Vice chair of the board of directors at the Atlantic Council of the United States, member of the Executive and Strategy Committees and the Advisory Council of the Scowcroft Center for Strategy and Security. Mirtchev also contributed to the international defense and global economic security policy realm as Vice President of the UK's Royal United Services Institute for Defense and Security, RUSI, and as Executive Chairman of RUSI International.

Mirtchev is a Distinguished Visiting Professor at the SCHAR School of Policy and Government at George Mason University. He is a founding council member of the Kissinger Institute on China and the United States at the Woodrow Wilson International Center for Scholars where he also served as a member of the Wilson National Cabinet and Senior Fellow.

Dr. Mirtchev is the President of Krull+, a macroeconomic consultancy focused on emerging economic security trends and policy challenges.

He is the author of several monographs and numerous policy articles, has served as editor and publisher of academic journals and has appeared as an analyst in major international media.

Mirtchev is a member of James Madison Council at the Library of Congress. He enjoys classical philosophy, opera, and painting, and is a curator of ancient Greek Tanagra figurines.

Visit www.krullcorp.com for additional information on Dr. Alexander Mirtchev.